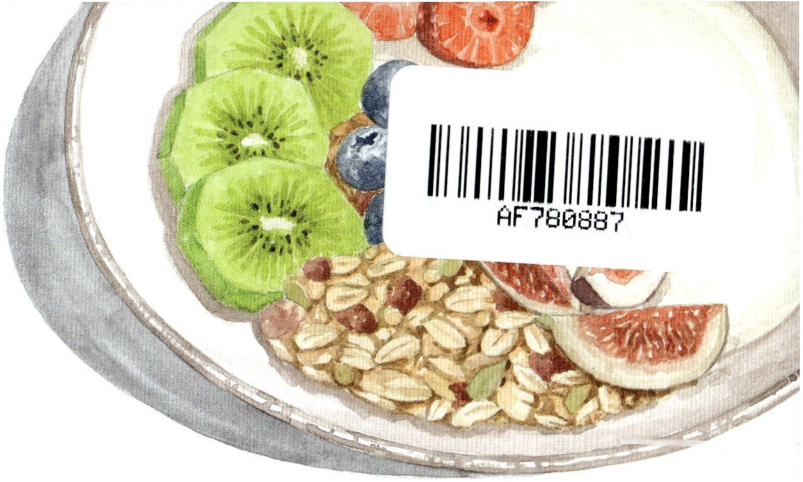

Watercolor Food Illustration

Learn to Paint Realistic Foods, Ingredients and Keepsake Recipe Cards

Thanh Huynh
Creator of Food Illustration Studio

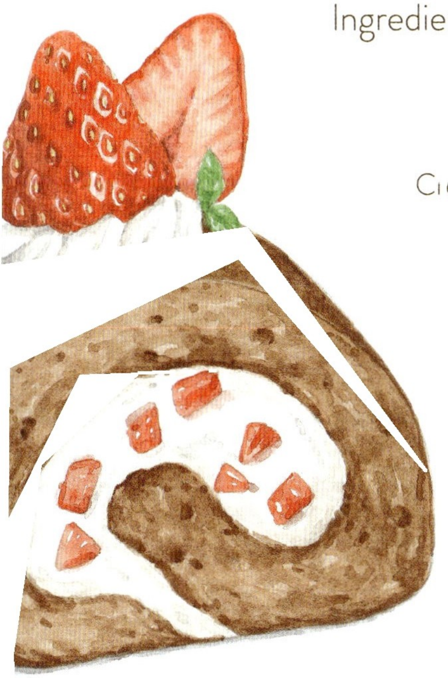

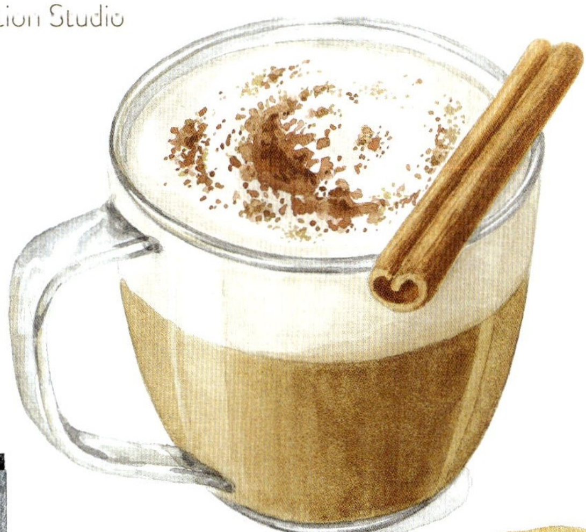

PAGE STREET PUBLISHING CO.

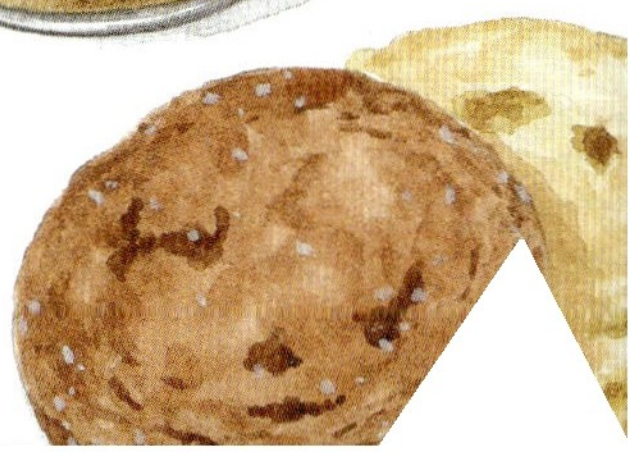

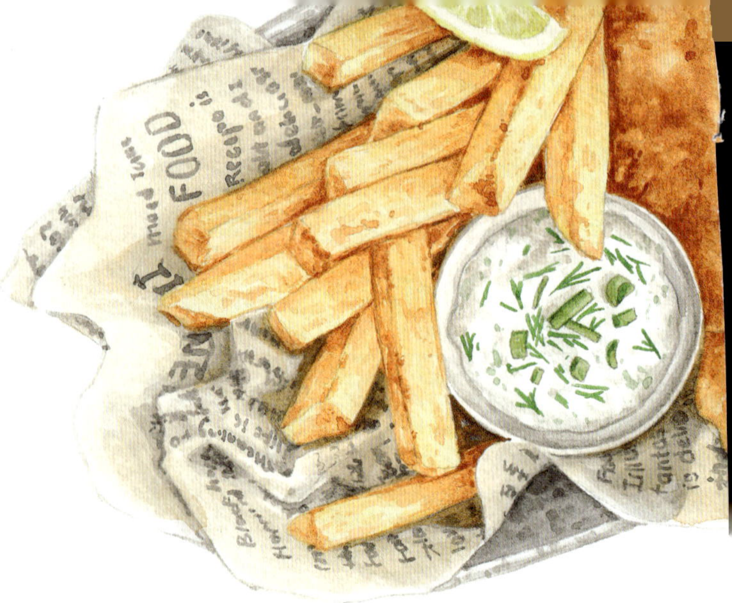

PAGE STREET
PUBLISHING CO.

First published in 2025 by
Page Street Publishing Co.
27 Congress Street, Suite 1511
Salem, MA 01970
www.pagestreetpublishing.com

Distributed by Macmillan, sales in Canada by The Canadian Manda Group.

29 28 27 26 25 2 3 4 5

ISBN-13: 979-8-890-03223-2

Library of Congress Control Number: 2024938036

Edited by Sarah Monroe
Cover and book design by Molly Kate Young for Page Street Publishing Co.
Artwork by Thanh Huynh

Printed and bound in the United States of America

trustees

Page Street Publishing protects our planet by donating to nonprofits like The Trustees, which focuses on local land conservation.

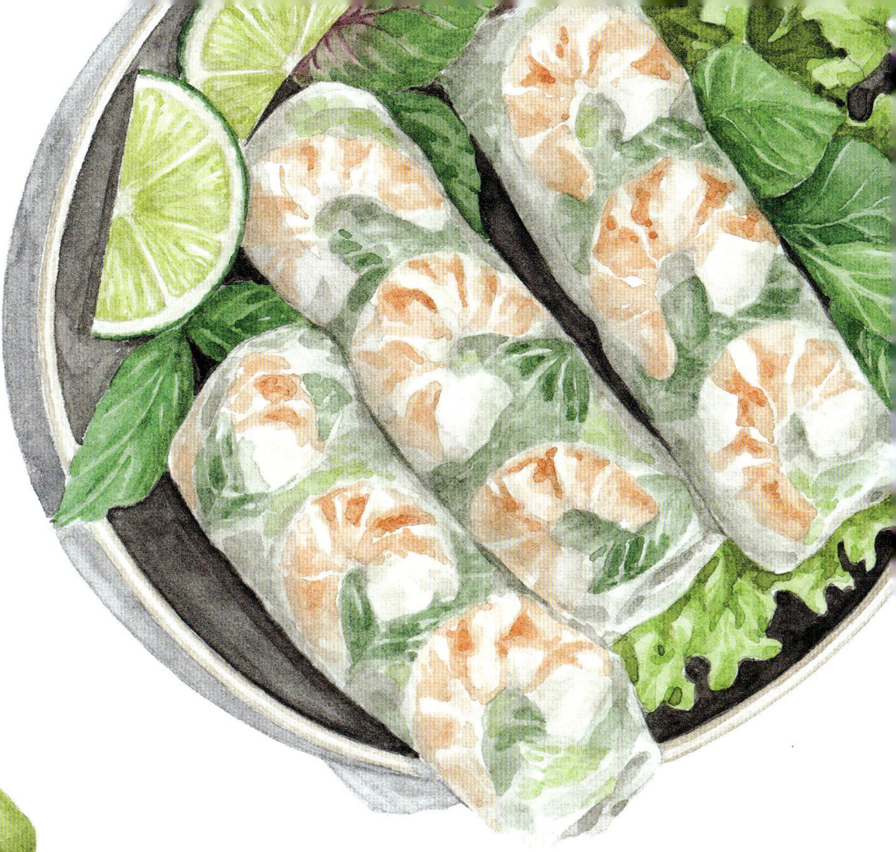

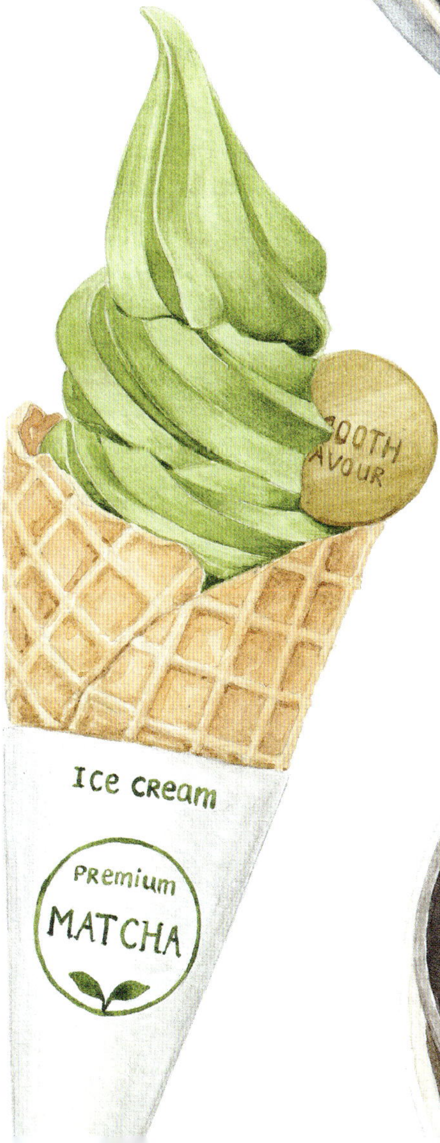

To Mom and Dad,
who recognized my passion for drawing
and wholeheartedly nurtured it.

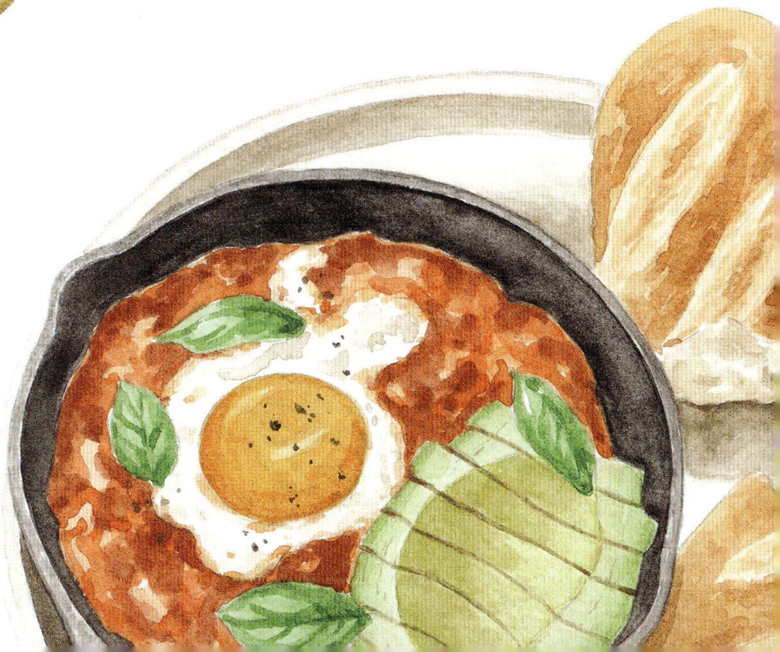

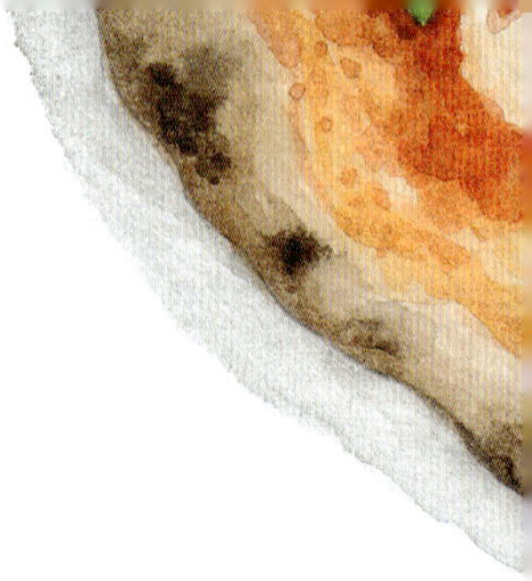

Contents

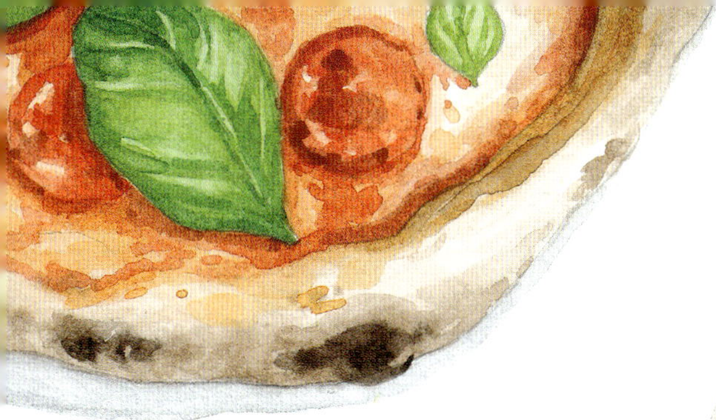

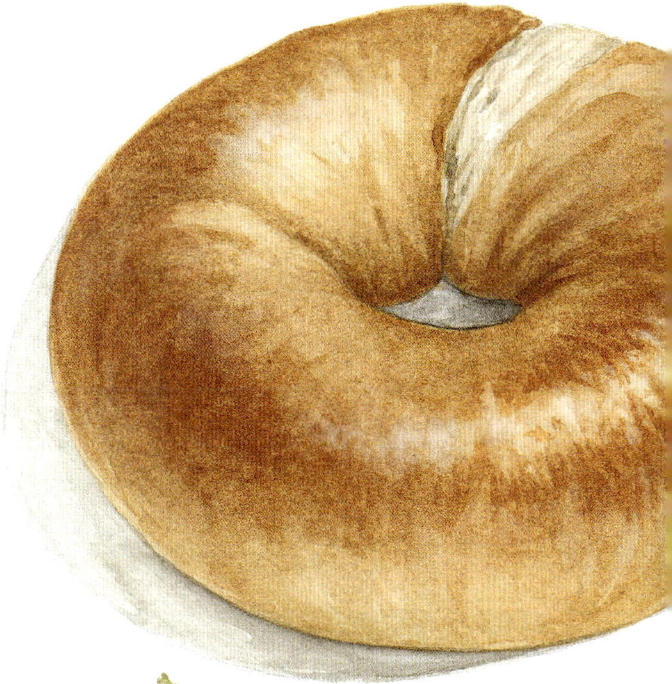

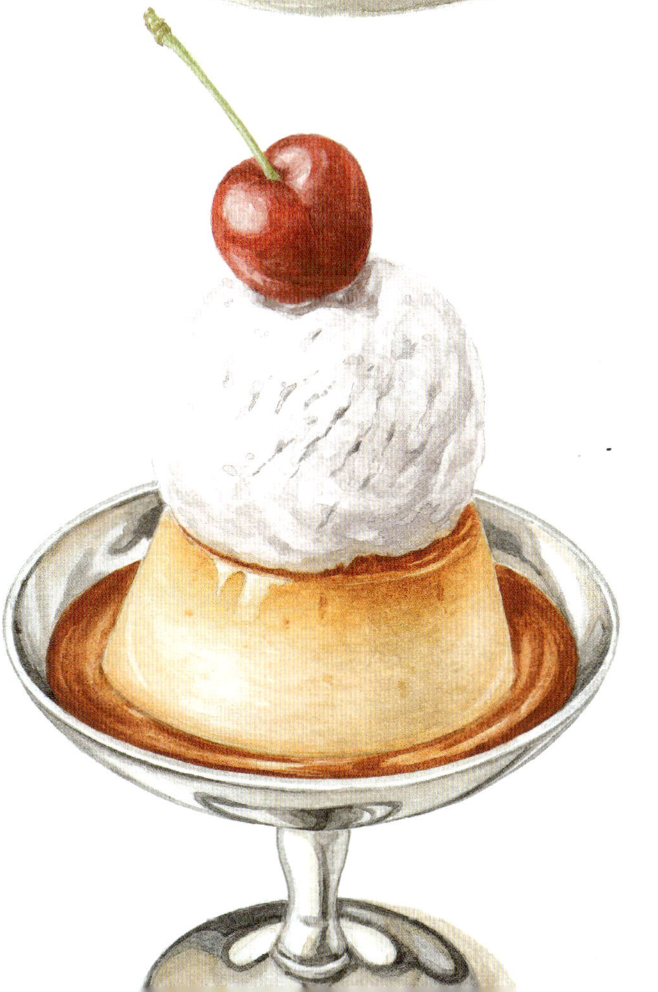

Introduction

Welcome to the fascinating world of Watercolor Food Illustration! In this book, you'll explore the fundamentals of creating a realistic piece of art featuring your favorite dishes using watercolor. Whether you're just starting out or looking to refine your skills, I'm confident you'll find valuable inspiration throughout.

As an alumnus of the University of Architecture, I received extensive training in shapes and lighting over 6 years, experimenting with various media to depict still-life subjects, including pencil, watercolor, chalk pastel, charcoal, sculpture and model making with materials such as paper, metal, foam and digital tools. After graduation, as I sought a unique career path, I began painting food that I encountered and fell in love with during my travels in and outside of Vietnam, building on the strong foundation of my training. This blend of experiences has deepened my appreciation for shapes, spatial relationships and global culinary cultures.

Painting food brings me great joy, as it feels like "cooking" with my hands and "eating" with my eyes. This process fosters a deep connection with each dish, honoring both its creation and the person who made it. My goal is to share the best of these insights and techniques with you, refined over years of practice.

Through these pages, I hope to motivate you to start painting and creating art, no matter your level of experience. Let's embark on this creative journey together and discover the joy and satisfaction of watercolor food illustration!

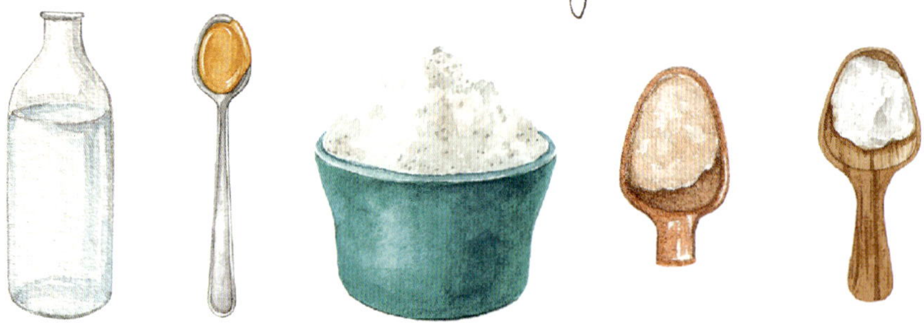

How to Use This Book

This book is organized to help you understand, practice and yield the best results from each chapter.

Chapter I covers the five essential skills needed to master this visual art: sketching, shading, building composition, mixing colors and depicting textures. Considerable effort has gone into making them accessible even to beginners. To make the most of this book, take the time to practice all the basic exercises. This will help you get familiar with your art supplies, become proficient in their use and gain the confidence to tackle more complex projects with ease. Believe me when I say: Practice leads to progress!

Chapter II is dedicated to 20 painting projects, ranging from beginner to advanced levels. I have selected these projects for their variety of shapes and textures, ensuring a valuable learning opportunity every step of the way. Each project has unique characteristics, reinforcing both the theoretical and practical aspects of the tips provided. There is no need to stress about making your painting look exactly like the sample. The key is to understand and practice the steps at your own pace and skill level. It's perfectly fine to revisit and redo a project multiple times. I encourage you to find your own inspiration and fully embrace the creative process.

In Chapter III, I will guide you in transforming your individual paintings into practical and engaging recipe cards. You can use any of the finished work from Chapter II or future projects, integrating them into nine attractive and functional layouts for gifts or as part of your journal. I also include my personal handwriting styles and step-by-step instructions.

Chapter IV serves as a worthy source of inspiration and ongoing reference for the artist in you. It features a broad selection of ingredients and items commonly found in the kitchen. This will also offer guidance on choosing colors and container shapes to enhance your work.

And what's more, I've given you a comprehensive library of ingredients: a collection of reference images you can refer to as you work. These are provided for your ongoing reference, ensuring you have the resources you need at any time.

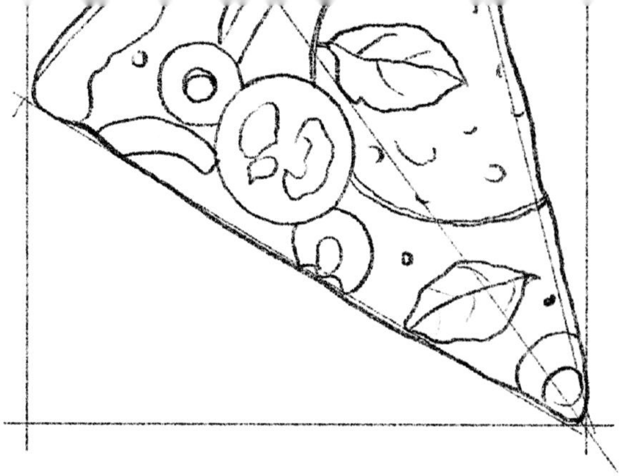

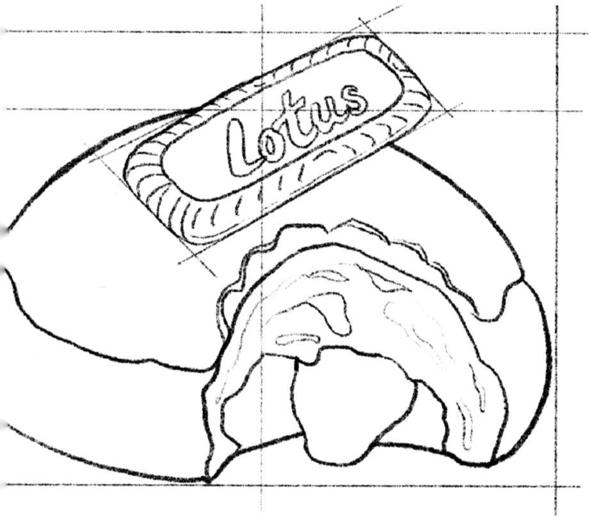
Lotus

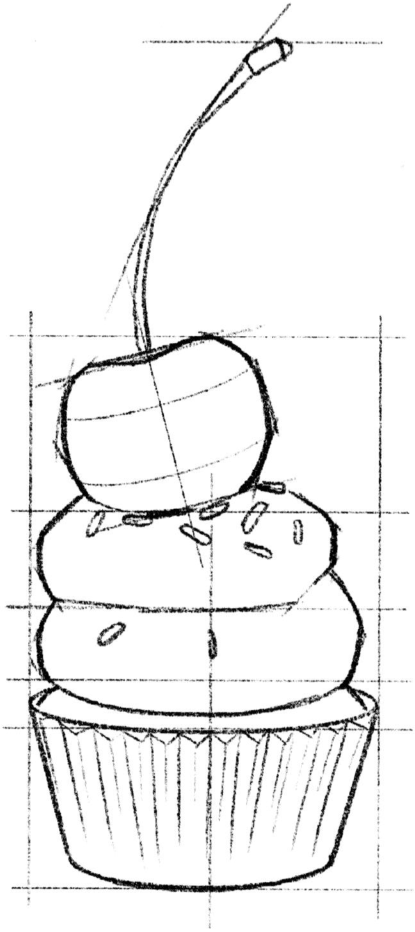

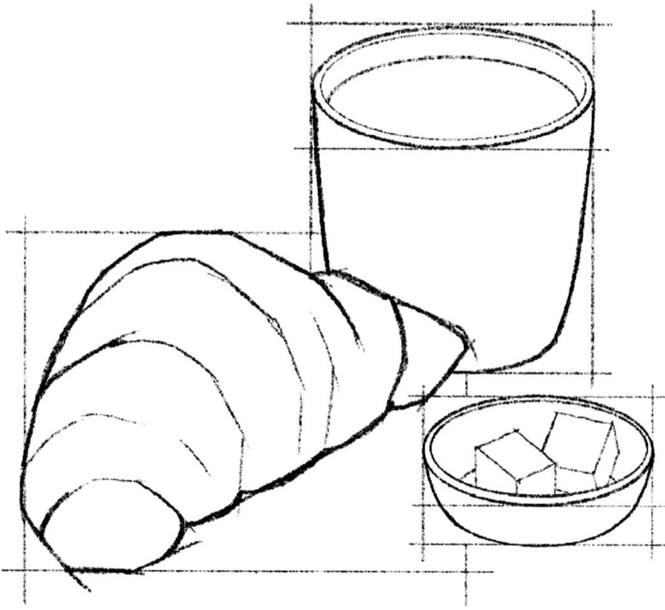

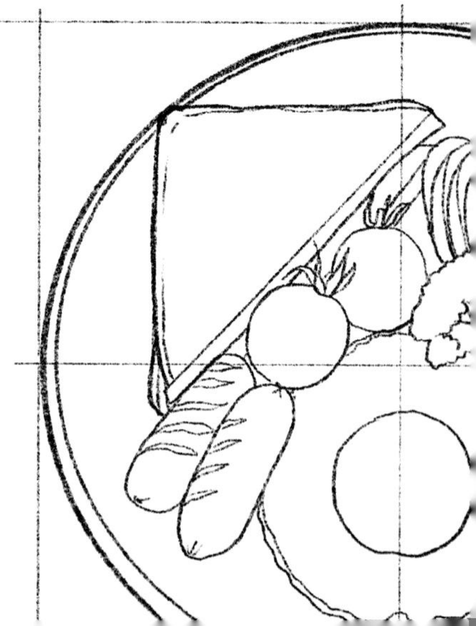

Chapter I

The Groundwork

If you find yourself irresistibly drawn to the projects in Chapter II and tempted to dive right in, I recommend taking a deep breath and starting your journey here instead. Investing time in mastering these foundational skills will be crucial for achieving realistic effects in your food paintings. By addressing these fundamentals now, you'll save time in the long run, avoiding the frustration of filling in gaps later, and you'll be able to enjoy the creative process more fully.

The coming pages will shed light on the five pillars of a realistic painting by watercolor: 1) sketching various shapes; 2) shading based on a solid understanding of how light interacts with the subject; 3) selecting the best angle and composition to highlight key elements of your chosen food item; 4) color mixing techniques using my custom palettes designed for food; and 5) illustrating common textures.

If you encounter any difficulties, identify which of these five skills might be the issue and review that section. This approach will help you pinpoint the problem and understand why your painting might not yet meet your expectations.

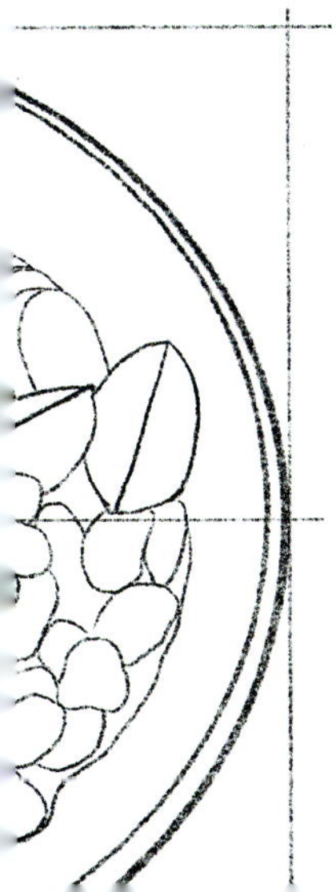

Sketching

Four Essential 3-D Shapes to Master

Sketching realistic food involves transforming 3-D shapes in space into 2-D representations on paper. Food may seem like a complex subject to sketch, but many organic forms in nature adopt basic geometric shapes: An orange is essentially a sphere, while a carrot has a cone-like structure.

To accurately sketch these forms, it's crucial to train your eyes to recognize and translate organic shapes into their basic geometrical equivalents. Doing so will not only help you sketch individual objects more easily, but also allow you to break down complex structures into manageable elements. Sketching plays a fundamental role in realistic painting. By serving as the skeleton of the subject, a sketch gives you the first sense of depth and perspective. Mastering this technique will provide a solid foundation for further detailed painting and help you achieve the desired level of realism.

Principles In Sketching Basic Shapes

Sphere

A sphere is unique among three-dimensional shapes because it appears perfectly round from any perspective. When drawn on 2-D paper, it's shown as a circle. While a compass or a round lid can be handy for drawing circles, the method I introduce here grants you the freedom to sketch a perfect circle anywhere, without the need for any tools.

Exercise: I usually begin by drawing a square that encloses the entire shape. From the center of this square, draw a horizontal line and a vertical line extending to touch each of the square's edges. Next, I draw arcs that connect the adjacent intersection points. This method ensures the accurate size, balance and symmetry of the subject being observed, providing a useful framework for shading and other details in subsequent stages.

Applying to food illustration: Although perfectly round spheres are rarely seen in everyday foods, many fruits and vegetables are sphere-like. For instance, tomatoes often have a slightly flattened top, watermelons are more elongated versions of the sphere and cabbageheads feature wavy, irregular edges.

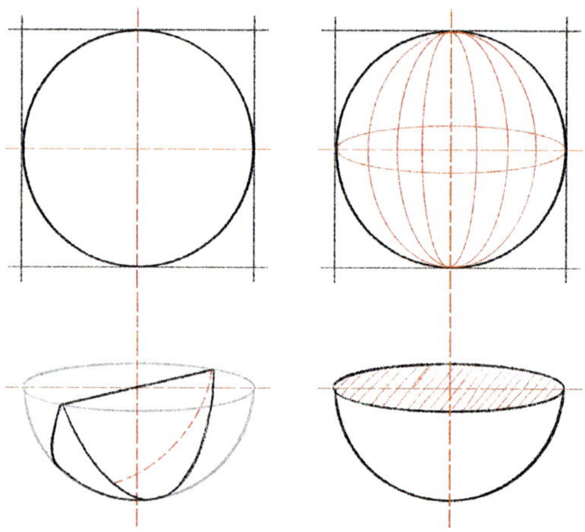

Depending on your subject, the sketch can begin with either a full sphere or just half of it. As long as the center lines are drawn correctly, all the other lines automatically fall into place.

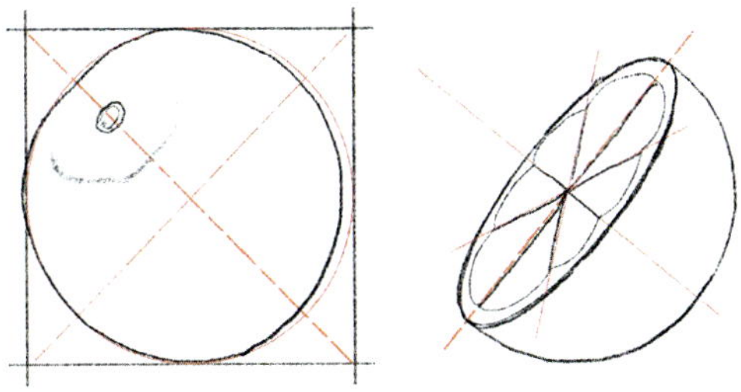

Sketching an orange: The key takeaway here is to accurately recognize the basic shapes present in everyday food items (in this case—a complete or half an orange within a sphere).

Advanced: Always pay attention to the proportion and ratio as you draw. By constantly comparing ratios during sketching, you can add distinctive details and character to the food in your painting without compromising its proportions. For instance, a cabbage might be slightly shorter than a typical sphere, while a watermelon could be longer. This awareness of unique proportions can add realism and playfulness to your sketches.

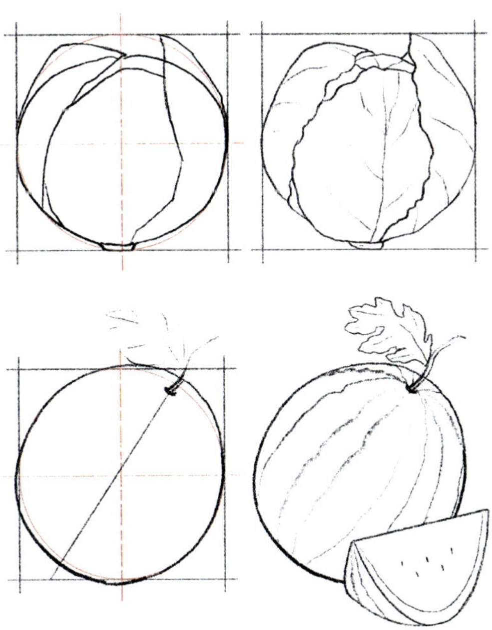

You can begin playing around with positioning your objects—draw them diagonally or "dissect" them into smaller pieces to highlight their interior.

Cylinder

You can recognize a cylinder by observing it from perspectives other than the top or side views. When viewed from the top, a cylinder will look like a circle; from the side, it looks like a rectangle. Preferably, a cylinder should be sketched from an eye-level perspective to naturally reveal the depth of the object.

Exercise: The first key step in sketching a cylinder is to draw a frame to define its boundaries. It could be a portrait or landscape rectangle, depending on the height of your object. Next, draw a vertical center line along the middle of the frame to help you maintain symmetry. Lightly indicate the width of the oval ends at the top and bottom of the cylinder. Identify the midpoints of the top and bottom edges of your frame where the ovals will be at their widest. Use your pencil to gently draw the ovals at the top and bottom of your cylinder, ensuring they pass through the midpoints.

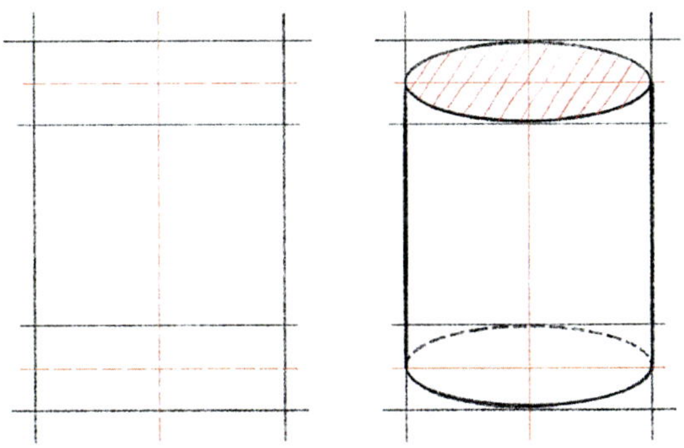

When sketching the oval ends, remember that the taller the cylinder is, the greater the difference in width between the top and bottom ovals (see A in the image). In contrast, ovals that belong to shorter cylinders (see B and C in the image) will have the same width but appear rounder when viewed from a higher angle. This guideline will help you create accurate and realistic sketches of cylindrical objects.

Applying to food illustration: Cylinder-like shapes may include cups, cucumbers, birthday cakes and so on. Once you understand the structure of a cylinder, try adding details into your food object based on it.

Advanced: Consider a piece of cake as a component within a larger cylindrical structure; let the shading process follow suit. Now, you can delve deeper into the nuances of the object's edges and rims: Dedicate careful attention to these irregularities, capturing them on paper with precision. This will provide a more refined groundwork for the next step—which is shading.

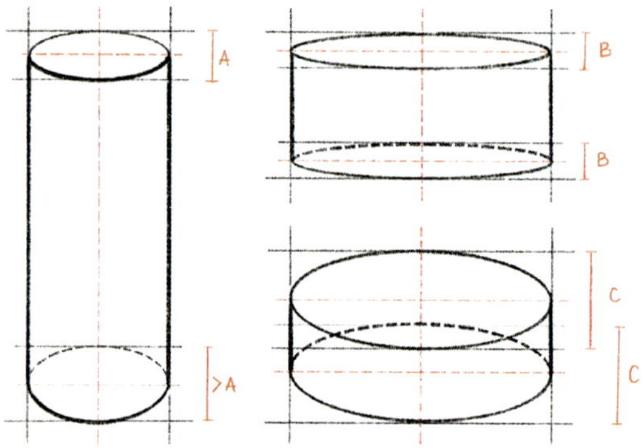

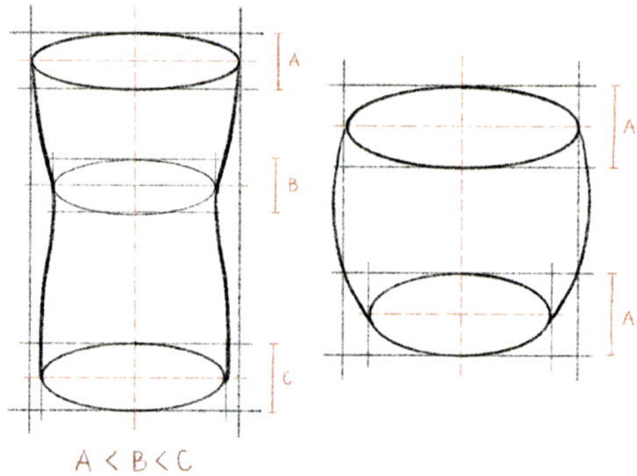

Cups can come with a variety of shapes in the middle, but they are mostly round on the top and bottom.

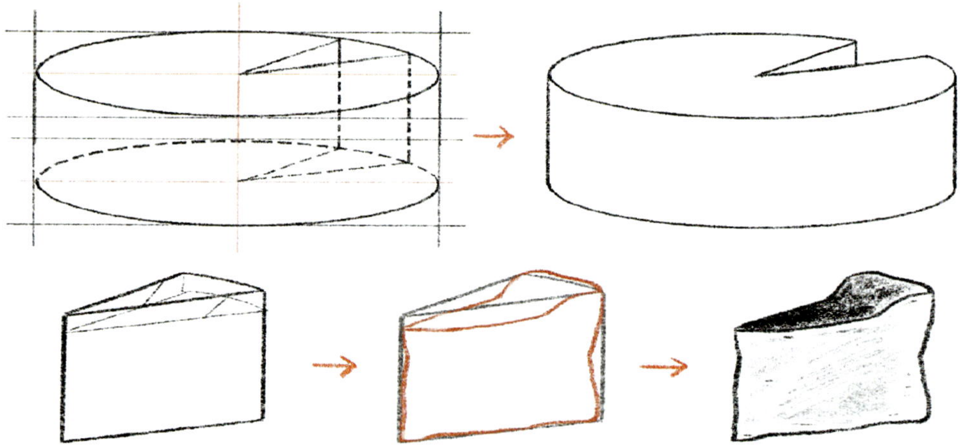

Cuboids

A cuboid has six faces and twelve edges. When a cuboid is viewed from the top and the side, it appears as a rectangle or a square (in the case of a cube), but from an angle, it reveals its three-dimensionality by showing three faces: top or bottom, and at least two sides. For the best sense of depth, I recommend sketching from an eye-level viewpoint.

Exercise: To draw a cuboid, begin with a vertical line to indicate the object's height. Then draw two diagonal lines that represent the width of the cuboid's side faces (see D in the image). At the ends of these diagonal lines, draw two shorter vertical lines, which will define the back edges of the cuboid (see B and C in the image). Next connect the top edges by finding the intersection of the parallel lines. Make sure the point of intersection is slightly lower than the original vertical line to account for perspective. This will give the top face its three-dimensional look, providing a realistic sense of depth and volume.

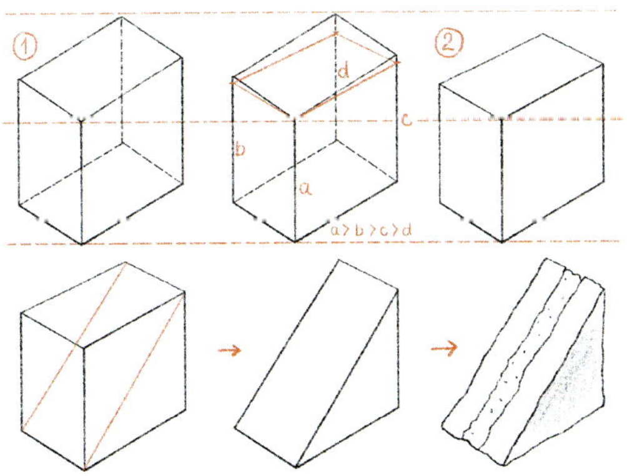

Applying to food illustration: Cuboid-like objects are commonly seen in everyday life, and in the context of food, they can take the form of a sandwich loaf, a block of butter or a carton of milk.

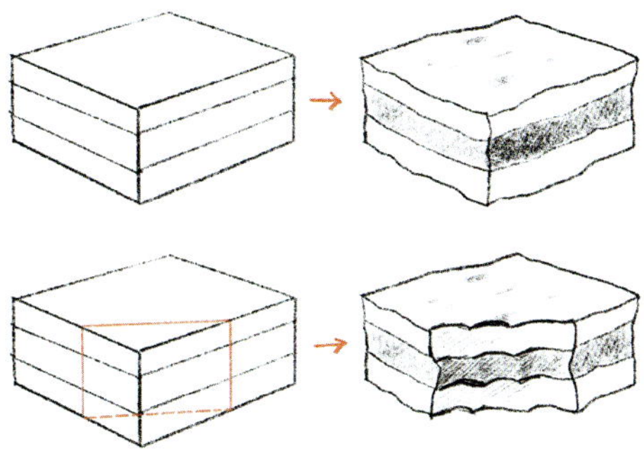

Consider different ways you can dissect the item to give viewers a better depiction. The cutline itself must be proportionally correct.

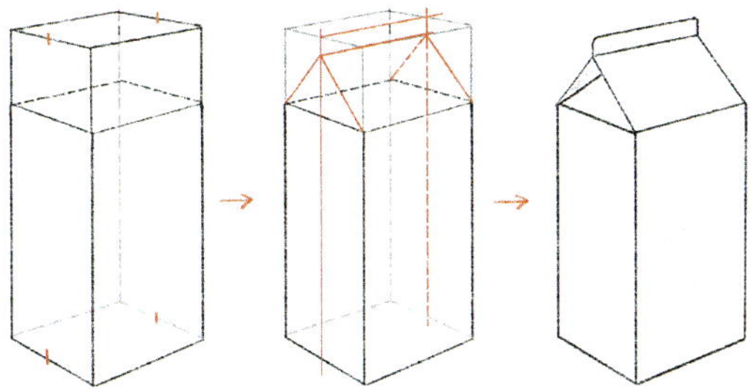

Advanced: A loaf of bread is potentially one of the most common objects in food illustration. Derived from a combination of a cube and a cylinder, its curved and soft lines can be adjusted accordingly to provide effective guidelines for shading later on.

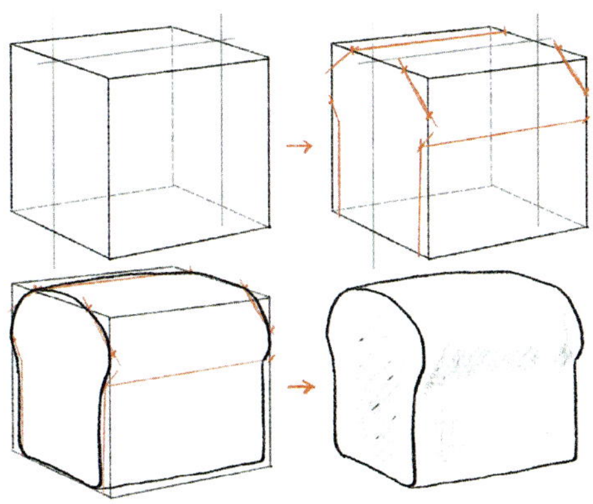

Cone

A cone shape is somewhat similar to a cylinder, as it has a circular base, but instead of having two flat ends, a cone has one pointed tip, creating a peak.

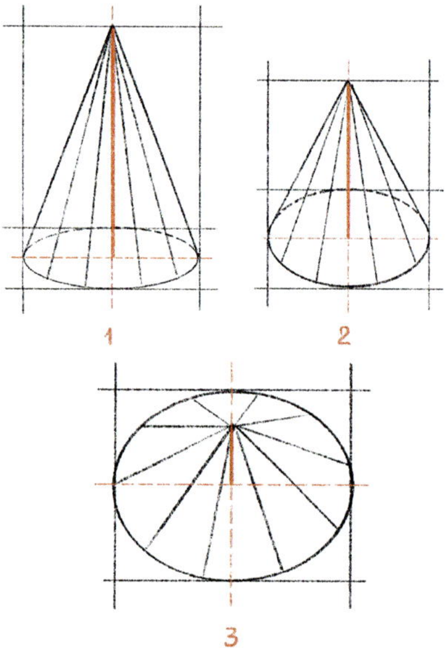

Exercise: To sketch a cone, start by drawing an oval to represent the base. Next, draw a vertical line from the center of the oval to indicate the cone's height. Finally, connect the top of this line to the widest points on the oval's sides with two straight lines, forming the cone's sloping sides.

Applying to food illustration: This shape can be found in several familiar food items, including carrots, waffle ice cream cones, conical mushrooms, figs, etc. Waffle ice cream cones have a pointed bottom tip and are hollow at the center, whereas Hershey's Kiss® chocolates have a rounded bottom and a solid interior. Despite these differences, both items share a common foundation in the cone shape.

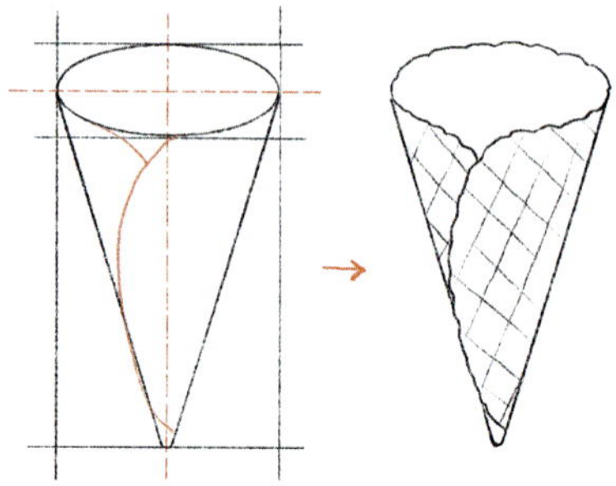

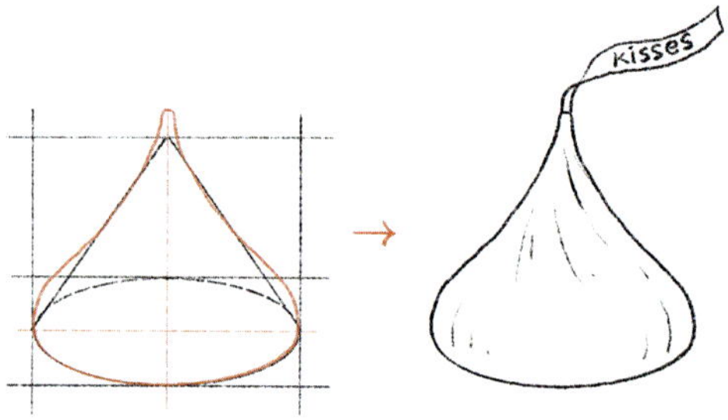

Advanced: I can't stress this enough—mastering the art of dissecting objects is a skill honed through consistent practice. Deriving its form from a basic cone shape, a fig can be depicted whole or broken into parts, or even as a blend of both approaches. Embrace the challenge and exploration!

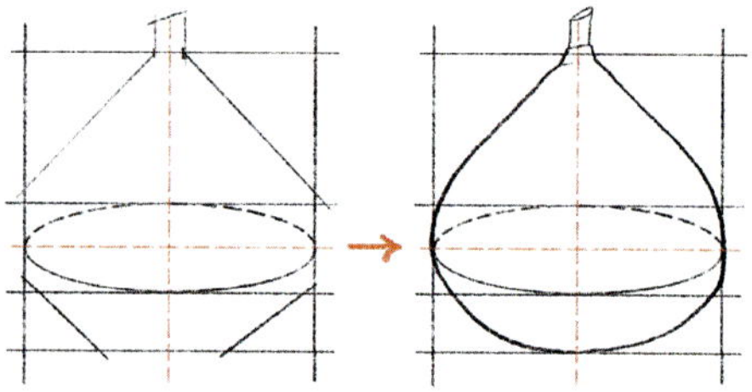

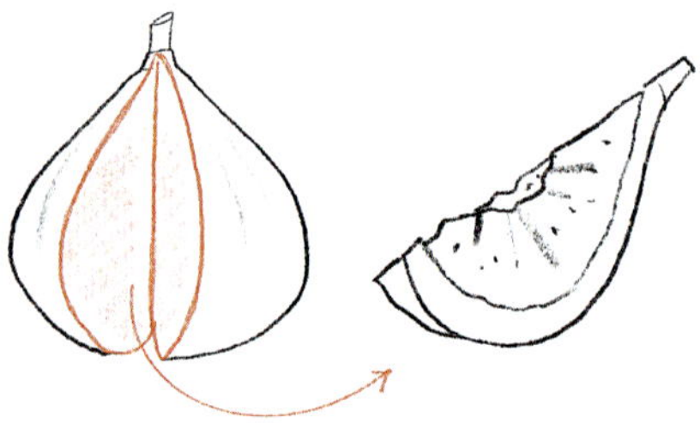

Shading

Understanding the Lighting in 3-D Shapes

In this section, we'll delve into shading techniques to transform your two-dimensional sketch into a lifelike, three-dimensional illustration. First, you have to familiarize yourself with how lighting works on an object. Lighting enables our eyes to observe an object in its environment. When light illuminates an object, it creates highlights, midtones and shadows, allowing the eye to perceive depth, form and shape. To replicate this effect on paper, we simulate a light source shining on our subject, in this case, food. The reason this acknowledgment is needed is because we don't always have the perfect lighting in real life and it can cause confusion while painting.

Depending on the features of your subject, choose the light source direction that illuminates the side with the most detail to emphasize in your painting. In addition to creating highlight, midtone and shadow areas, the cast shadow on the surface by the subject also plays a crucial role in adding depth and dimension to your artwork.

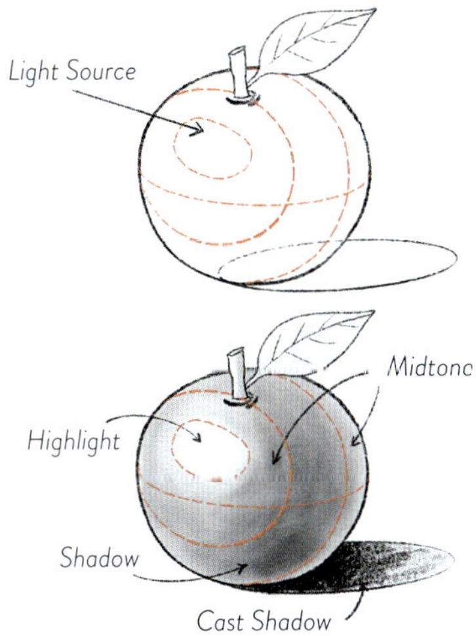

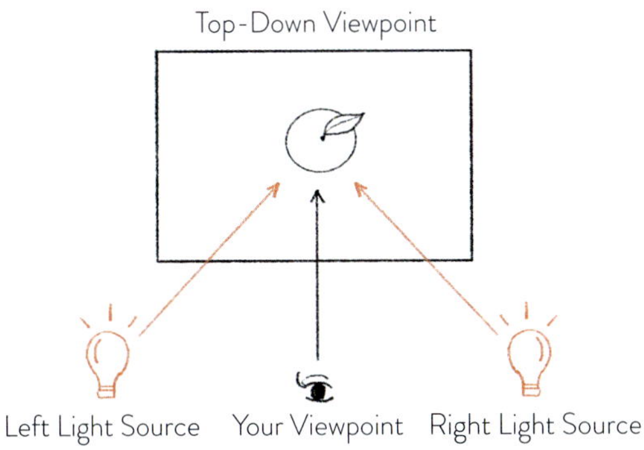

Two light source placements that provide optimal highlights on an object (choose one).

Principles In Shading Basic Shapes

We'll place the four essential shapes you learned to sketch in the previous section under a light source and observe how shading techniques can render them three-dimensional on paper.

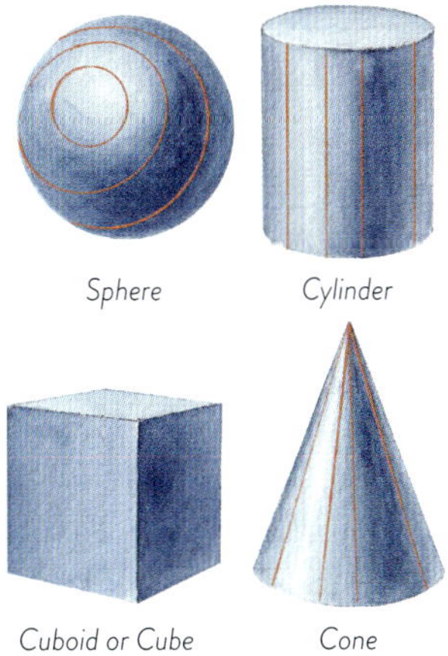

Create your own shading guidelines for organic forms: To better understand the transition and movement of 3-D shapes, I find using contour lines particularly helpful. These lines can capture the three-dimensional form on paper, providing a visual guide to the structure of the shape. Additionally, they can assist in identifying where the highlight and shadow areas will occur naturally.

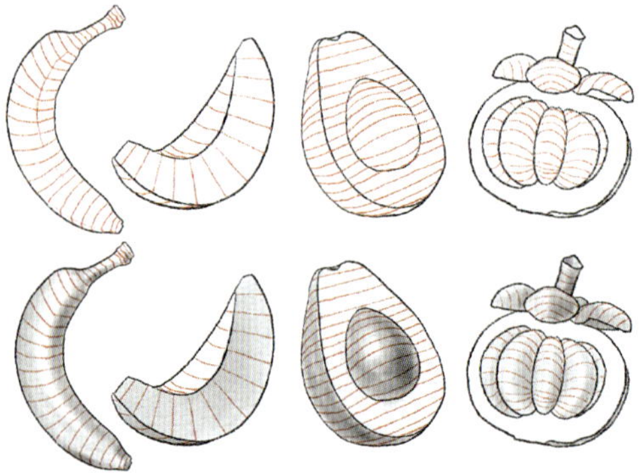

Artist's Tip: Choose a fruit from your kitchen and use a marker to draw contour lines around it to understand its 3-D structure. Once you've done that, sketch the fruit on paper as you see it from your perspective, incorporating the contour lines to guide your shading and depth.

Composition

Optimal Angles for Food Placements

In this section, I'll guide you on selecting the best angle from which to sketch food based on its composition. The angle you choose is crucial for a successful painting, as different foods have unique compositions. It's important to choose an angle that highlights the most distinctive elements or characteristics of your subject. By taking advantage of the right angle and suitable composition, the painting process becomes easier to manage. Firstly, I'll introduce you to the three primary viewpoints commonly used in food illustration. They are the eye-level viewpoint, side viewpoint and top-down viewpoint.

Eye-Level Viewpoint

Widely employed in food illustration, this angle offers a view from your table, allowing for natural sketching from a seated position. However, from my own experience, I divide this viewpoint into two subcategories: a sitting perspective and a standing perspective. In both scenarios, the object is situated on a table.

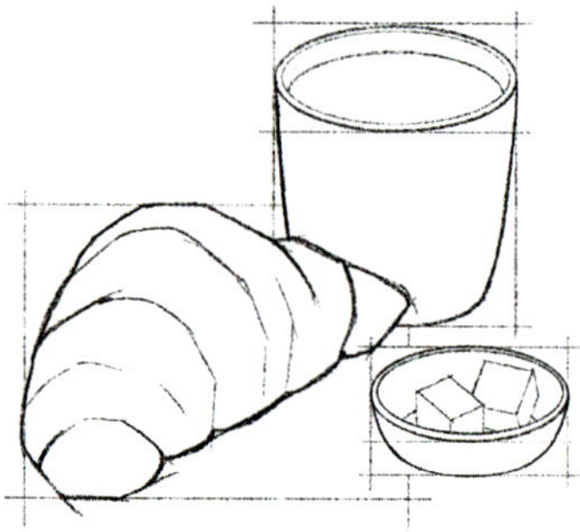

This angle is perfect for compositions featuring multiple objects arranged in order, with shorter objects in the front and taller ones further back.

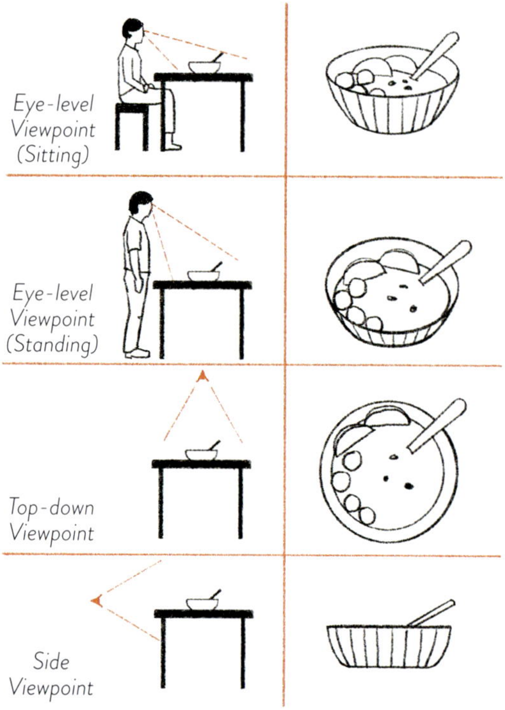

From a sitting perspective, your eyes capture less of the top surface of the food and slightly more from the side.

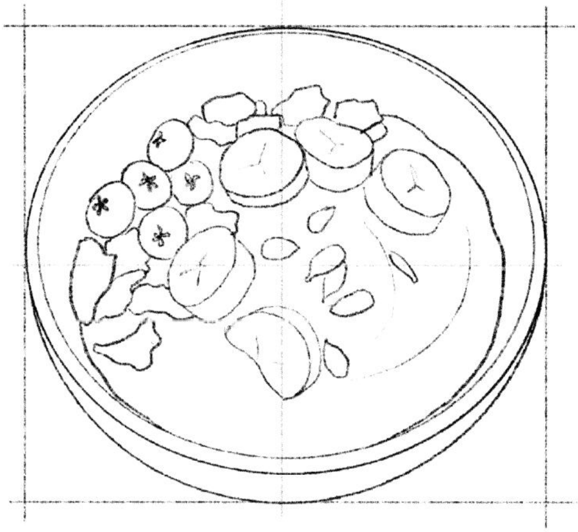

From a standing perspective, your eyes capture more detail on top. I find this view suitable for compositions with multiple objects, particularly those that are relatively flat or fairly uniform in height (such as a breakfast plate) or that contain smaller objects among larger ones (such as a yogurt bowl). This view is similar to the top view; however, as shown in the example below, the plate is not completely round and we can still see a bit of depth/side of the food. This example can be interpreted as a trick using the top view but a little lower to see the depth of the food.

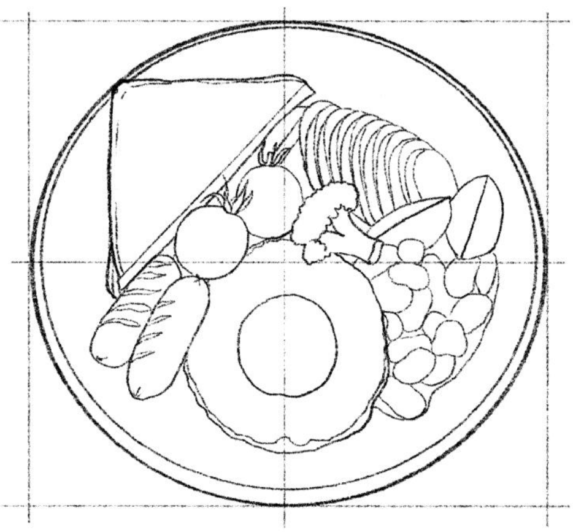

Side Viewpoint

This angle has limitations in conveying depth in food illustrations, which is also the case with the top-down perspective. However, it is ideal for technical illustrations. I often use this view to depict cross-sections of cakes or foods with multiple layers of toppings, such as cupcakes or decorated pastry.

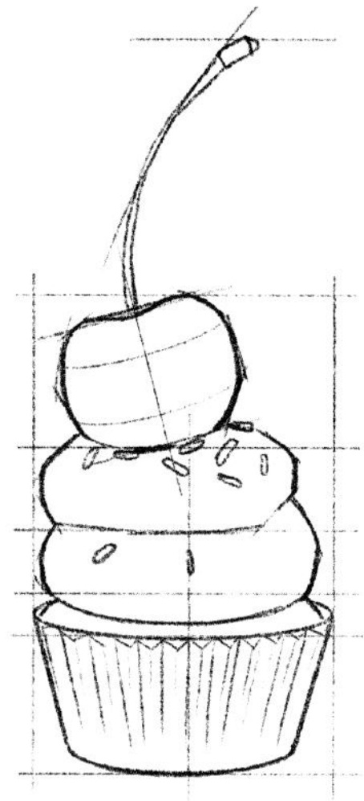

Top-Down Viewpoint

This angle offers a bird's-eye view of the dish, focusing solely on its top surface. The drawback is that it lacks any visible side details, giving the illustration a flat appearance. However, this angle is excellent for foods with flat surfaces and limited side features, such as pizza or toasted bread. Occasionally, I use this perspective to sketch noodle bowls or plates to highlight their toppings, as it provides a clear view of what's on top.

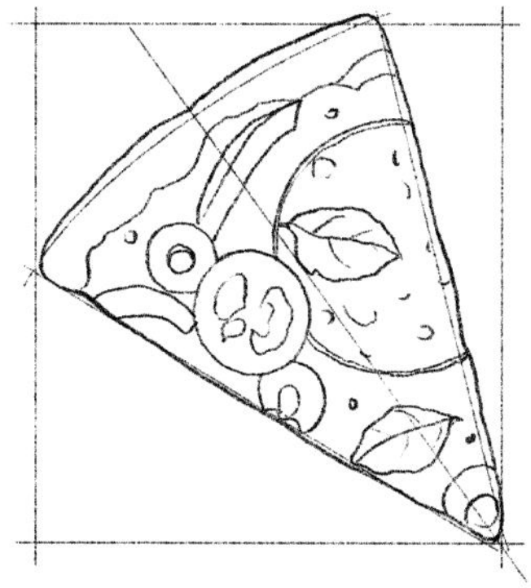

Mixing Colors

Ultimate Food Palettes

Sketching serves as the "skeleton" of your illustration, shading acts as the "skin," and finally, watercolor is like the "clothing" that completes it. When the sketching and shading are done correctly, this final step becomes much easier.

Let's swiftly review the art supplies I typically use, followed by an explanation of basic terms and the much-anticipated color palettes tailored for food illustration.

Water-to-Pigment Mixing Ratios

In watercolor painting, the consistency of your mixture plays a pivotal role in achieving diverse effects. Through careful adjustment of the water-to-pigment ratio, you can manipulate opacity and texture with precision. To help you get a good grasp of this concept, I have created a simple yet effective scale which ranges from level one to five, employing familiar beverage and dairy products to symbolize the thickness of the mixture:

"Tea" Value: The lightest and most diluted mixture, with a high water-to-pigment ratio. It's ideal for light washes and subtle gradients.

"Coffee" Value: Slightly thicker than "Tea," with a bit more pigment but still a translucent quality. It's useful for creating soft tones and light shading.

"Milk" Value: A great balance between transparency and opacity. It's more opaque than "Coffee" and can be used for defining midtones and gentle shading.

"Cream" Value: Higher pigment concentration, resulting in a thicker mixture with greater opacity than "Milk." It's suitable for deeper midtones and more defined areas of shading.

"Butter" Value: The thickest of all, it contains minimal water and is highly opaque. It's used for bold strokes, strong shadows and detailing that requires rich color.

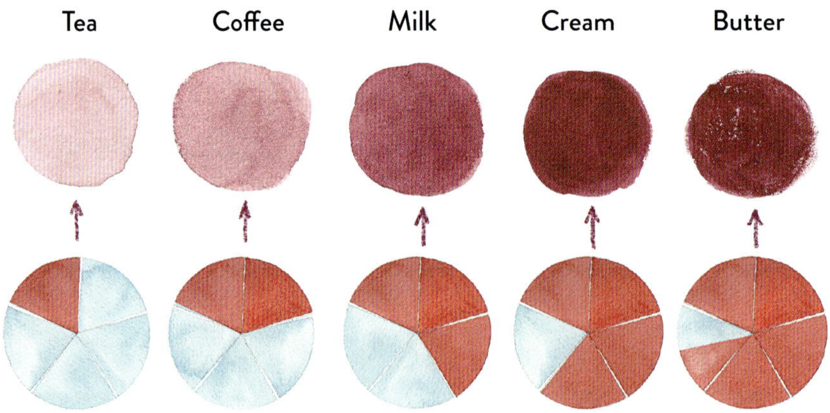

Utilizing this scale, you can easily determine the optimal water-to-pigment ratio for your watercolor endeavors. This method also aids in identifying the lightest and densest values within your watercolor palette. Henceforth, I'll incorporate these names into my instructions.

Water-to-Pigment Mixing Ratios

Color Mixture

This term indicates a blend of one or more color pigments combined with water. I frequently mix these solutions as I paint to fine-tune the colors and attain the desired tones for my illustration.

Following are thematic palettes revealing the hues used for each color mixture, their potential values and their application in food illustration. These color palettes will be your helpful guide whenever you need to find the right mixtures for your food paintings.

Pastry Palette

Quinacridone Gold, Burnt Sienna, Raw Umber, Pyrrol Orange, Burnt Umber, Permanent Violet

COLOR / VALUE	MILK-CREAM	COFFEE	TEA	APPLIED TO
Raw Umber				Bread Crumbs
Quinacridone Gold Pyrrol Orange				Pancakes Pastries Honey Tea
Quinacridone Gold Raw Umber				
Quinacridone Gold Burnt Sienna Raw Umber				Bread Crust Roasted Nuts
Quinacridone Gold Pyrrol Orange Burnt Umber				
Pyrrol Orange Burnt Umber				Wooden Texture Chocolate Coffee
Burnt Umber Raw Umber Permanent Violet				

Green Produce Palette

- Cadmium Yellow
- New Gamboge
- Quinacridone Gold
- Sap Green
- Phthalo Green (Yellow shade)
- Phthalo Green (Blue shade)
- Phthalo Blue (Green shade)
- Burnt Umber
- Raw Umber

COLOR / VALUE	MILK-CREAM	COFFEE	APPLIED TO
Cadmium Yellow Phthalo Green YS			Lettuce Cabbage Avocado
New Gamboge Phthalo Green BS			Green Onions Chives Herbs Beans
Phthalo Blue GS Quinacridone Gold			
Phthalo Green BS Burnt Umber			Watermelon Skin Kale Broccoli Rosemary Sage
Phthalo Green BS Raw Umber			
Phthalo Green BS Quinacridone Gold			Olives Cantaloupe Skin Cooked Bitter Melon Cooked Mustard
Sap Green Raw Umber			

Fruity Palette

Hansa Yellow	Pyrrol Scarlet	Quinacridone Rose	Phthalo Blue (Green shade)
New Gamboge	Permanent Alizarin Crimson	Permanent Violet	Cold Grey
Permanent Orange	Quinacridone Magenta	Ultramarine Blue	Raw Umber

COLOR / VALUE	MILK-CREAM	COFFEE	APPLIED TO
Phthalo Blue GS Quinacridone Rose			Blueberries Purple Figs Concord Grapes Dark Purple Plums
Ultramarine Blue Cold Grey			
Pyrrol Scarlet Quinacridone Rose Ultramarine Blue Phthalo Blue GS			Purple Grapes Purple Carrots Plums Figs
Quinacridone Rose Cold Grey			
Permanent A. Crimson Cold Grey			Purple Cabbage Red Grapes Mangosteen Passion Fruit Skin Beets Dragonfruit Raspberries
Quinacridone Rose Raw Umber			
Permanent A. Crimson Quinacridone Magenta			
Permanent A.Crimson Quinacridone Magenta Permanent Violet			
Pyrrol Scarlet Permanent Violet			Pink Grapefruit Blood Orange

Surf to Turf Palette

	Pyrrol Orange	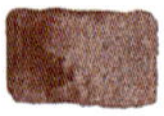	Indian Red	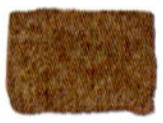	Burnt Umber
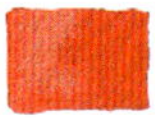	Pyrrol Scarlet	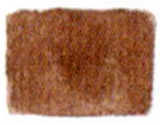	Burnt Sienna	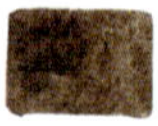	Raw Umber

COLOR / VALUE	MILK-CREAM	COFFEE	TEA	APPLIED TO
Indian Red				White Fish Raw Chicken Grilled Beef
Indian Red Raw Umber	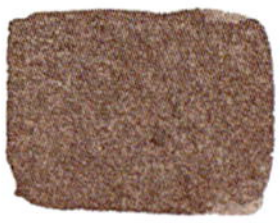			
Pyrrol Orange	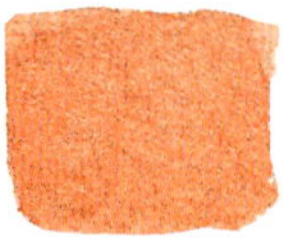	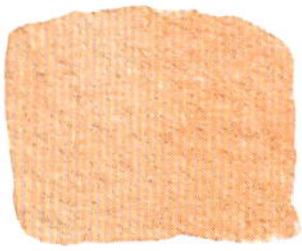		Grilled Shrimp Char Siu Pork Meatballs Crispy Pork Skin Salmon
Pyrrol Orange Pyrrol Scarlet Burnt Umber	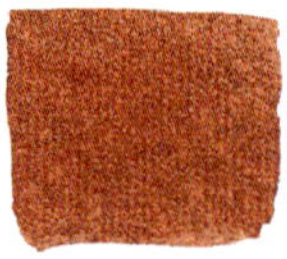	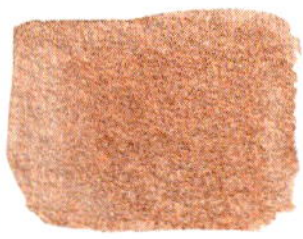		
Burnt Sienna	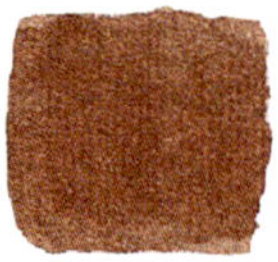	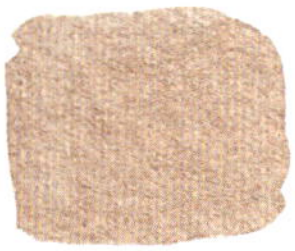		BBQ Meat Cooked Pork Fried Bacon
Pyrrol Scarlet Burnt Sienna Burnt Umber	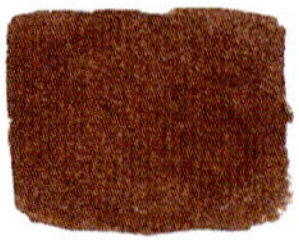	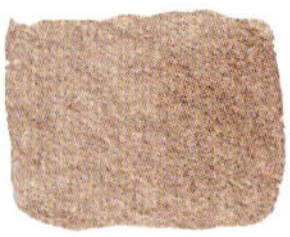		
Pyrrol Scarlet Indian Red	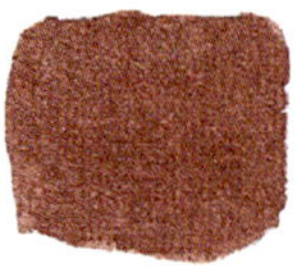	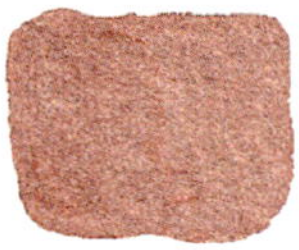		Bacon Ham Raw Meat Tuna

Depicting Texture

Common Brushstrokes in Food Illustration

Now that you've grasped the ideas of color mixtures and their values, let's get into the captivating realm of textures—exciting, isn't it? To effectively capture food textures on paper, you need to become familiar with two fundamental techniques: wet-on-wet (WOW) and wet-on-dry (WOD). There are no strict rules for combining these techniques; instead, focus on how to leverage their unique effects on the paper using the right amount of water and the appropriate brush. The key takeaway is learning how to translate the observed textures of food into the techniques needed to depict them, rather than simply perfecting your painting skills.

Principles In Watercolor Painting

Remember: Dry paper, a dry brush and dry tissue *absorb* liquid (water/color mixture). Dry paper absorbs color from the brush. On the other hand, wet paper and a wet brush tend to *repel* liquid. A clean dry brush or tissue can remove excess water or color from the paper. Understanding how much water your paper and brush can hold is essential for mastering your skills. Always take some time to experiment with your new set of art supplies, engaging with your brush, paper and colors. This experimentation phase is crucial for acquainting yourself with your materials and exploring their capabilities in painting.

The **wet-on-wet (WOW) technique** involves applying color or water onto a moist paper surface. This technique creates a soft spread of color, ideal for blending or moving colors on the paper. I primarily use WOW in the initial stages of painting food to establish base layers.

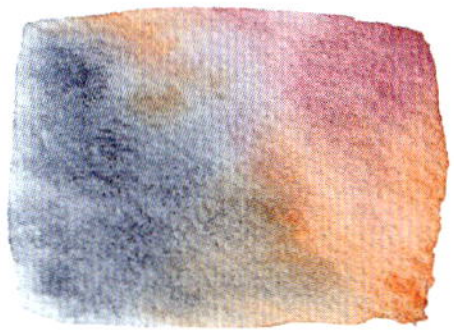

Color blending

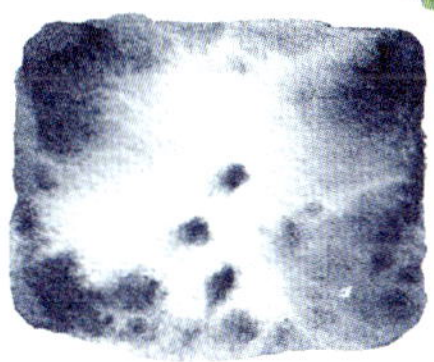

Bloom effect

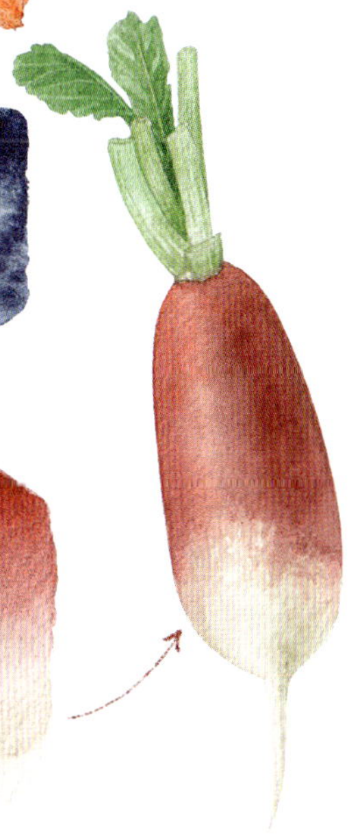

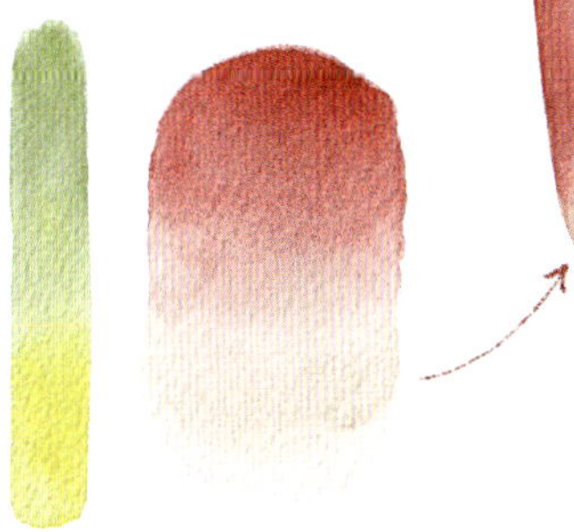

Gradient effect

Artist's Tip: In my food illustration practice, where most objects are small and delicate, I typically don't wet the paper before applying color. Instead, I begin by applying a subtle wash of light value (resembling Milk or Tea) as the first layer and work on the next step while it's still damp.

Conversely, the **wet-on-dry (WOD) technique** entails applying color or water onto a dry paper surface. This method allows for precise control of the mixture on the paper, as it doesn't spread out. I typically employ WOD toward the end of the painting process when adding delicate details or casting shadows. For example, the WOD technique can be effectively used to depict both glossy stainless steel and wooden textures, despite their very different appearances.

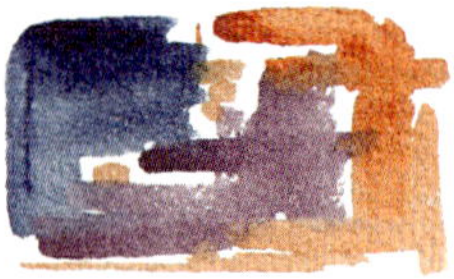

Sharp edges

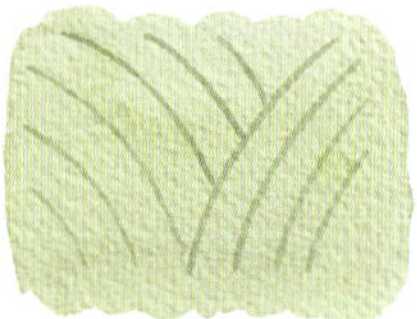

Sharp detail on dry background

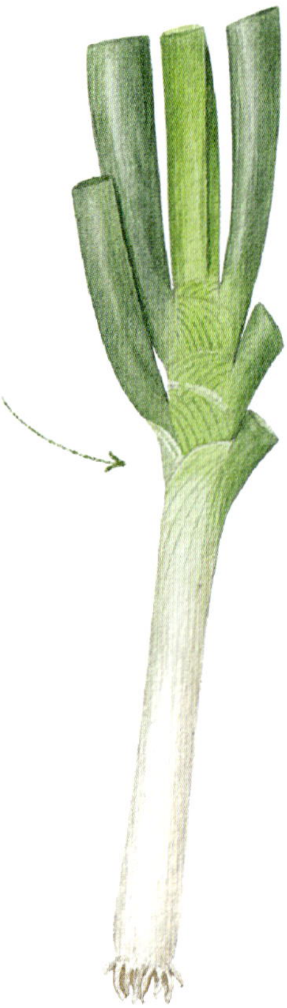

Scumbling effect

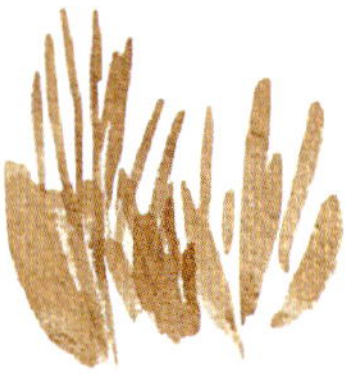

Hatching lines

Flat Wash

Applying to food illustration: A flat wash is used to achieve a seamless coverage, devoid of puddles or discernible strokes, especially to convey the initial base for food items with a smooth appearance.

Exercise: Prepare a Milk value mixture of any color. Take a good amount of this mixture onto a filbert brush #4 and apply it on dry paper. Move and press your brush gradually on the surface to fill the shape that you want (a square, in my example) without leaving any puddles. If your brush feels dry and is unable to leave the same shade of color, avoid exerting excessive force to drag the brush across the paper as it may result in coarseness. Instead, quickly dip it again into the palette to get more mixture and come back to where you left off. Repeat these steps until you finish.

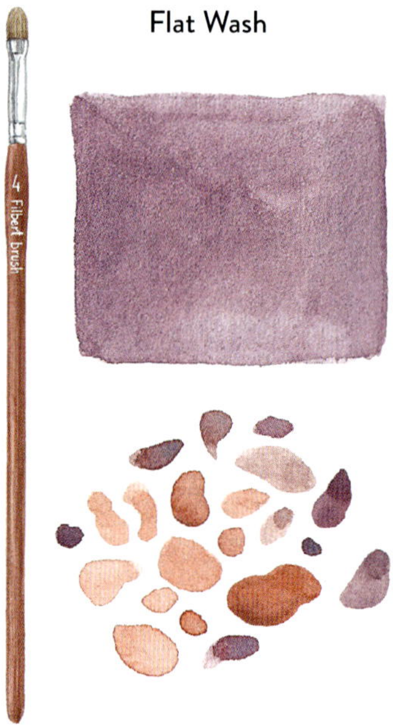

Advanced: Use the same technique with different brushes to explore an array of shapes and sizes to enhance your understanding of the aptness of each brush.

Gradient Wash

Applying to food illustration: Widely used in food illustration, this type of wash captures the gradient base layer and smooth transitions between highlight, midtone and shadow areas.

Exercise: Prepare a mixture of colors in "Cream" value. Select a filbert brush #8 and load it generously with the mixture. Apply the mixture onto the paper from left to right to create a thick, straight line. Next, dip the brush into a rinse jar to remove excess pigment, then gently blot it with a paper towel to ensure it remains damp and has enough pigment. Return to the paper and wash another straight line below the first one, leaving a gap between the lines. Repeat this process several times, each time with less pigment on the brush and ensure it maintains proper dampness, to create lighter values.

Gradient Wash

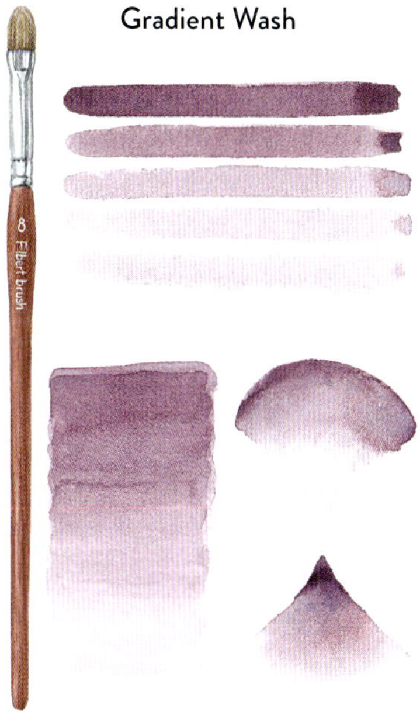

Advanced: This exercise helps you control the water and pigment on your brush while painting. Once you get familiar with it, try to put the lines together and create a gradient background. You can change the way you move your brush to create more interesting gradient forms.

Scumbling Brushstrokes

Applying to food illustration: Commonly used in food illustration during the detailing phase, this brushstroke effect can easily express textured gradation of colors or values, such as in depicting bread crumbs or bumpy surfaces.

Exercise: Prepare a "Cream" value mixture on your palette. Using a filbert brush #4, apply the mixture to dry paper by gently scumbling the brush's tip to create a pattern of random dots. Dip the brush in water to dilute the solution, then return to the paper and continue scumbling to produce various shades. These can be overlapped and applied randomly on the paper.

Scumbling

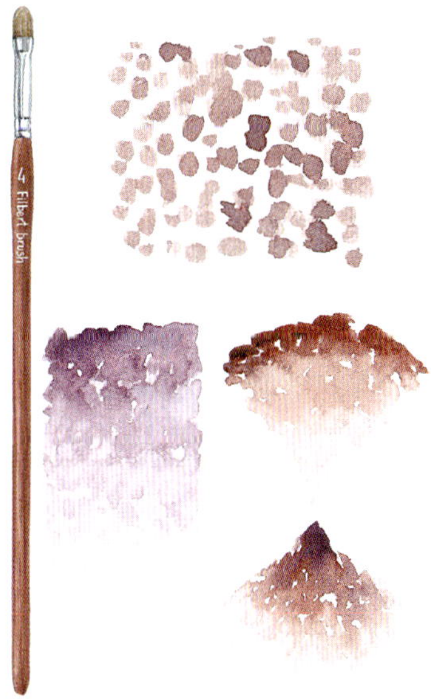

Advanced: Later, try to combine this scumbling brushstroke with flat wash technique, and voila! You are already creating interesting and practical texture with different values!

Hatching Lines

Applying to food illustration: Hatch lines are extensively used in the detailing phase to achieve textured gradations of colors or values, particularly for surfaces that are coarse, furry or hairy, such as wood grains, rambutan or coconut shell.

Exercise: Prepare a mixture in "Milk" value. Using round brush #1 or #2, stroke multiple short vertical lines on dry paper. Swiftly move your wrist from left to right after each downward movement to create lines of varying length and size. Ensure that the lines do not touch each other to prevent blending.

Now, employ the same technique, but after the intended space is filled, lightly wash your brush. Return to the paper and add lines so that their heads overlap with the tails of previous lines. Perform this step swiftly to allow slight color blending and create a bloom effect. Repeat this process several times until the mixture on your brush approaches the color of the white paper. This brushstroke demonstrates another method for creating a gradient background with straight lines.

Hatching

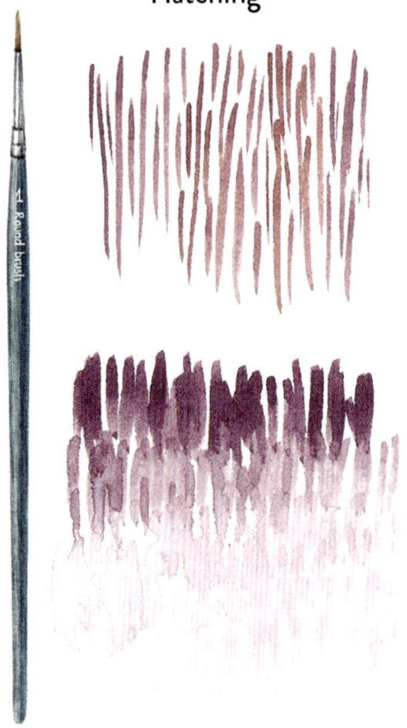

Thick-and-Thin Brushstrokes

Applying to food illustration: This brushstroke effect can be used for both the initial base layer and detailing, aiming to achieve a serene, water-like flow suitable for painting liquids and their reflections.

This technique is all about learning how to control pressure points on your brush by pressing and lifting. While this exercise primarily focuses on the left-right direction, this style can be employed in any direction you desire.

Exercise: Prepare a mixture in "Milk" value on your palette. Using round brush #2, gently draw a zigzag line on dry paper. This step helps your wrist become accustomed to the left-right movement. Next, draw another line straight from left to right, varying the pressure points along the way as long as the tip still touches the paper. This exercise enhances the flexibility of your wrist as it moves across the paper.

Advanced: Now, combine these two movements and create a zigzag pattern with varying thickness. While painting, you can dip the brush in a different color to achieve a nice blend. The key here is to move your wrist quickly but gently.

Thick-and-Thin Strokes

Principles In Creating Food Textures

The texture of any object is a result of how light interacts with its surface—whether it's reflected back into the environment, absorbed by the object or a combination of both. Glossy and smooth surfaces, such as cherry skin, excel at reflecting light, creating bright highlights. In contrast, matte or bumpy surfaces, like orange peel, have subdued highlights and deeper shadows in some spots. Materials like metal or glass not only reflect light but also capture reflections of their surroundings.

What follows are some of the most common textures found in food items. While there are many more textures than these, they are typically combinations of the ones introduced here. Feel free to revisit this section whenever you have doubts.

Glossy & Semi-Glossy Surfaces

These textures reflect a significant portion of the light that strikes their surface back into the environment. This characteristic results in high contrast on areas directly facing the light source.

Round brush size 1
Filbert brush size 4

Techniques: Gradient wash, small scumbling brushstrokes

Color Palette

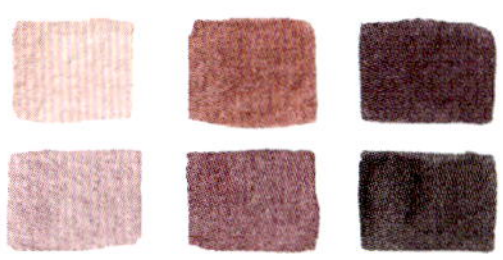

Featured Brushstrokes

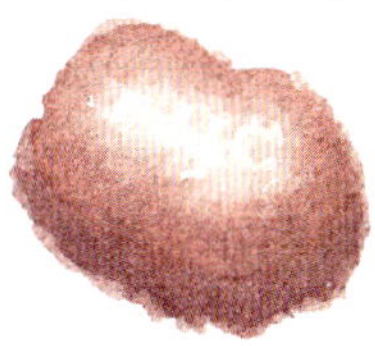

In food illustration, this texture is evident in smooth-skinned fruits such as cherries, apples, strawberries and oranges, as well as in certain condensed liquids like melting chocolate, jam, boba pearls, etc.

Exercise: I typically begin by painting the entire designated area using the WOW technique, except for the highlight zone. Then, I gradually add more layers in "Milk" value to create the deep shade of the shadowed side. To soften the edge where the color meets the highlight zone, I pick up a clean, damp brush and begin scumbling from the colored side toward the lightest area. This technique allows me to achieve a blending effect while retaining high contrast between the two zones. Despite the smooth appearance of cherry skin, I choose the scumbling technique to infuse character into the blending process, since overly smooth wash can inadvertently give the texture a plastic-like appearance.

> **Artist's Tip:** The highlight area is often seen as white but in this cherry illustration, I put a thin layer of light pink to enhance its natural appearance.

For smoother and glossier surfaces like melting chocolate, I prefer using the gradient wash technique (page 25) instead of scumbling to achieve a shinier effect.

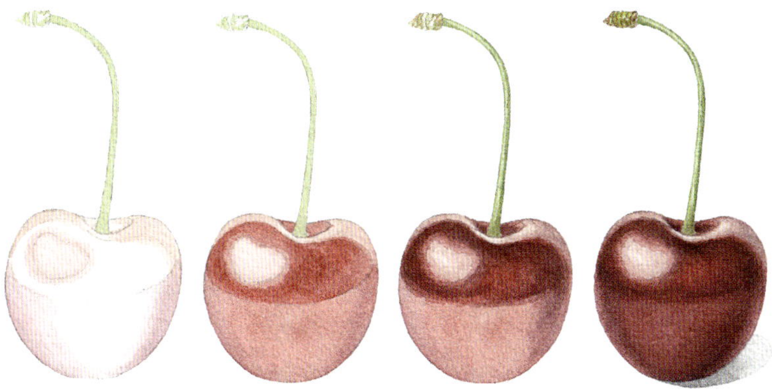

Wood

In nature, each wood grain is unique, akin to snowflakes or human fingerprints, boasting a diverse array of patterns and colors. It's essential to understand the specific type of wood grain you are depicting and its inherent properties. For instance, bamboo wood grain tends to be more streamlined and duller compared to hardwood.

Common wooden items found in the kitchen include cutting boards, mixing spoons, mixing bowls, coasters and more.

Exercise: First, employ the WOW technique for the base layer, establishing the basic shading for the object. Colors used for wooden texture can vary from light yellow to dark brown. Once the shading is complete, apply the WOD technique to paint the wood grain and/or knots. Pay careful attention to the direction of the grain, considering how it may differ on each surface, as well as its irregularities in width and hues to mimic its natural arrangement.

Artist's Tip: The grain must remain seamless and continuous, even when the object is cut through or manipulated. Always keep your wrist relaxed and ensure your brush absorbs enough solution to preserve the natural depiction of the texture.

Filbert brush size 4
Round brush size 1
Spotter brush size 3/0

Techniques: Gradient wash, hatching small and sharp details

Color Palette

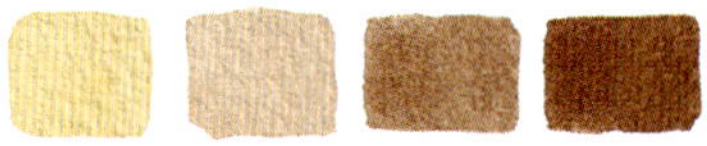

Featured Brushstrokes

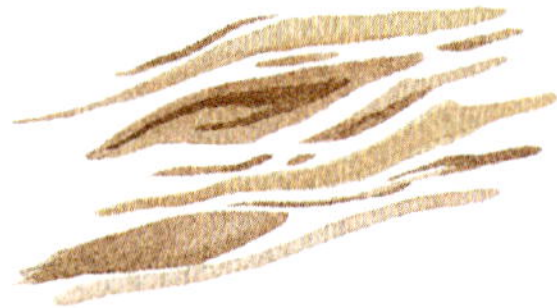

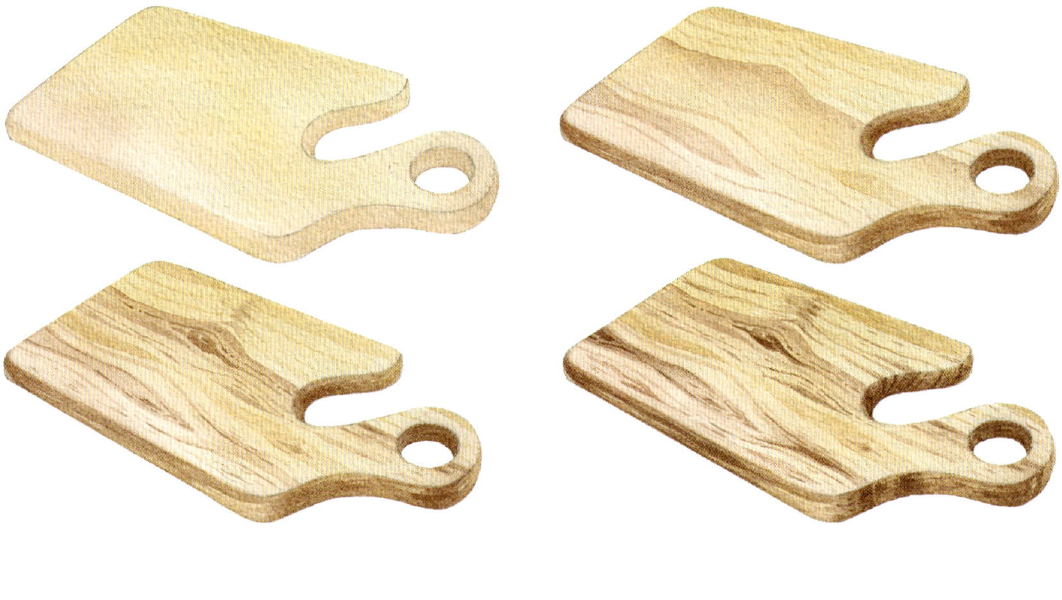

Filbert brush size 4
Spotter brush size 3/0

Techniques: Flat wash, gradient wash, hatching thin lines

Color Palette

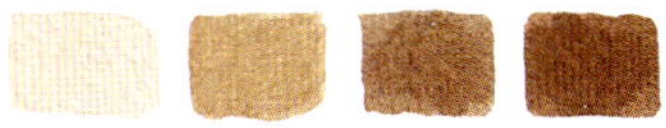

Featured Brushstrokes

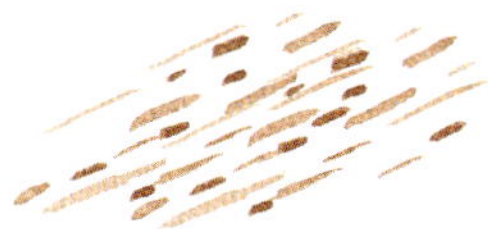

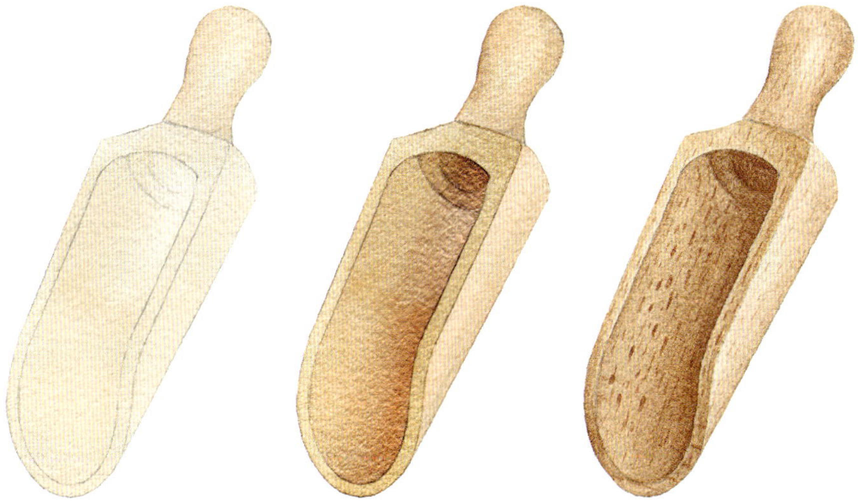

Liquids

Liquids have the capacity to reflect light, and their transparency allows them to adopt the characteristics of their container, as demonstrated in the example of honey on the next page. There is no universally applicable shading technique for liquids; it varies greatly depending on the surrounding environment and the interaction of light with and through the liquid. This exercise demands meticulous and ongoing observation of your object or reference photo while you work on it.

The most commonly depicted liquid textures in food illustration include honey, caramel, chocolate sauce, etc.

Exercise: There are two separate steps involved here. First, I use the WOW technique to apply basic shading to all elements, excluding the reflective highlight zone of the honey. After that, I gradually add more layers for midtone and shadow areas using the WOD technique, working on new layers only after the previous one has completely dried out.

Artist's Tip: It's best to use a spotter brush #3/0 and round brush #1 for the areas surrounding the reflective highlight. This helps to create sharp boundaries between the brightest and darkest tone, boosting the reflective property of the liquid.

Round brush size 1
Filbert brush size 4
Spotter brush size 3/0

Techniques: Gradient wash, wet-on-dry

Color Palette

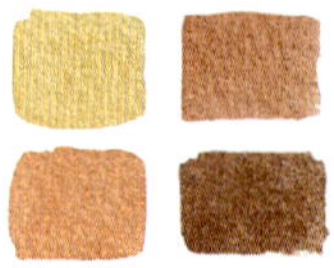

Featured Brushstrokes

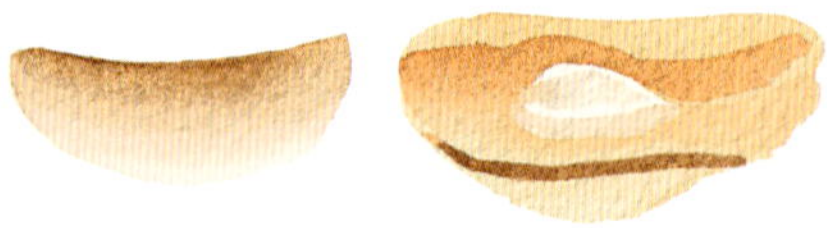

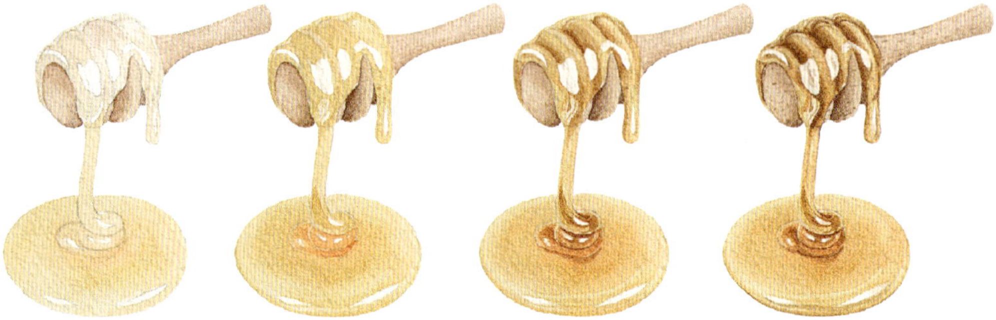

Round brush size 1, 2

Technique: Gradient wash

Color Palette

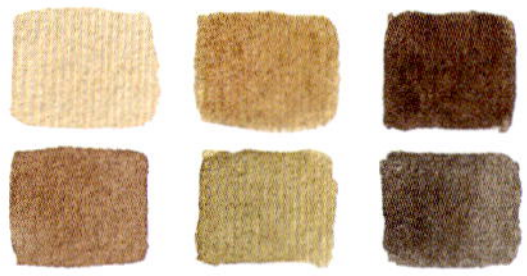

Featured Brushstrokes

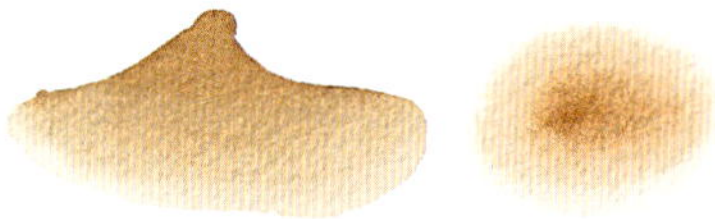

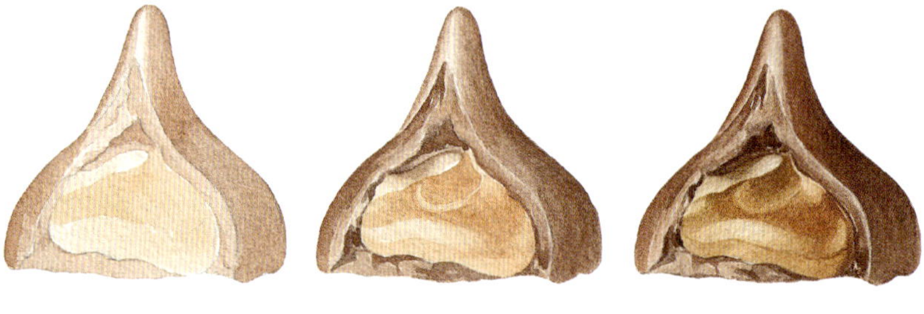

Caramel is much more opaque than honey, so the contrast and sharp boundaries between highlights and shadows should be toned down.

Metal

Metal surfaces reflect the majority of light that strikes them, resulting in a mirror-like effect. This characteristic makes them highly influenced by lighting and any surrounding objects.

In food illustration, commonly depicted metal items include utensils, pots and pans made of silver, bronze or stainless steel.

Exercise: Metal necessitates a pronounced contrast between the highlights and shadows of the object. Notably, there will be a clear bright spot within the shadow area and a clear dark spot within the highlight.

Pay close attention to the reflective properties, which are much more apparent than in liquids. I exclusively employed sharp WOD and sharp edge brushstrokes for this material. What's more, I introduced a dark-brown spot (featured in the enlarged circle) in the shadow area to depict a reflection from a nearby brown object.

Artist's Tip: Depending on the mood you want to set for the environment where your object is placed, mix either cool or warm colors into your gray solution. I recommend using Raw Umber for warmth and Ultramarine Blue for coolness.

Round brush size 1, 2
Spotter brush size 3/0

Techniques: Gradient wash, flat wash

Color Palette

Featured Brushstrokes

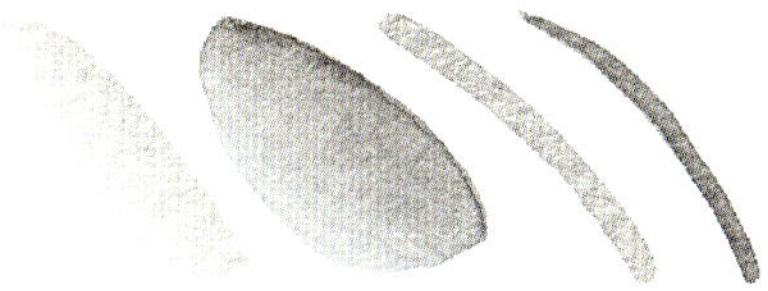

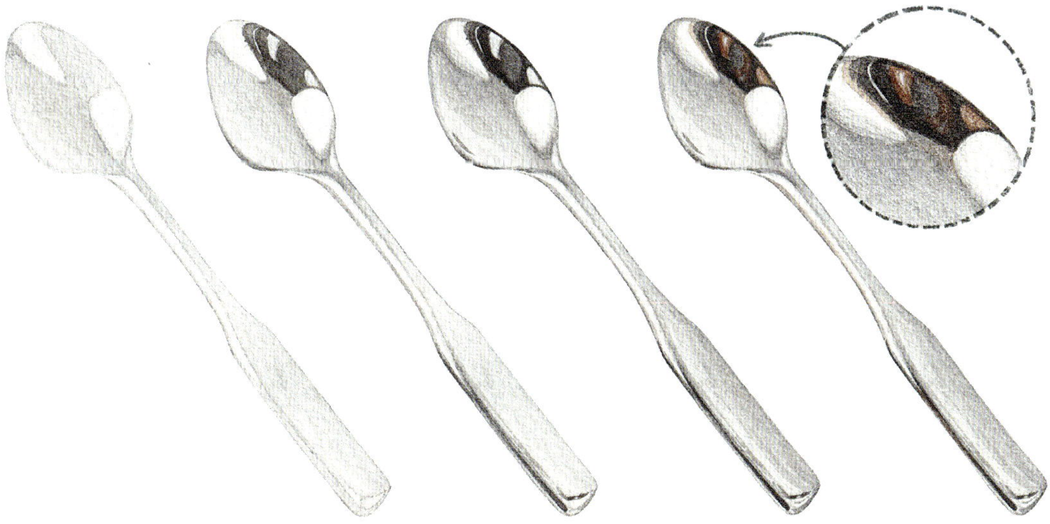

Glass & Transparent Materials

Essentially, to render transparent materials effectively, we focus on painting the objects contained within them rather than the material itself. The clearer these objects are depicted, the more transparent the container appears. For example, a glass cup is more transparent than the ice cubes within it, so greater attention should be paid into detailing the ice cubes. Conversely, ice cubes are more opaque than pure glass, thus they will partially obscure anything behind them.

Some of the most common transparent items (ranging from clear to slightly opaque) in food illustration include cups, glasses, ice cubes, glass containers, jars, rice paper, plastic wrap, etc.

Exercise

For the glass, I use the WOD technique to establish bold contrast between highlight and shadow for the rim. The midtone area at the back should be blended with a damp brush.

For the ice cubes, begin with the WOW technique for the initial base layer, then transition to WOD to depict how shadows move within water. It's essential to place highlights and shadow zones randomly, sometimes juxtaposing them to emphasize the brightest and darkest spots, thus enhancing the realistic reflective properties of the material. I recommend using a thick-and-thin brushstroke for this step.

Artist's Tip: Everything looks a bit bigger and shows less detail when submerged underwater. Therefore, it's important to create a subtle difference in size between the floating and submerged parts to enhance realism.

Round brush size 1, 2, 4
Spotter brush size 3/0

Techniques: Gradient wash, thick-and-thin brushstrokes

Color Palette

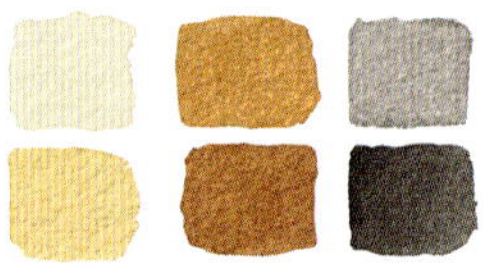

Featured Brushstrokes

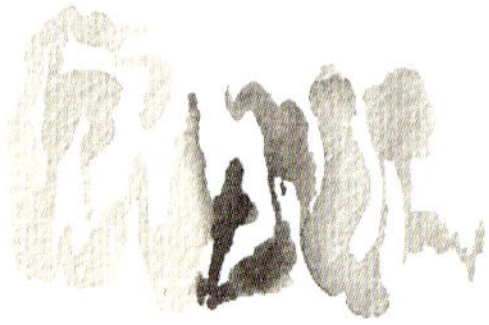

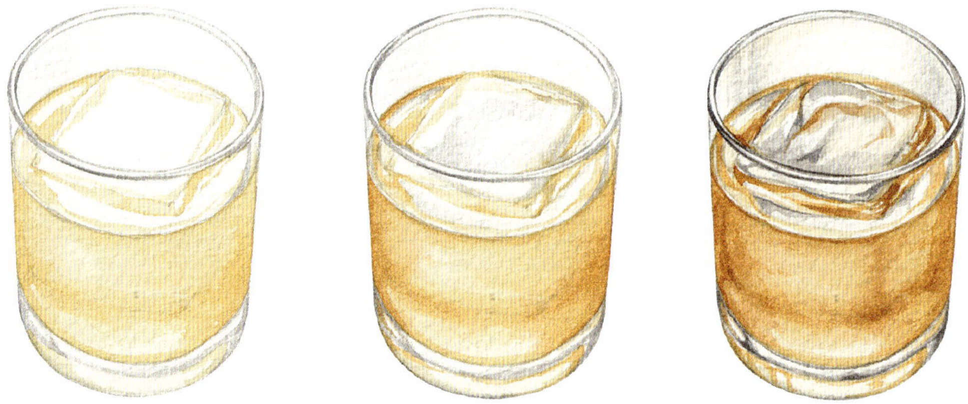

Bread

Bread is such an essential and diverse element in food illustration that I've given it its own dedicated section on texture. Importantly, every type of bread will have a crust and crumb, each with its own unique structure and texture depending on the specific type of bread you are painting.

The Crumb

This part will only become apparent when you "dissect" the bread, a common illustration technique that unveils the appealing aspects of food items. Bread structure varies, from very airy with different-sized cells in sourdough bread, to denser with more uniform holes in sandwich or soft bread.

Airy texture: A sourdough toast showcases cells in irregular shapes and sizes, arranged seemingly at random. As a result, deeper cells receive less light, resulting in darker shadows. In this example, I employ the WOW technique for initial shading, followed by multiple layers of WOD to add darker shades for the cells.

Soft/fluffy texture: Given that the air pockets in sandwich toast are smaller and shallower, I opt for lighter hues. These pockets typically encircle an imaginary center and increase in size as they approach the center of the loaf. I exclusively use "Tea–Coffee" values to avoid over-layering. Initially, I apply the "Tea" value solution with a larger brush for the base shading, then switch to a smaller brush and "Coffee" value, or slightly thicker if needed, for finishing layers.

Round brush size 1, 2
Filbert brush size 4

Techniques: Gradient wash, flat wash, scumbling

Color Palette

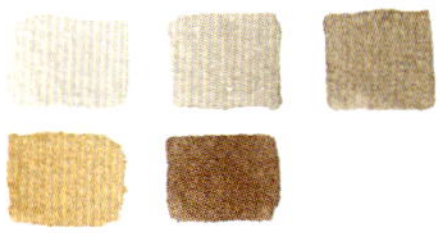

Featured Brushstrokes

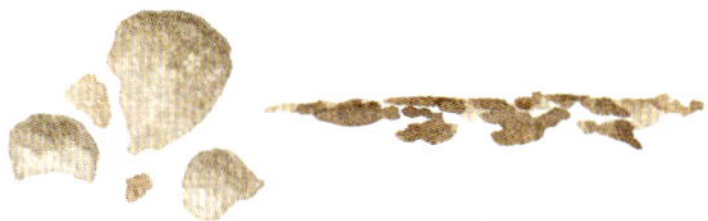

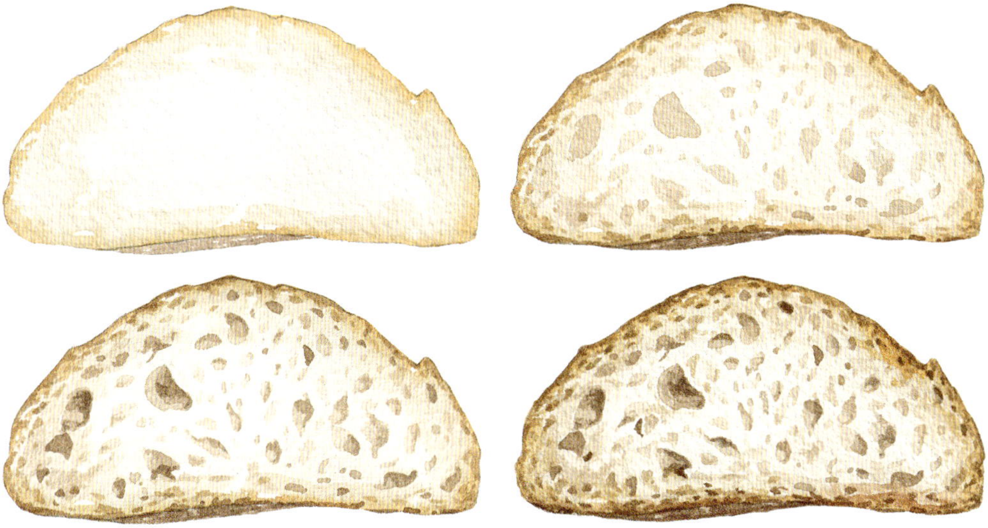

Round brush size 1, 2
Filbert brush size 4

Technique: Scumbling

Color Palette

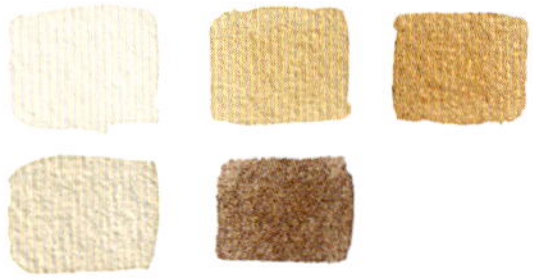

Featured Brushstrokes

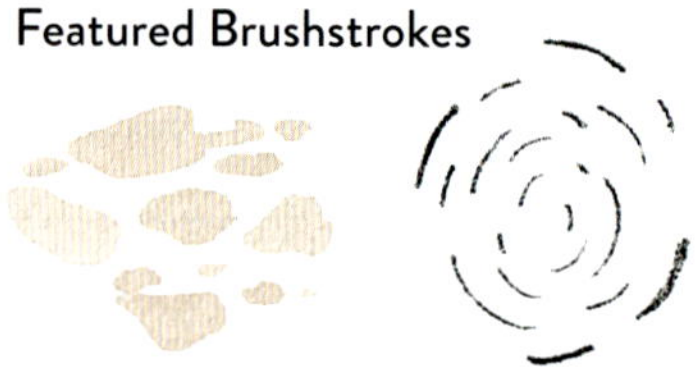

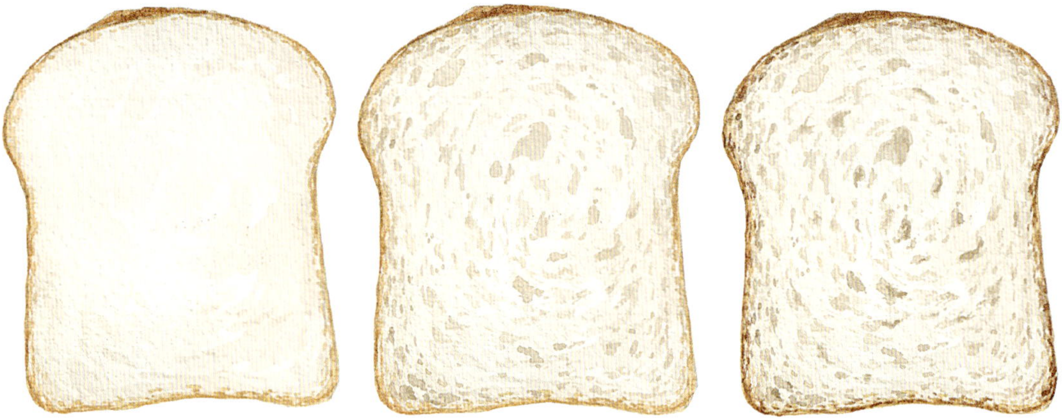

The Crust

Crispy and powdery texture: In this sourdough crust example, I incorporate two types of texture. To portray the crunchiness of the crust, I add layers using the WOD technique. Upon closer observation, you'll notice the structure expands in one or two main directions, depending on how the bread is scored. Therefore, you'll need to move your brush in these directions to enhance the effect.

For areas covered by powder, the texture should be more refined and matte, resulting in reduced contrast between shades and hues compared to the crispy crust. The dark-brown cracks on the powdery surface are crucial details to enliven the appearance.

Begin by applying a gray flat wash, then dab a darker shade on damp paper near the outline to create a 3-D shape. Once this layer has dried, use a smaller brush to paint the cracks randomly, with a few extending to the boundaries, accentuating the bread's ultimate rise.

Flaky texture: Let's use croissants as an example. Their surface is typically wavy with multiple layers, and their buttery dough gives them a more reflective quality compared to other breads, with highlights scattered throughout. Use the thick-and-thin brushstroke technique, moving your wrist back and forth in an arc. Layering should be done on damp paper to achieve a soft blend between shades. Use darker shades and apply lesser pressure with each step to emphasize the folds without making them appear "burned."

Round brush size 1, 2
Filbert brush size 4

Techniques: Gradient wash, scumbling

Color Palette

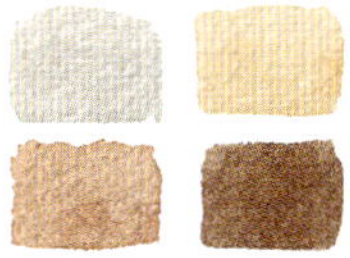

Featured Brushstrokes

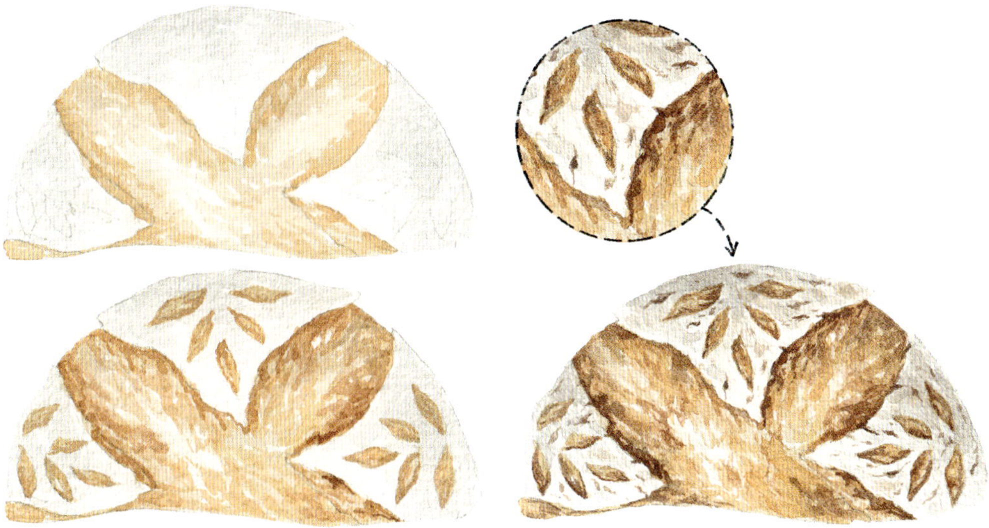

Round brush size 1, 2
Filbert brush size 4

Techniques: Gradient wash, thick-and-thin brushstrokes

Color Palette

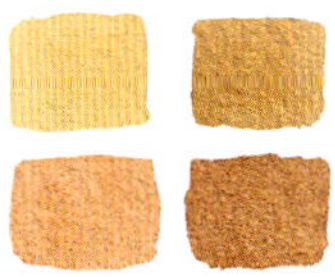

Featured Brushstrokes

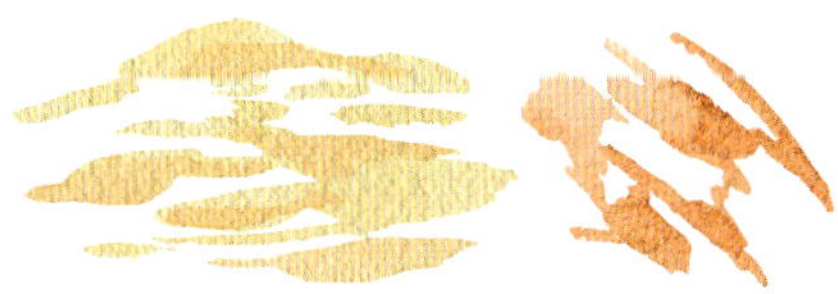

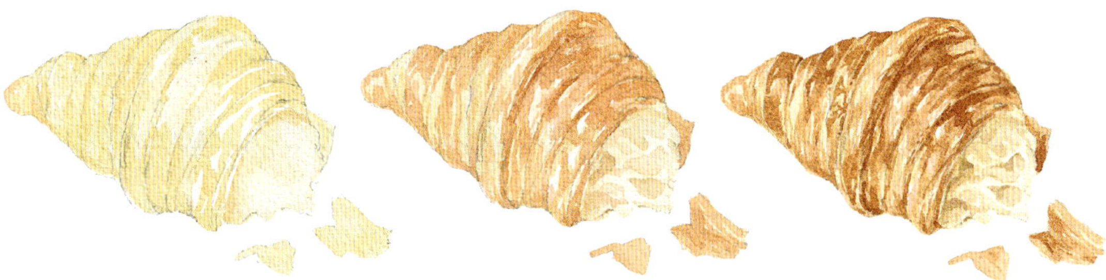

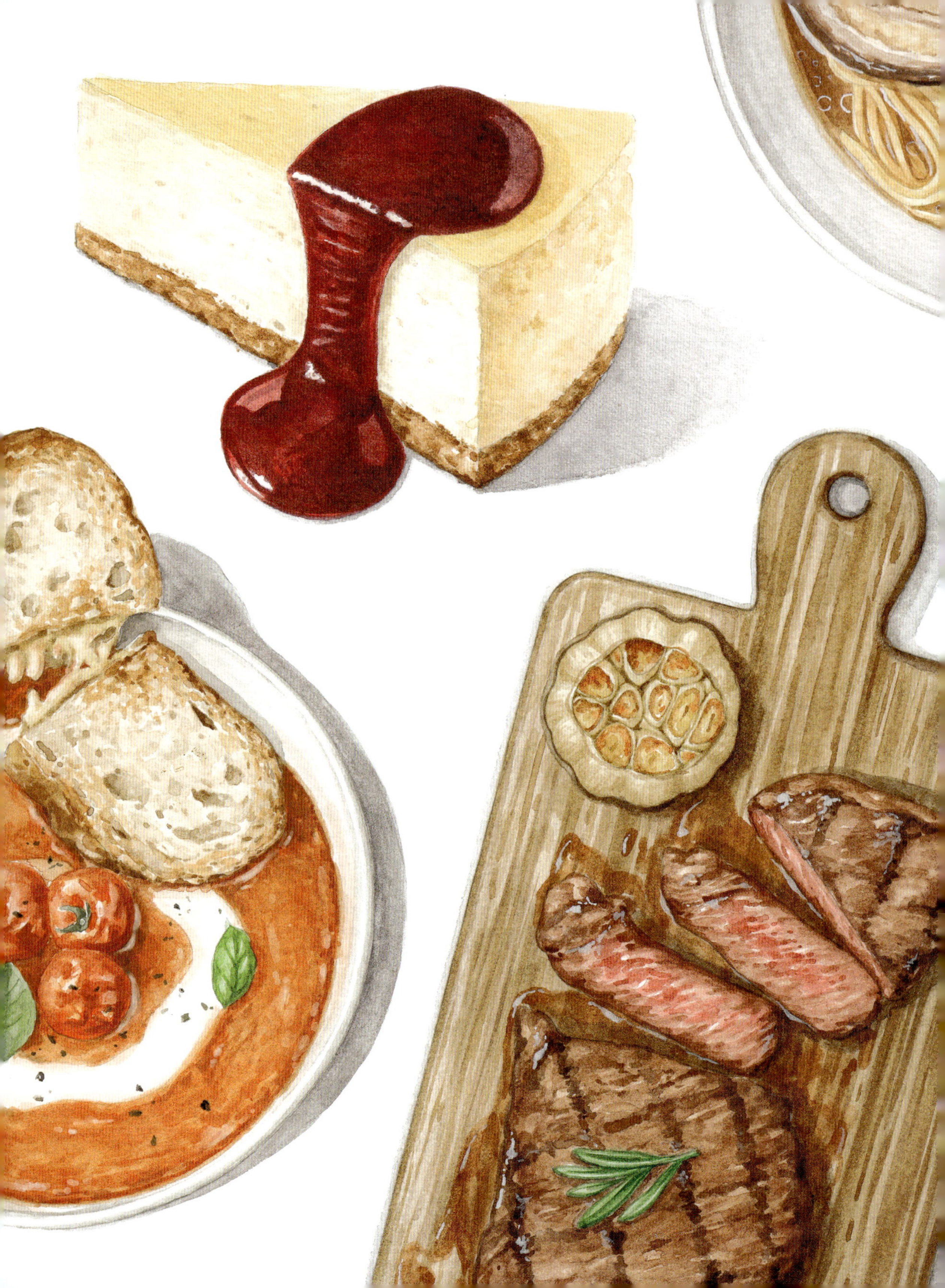

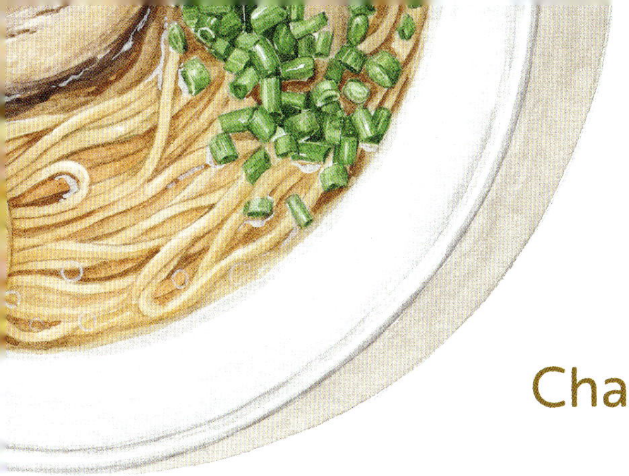

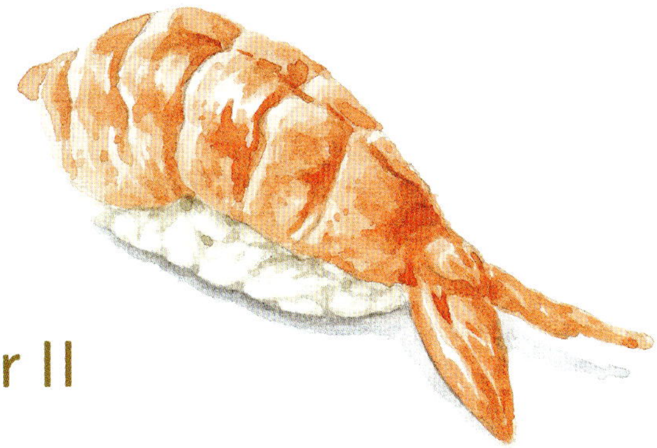

Chapter II

The Painting Projects

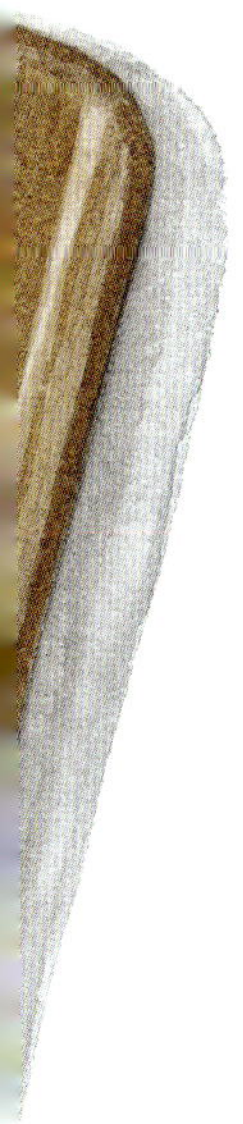

Welcome to Chapter 2, where we delve deeper into the art of food illustration with watercolor. In this section, I'll guide you step-by-step through each project, revealing techniques in greater detail. The dishes featured here have been carefully chosen to highlight the most common shapes and textures you'll encounter in food illustration. As we move forward, you'll discover new skills and insider tips drawn from my personal experience.

This chapter is designed to build your confidence gradually, helping you master sketching and painting techniques as well as the art of selecting the ideal angle based on composition and light source. Patience is key on this journey, so take your time with each project to fully absorb the lessons. As your skills develop, you'll find that painting food becomes an exciting and joyful adventure.

Let's embark on this delicious artistic exploration together. Relax, enjoy the process and watch your abilities flourish with each brushstroke.

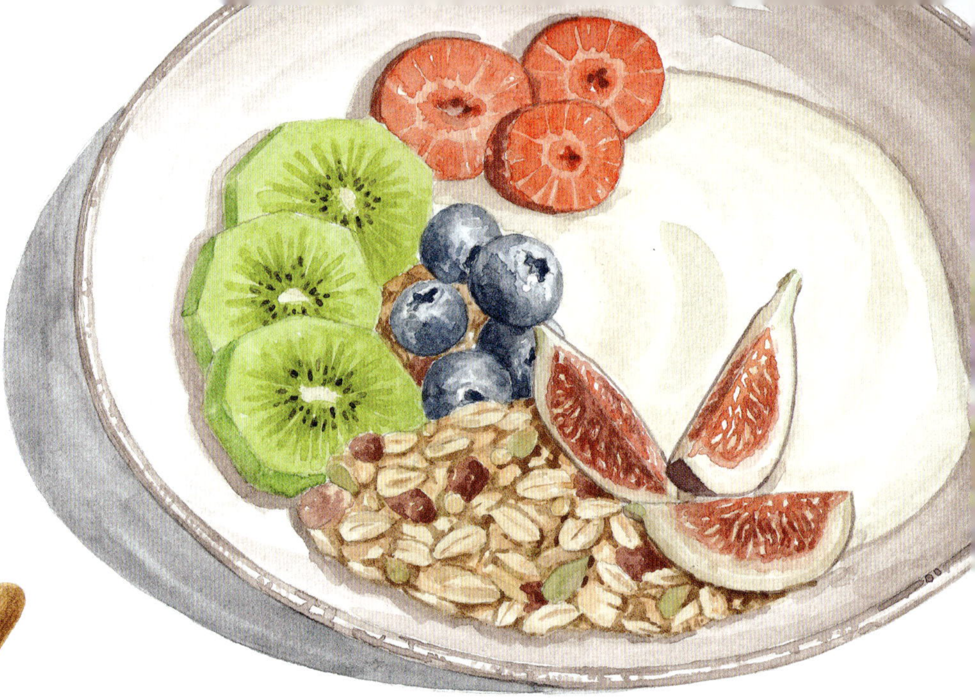

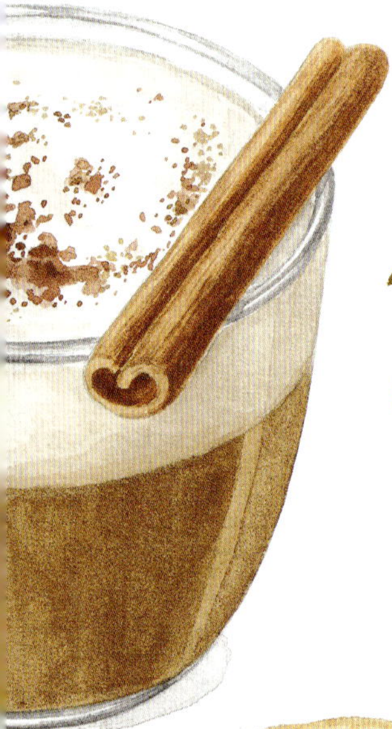

Breakfast & Brunch

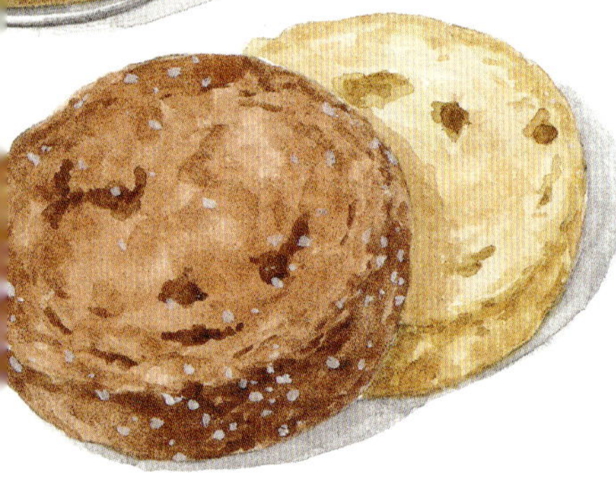

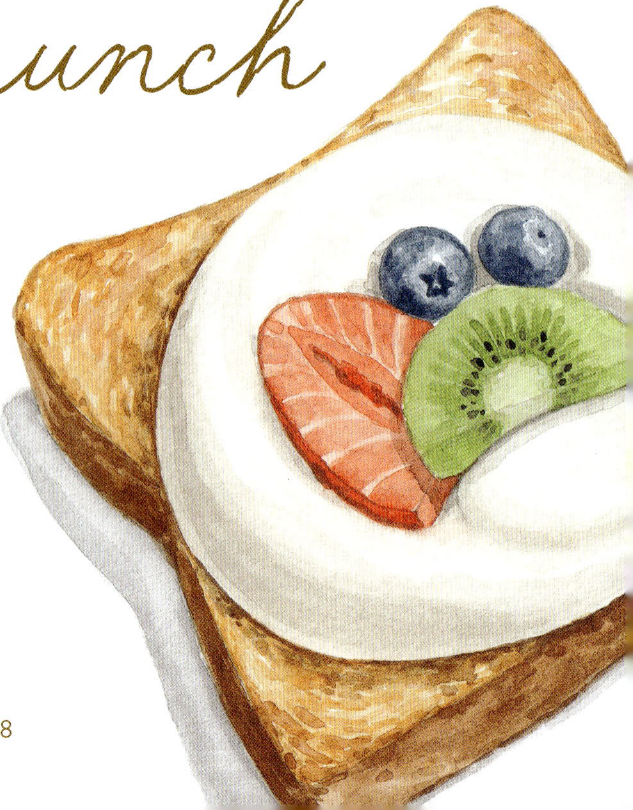

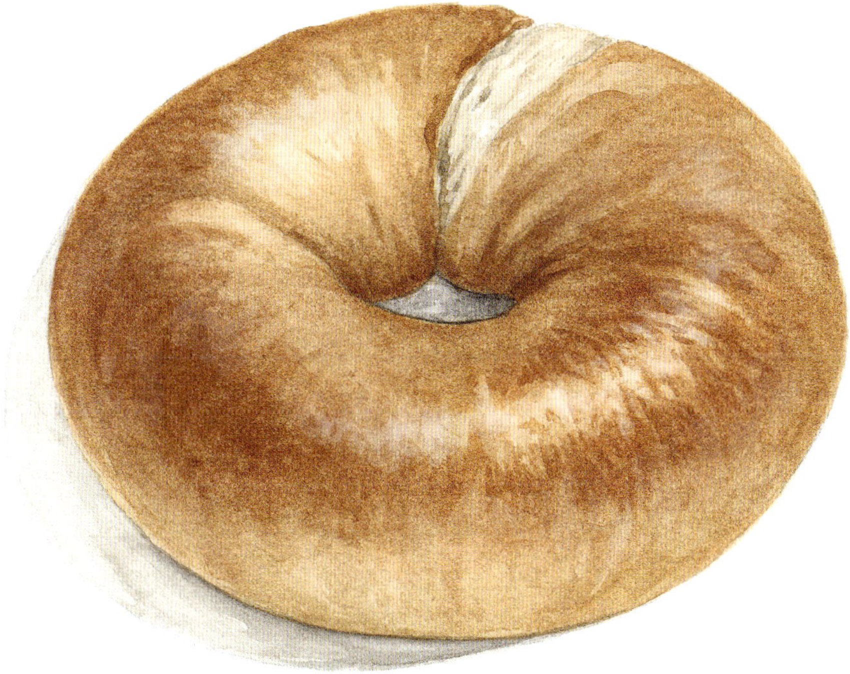

Project 01

New York Bagel

(Dimensions: W 4⅛" x H 3¼" / W 10.5 cm x H 8 cm)

Our initial phase of exploring food illustration starts with a beloved breakfast staple—the bagel, a familiar choice for many. While its appearance may seem straightforward, it presents an invaluable opportunity to master the art of sketching and shading a donut-like shape, skills transferable to various other food forms. I'll guide you through using both wet-on-wet and wet-on-dry techniques (page 23) to capture the distinctive leathery and glossy skin of this delightful breakfast. You'll also become adept at managing different brush sizes to ensure a seamless workflow, preparing you for even more engaging projects in the future.

Brushes

Round brushes: sizes 1, 2 and 4
Filbert brushes: sizes 4 and 8

Color Palette

OBJECT		COLOR NAME	COLOR VALUES		
			Tea/Coffee	Milk	Cream
Bagel	*Mixture 1*	**Pyrrol Orange Quinacridone Gold Burnt Umber**			
	Mixture 2	**Mixture 1 Burnt Sienna**			
	Mixture 3	**Mixture 1 Raw Umber**			
Expanded bread		**Raw Umber**			
Shadow		**Ivory Black**			

Note that there are three mixtures for the bagel body: Mixture 1 is mainly for the initial base; Mixture 2, with a warmer brown tone, is used primarily around the highlighted area of the bagel; and Mixture 3, a colder and deeper brown, is mainly used for the shadowed areas. Since there's only one object, we should aim to vary its colors according to the light source: The closer to the light source, the more vibrant the colors and the greater the contrast should be.

Viewpoint & Light Source

Viewing a bagel from above or the side won't reveal its iconic hole in the center. Therefore, an eye-level viewpoint is ideal for showcasing all its elements and emphasizing its plumpness. The light source should come from the right side, casting shadows to the left onto an imaginary surface.

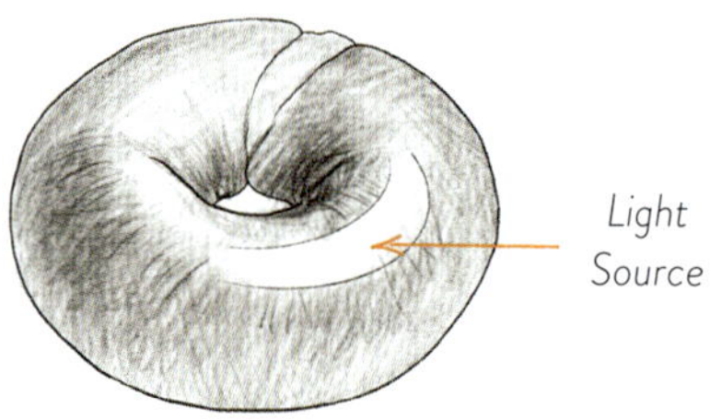

These Light Source Shading Sketches serve as crucial references for determining the highlight, midtone and shadow areas at any stage during the painting phase.

Composition

In this artwork, the composition isn't complex with multiple objects. However, it's crucial to focus on the composition *within* the object itself, ensuring a balanced arrangement of all elements for visual coherence. One technique I use here is creating a scoring slash at the farther top half where the dough expands, adding visual interest to its overall shape. Placing this detail in a distant corner helps balance the focal point, which is the glossy surface closest to the viewer's perspective. This also provides an opportunity to practice depicting both the crusty outside and the soft, expanded interior.

Let's Sketch!

Artist's Tip: When shading donut-like shapes, think of them as cylinders bent around a full circle, with a hole in the middle. This allows you to apply basic shading principles used for cylindrical objects.

Start by defining the central lines for two ovals, one directly below the other. The distance between their centers should be equal to the desired height of the bagel. Next, connect the sides of these ovals with curved lines to outline the thickness of the donut. Then, create a smaller oval inside the upper oval to represent the central hole, ensuring it shares the same center. Visualize the plumpness of the bagel with contour lines, and then connect a small curve below to indicate the bottom of the hole.

Next, consider adding details such as folds, boundaries for the expanded bread and subtle imperfections to the ovals to achieve a more realistic appearance. Finally, use the eraser to lighten the sketch if needed.

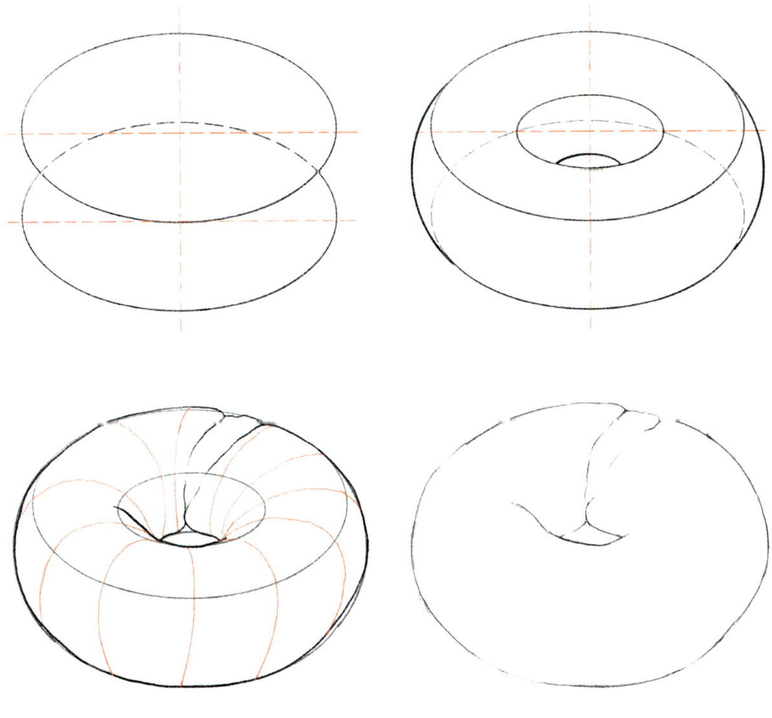

This is a simplified approach to sketching a donut-like shape. Some might argue it lacks technical precision, but I find it suitable for beginners. While bagels come in various shapes, I personally sketch them with a wide center hole that shows both the opening and bottom, which I believe is an effective way to shade and depict their form.

Let's Paint!

First & Second Layer

Use a filbert brush #8 to apply a "Tea" value of Mixture 1 to the entire bagel. For the expanded bread area, rinse and dry your brush, then apply the "Tea" value of Raw Umber to it. Apply this solution to the lowermost corner and blend it upward.

Wait until the first layer is completely dry, then pick up round brush #4 to apply a layer of Mixture 3 in "Tea" value to the bagel, focusing on the shadow areas this time. Employ the gradient wash technique (page 25) as follows: Start from the left edge and move your brush up and down, following the vertical curve of the object (indicated by red arrows).

The bottom half of the object, which receives less light than the top half, will appear darker in shade. Switch to a smaller brush to apply a thicker "Milk" value of the same mixture to the right side and the folds of the inner ring. This will establish the initial sense of depth for your object and indicate where you'll later need to darken to enhance the bagel's three-dimensional shape.

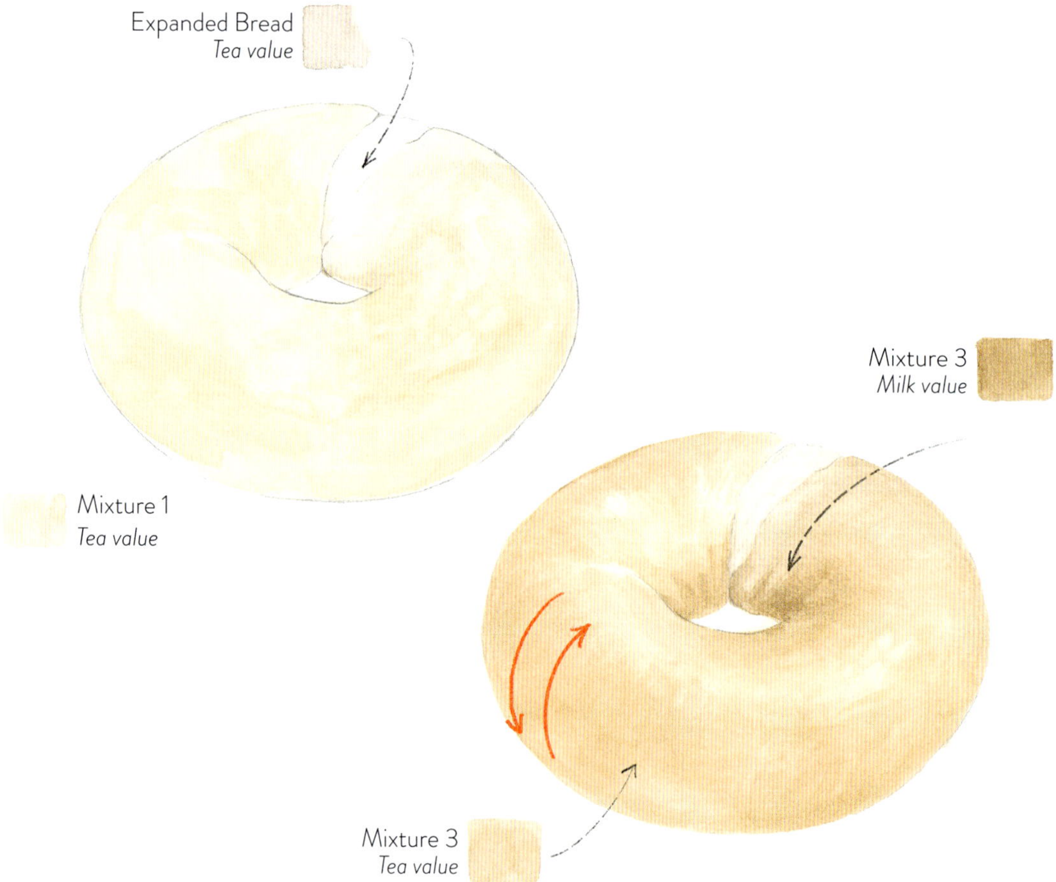

Third Layer

Expanded bread: Use the "Tea" value and round brush #2 to dim the whole area down gradually. When it's dry, switch to round brush #1 and the "Milk" value to add some short strokes along the curve to depict the texture.

Now, make sure the paper is dry, and use a filbert brush #8 to add a "Milk" value layer of Mixture 2 to the entire bagel, except the highlight area (refer to the Light Source Shading Sketch on page 40). While it's still wet, switch to filbert brush #4 to apply the "Cream" value of the same mixture to the shadow areas, employing the same technique used in the second layer. Next, use round brush #1 to add the same "Cream" value solution to deepen the crusty line near the expanded bread.

Add a "Tea" value of gray for the center hole to dim this area down as the light can't reach here.

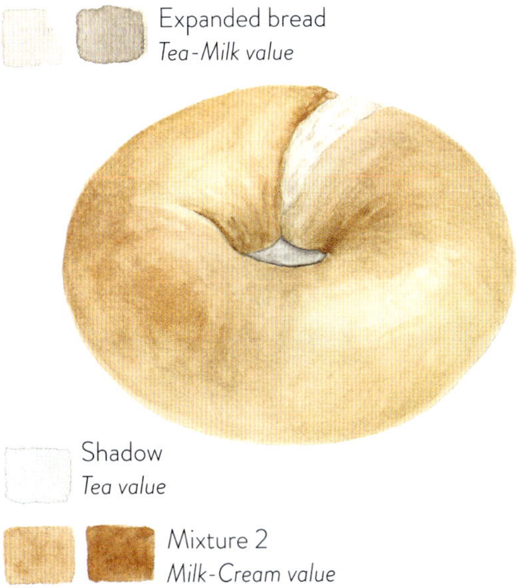

Fourth Layer

Use filbert brush #4 to apply the "Cream" value of Mixture 2 to the midtone areas and Mixture 3 to the shadow areas to deepen the whole donut (refer to the Light Source Shading picture on page 40). Focus especially around the highlight (within the red dotted area) to bring out the brightness of this area, where it's closer to the viewpoint. Turn to the thin side of the filbert brush and make hatching lines to create a soft transition between the midtone and highlight areas.

> **Artist's Tip:** To create a leathery yet glossy surface, you'll need to soften the hatching lines: Apply the "Cream" value to the darker area, then dip the tip of your brush in clean water or the "Tea" value of the same mixture to dilute it slightly. Return to the paper and blend the "Cream" value out, also using hatching lines. This method deepens the darker areas, creates the bagel crust texture and makes a soft transition toward the brighter areas.

Repeat the same process done in the previous layer for the expanded bread area. Use the same "Milk" value of Raw Umber to deepen some of the lines, and feel free to pick some brown tone on your palette and add a touch of it on this area, too.

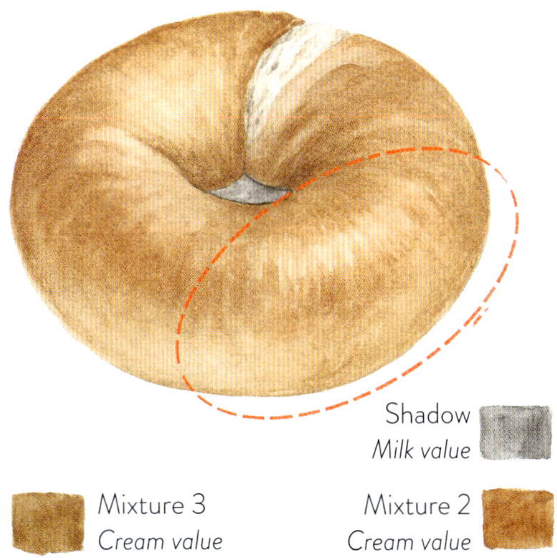

Finishing Touches

Repeat the previous step using round brush #2 to apply the "Cream" value of Mixtures 2 and 3 until you achieve a nice deep brown shade for the shadow areas, especially the right side of the central hole and the left side of the outer wall. At this step, you can move the brush along the vertical curve direction, hatching small brushstrokes, and create the texture at the same time. To create a sharper contrast and define the shape more, use the "Butter" value from Mixtures 2 and 3 to darken both the areas around the highlight and the shadow areas of the bagel.

Artist's Tip: While the bottom half of the object is technically darker than the top half, it appears to be in lighter shade in this painting. This effect is due to the color of the bagel itself. During baking, the top half receives more heat and can sometimes become slightly burnt. The bottom half, receiving less direct heat, retains a lighter color, though it should not be lighter than the highlight.

Use a filbert brush #4 to add the cast shadow, using the "Coffee" shade of Ivory Black with a touch of brown for color harmony. The shadow should be darker and have a sharper border when closer to the light source, fading out as it moves farther back.

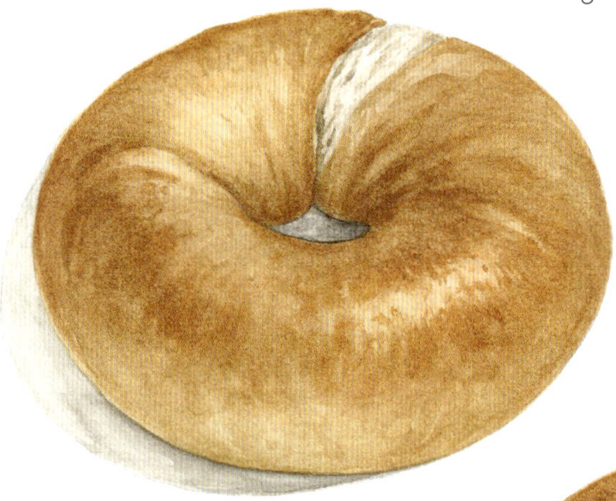

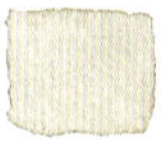

Shadow
Coffee value

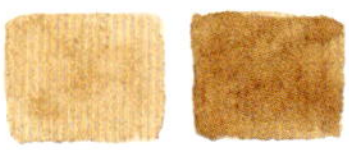

Mixture 2
Milk-Cream value

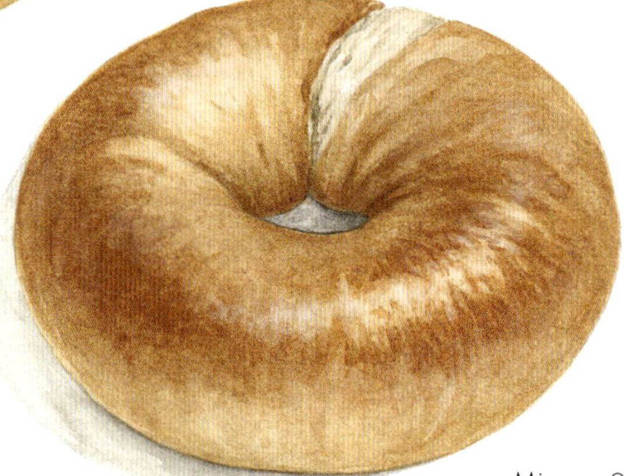

Mixture 2, 3
Butter value

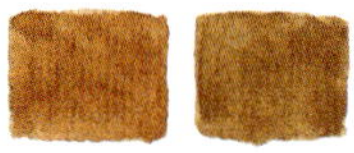

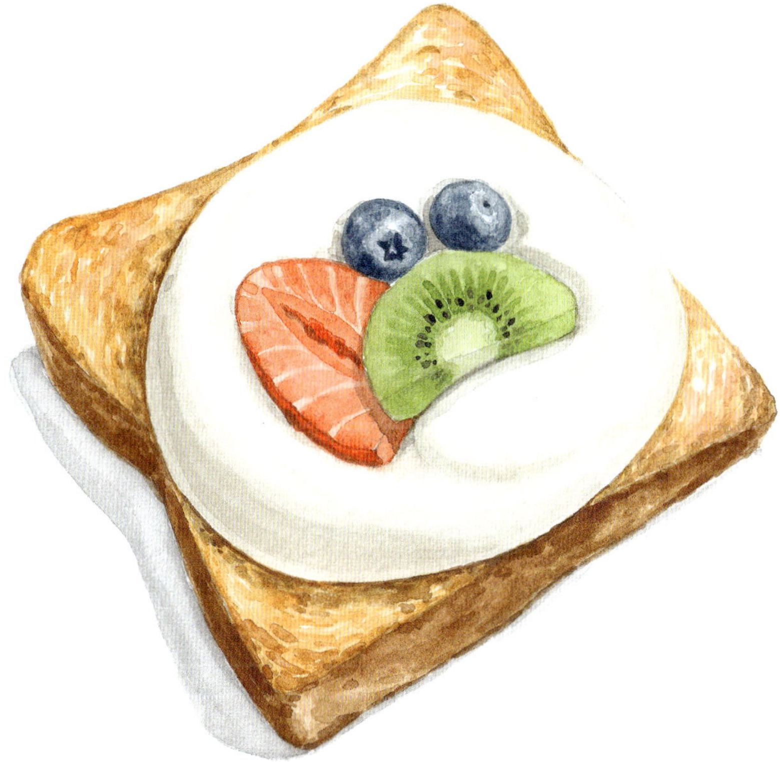

Project 02

Toasted Bread With Fruits & Cream

(Dimensions: W 4¾" x H 4¾" / W 12.5 cm x H 12.5 cm)

Toasted bread is undoubtedly a comfort food for many of us and is enjoyable to depict through painting thanks to its rich texture. It demands minimal effort yet yields visually captivating results on paper. In this project, you'll discover specialized techniques aimed at capturing the fluffiness of the whipped cream with subtle layering and gentle blending, achieving a lifelike appearance. Additionally, we'll explore methods to depict the toasted bread texture, focusing on creating a warm, crispy look through controlled brushstrokes and color variation.

Brushes

Round brushes: sizes 1, 2 and 4
Filbert brushes: sizes 4 and 8
Spotter brush: size 3/0

Color Palette

OBJECT	COLOR NAME	COLOR VALUES		
		Tea/Coffee	Milk	Cream
Bread crumb	Quinacridone Gold Pyrrol Orange			
Bread crust	Quinacridone Gold Pyrrol Orange Burnt Umber			
Blueberry	Ultramarine Blue Grey (a touch of black)			
Strawberry	Pyrrol Orange Pyrrol Scarlet Permanent Alizarin Crimson			
Kiwi	Sap Green Quinacridone Gold			
Cream	Jane's Grey Raw Umber			
Kiwi seeds	Ivory Black			

Viewpoint & Light Source

In this project, I opted for a relatively high viewpoint to accentuate the details on the toast's surface, with the light source coming from the right side.

Composition

We still stick with something simple in this project: All toppings are entirely confined within the edges of the toast and positioned centrally.

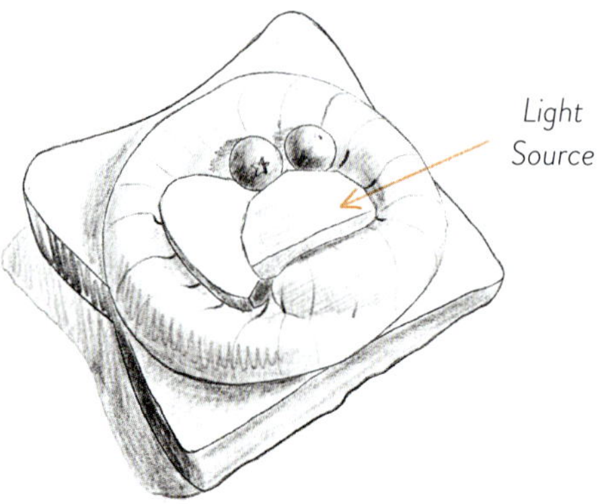

Let's Sketch!

I start by sketching a very short cube, or cuboid. From there, I add curved edges and round the corners for a more realistic look.

Next, I gently sketch an irregular circle on the top face of the toast to indicate where the cream will be, which slightly extends beyond the right side of the toast to suggest the thickness of the cream later in the painting phase. Inside the cream boundary, I draw the fruits, including a blueberry, a slice of strawberry and a kiwi. The kiwi slice is placed atop the others, with one corner overlapping the strawberry.

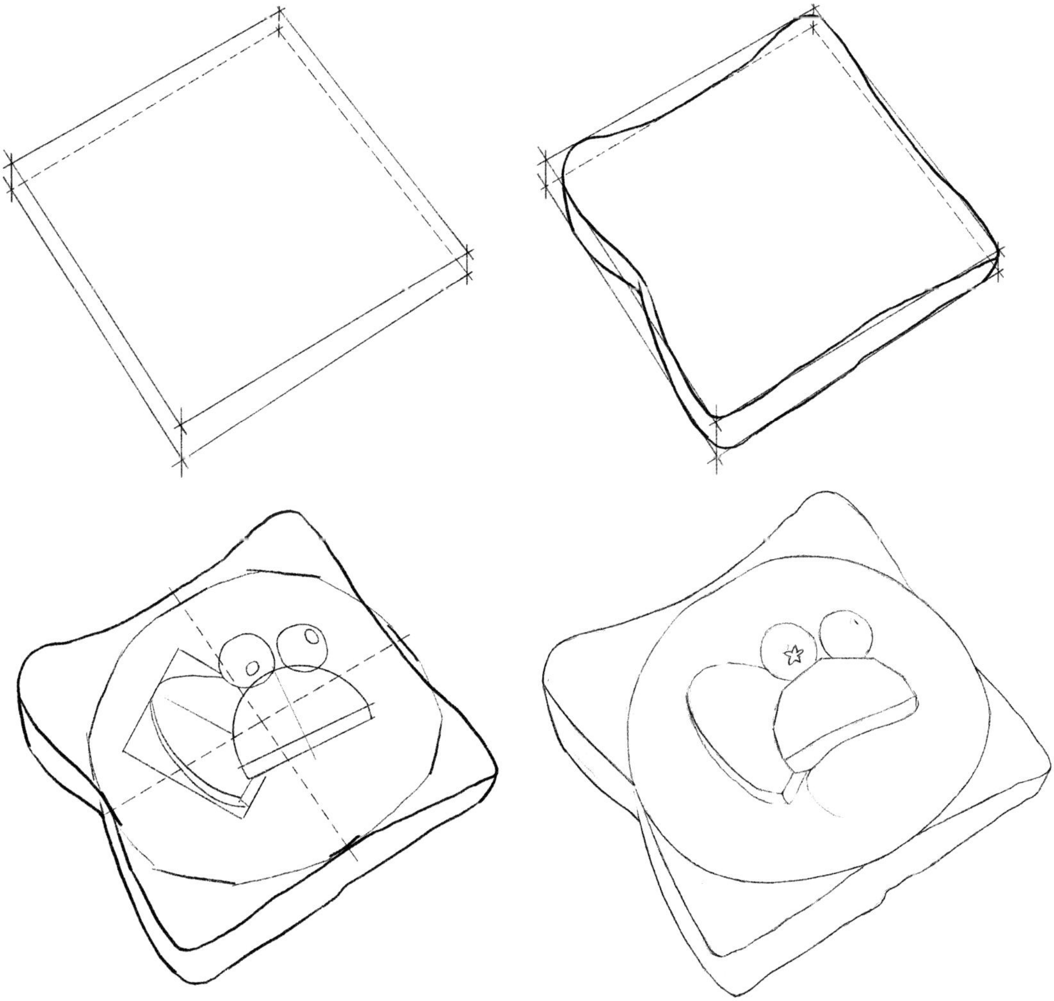

Let's Paint!

First Layer

The Toast: Prepare a highlight mixture in "Tea" and "Coffee" values. Select the round brush #4 for applying the "Tea" mixture to the top surface, using a scumbling brushstroke technique. Keep switching between the "Tea" and "Coffee" values to make some darker color bleed onto the paper. Aim to maintain gaps between brushstrokes and allow each layer to dry before applying the next. For the crust, use filbert brush #4 to apply the Bread Crust mixture in "Coffee" value to the two visible sides.

Artist's Tip: Make sure you prepare an ample amount of mixture beforehand to avoid interruptions for remixing while painting. Don't try to control the brush, relax your wrist and just make loose strokes around the edges.

Fruits: Use round brush #1 to apply the base layer on the blueberries and a size 4 filbert brush for the strawberry and kiwi. Keep in mind that the light source will determine the highlight areas, which will be on the right side.

Whipped Cream: Mix a very light value of Raw Umber and pick up the filbert brush #8 to apply the solution on the left side of the cream, using long brush strokes. Do the same for the area around the fruit on the left, indicating their weight onto the cream. Try to keep the other areas white in this step to maintain the contrast between the objects.

Artist's Tip: If you feel a bit confused, refer to the shading guidelines (page 15) from the sketching phase to determine where you should place the solution.

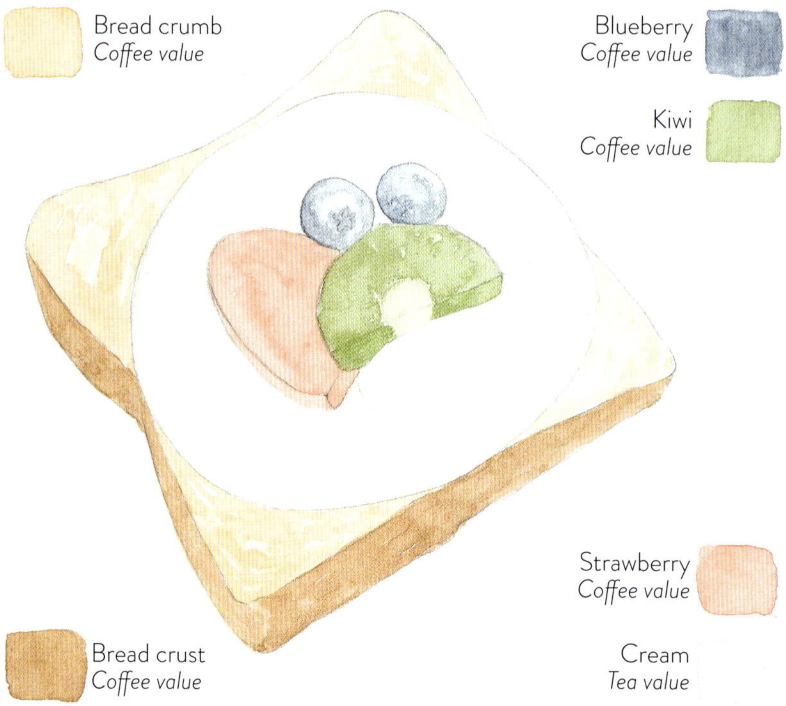

Second Layer

Artist's Tip: Exercise patience and apply each layer slowly to preserve the correct contrast throughout the painting process. Remember, with watercolor, you can always add darker mixtures later, but once it's overdone, you can't remove it as easily as you can in other mediums.

Toast: Use round brush #1 to apply the Bread Crumb mixture in "Milk" value to the top surface. Gently press and lift the brush while you move the solution around the cream to create the bread texture. Leave a bit more mixture in areas close to the cream to depict its shadow on the bread.

Apply a Bread Crust mixture in "Milk" value to the sides of the bread, intentionally painting the left side darker by using a more concentrated mixture on it.

Fruits: Apply the Blueberry mixture in "Milk" value to the left side of the blueberries with a size 1 round brush, deepening the stem area. Gently dampen the brush in between to leave an uneven wash, creating the characteristic texture of the blueberries.

Use round brush #2 to paint the strawberry flesh, leaving a thin gap between the segments to portray the details.

Prepare the Kiwi mixture in "Milk" value and use round brush #1 to paint thin lines toward the center of the slice.

Whipped Cream: Continue using the "Tea" value to add another wash on the shadow side, then blend it out using the gradient wash technique (page 25). Remember to leave ample space for the reflected highlight on the far left, employing the shading technique akin to a sphere-like object. Apply a thicker value solution on the right side of the blueberry and kiwi to enhance the sense of fluffiness in the cream.

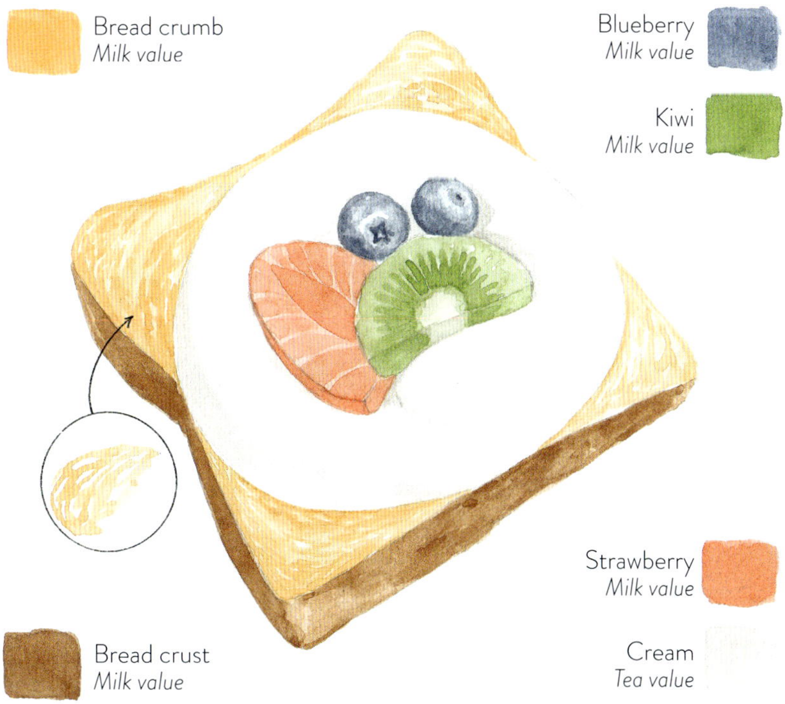

Third Layer

Toast: Use round brush #1 to apply the Bread Crumb mixture in "Cream" value to the bread, repeating the same brushstrokes as in the second layer. While painting, incorporate a hint of the Bread Crust mixture to deepen the tone on the surface and depict the cream's shadow on the toast.

Apply the Bread Crust mixture in "Cream" value to the sides. Use the tip of the brush to depict some darker lines for added texture.

Fruits: Add another layer to the blueberries and strawberry using their "Cream" mixture values, focusing on the shadow areas on the left side of the objects.

Using a spotter brush, apply some Ivory Black in "Cream" value to the center of the kiwi to depict its seeds. Leave some dots darker than others to create a sense of depth.

Whipped Cream: Add another layer of "Tea" value using a filbert brush #8. Apply a subtle wash to the farther half to tone down the contrast. Continue adding additional layers for the shadows of the kiwi and strawberry on the cream.

> **Artist's Tip:** In watercolor painting, depicting white objects is more about painting the shadows and the objects surrounding them.

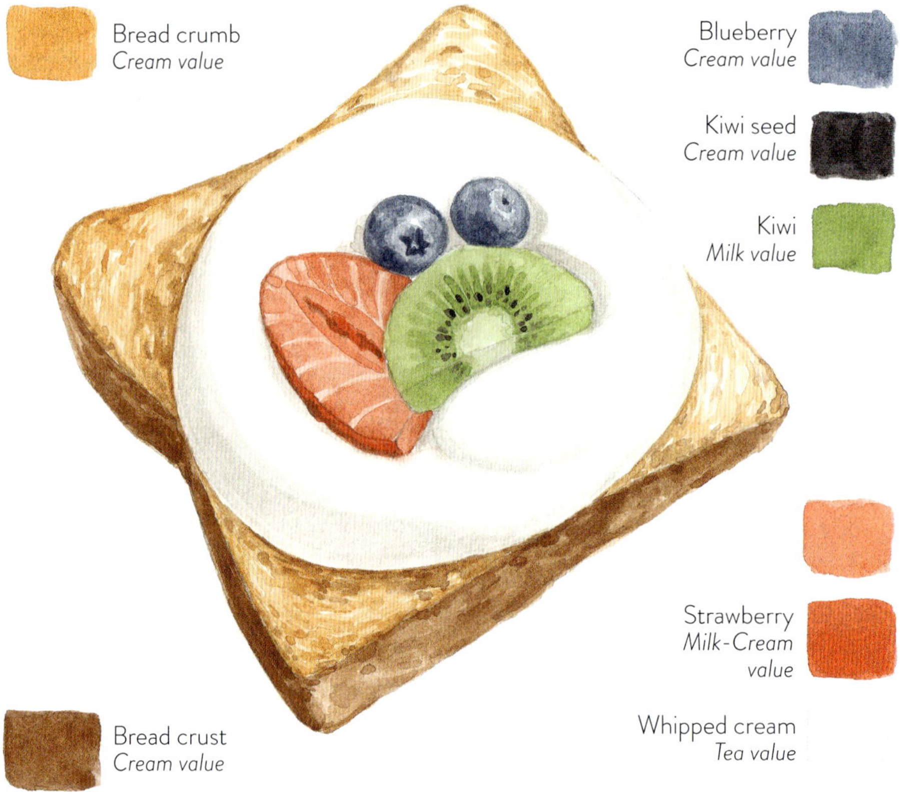

Finishing Touches

Using a filbert brush #4, apply a gray mixture in "Coffee" value to the left side of the toast to create a cast shadow.

With the spotter brush, apply dark-brown color in "Cream" value to the edge of the cream, focusing solely on the left half, as it's closer to your viewpoint. Leave the further half with a softer contrast to blend more seamlessly into the background.

Artist's Tip: Squint your eyes to check the contrast between the cream and toast. If the cream appears too bright, use a large brush to wash a very thin layer of its mixture over the whole cream to help tone it down.

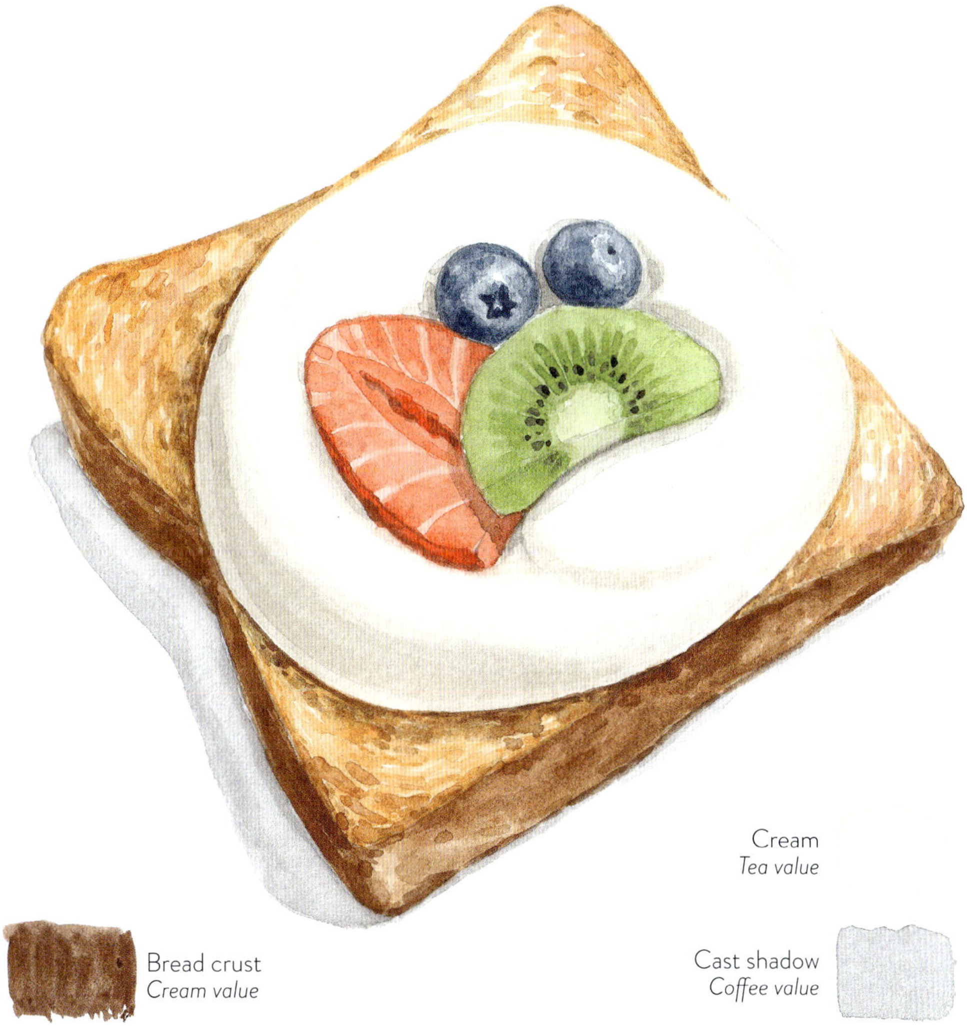

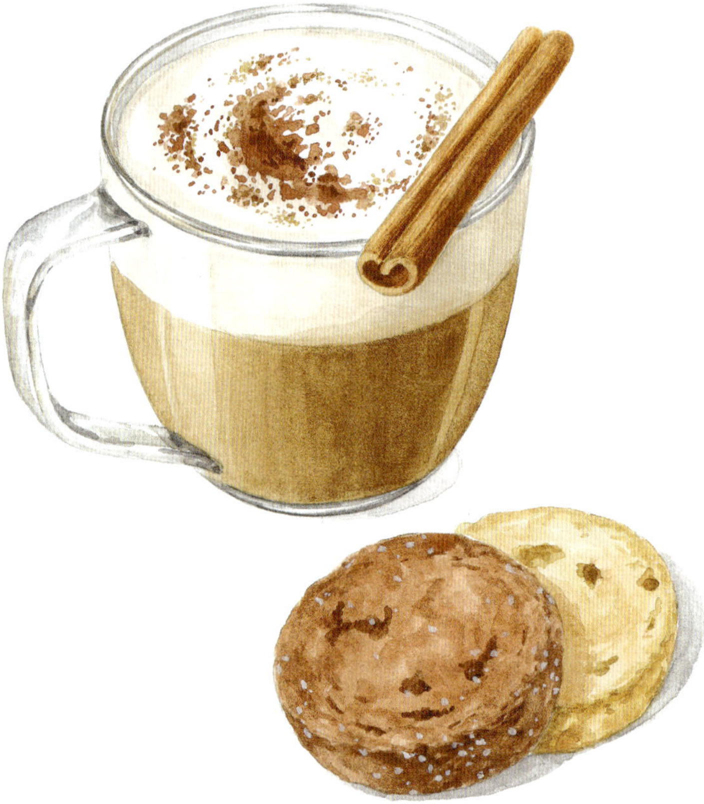

Project 03

Cinnamon Latte & Shortbread Cookies

(Dimensions: Coffee: W 3½" x H 3¼" / W 9 cm x H 8 cm;
Cookies: W 2½" x H 1¾" / W 6.5 cm x H 4.5 cm)

Breakfast is not complete without coffee. Let's learn how to paint a cup of coffee and some shortbread cookies in this project. Through the process, you'll gain valuable insights into portraying simple drinks in a glass cup and depicting the intricate texture of cookies.

Brushes

Round brushes: sizes 1 and 2

Filbert brushes: sizes 4 and 8

Spotter brush: size 3/0

Color Palette

OBJECT	COLOR NAME	COLOR VALUES		
		Tea/Coffee	Milk	Cream
Milk foam	**Raw Umber**			
Coffee	**Quinacridone Gold** **Burnt Sienna** **Raw Umber**			
Glass cup	**Ivory Black**			
	Jane's Grey			
Cinnamon stick	**Quinacridone Gold** **Pyrrol Orange** **Burnt Umber**			
Butter cookie	**Quinacridone Gold** **Pyrrol Orange**			
Chocolate cookie / Cinnamon powder	**Pyrrol Orange** **Burnt Umber**			

Artist's Tip: When selecting a reference for your drink painting, opt for one taken in natural light to capture the truest colors of the cup and beverage. Studio photos may cast harsh lighting on the object, resulting in an unnatural appearance in your painting.

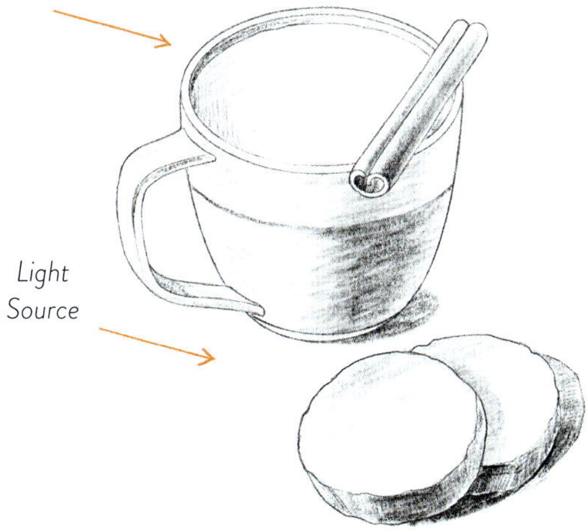

Viewpoint & Light Source

In this project, adopting an eye-level viewpoint from a sitting perspective is optimal, as it captures the cup's profile more compared to a standing perspective. I choose a light source from the left side, ensuring that shadows cascade to the right, enhancing depth and dimension in the scene.

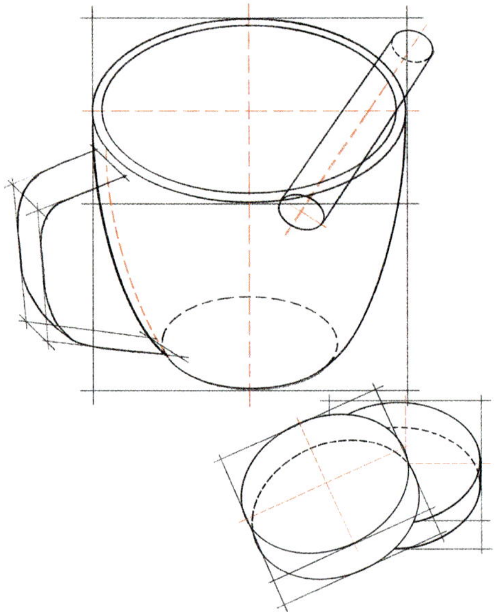

Imagine the handle of the glass resembling a flat bar attached to the glass at two points, forming lines that trace the curvature of the glass.

Composition

From this point on, you'll gradually learn how to place objects on paper to achieve optimal positioning. In this project, for instance, the objective is to achieve a balanced composition between two objects—the cup and the cookies—without compromising the unique characteristics of each. In this particular case, I intentionally positioned the handle of the cup to the left to balance the presence of the cinnamon stick and the cookies.

On a different note, always pay attention to the total length and width of your painting to decide which paper orientation to sketch on. If the total length is greater than the width, a horizontal (landscape) layout would be most suitable. Conversely, as observed in this painting, if the total length is less than the total width, you should opt for a vertical (portrait) layout.

Let's Sketch!

All three objects (the cup, the cinnamon stick and the cookies) are cylinder-related shapes. Start with the general frame to locate them on paper. Next, draw the central lines and determine the width for the ellipses of each object. From there, add details as you see fit.

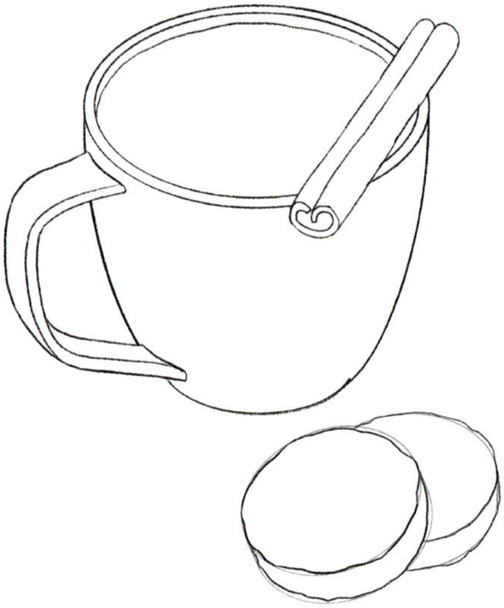

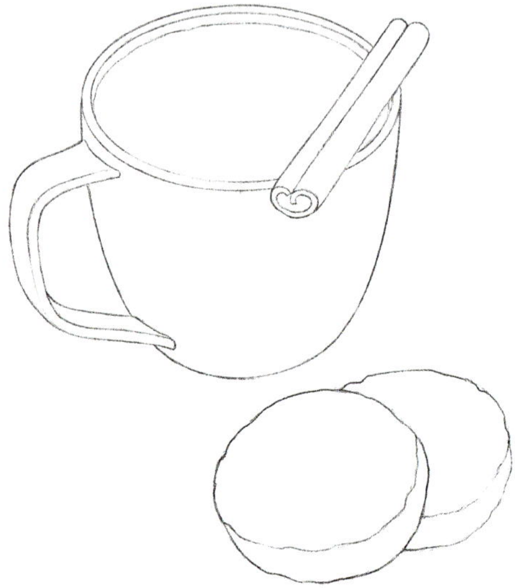

Let's Paint!

First Layer

Cinnamon Stick: Pick up round brush #2 and apply a flat wash of "Coffee" value to the whole cinnamon stick.

Glass Cup: Use round brush #1 and gently apply the gray mixture in "Tea" value to the rim of the cup and where the handle connects with the glass.

Milk Foam: Use filbert brush #8 to apply thick and long strokes of "Tea" value, covering the left edge of the top oval and applying shorter strokes in the middle and on the right. Its vertical section will adhere to cylinder shading rules, with the shadow area situated on the right. Therefore, give this section a subtle flat wash.

Artist's Tip: You needn't coat the entire top surface with color. The left side appears darker because of the shadow cast by the glass.

Coffee: Employing the cylinder shading rule and gradient wash technique (page 25), apply the "Coffee" value to the lower part of the glass.

Cookies: Choose filbert brush #4 and use a scumbling brushstroke to apply the "Tea" shade to the entire chocolate cookie. Then, add some "Milk" value of the same brown mixture to the cookie's thickness to enhance the sense of depth. For the butter cookie, first apply a thin layer of water on top, and then apply a very thin layer of the "Tea" value to create a very light brown blend. Intentionally leave more of the mixture on the side to further enhance the sense of depth.

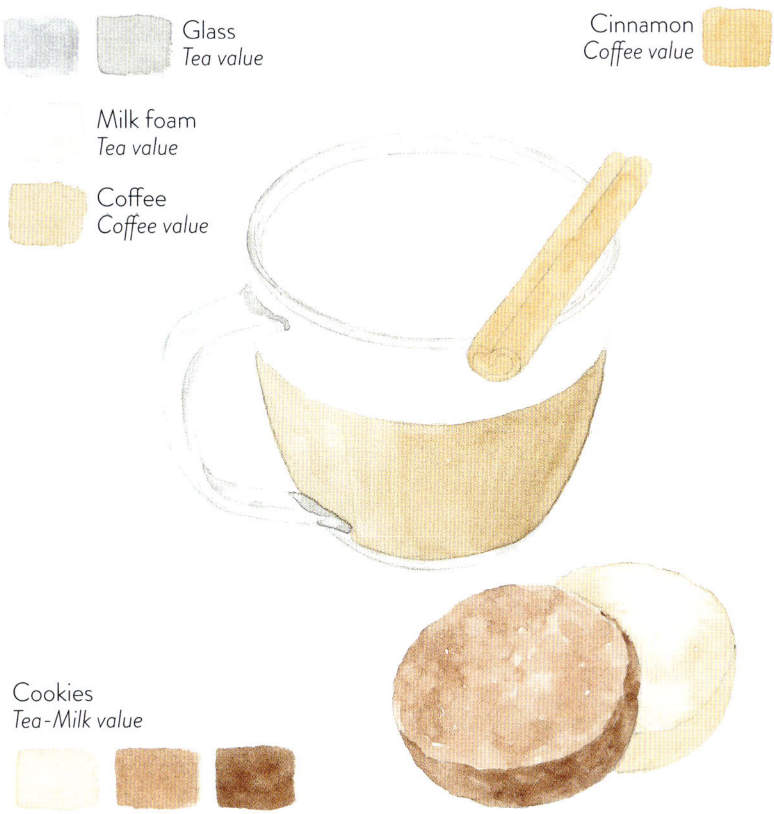

Second Layer

Cinnamon Stick: Use round brush #1 to wash another layer of "Milk" value over the entire stick. Then, lightly hatch some lines along the right edges, leaving the left side brighter.

Glass Cup: Switch to "Milk" value solution and use spotter brush #3/0 to add sharp lines along the rim, the handle and the bottom.

> **Artist's Tip:** Try to manage your strokes well to gradually intensify smaller areas. The interweaving of the layers will create a glass-like appearance.

Milk Foam: For the top surface, apply a fresh set of thick strokes of "Tea" value to the same area as the initial layer, utilizing filbert brush #8. As for the side view, allow the first layer to fully dry before adding another one, making sure to leave brighter sharp lines that follow the cup's shape. This helps to enhance the glossiness of the cup that contains it.

Coffee: Use filbert brush #8 and move on to the "Milk" value to deepen the gradient wash. Be sure to leave brighter, sharp gaps, mimicking the effect created when painting the milk foam.

Cookies: Choose filbert brush #4 and begin scumbling the "Milk" value onto the top to further enhance the texture. Since cookies usually don't have large air pockets like bread, their surface is smoother. Lightly suggest some darker small spots to represent chocolate chunks. For the sides, apply a mixture of "Cream" value for each color using a gradient scumbling wash, with the shading darker on the right and gradually brighter toward the left.

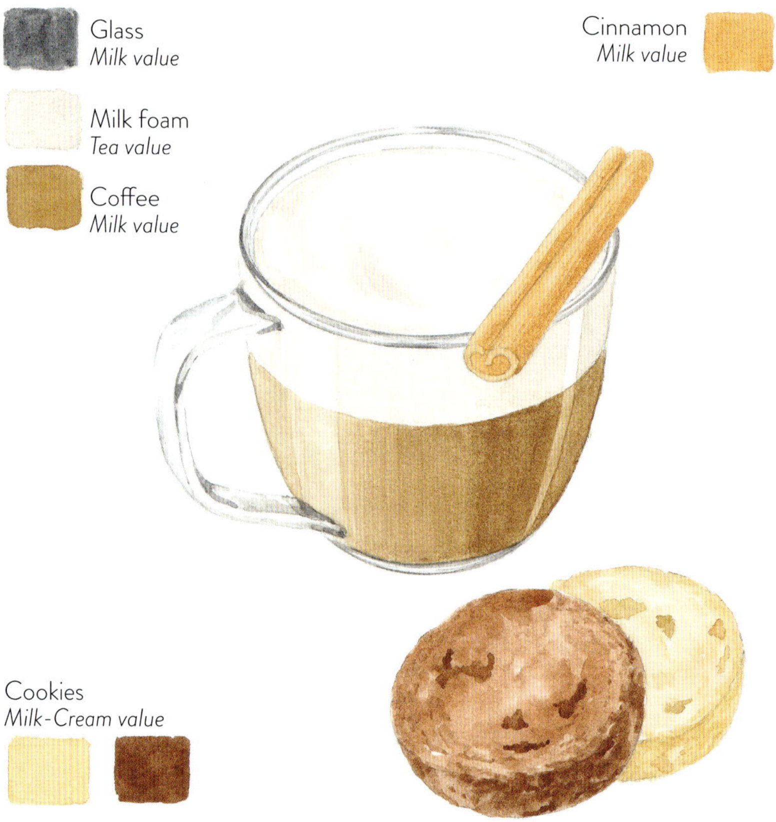

Third Layer

Cinnamon Stick: Pick up round brush #1 and apply the Chocolate Cookie color in "Cream" value to the shadow area as well as the hollow inner part. Switch to a spotter brush to hatch very thin lines along the stick to create texture and darken the shadow part at the same time.

> **Artist's Tip:** Alternatively, you can create the darker shade by adding more Burnt Umber pigment to the mixture.

Cinnamon Powder: On top of the milk foam, use round brush #1 to apply the Cinnamon Powder color in "Cream" value, employing short scumbling brushstrokes. Make sure to leave random spaces between the strokes. You can add another layer once the previous one has dried out to create darker spots as desired.

Keep deepening the glass, milk foam and coffee in the cup with the same value mixture.

Cookies: Apply some darker strokes around the rim and onto the chocolate chunks. Squint your eyes to see if the edges are dark enough. If they don't really pop out, add more of the "Cream" value mixture to it.

Indicate the first layer of cast shadow for all objects using the "Coffee" value.

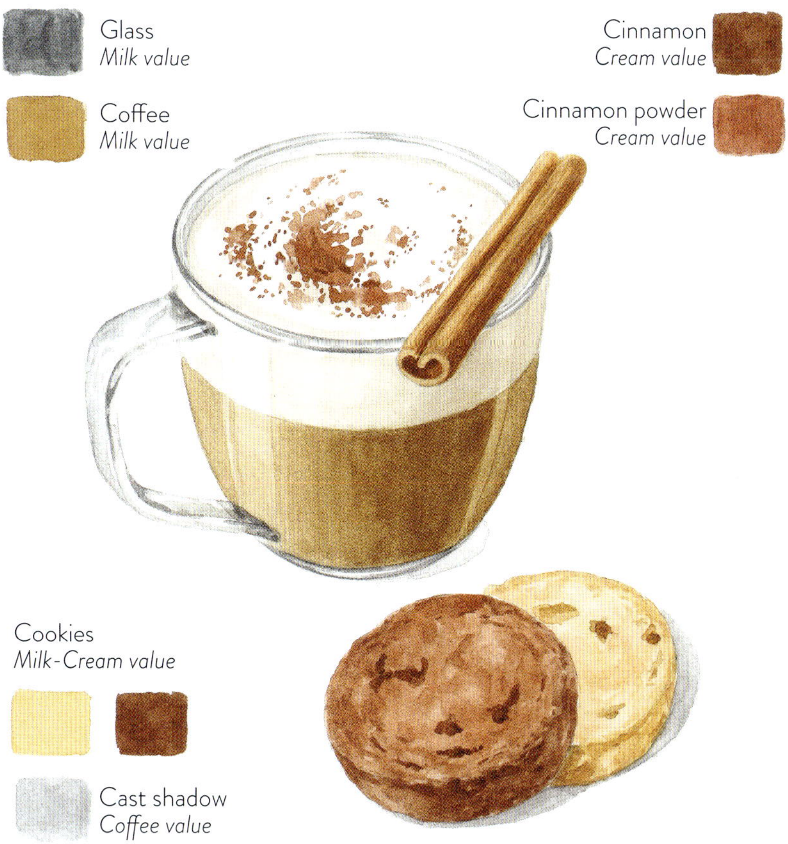

Finishing Touches

Give the cinnamon powder another layer of the same routine.

Provide a light wash of Raw Umber in "Milk" value to indicate the shadow of the cinnamon stick on the glass.

Add a touch of light brown from the Coffee color to the glass's handle to show the reflection of the coffee on it.

Sugar Grains: Use a spotter brush to apply small dots of a concentrated mixture of white pigment onto the cookies. Ensure that the paper is dry at this stage.

Deepen the cast shadows of all objects with a "Coffee" value mixture.

Check the whole painting to adjust the contrast one last time.

> **Artist's Tip:** Your eyes are adept at detecting when the contrast is not right between objects—where one might be too bright or too dark compared to others. They serve as an excellent tool for identifying areas that need to be darkened or toned down.

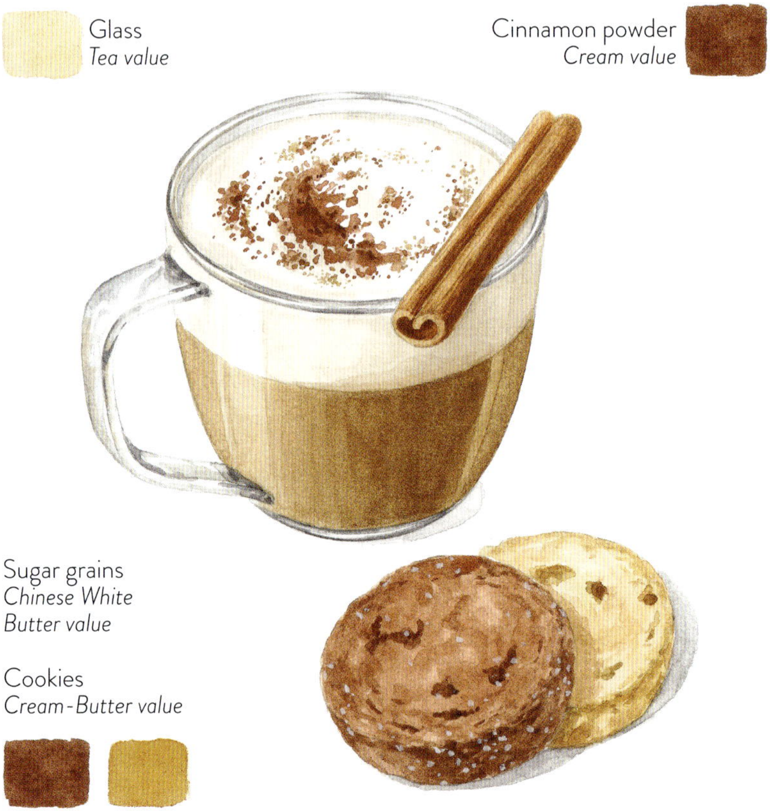

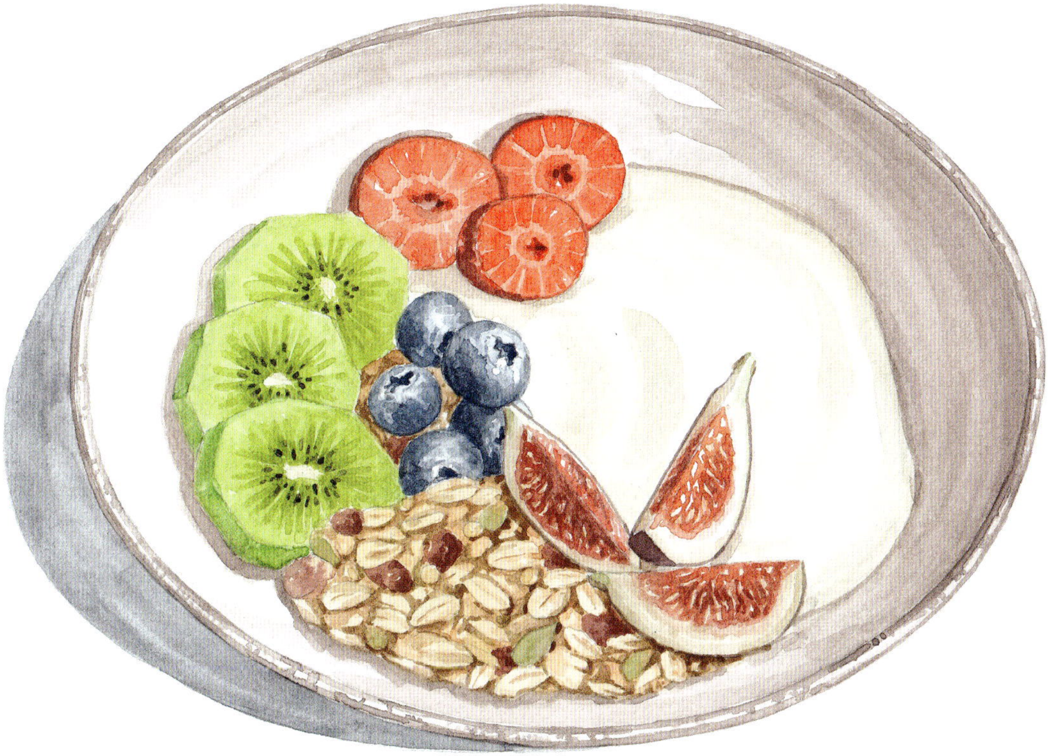

Project 04

Yogurt Bowl

(Dimensions: W 6" x H 4½" / W 15.3 cm x H 11.3 cm)

The yogurt bowl is one of my favorite breakfast or snack options, thanks to its refreshing taste and nutritious ingredients. However, when it comes to painting it, I often find the small details of the toppings challenging to capture accurately. Nevertheless, when arranged thoughtfully, the effort becomes entirely worth it. In this project, you'll learn how to utilize the "negative painting" technique (in which you paint around the subject rather than on the subject) to depict granola and practice your brushstroke techniques to create a vibrant and colorful yogurt bowl.

Brushes

Round brushes: sizes 1 and 2
Filbert brushes: sizes 4 and 8
Spotter brush: size 3/0

Color Palette

OBJECT	COLOR NAME	COLOR VALUES		
		Tea/Coffee	Milk	Cream
Strawberry Fig's flesh	**Pyrrol Orange Pyrrol Scarlet Permanent Alizarin Crimson**			
Kiwi	**Sap Green Hansa Yellow**			
Blueberry	**Ultramarine Blue Jane's Grey**			
Dried cranberry Fig's flesh	**Permanent Orange Permanent Violet Permanent Alizarin Crimson**			
Fig's skin Bowl	**Permanent Violet Permanent Orange Jane's Grey**			
Yogurt	**New Gamboge Raw Umber**			
Granola	**Quinacridone Gold Pyrrol Orange Burnt Umber**			

As your palette becomes more complex, it offers a valuable opportunity to refine your skill in managing mixtures and experimenting with blending leftovers. This process helps you achieve a more harmonious color scheme in your painting.

Viewpoint & Light Source

In this project, we'll be painting a wide bowl adorned with small toppings, so I opt to sketch it from a standing viewpoint. This angle showcases all the intricate details within the bowl, avoiding the flat appearance of a top-down view.

The light source positioned on the upper right side will effectively highlight the details present on the left side of the bowl.

Artist's Tip: Kindly observe that the recessed or hollowed components, including the centers of strawberries, stems of blueberries and the bowl, will have their highlight and shadow areas positioned in reverse of those applied to the protruding parts of the objects.

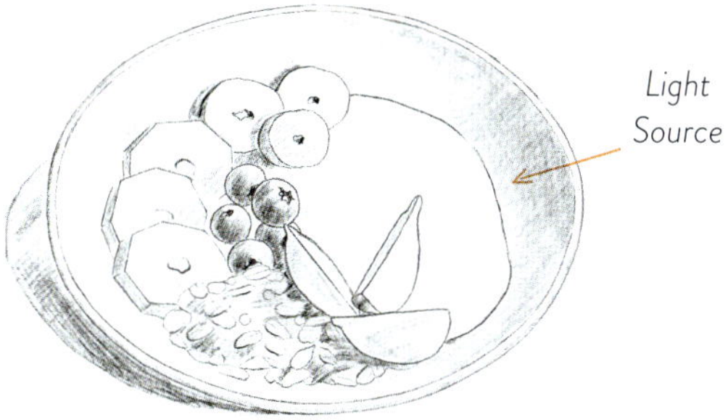

Composition

For the toppings, I have arranged slices of kiwi and strawberry against the bowl, with blueberries positioned next to them on the right side. The two toppings nearest to the viewpoint are granola and figs. Granola boasts intricate details such as oats, dried cranberries and nuts, so I've placed it closer to the viewer to enhance visibility. The remaining space will be filled with yogurt, creating a visual resting place amidst the array of small elements, contributing to a more balanced overall composition.

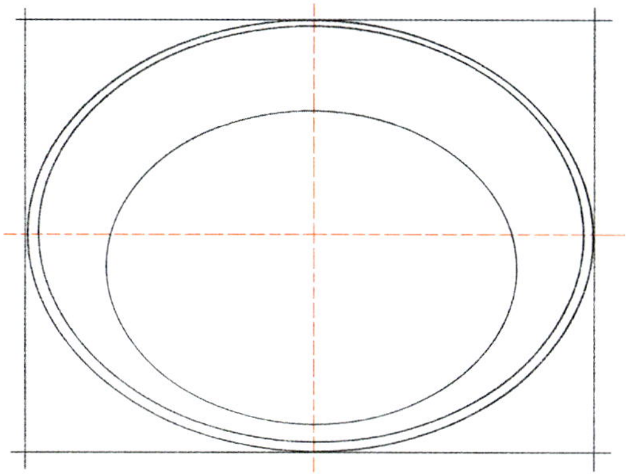

Let's Sketch!

Because there's no side view to show, simply draw a horizontal rectangle, mark its central lines and outline an ellipse to depict the bowl's rim. Then, draw a smaller ellipse with its center positioned below the previous one to delineate the area for the toppings. Finally, add details for each topping according to the inner ellipse and the discussed composition.

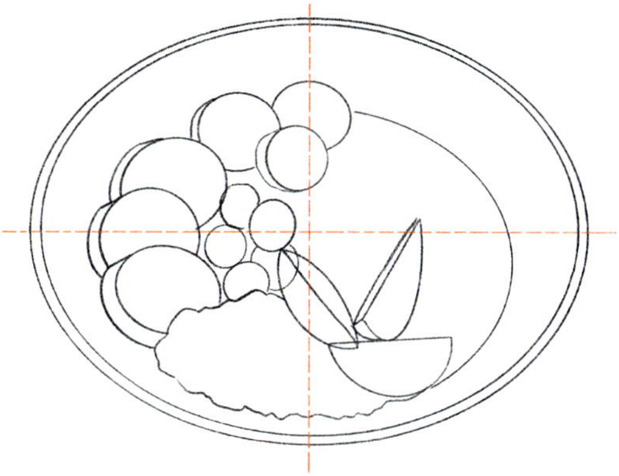

Avoid dedicating excessive time to intricately detailing each granola piece; instead, lightly suggest some on the surface. The remaining detailing will be accomplished through the negative painting technique, which we'll explore later.

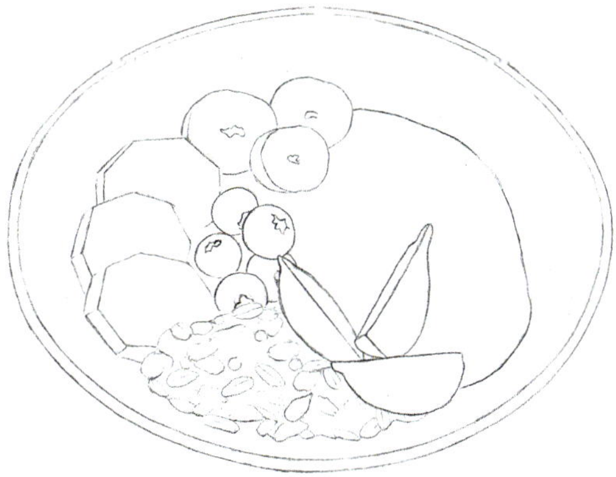

Let's Paint!

First Layer

Strawberries: Use filbert brush #4 to wash the first layer of the Strawberry mixture in "Coffee–Milk" value. The brush strokes should move inward toward the center, avoiding complete flatness to allow for a subtle bleeding effect, which will serve as a foundation for texture indication. Once it's slightly dry, dab some more solution to the center and the left side of the slices.

Kiwi: Use the same brush and brush strokes to apply the Kiwi mixture in "Coffee" value onto the paper, and make sure to leave some white space at the center.

Figs: Blend the "Tea" value of the Yogurt mixture with a hint of Raw Umber to craft the color for the base layer, and then apply additional mixture to the side not facing the light source for a darker tone. Once it has dried completely, switch to round brush #1. Load it with the Fig's Skin mixture in a "Cream" value and paint thin lines encircling the flesh to denote the skin.

Granola: Prepare a Granola mixture in "Tea" value. Use filbert brush #4 to apply an uneven wash over the entire section.

Yogurt: Prepare a Yogurt mixture in "Tea" value. Use filbert brush #8 to apply a watery wash over most of the area.

Bowl: Use filbert brush #8 to apply a watery wash of the Bowl mixture in a "Tea" value over the entire bowl. While it's still damp, add some extra brush-strokes on the right wall to darken it, indicating the shadowed side due to the light source coming from the right.

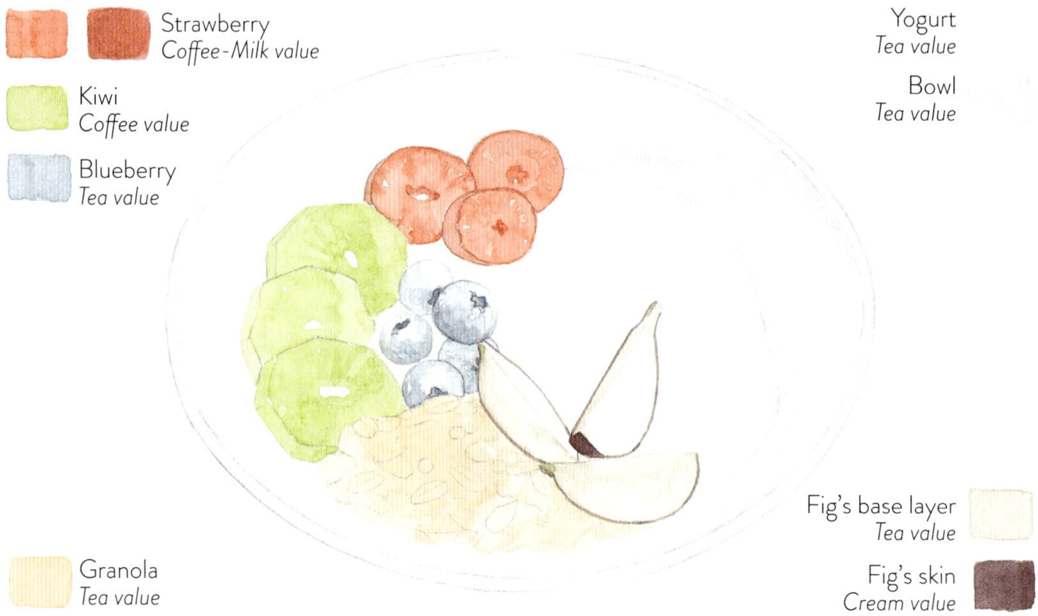

Second Layer

Blueberries, Strawberry and Kiwi Slices: Use round brush #1 and #2 to apply a second layer with a thicker value. Make sure to give the slices a slightly darker shade on the left to indicate their thickness, as they are not directly facing the light source. During this step, the way you apply the colors will also help portray the texture. Therefore, pay attention to the characteristics of each object to move your brush accordingly. Simultaneously, remember to adhere to the shading rules outlined for the recessed elements as described in the Light Source section on page 60.

Artist's Tip: Avoid applying the mixture evenly all around to create a more natural and realistic look.

Figs: Load the Fig's Flesh mixture with a "Milk" value onto round brush #1. Apply the solution by painting small, thin lines toward the uppermost edges of the wedges, leaving some white spaces to denote the fig seeds. Use the tip of the brush to drop some darker mixture onto the flesh to enhance visual interest.

Granola: Prepare the recommended mixture in "Coffee" value. Load it onto round brush #1 and apply the darker value to the area closer to the figs. Since the negative painting technique involves darkening the space surrounding the object (in this case, the oat grains) rather than the object itself, start by drawing thin lines around the grains using the tip of the brush. Apply similarly sized lines in random positions, leaving gaps between them. Darken those gaps further so that the unpainted grains in this second wash will stand out as the grains on the top layer. Among the oats, incorporate some larger chunks to represent dried cranberries using the corresponding color and value.

Yogurt and Bowl: Use a filbert brush #8 to apply an additional wash of the recommended color in "Tea" value for each object. Apply these layers gradually and with patience, as white objects will become more appealing only after two to three layers.

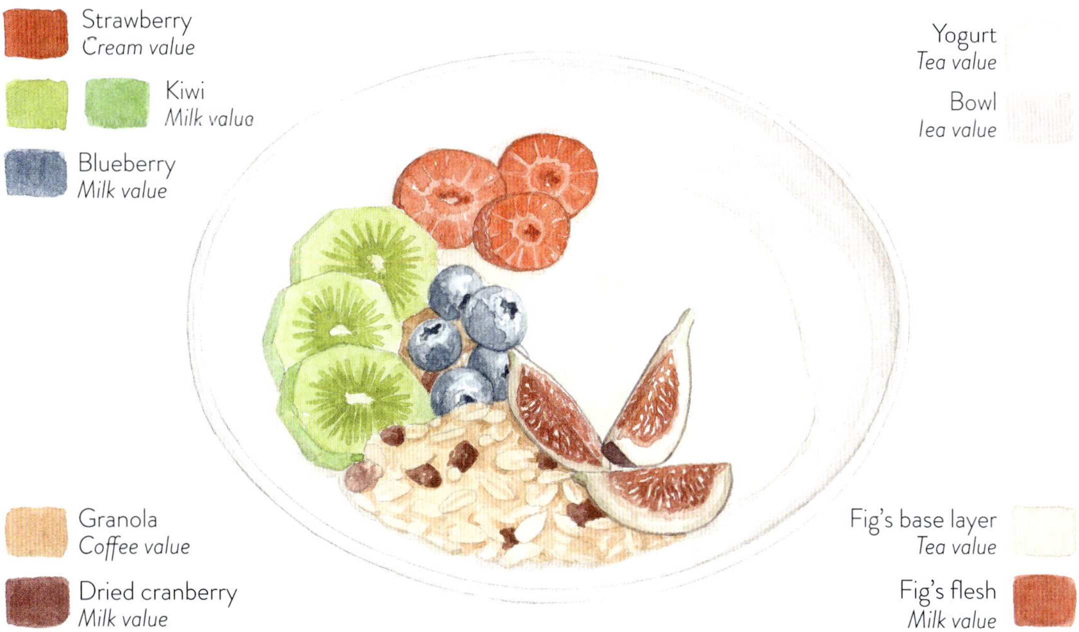

Third Layer

Blueberries, Strawberry and Kiwi Slices: Continue applying another layer of thicker mixture to all objects while darkening the recessed parts. Carefully add meticulous details, such as kiwi seeds, using spotter brush #3/0.

Granola: Use round brush #1 to deepen the gaps between oat grains with a more concentrated value. Do the same to the dried cranberries. Additionally, observe that I blend some Kiwi mixture with light brown to produce a new color for the pumpkin seeds.

Artist's Tip: As I mix colors, I always take advantage of what's available on the palette and don't hesitate to explore different combinations. For instance, you can experiment by blending the "leftover" Blueberry mixture with the Strawberry mixture to achieve a rich, cooler red for the cranberry's shadow.

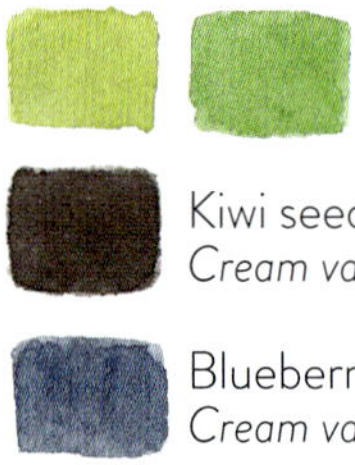

Kiwi
Milk value

Kiwi seeds
Cream value

Blueberry
Cream value

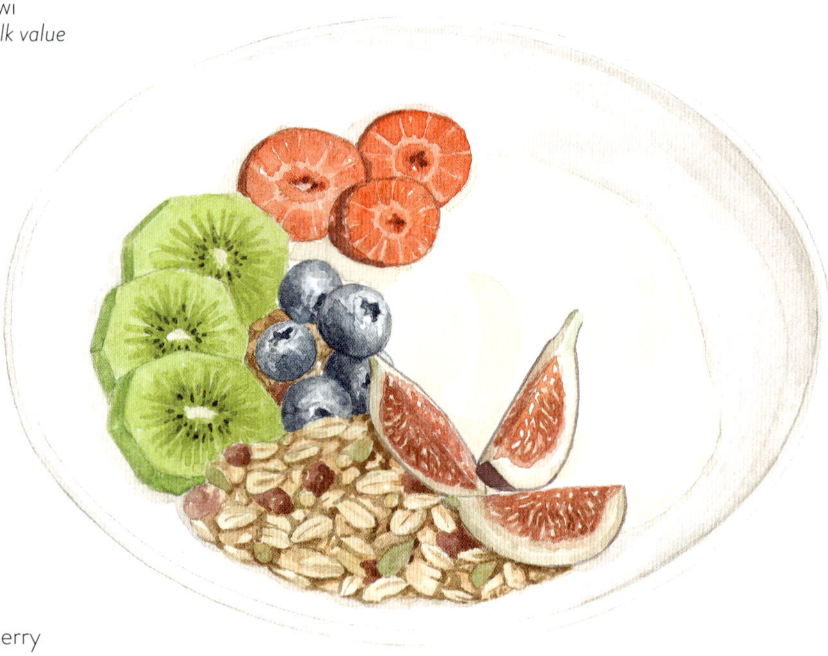

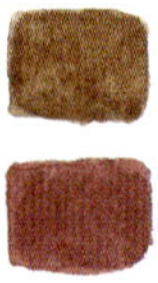

Granola
Cream value

Dried cranberry
Cream value

Finishing Touches

Yogurt: With a filbert brush #8, add another layer in "Tea" value. Feel free to add one to two more layers of the same value until you achieve the desired tone.

Bowl: Continue applying multiple layers using a filbert brush #8, concentrating thicker value on the right wall and blending it out toward the upper left side, which is the brightest area. Then, switch to round brush #1 and use "Milk" value for the lip, applying medium-long arc strokes and connecting them randomly to evoke a handmade pottery feel.

Lastly, add a cast shadow for the whole bowl using a gray mixture in "Coffee" value.

Artist's Tip: In some references, cast shadows may appear very dark. However, when painting, I restrict the amount of pigment used to the level of "Coffee" consistency. Shadows that are excessively dark or too solid can be visually disturbing and disrupt the overall harmony of the painting.

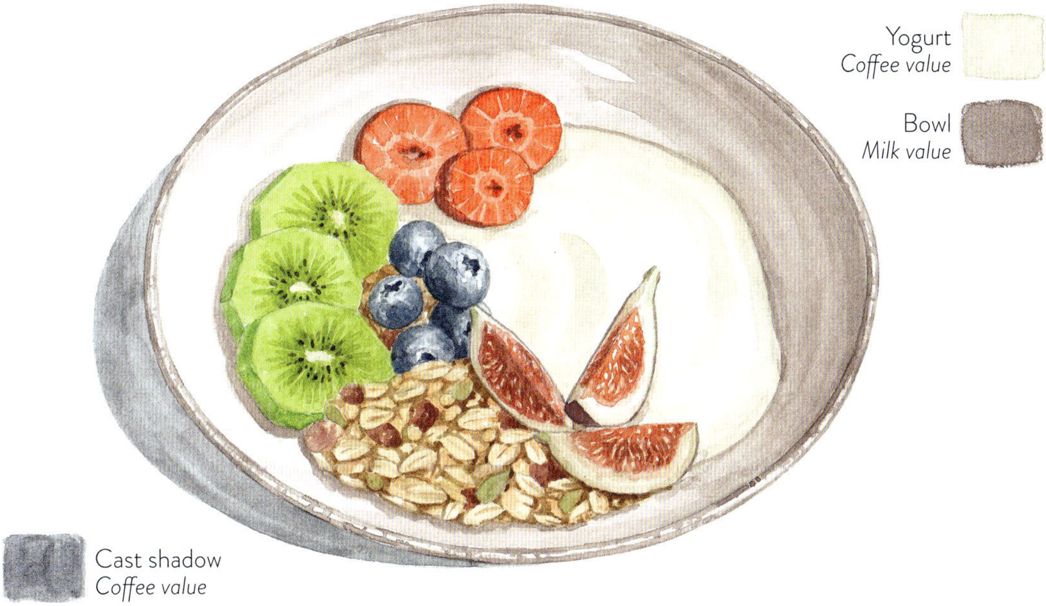

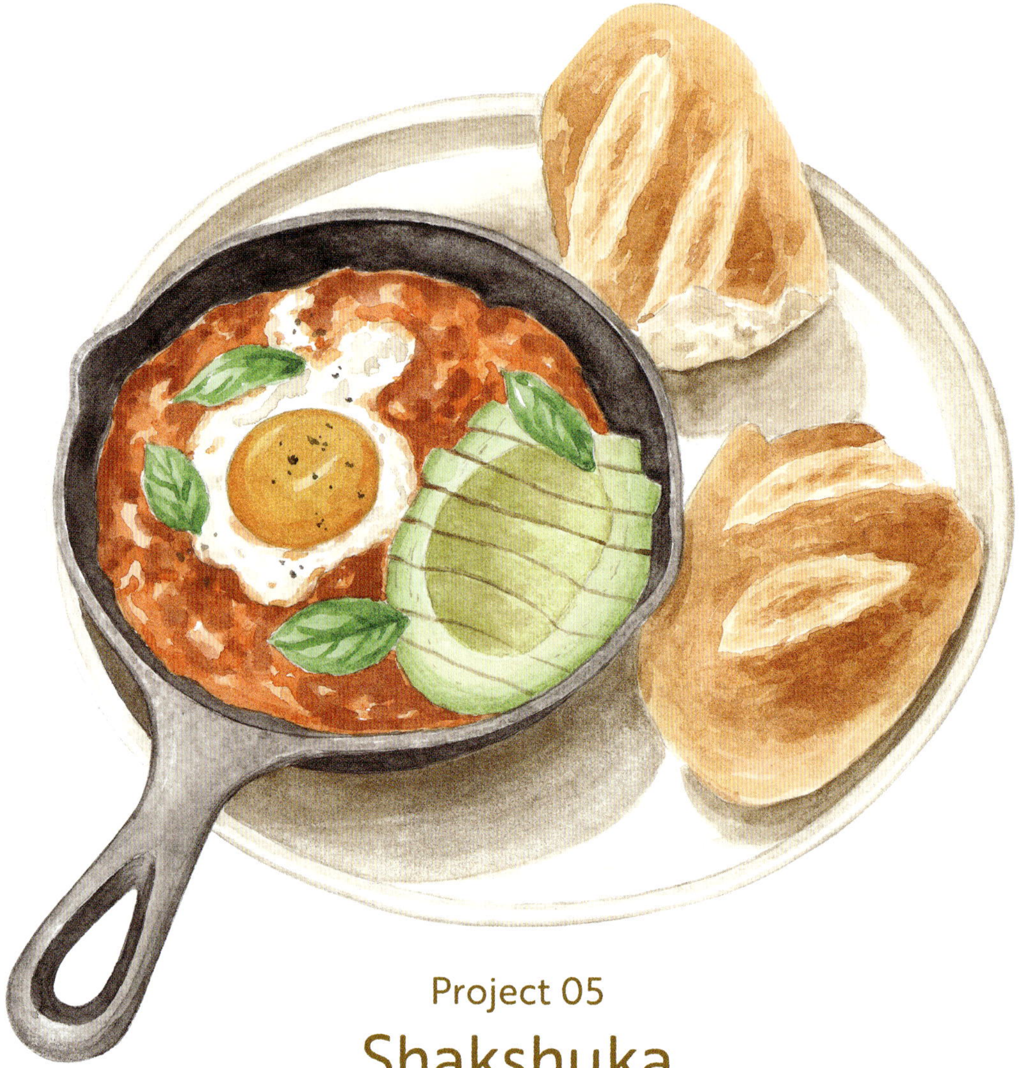

Project 05

Shakshuka

(Dimensions: W 5¾" x H 5⅞" / W 14 cm x H 15 cm)

In this project, we'll learn how to depict the texture of cast-iron cookware and a tomato-based dish such as shakshuka. Mastering the technique involves practicing gentle brushstrokes and making sure not to overwork the paint before it dries. Knowing when to pause and refrain from rubbing the paper is crucial for achieving the desired watercolor effect in food illustrations.

Brushes

Round brushes: sizes 1 and 2
Filbert brush: size 4
Spotter brush: size 3/0

Color Palette

OBJECT	COLOR NAME	COLOR VALUES		
		Tea/Coffee	Milk	Cream
Tomato sauce	Quinacridone Gold Pyrrol Orange Permanent Alizarin Crimson			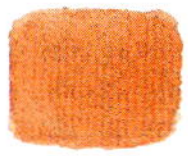
Avocado	Sap Green Quinacridone Gold Raw Umber		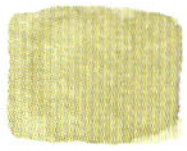	
	Hansa Yellow Hooker's Green	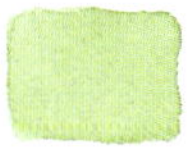	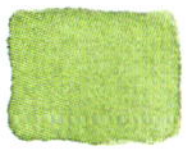	
Herbs	Sap Green Hooker's Green	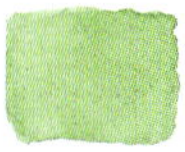		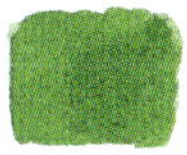
Egg yolk	Quinacridone Gold Permanent Orange New Gamboge		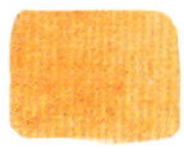	
Bread	Quinacridone Gold Pyrrol Scarlet Pyrrol Orange Burnt Umber		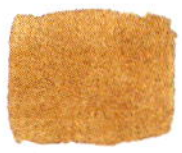	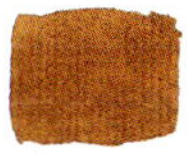
Plate Egg white	Raw Umber	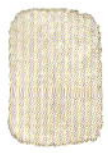	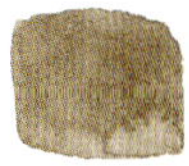	
Skillet	Ivory Black		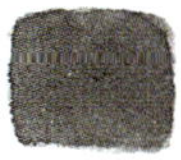	

Viewpoint & Light Source

Since the elements in this dish are quite flat, I choose a standing viewpoint to effectively capture the items within the skillet. The light source will come from the left side, enhancing the visibility of these details.

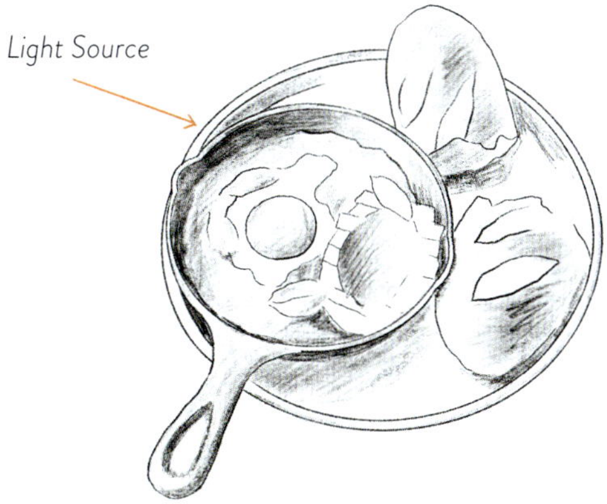

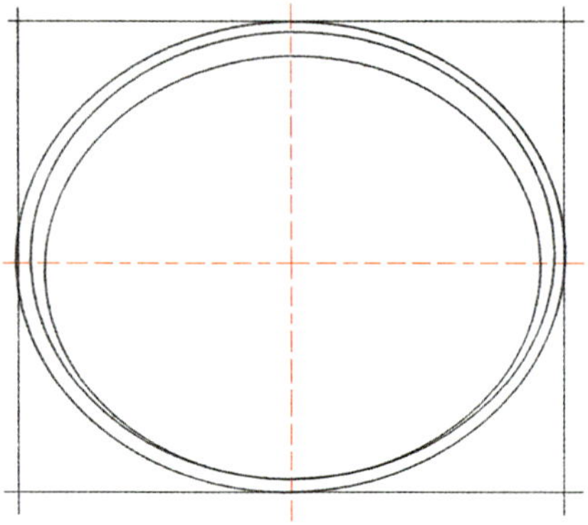

Composition

The dark-colored skillet will act as the backdrop, allowing the food inside to stand out effectively. In this composition, a halved avocado will occupy space in the large skillet, complementing the warm tones of the entire dish. Notice how I deliberately split the baguette in half rather than leaving it whole, enhancing the visual interest and balance of the composition. To ensure all elements are visually linked, I also include a serving plate.

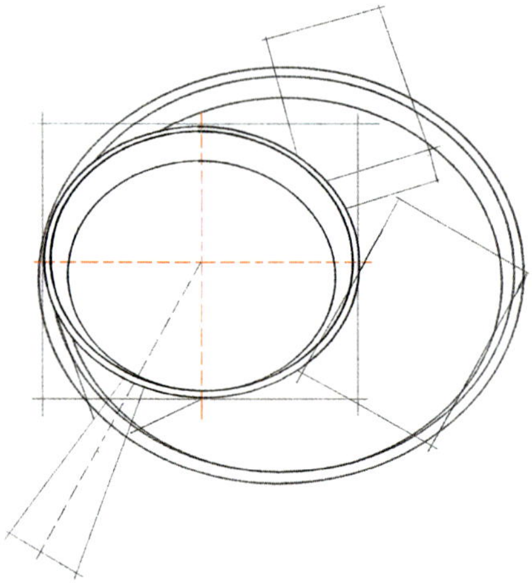

Let's Sketch!

As always, begin by defining rectangular frames and central lines for each item. Applying the rule of thirds can be advantageous when arranging multiple objects. Since the skillet is the focal point here, I allocate approximately two-thirds of the overall width to it, with the remaining items scattered around. Notice how I intentionally position one piece of baguette to extend beyond the plate's edge, enhancing visual interest and balancing the skillet's handle on the bottom left.

Draw ellipses for the plate and the skillet and base the baguette pieces on cylindrical shapes. Once you are satisfied with their placement, add more details to all the objects.

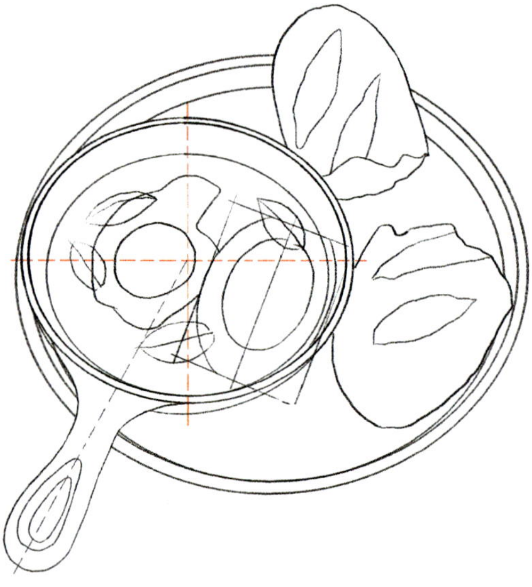

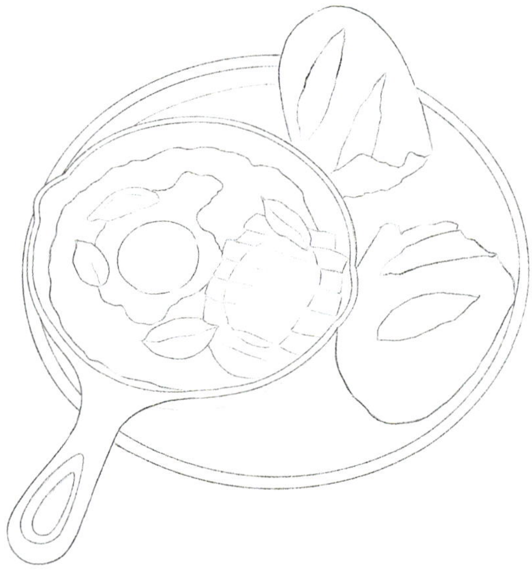

Let's Paint!

First Layer

Tomato Sauce: Select round brush #2 and apply the "Coffee–Milk" value onto paper. Occasionally dip the brush into water and go back to blending the solution directly on the paper. This technique will create a bleeding effect due to the excess water on your brush. It's also beneficial to leave some tiny white spots at this stage.

Avocado: Wash the whole avocado with a "Tea" value mixture of warm green. While the paper is still damp, use round brush #1 to dab some warm green mixture to the right of the recessed part. Apply the more vibrant green to the areas closer to the skin. Ensure the second layer transitions quite smoothly with the first. Allow it to dry completely.

Herbs and Egg: Use round brush #2 to apply the "Coffee" value for the herbs. Give the egg yolk a first wash, then apply a bit more mixture on the right side around it to create the initial sense of a 3-D shape.

Bread and Plate: Use filbert brush #4 to wash the first layer of the bread, employing the dilute-and-blend technique used for the tomato sauce to indicate texture. Use a filbert brush #8 for the plate, focusing on depicting shadowed areas according to the light source's direction, and leaving white spaces for highlights.

Skillet: Use filbert brush #4 to apply the "Milk" value of the black mixture on the inside and outside parts of the skillet. Later, switch to a smaller brush to apply the "Tea" value on the lip and handle.

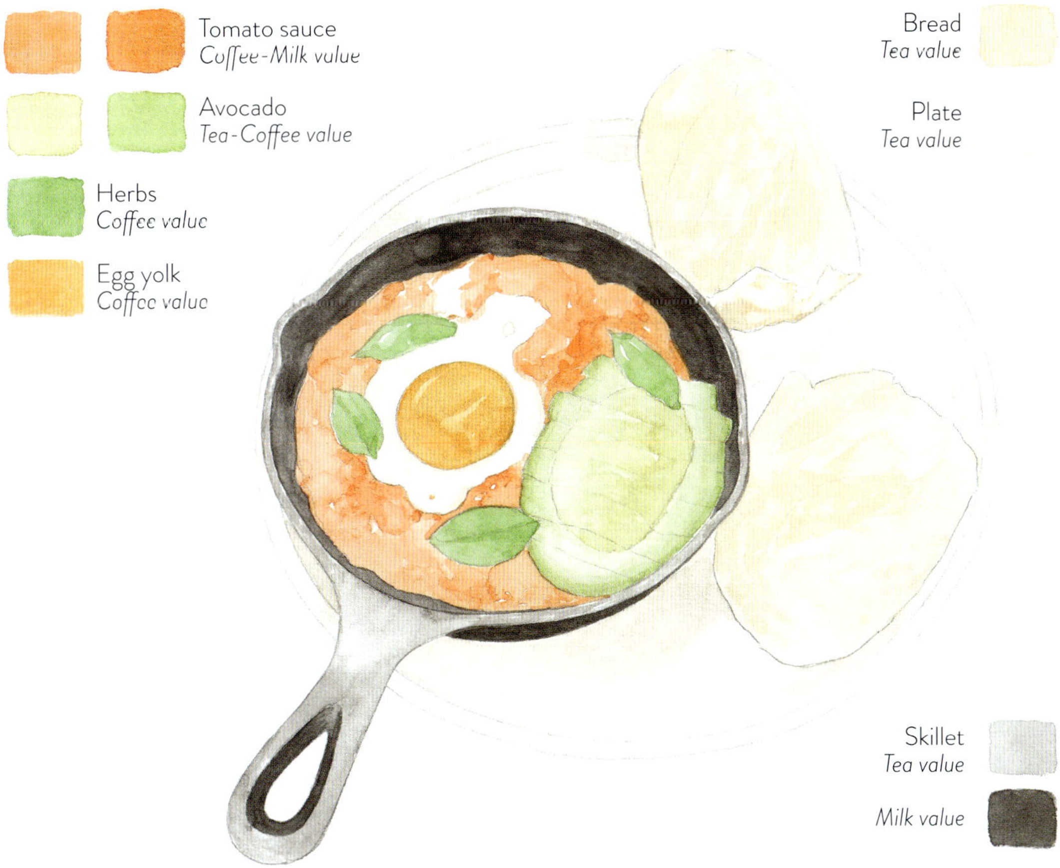

Second Layer

Tomato Sauce: Prepare a "Milk–Cream" value mixture and use round brush #2 to apply it over the first layer. Move your brush freely, allowing some areas to remain lighter to create contrast.

Avocado: Use round brush #1 to apply the "Coffee" value of warm green (the color in the upper row of the "Avocado" color palette rows) to the recessed part, focusing on deepening its left side. Make sure to leave some lighter lines to indicate the cuts. Add another layer of vibrant green (the color in the lower row of the "Avocado" color palette rows) in the same value as the first layer.

Herbs: Deepen the stems using round brush #1 and the "Cream" value. Lightly depict the midribs and veins, applying gentle pressure to maintain their delicate appearance.

Egg: Add a deeper layer of "Milk" value to the egg yolk with round brush #2, making it darker at the right edge. Rinse your brush slightly to reduce pigment load, then dab it around the edge of the egg white to create a soft blend into the tomato sauce. Leave a sharp, bright area on the egg yolk to give it a shiny appearance, reflecting the light source.

Bread: Use a filbert brush #4 and apply the "Milk" value of the warm brown mixture to the bread crust with a scumbling brushstroke. Employ the same brushstroke style for the scored areas, but use a brighter mixture.

> **Artist's Tip:** You can twist the filbert brush to its thinner side to reach narrow areas. This technique also helps create finer texture for the bread.

Plate: Use a filbert brush #8 to add a new layer of the "Coffee" value mixture to the shadow areas of the plate, including those cast by the skillet and bread.

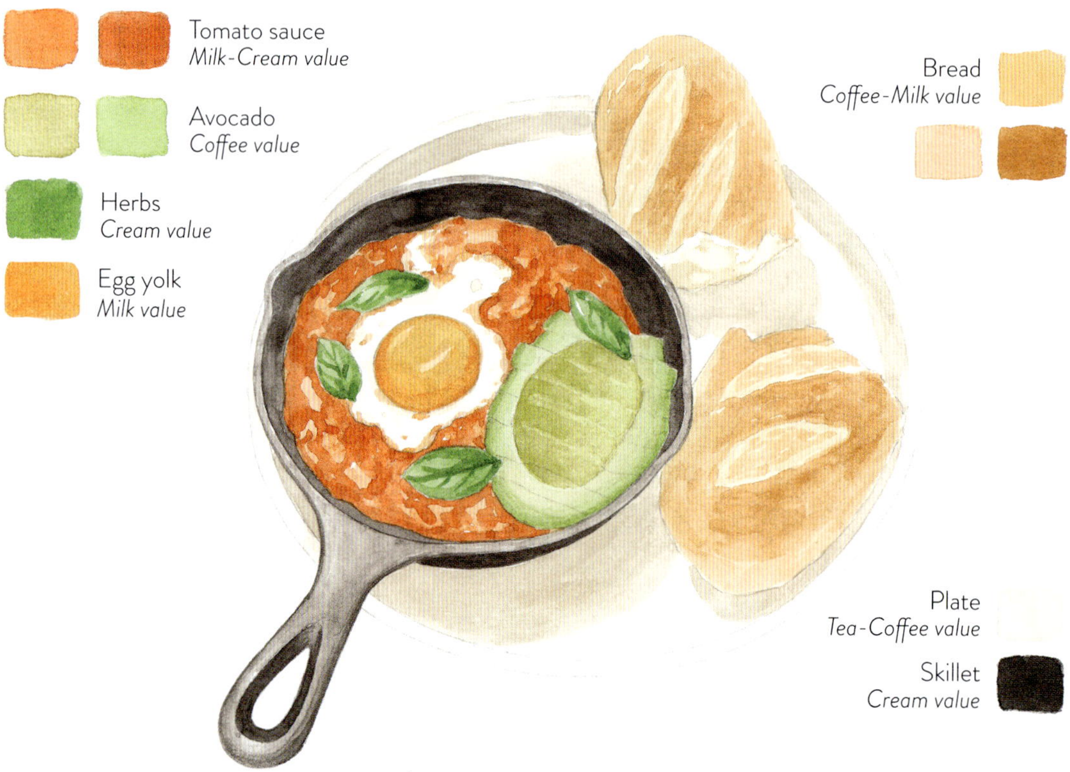

Third Layer

Tomato Sauce: Pick up round brush #1 to apply a deep-toned red in "Cream" value, following the same technique used for the second layer. Add a bit more shade for the corners around the avocado and egg white.

Avocado: Blend Raw Umber with a touch of the Tomato Sauce mixture, then load it onto a spotter brush to draw thin lines between the avocado slices. Apply thicker value at the two ends of each line, leaving the middle section lighter.

Bread: Enhance the current depiction with "Cream" value for both colors as needed, using a filbert brush #4 and a scumbling brushstroke.

In addition to applying the darkest shade according to the cylinder shading rule, dab some more color onto the highest part of the bread crust where it's more burnt. Also, apply touches of the same mixture along the middle of the score marks.

Plate: Use a filbert brush #8 to apply the "Milk" value to the shadow areas, blending it gradually to thin the mixture as it moves toward the highlight areas. Ensure that the shadow appears darker closer to the object.

Skillet: Add a layer of the black mixture in "Cream" value to the left side of the skillet's interior wall using a filbert brush #4, as this side is not facing the light source.

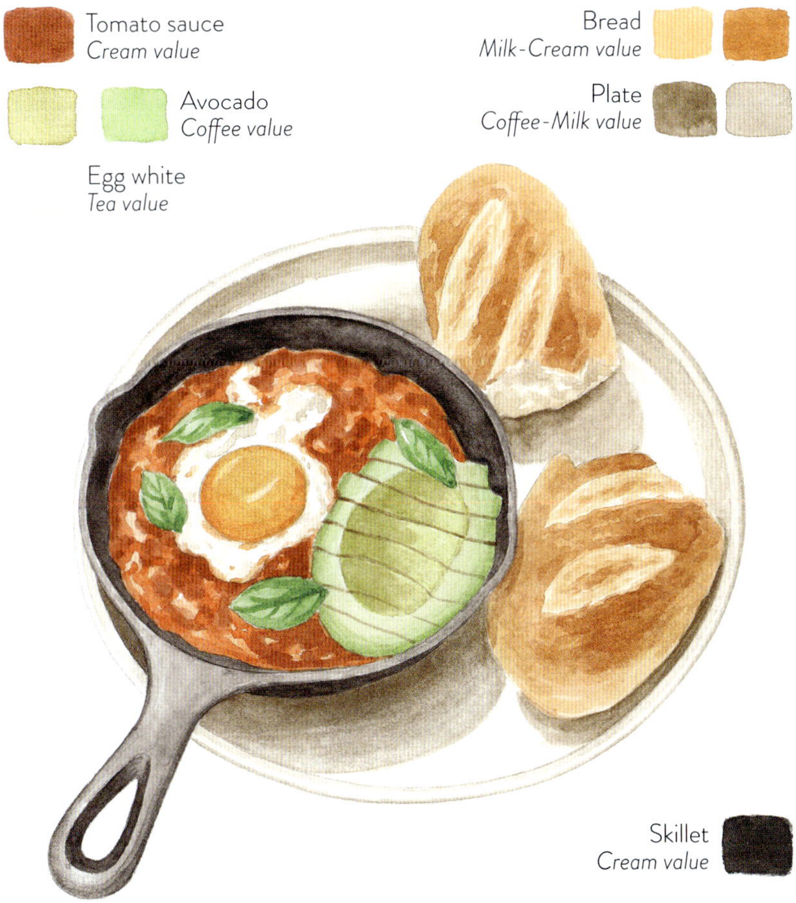

Finishing Touches

Bread: Squint your eyes to check if the more burnt spots are standing out. If not, apply an extra layer of "Cream" value on them to enhance the contrast.

Skillet: Load a light-gray mixture onto round brush #1. To create the cast-iron texture where the light hits, scumble short strokes on the handle, leaving slight gaps between the strokes.

Add some black pepper on top of the egg yolk with a spotter brush, using a "Butter" value of Ivory Black. Vary the size of the cracked pepper pieces to achieve a natural look.

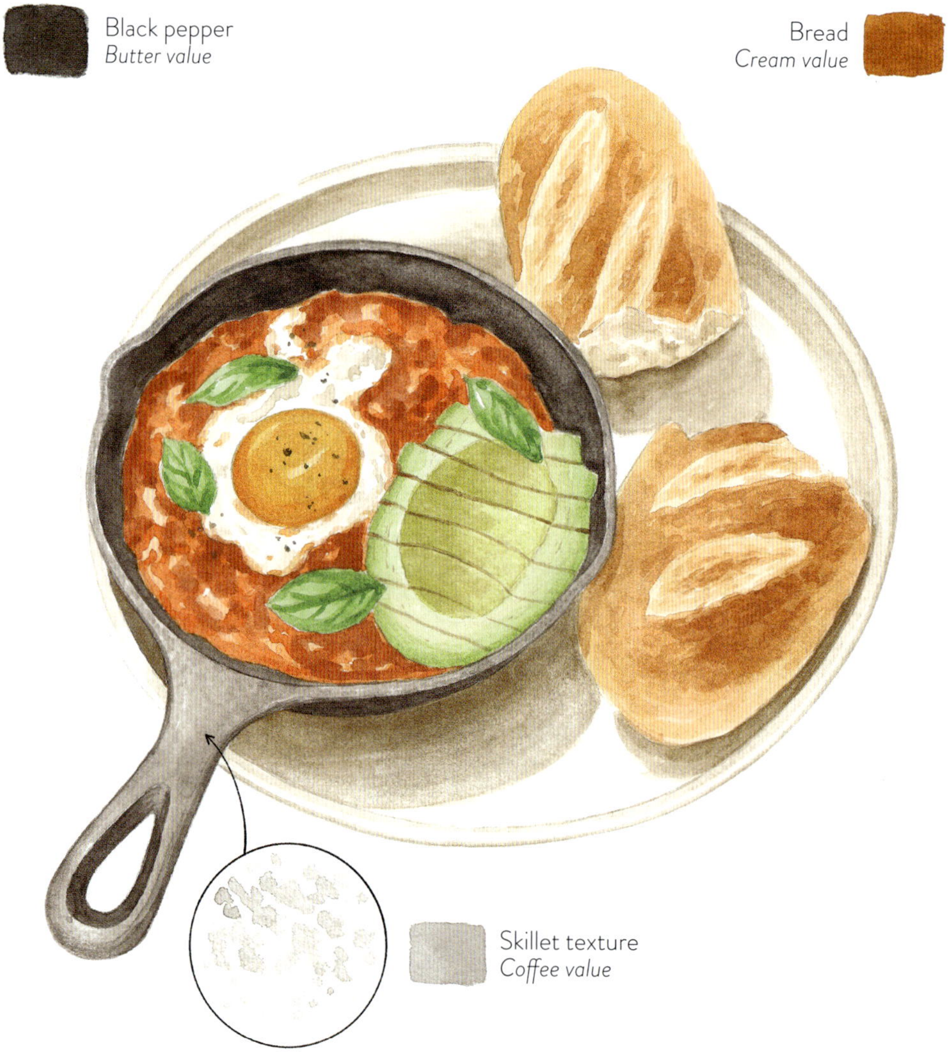

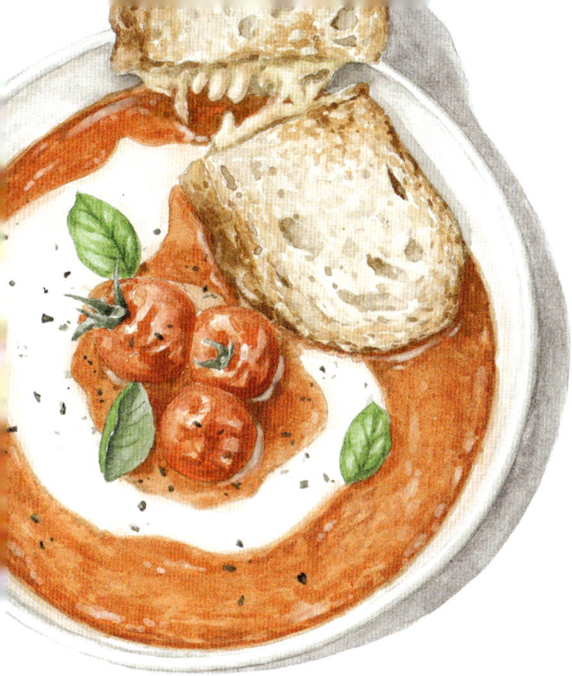

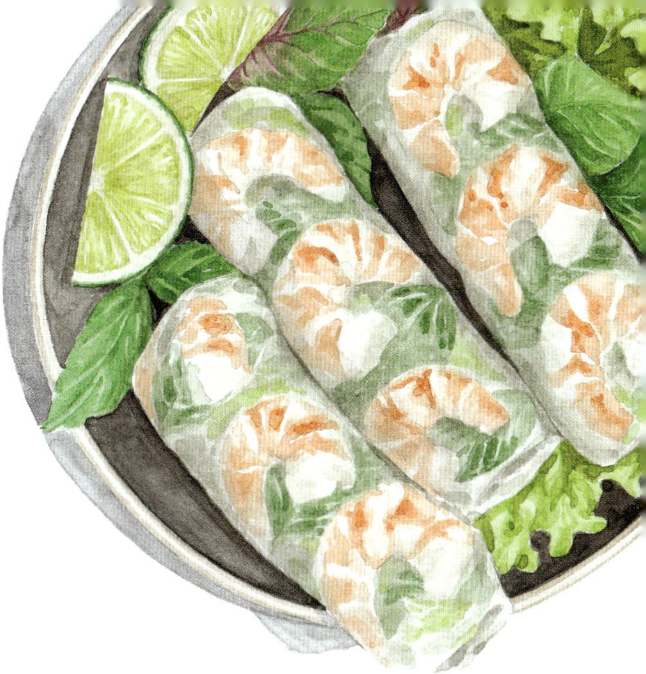

Soups, Salads & Small Bites

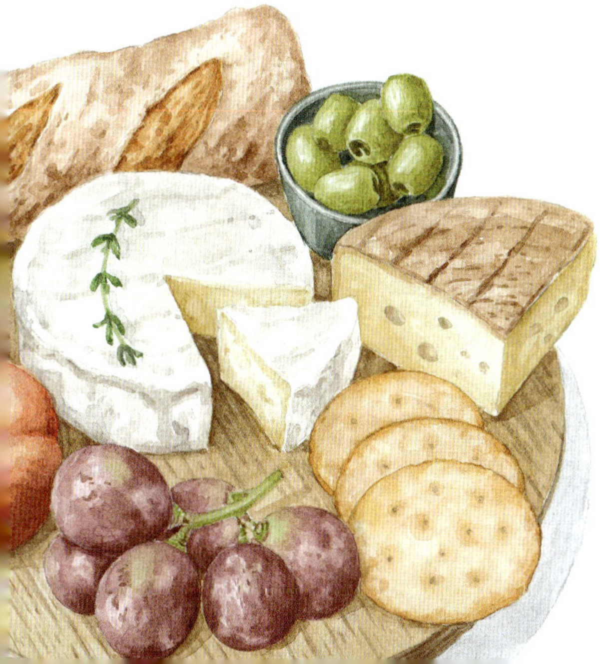

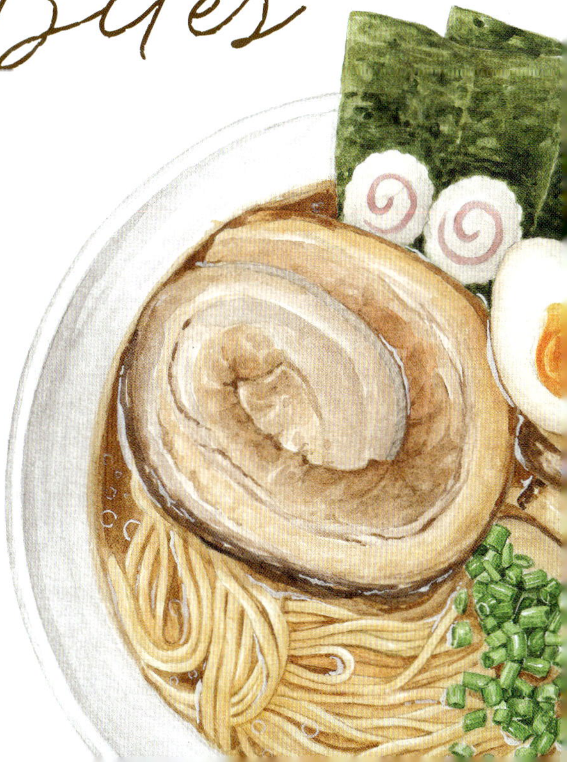

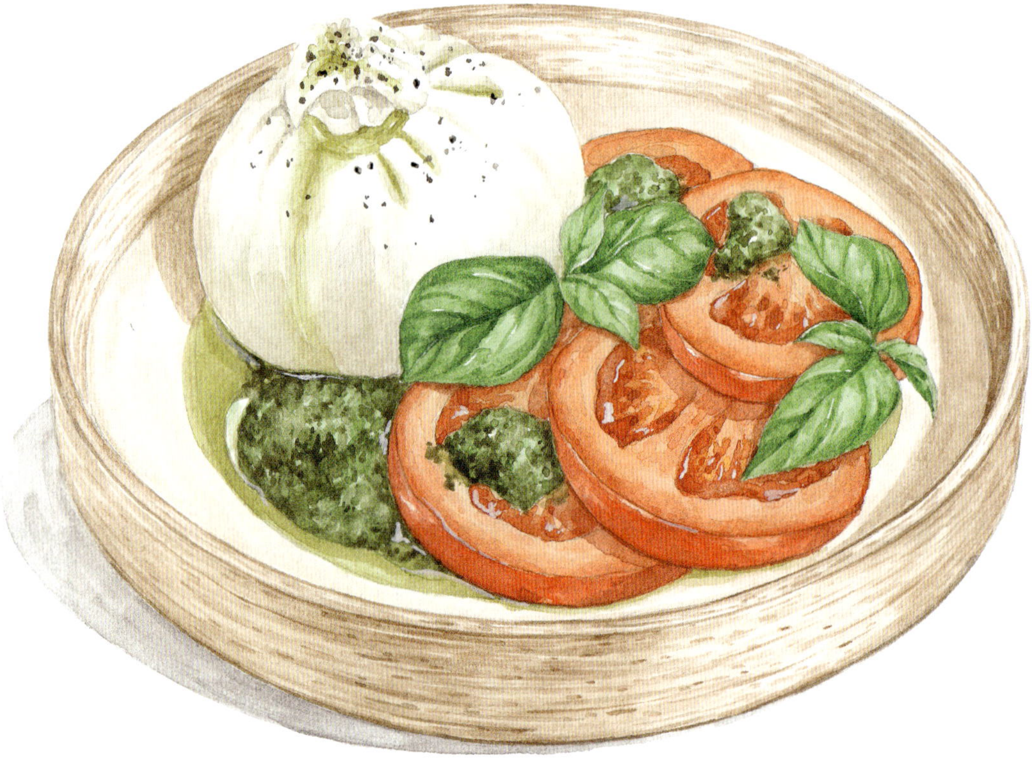

Project 06

Tomato Caprese

(Dimensions: W 6" x H 4½" / W 15.3 cm x H 11.3 cm)

This project centers around tomatoes, featuring vibrant, juicy slices that showcase their seeds and flesh, accompanied by a luscious burrata cheese knot. It is perfect for those who adore creamy white cheese and crave a wholesome yet simple salad experience. Additionally, I aim to emphasize the role of an attractive serving plate in food illustration, underscoring how it can elevate the overall appeal and value of the dish.

Brushes

Round brushes: sizes 1 and 2

Filbert brushes: sizes 4 and 8

Spotter brush: size 3/0

Color Palette

OBJECT	COLOR NAME	COLOR VALUES		
		Tea/Coffee	Milk	Cream
Basil leaves	**Sap Green** **Hooker's Green**	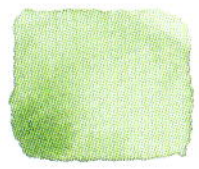		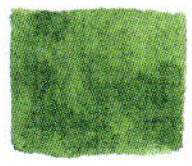
Pesto sauce	**Quinacridone Gold** **Sap Green** **Phthalo Green** **Raw Umber**		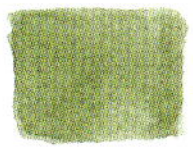	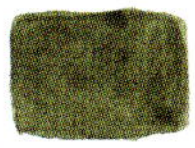
Olive oil	**Sap Green** **Quinacridone Gold**		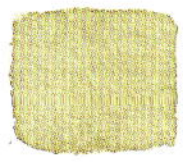	
Tomato flesh	**Pyrrol Orange** **Pyrrol Scarlet** **Quinacridone Gold**		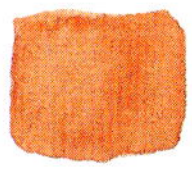	
Tomato skin	**Pyrrol Scarlet** **Quin. Burnt Scarlet**			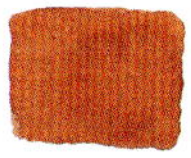
Burrata cheese	**Raw Umber**		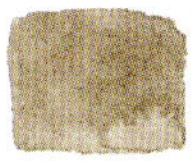	
Plate	**Raw Umber** **Goethite**			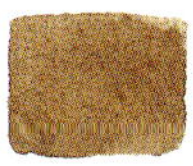

Viewpoint & Light Source

Here, a sitting eye-level viewpoint is employed to display the various levels of the ingredients. A higher viewpoint would flatten the whole composition, showing only the tops of the elements without depth.

Because the heavier element, the burrata cheese, is positioned more toward the left side, I choose to have the light source come from the right side to complement all the ingredients displayed on the plate.

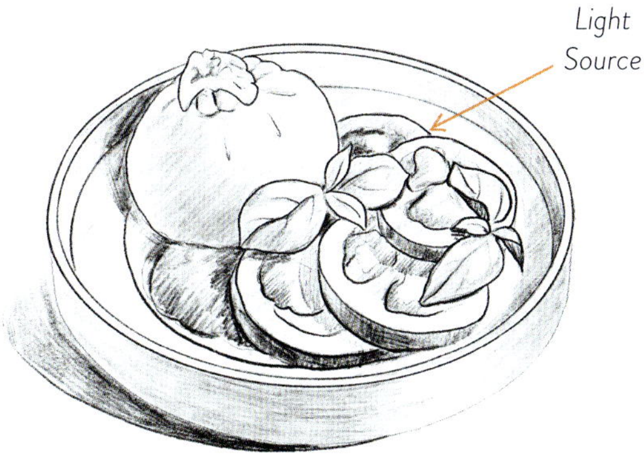

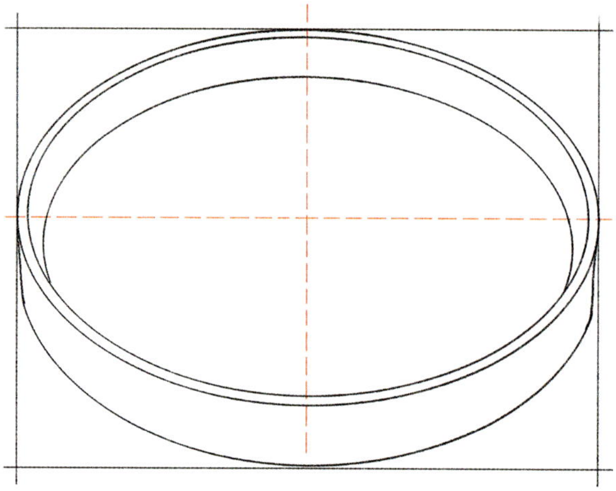

Composition

Due to the thinness of the tomato slices, a straight-walled flat plate effectively showcases the ingredients from this angle as well as presents the tomatoes' attractive texture. Additionally, I stack the slices up to add depth to the composition. The placement of the basil leaf garnish is flexible, provided it features various angles and contributes harmoniously to the overall balance and presentation of the dish.

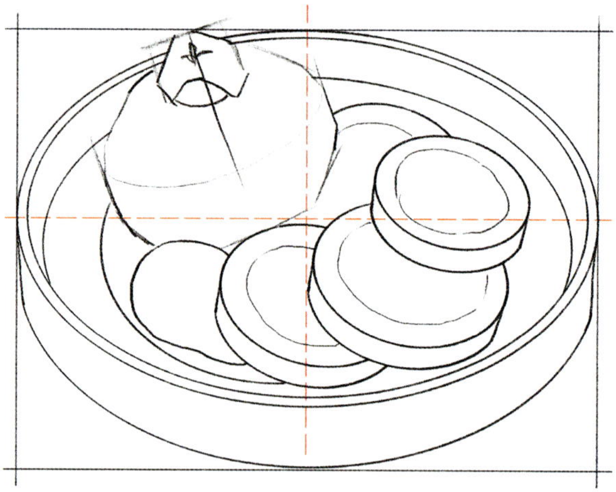

Let's Sketch!

Begin by sketching a frame and its central lines to outline the shape of the plate. Since the plate has straight walls, it resembles a simple cylinder with a recessed bottom and a slightly thick rim. The burrata cheese is derived from a sphere, while tomato slices are based on thin cylinder blocks. From there, add the necessary details to each item.

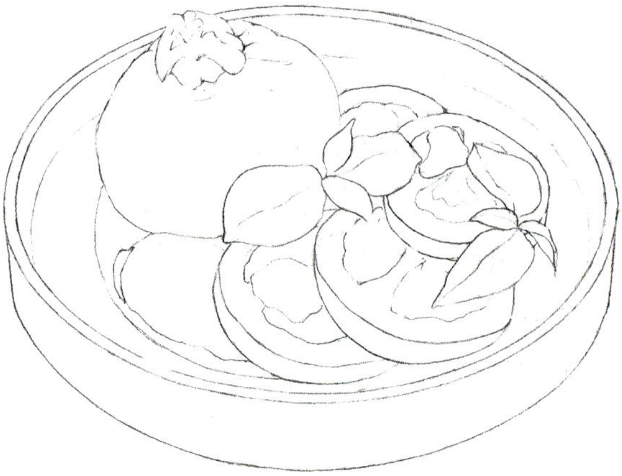

Let's Paint!

First Layer

Burrata Cheese: Use a filbert brush #8 to wash a "Tea" value base layer of Raw Umber to the shadow area of the cheese and leave the highlight area white.

Tomato Slices: Load a filbert brush #4 with Tomato Flesh mixture in "Coffee" value and apply a base layer for the top surfaces. While still damp, blend the Tomato Skin mixture onto the rim for a soft color transition. Once the top surfaces are completely dry, use a smaller brush (like round brush #1) to apply the Tomato Skin mixture to the sides of the slices, ensuring precise application in narrow areas. Apply more pressure with the brush in wider areas to achieve a richer pigment. Carefully leave a thin line of lighter shade near the surface to create a shiny effect later.

Pesto Sauce: Give the entire section a base wash with Basil Leaf mixture in "Tea" value, using round brush #2. When the paper is still damp, add the "Milk" value solution using a scumbling brushstroke.

Olive Oil: Use round brush #2 to apply a flat wash of Olive Oil mixture in "Coffee" value, deliberately leaving a thin white stripe where it meets the pesto sauce to depict the glossiness of the oil later.

Basil Leaves: Use round brush #2 to apply "Coffee" value across all the leaves, then quickly add a bit more mixture to the edges to create shading. Once the paper is less damp, switch to round brush #1 and use the same mixture to add details of the veins and midribs.

Bamboo Plate: Select filbert brush #8 to apply the Bamboo mixture in "Tea" value to the paper. Be particularly mindful of the lighting direction around the object; the shadow will fall to the right on the inner wall and to the left on the outer wall.

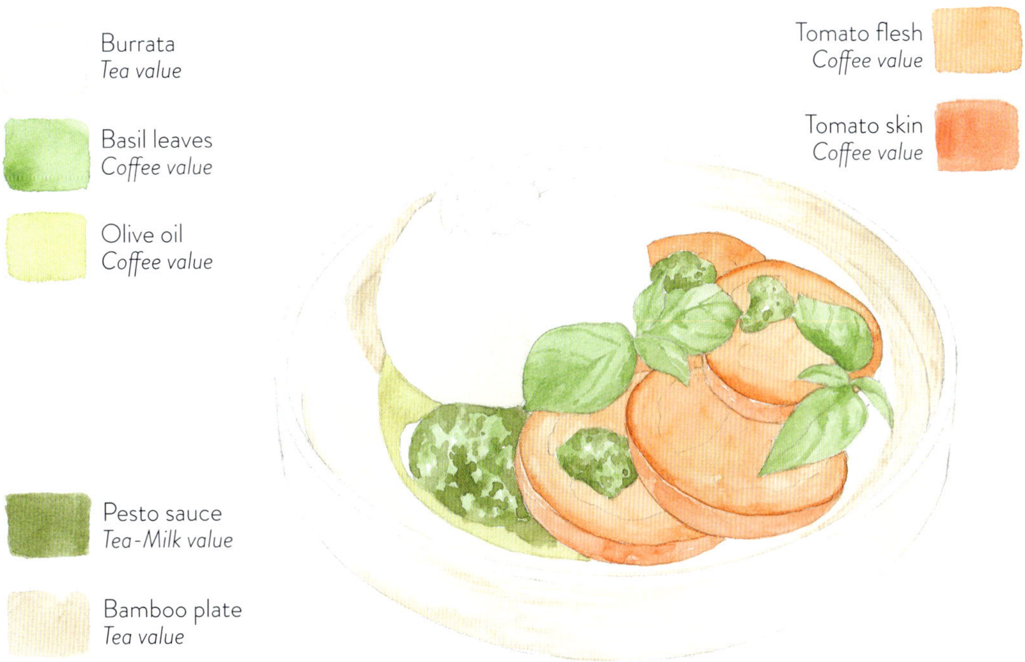

Second Layer

Burrata Cheese: Slowly darken the shadow area to avoid overdoing it, as it's harder to remove color from the paper than to add more layers. Once it dries, switch to round brush #1 to apply the Olive Oil mixture on top and around the knot. You can gently pull this color down toward the bottom of the cheese, following its curve. Now, employ the gradient wash technique (page 25): Dip your brush into a clean water jar to rinse off excess pigment, then return to the paper to soften the edge of your brushstroke.

Tomato Slices: Use filbert brush #4 to apply the "Milk" value to the locules, dropping a thick mixture along the curve, then using the thin side of the brush to blend it toward the center. Work on each section at a time to better control the colors on the paper. Once they are all dry, apply the "Milk" value of the Tomato Skin mixture to the sides, ensuring that shadow areas follow cylinder shading rules.

> **Artist's Tip:** For larger objects, prepare ample quantities of all the mixtures in advance to avoid having to stop in the middle of the process to mix more colors.

Olive Oil: Repeat the process from the first layer, ensuring that the area close to the burrata cheese is slightly darker to depict the shadow cast by the cheese.

Basil Leaves: Apply the "Cream" value to the midribs and veins of each leaf using round brush #1, blending it gently toward the outer edges. Ensure darker shades remain at both the center and edges to emphasize the basil leaves.

Bamboo Plate: Use filbert brush #8 to apply "Coffee" value to further darken the shadow areas. Change to the thin side of the brush to depict the texture at the same time by hatching long, thin lines following the oval shape. Blend the solution toward the highlight areas using a clean, damp brush.

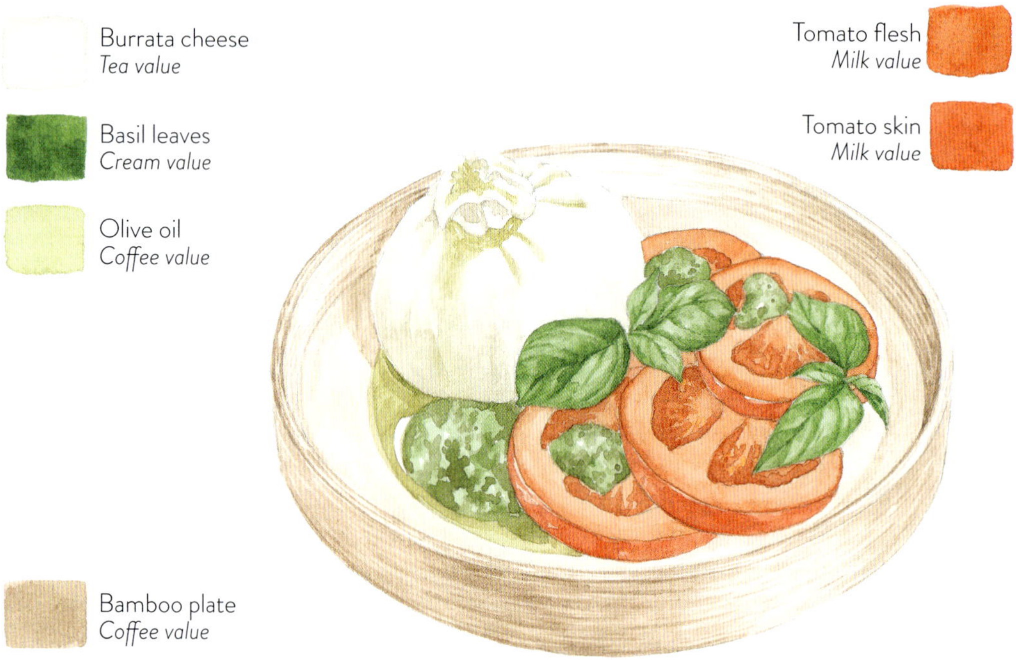

Third Layer

Burrata Cheese: Deepen the shadow areas further with another layer of "Tea" value using a filbert brush #4. Switch to round brush #1 and apply a thicker value to the knot area, focusing on the creases. Add the "Milk" value of Olive Oil mixture around the knot. Pay attention to preserving the contrast between the white and olive tones when increasing the values.

Tomato Slices: Add some Tomato Skin mixture to Tomato Flesh mixture to create a deeper shade for the locules, leaving the core lighter. Then, apply the "Cream" value of the Tomato Skin mixture to the thickness of the slices, ensuring a smooth transition toward the narrow ends to enhance their 3-D appearance.

Basil Leaves: Repeat the process from the second layer until the midribs are a deep green shade and the blades stand out. Maintain a balanced contrast between highlight and shadow areas by adding small amounts of mixture at a time.

Pesto Sauce: Use round brush #1 to apply scumbling strokes of the "Milk" value, creating texture for the pesto. Add more mixture on the left side and the area close to the tomato slices to darken these shadow areas.

Bamboo Plate: Repeat the technique used in the second layer, with darker value and filbert brush #4 this time. Vary the length of your strokes more in this step. For very thin lines, switch to round brush #1.

Artist's Tip: Carefully add darker lines to the highlight areas to enhance the natural look, ensuring they remain lighter than the lines in shadow areas. Soften the details at the farther end of the plate to create a greater sense of depth.

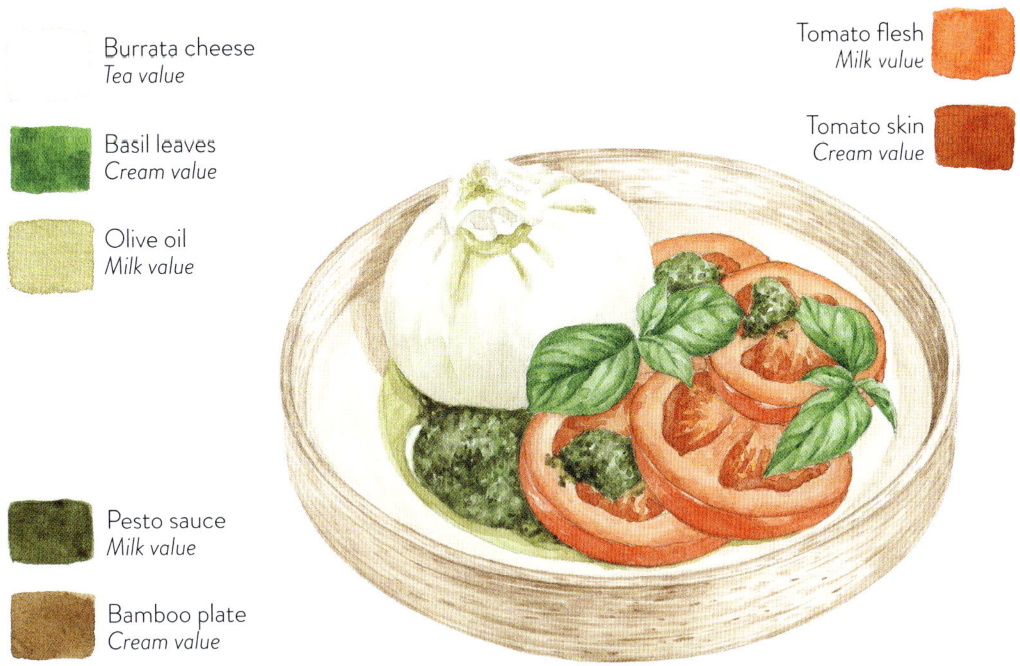

Finishing Touches

Add some black pepper on top of the burrata cheese using a spotter brush #3/0 and "Cream" value of Ivory Black.

Wash your spotter brush thoroughly and load it with some White pigment in "Cream" value. Apply it to the shiny spots that were left untouched across all the layers for the tomato slices. Add a few additional strokes to the locular gel to depict its jelly-like consistency.

Add a cast shadow with a "Coffee" value of a warm gray mixture.

Squint your eyes to check the contrast between the objects and the highlight-shadow balance. Repeat any of the previous steps to adjust the tone until you are happy with it.

Artist's Tip: If a certain area ends up too dark, you can lighten the color following these steps: Apply a moderate amount of clean water to the area with a clean brush. Gently rub the brush on the paper to dilute excess color, avoiding overuse that might wear the surface out. Quickly clean and dry the brush (or use a different clean, dry brush) to absorb the excess solution. For larger areas, use a paper towel instead. Please note that this technique is effective only on fresh or slightly damp layers.

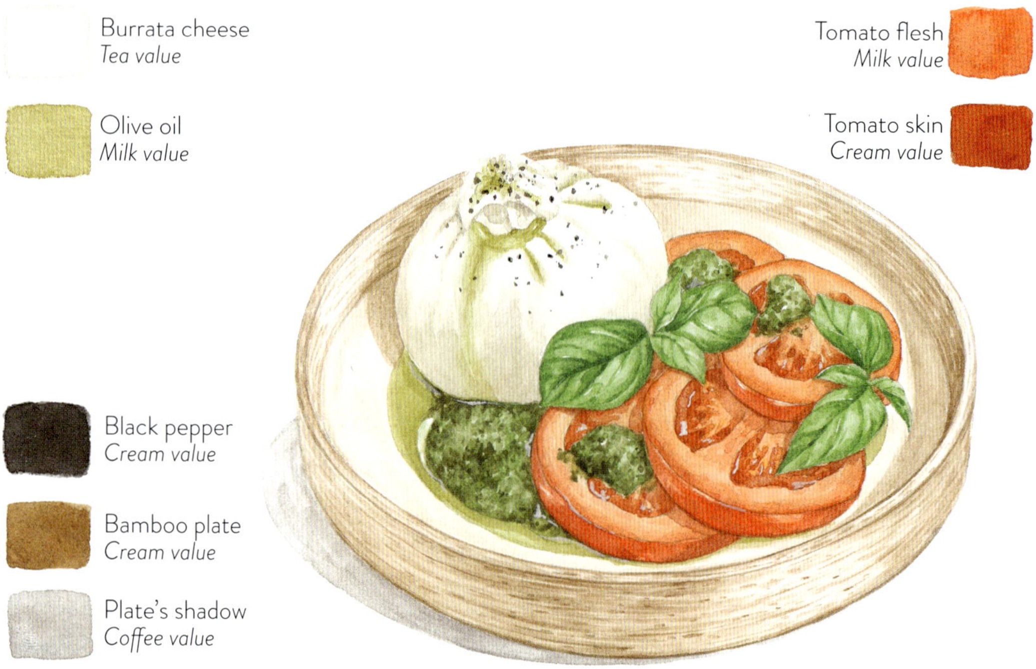

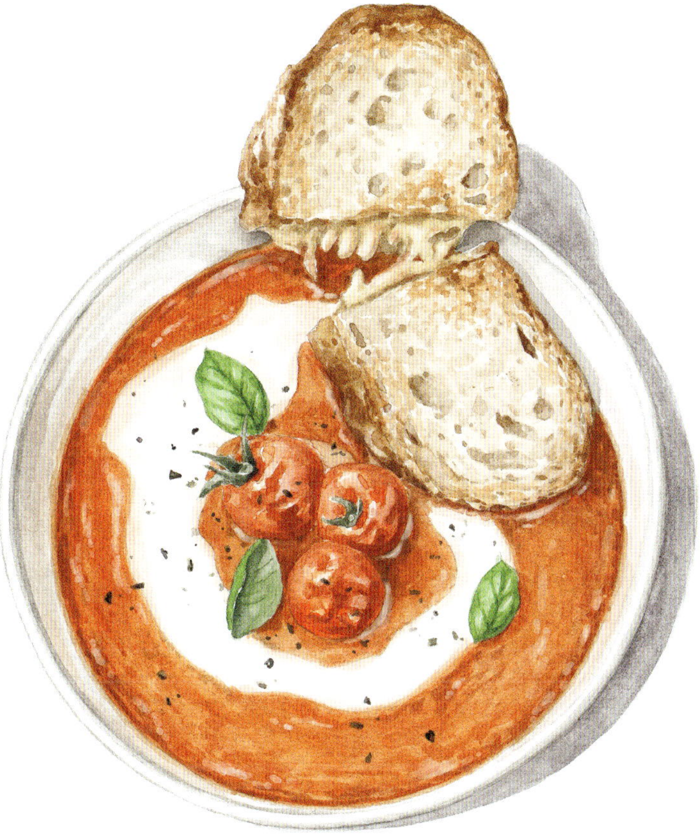

Project 07

Tomato Soup

(Dimensions: W 5⅛" x H 6¼" / W 13 cm x H 15.8 cm)

You might question whether it's possible to effectively depict food in a flattened, overhead style. The answer is a resounding yes! In this project, I showcase a flat representation of a tomato soup bowl adorned with cooked tomatoes and basil leaves, served with cheese toast on the side. The diverse textures—ranging from smooth, thick soup and light, airy bread to the skin of the cooked tomato and melted cheese—represent another advancement in your journey of food illustration.

Brushes

Round brushes: sizes 1 and 2
Filbert brush: size 4
Spotter brush: size 3/0

Color Palette

OBJECT	COLOR NAME	COLOR VALUES		
		Tea/Coffee	Milk	Cream
Bread crumb	**Raw Umber**			
Bread crust	**Burnt Sienna Burnt Umber Quinacridone Gold**			
Basil leaves	**Sap Green Hooker's Green**			
Tomato soup	**Quinacridone Sienna Burnt Sienna Pyrrol Scarlet**			
Tomato	**Quinacridone Sienna Pyrrol Scarlet Permanent Alizarin Crimson**			
Tomato stem	**Phthalo Green Raw Umber Sap Green**			
Bowl Black pepper	**Ivory Black**			

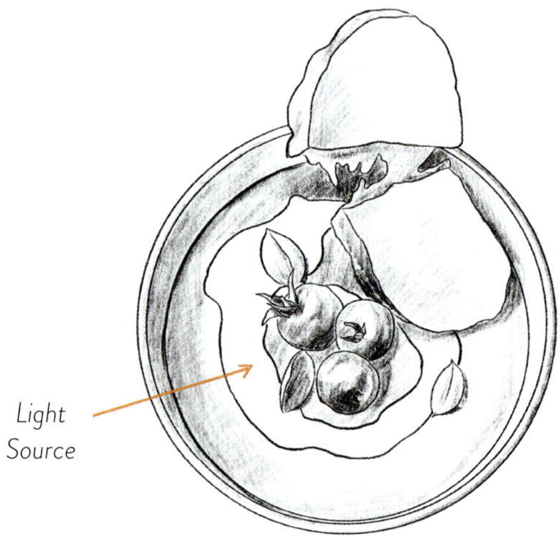

Viewpoint & Light Source

Chosen for learning purposes, a nearly top-down perspective will capture a flat view of the soup, tomatoes and accompanying elements. I position the light source higher and to the left to emphasize the texture of the bread positioned on the right side. This setup allows shadows to fall on the bowl, enhancing the perception of depth within the flat composition.

Composition

I place some roasted cherry tomatoes at the center of the bowl as a focal point. On the side, there are two pieces of grilled cheese "dissected" to reveal the melted cheese inside. To create color harmony, I garnish the soup with some basil leaves and a drizzle of white cream.

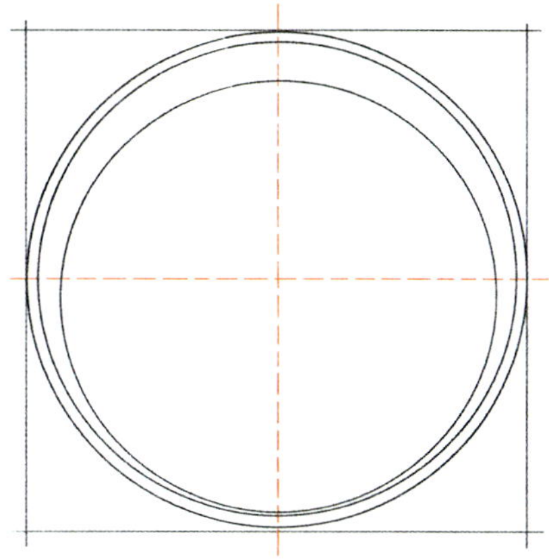

Let's Sketch!

Due to the nearly top-down viewpoint, the bowl appears as a circle neatly placed within a square. To enhance depth perception, the contents within the bowl can be contained within a wide ellipse, with its center slightly lower than the center of the circle.

Next, sketch all the other elements with their basic shapes: tomatoes as spheres and toast slices as short cuboids. As always, extending one or a few elements—such as one of the toast slices—beyond the bowl's boundary can enhance visual appeal. Then, add necessary details. Once satisfied, use an eraser to lighten the sketch, ensuring bold pencil lines do not obscure the painting phase.

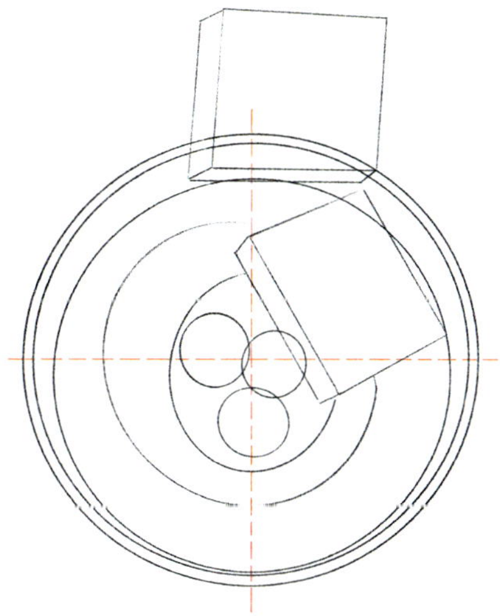

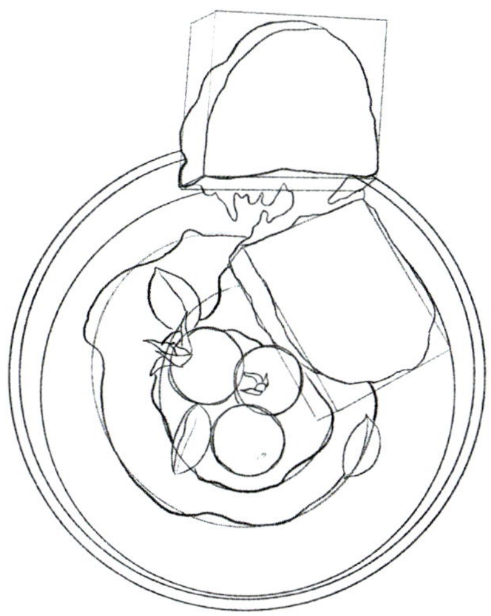

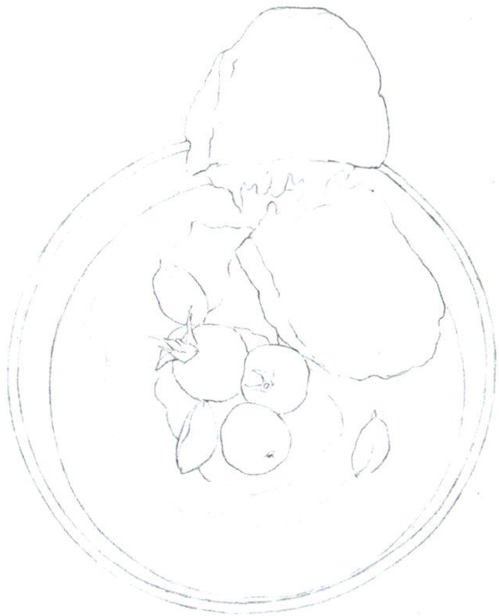

Let's Paint!

First Layer

Tomato Soup: Use round brush #4 to apply the "Tea" value across the entire area, loading the mixture generously for several strokes at a time. Near the edge closest to the white cream, dip the brush tip in clean water to slightly dilute the mixture and blend it toward the cream, creating softer edges. Lightly suggest the toast's shadows with another layer of the mixture while the paper is still damp.

Bread: Using filbert brush #4, apply a watery wash of Raw Umber to the bread crumb, employing a scumbling brushstroke. While it's still wet, switch to round brush #2 and scumble a darker brown in "Tea–Coffee" value onto the crust. Dilute the mixture slightly with clean water and gently blend the edge of the crust.

Bowl: Given the predetermined light source, the left interior wall of the bowl will appear darker as it's not directly illuminated. Apply a light-gray wash to this area with a filbert brush #4. The lip of the bowl will be darker on the right half, so use round brush #1 to dim this area down with the same mixture.

Cherry Tomatoes: Use round brush #2 to apply mixtures of both warm and cool in "Tea" values. The cool value can be made from Permanent Alizarin Crimson. Place the cool mixture on the shadow area, which is the right side in this case, while the warm color goes on the highlight area. Despite their generally spherical shape, these are cooked tomatoes, so their skins are wrinkled and less smooth than fresh ones. Hence, place reflections randomly to depict this distinctive skin texture. After that, switch to round brush #1 to apply dark green to the stems, which also darken when they are cooked.

Basil Leaves: Use round brush #2 to apply "Coffee" value across all the leaves, then quickly add a bit more mixture to the edges to create shading. Once the paper is less damp, switch to round brush #1 and use the same mixture to add details of the veins and midribs.

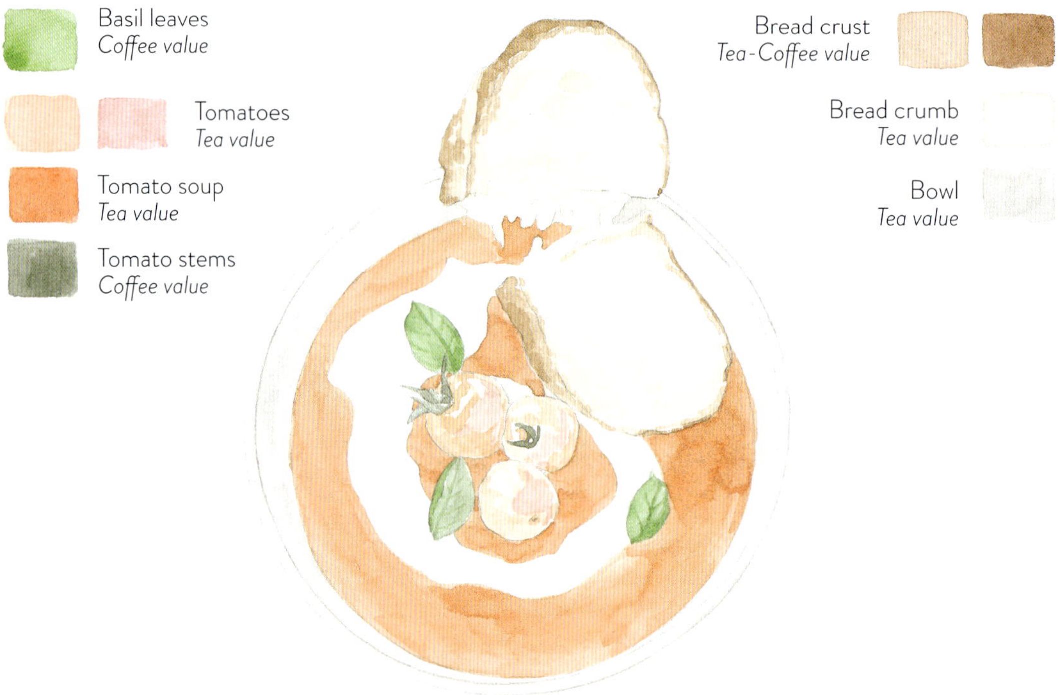

Second Layer

Tomato Soup: Use filbert brush #4 to add a layer of "Cream" value, employing the same technique as the first layer. Apply additional brushstrokes to the left side of the soup where the bowl casts a shadow to darken that area.

Bread: Apply "Milk" value mixture to the air pockets or cells with a filbert brush #4, making sure to darken the left edge of the larger ones with additional brush strokes.

Use the same brush to apply the dark-brown mixture to the crust. Note that toasts are unevenly burnt, so I suggest dabbing a thick solution onto one corner and then using a damp clean brush to scumble it out. This approach will enhance their natural appearance and prevent a uniformly applied hue around the entire edge.

Add the Bread Crumb mixture to the cheese, ensuring the right side remains slightly darker.

Bowl: Repeat the step from the first layer with the same "Tea" value solution.

Cherry Tomatoes: Keep the cold "Tea" value shadow spots from the first layer as they are in this step. Pick up round brush #1 and add "Cream" value to the other shadow areas following sphere shading rules, then thin it out toward the highlights. Relax your brush to let it bleed randomly. Add "Cream" value for the stems, leaving some areas as highlights to maintain detail visibility.

Basil Leaves: Apply the "Cream" value to the midribs and veins of each leaf using round brush #1, blending it gently toward the outer edges. Ensure darker shades remain at both the center and edges to emphasize the distinctive curved appearance of the basil leaves.

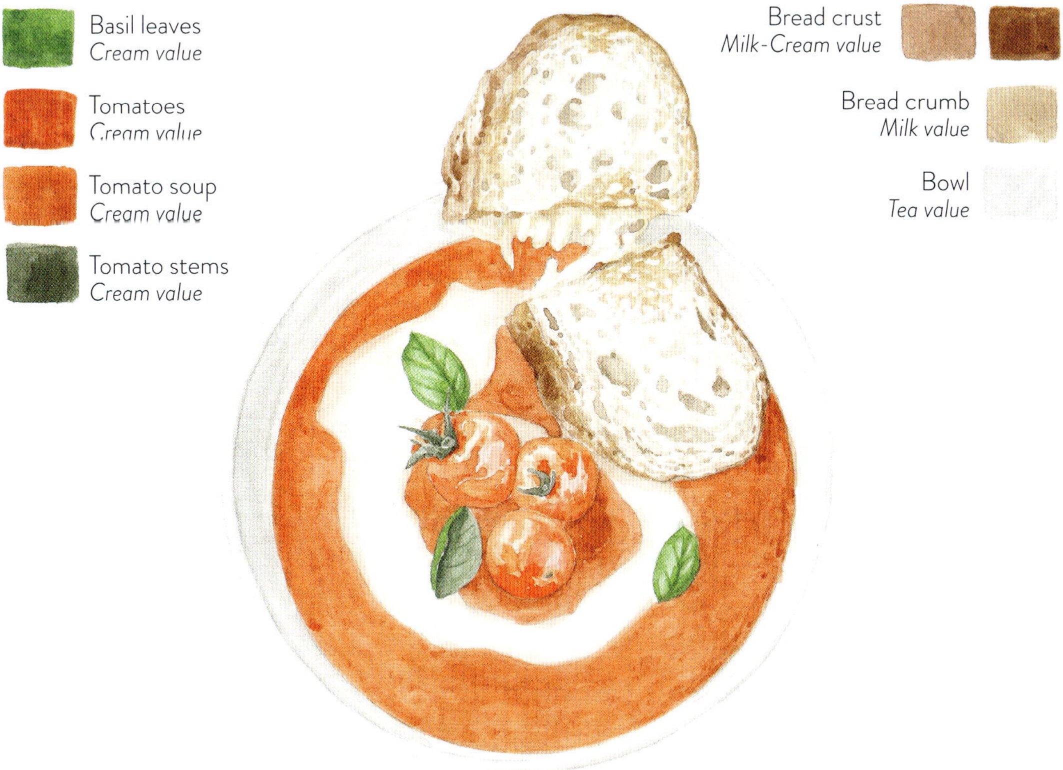

Third Layer

Tomato Soup: Repeat the steps from the second layer, using a "Cream" value this time. Turn to the thin side of the filbert brush and use a combination of hatching and scumbling strokes along the curve of the bowl to create a thick fluid texture for the soup. Apply extra mixture on the left side and in the shadows cast by the toast to increase depth.

Bread: Repeat the steps from the second layer with thicker mixture for both the crumb and the crust. To enhance the texture for the crumb, use the warm brown mixture of the crust and apply thick-and-thin strokes here and there. Add a touch of warm yellow color to the mixture to give the cheese a yellow tint.

Bowl: Further darken all the shadow areas mentioned in the second layer with thicker value. Prepare a new mixture combining Tomato Soup color in "Tea" value with the current gray, then wash it over the shadow side of the bowl. This will create a subtle reflection of color between the objects.

Cherry Tomatoes: Prepare a thicker and colder red by adding Permanent Alizarin Crimson to the previous mixture. Still using round brush #1, apply it to the shadow areas to create a deeper tone. While using this mixture, you can always dip your brush into the warm red mixture from the second layer and blend it toward the highlight area to improve the color harmony on the wrinkled skin. Soften the reflection areas by using a clean, damp brush to pull the color around.

Basil Leaves: Repeat the process from the second layer until the midribs are a deep green shade and the blades stand out. Maintain a balanced contrast between highlight and shadow areas by adding small amounts of mixture at a time.

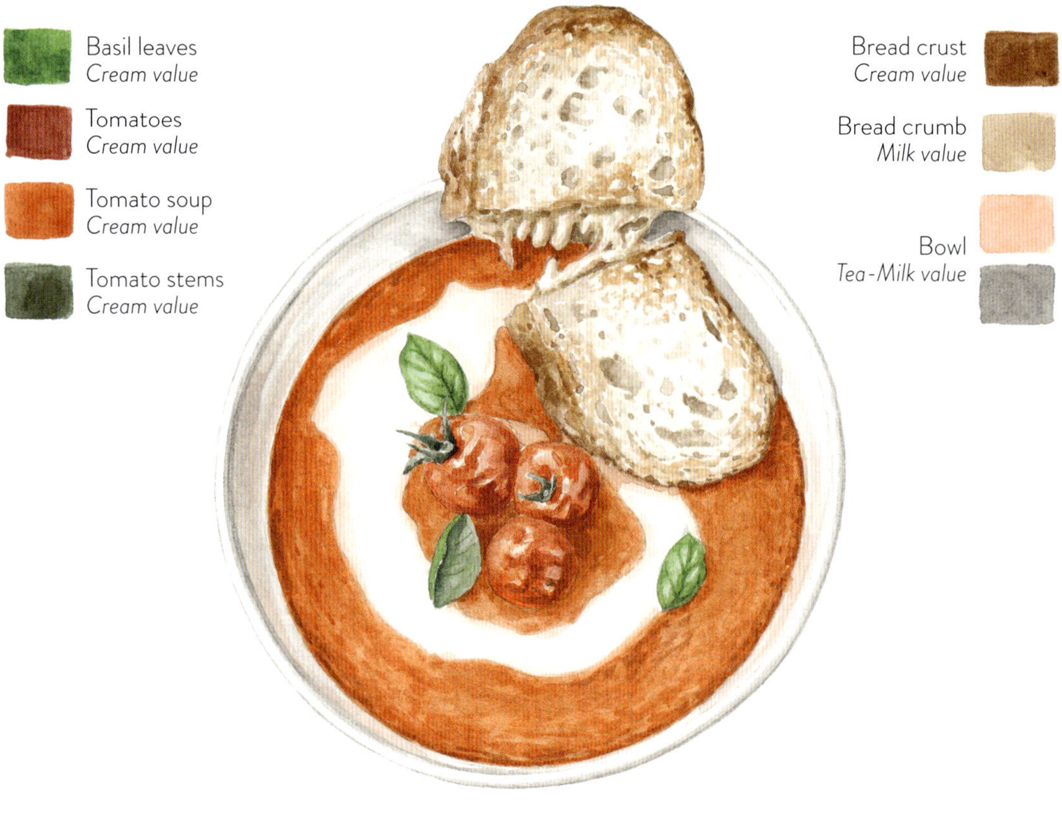

Finishing Touches

Add a cast shadow to the upper right side of the bowl and a part of the toast with a cool gray color in "Coffee" value. I add a hint of purple to the mixture to balance the warm look of the whole bowl.

Use a spotter brush and Ivory Black to sprinkle black pepper onto the soup. Vary the intensity of some spots to make them look more natural.

Tomatoes
Cream value

Tomato soup
Cream value

Black pepper
Milk-Cream value

Bread crust
Cream value

Bread crumb
Milk value

Cast shadow
Coffee value

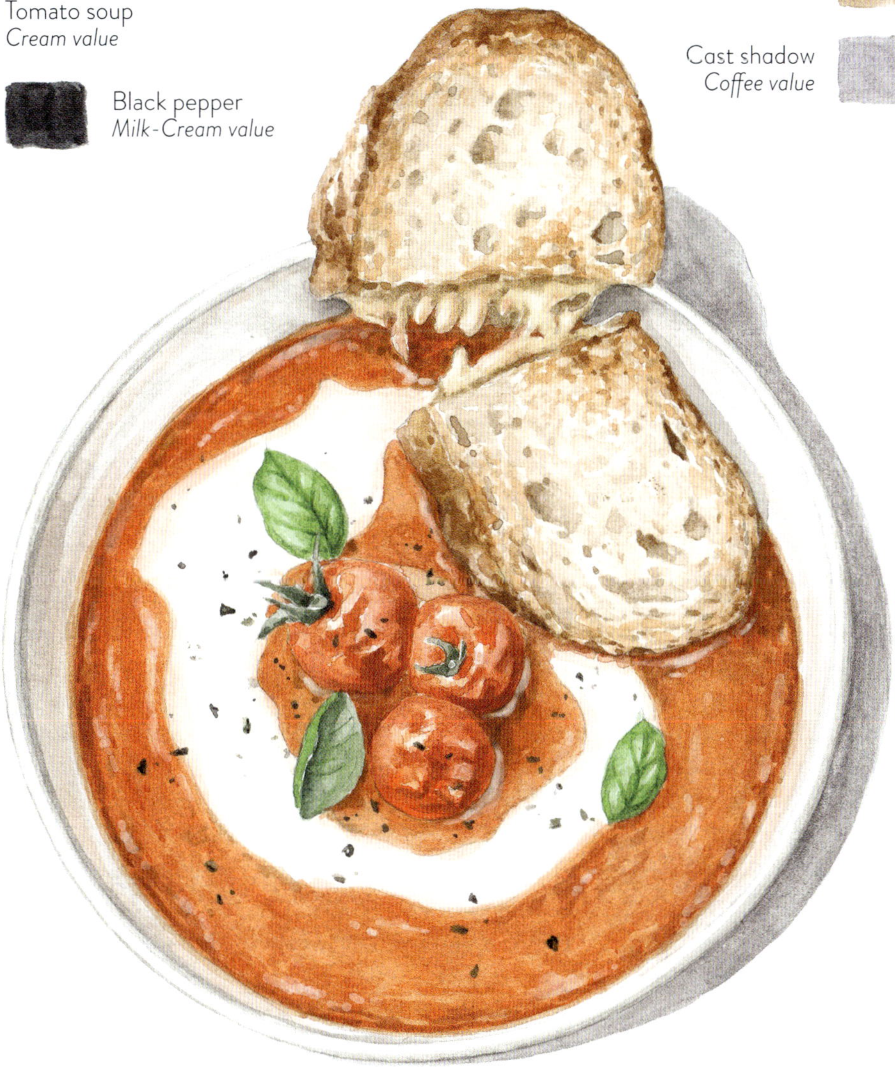

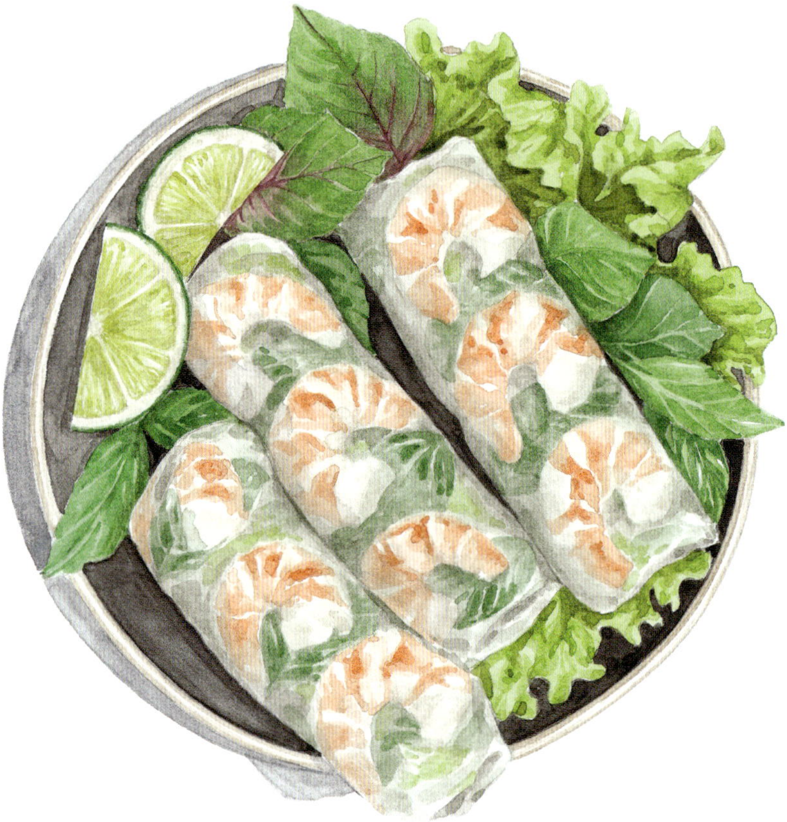

Project 08

Vietnamese Spring Rolls

(Dimensions: W 5¼" x H 5¾" / W 13.5 cm x H 14 cm)

As someone who is proudly Vietnamese, I'm filled with enthusiasm for this project, which also embraces the top-down viewpoint. It not only showcases one of the finest dishes I've ever tasted, known for its perfectly balanced flavors, but also utilizes a technique ideally suited for watercolor art—depicting transparency. Additionally, we'll tackle a new challenge: depicting various types and layers of leafy greens in the same display while maintaining color harmony among all the objects.

Brushes

Round brushes: sizes 1 and 2

Filbert brush: size 4

Spotter brush: size 3/0

Color Palette

OBJECT	COLOR NAME	COLOR VALUES		
		Tea/Coffee	Milk	Cream
Shrimp	**Pyrrol Orange**			
Lettuce	**New Gamboge** **Hansa Yellow** **Phthalo Green YS**			
Herbs Lime peel	**Sap Green** **Hooker's Green**			
Herbs' shadow	**Hooker's Green** **Raw Umber**			
Lime Lettuce's shadow	**Quinacridone Gold** **Sap Green**			
Perilla leaves	**Rose of Ultramarine** **Permanent Alizarin Crimson**			
Bowl's lip Spring roll's shadow	**Raw Umber**			
Bowl Spring roll's shadow	**Ivory Black**			

Viewpoint & Light Source

The top-down viewpoint allows a full view of all objects in the bowl. The light source is from the right. While the shadow of the rolls is not clearly visible due to the transparent rice paper, understanding the light source helps position the cast shadows of all objects within the bowl and onto the imaginary plane on which the dish is placed, thereby creating depth from this angle.

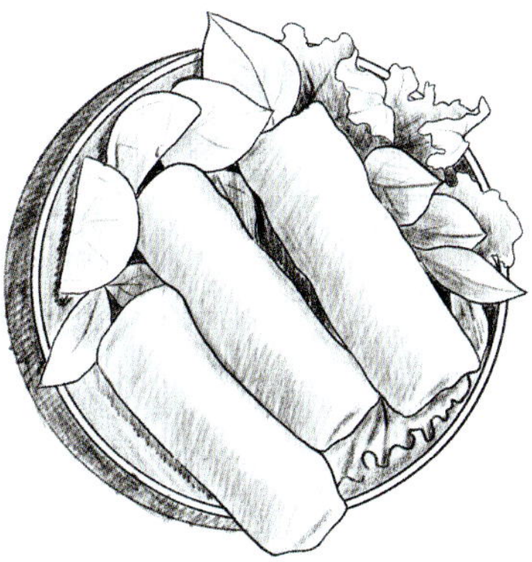

Light Source

Composition

Our main subject in this composition is the fresh rolls, where the fillings are visible through the transparent rice paper. Depicting this material requires focusing on what is seen through it. Vibrant layers of green lettuce and herbs, complemented by the dark, flat bowl, define clear boundaries for the main elements, which are mainly in neutral colors.

Let's Sketch!

Start with a square frame, then draw a full circle using its center lines as a guide. Position the cylindrical shape representing the rolls slightly closer to the bottom. It's beneficial to allow some parts to extend beyond the large circle to increase visual appeal.

The lettuce does not adhere to strict 3-D rules, so it's crucial to observe and understand its organic form, noting how it bends and curves. Then, add additional details to all items as needed. Finally, erase any excess lines and lighten the entire sketch.

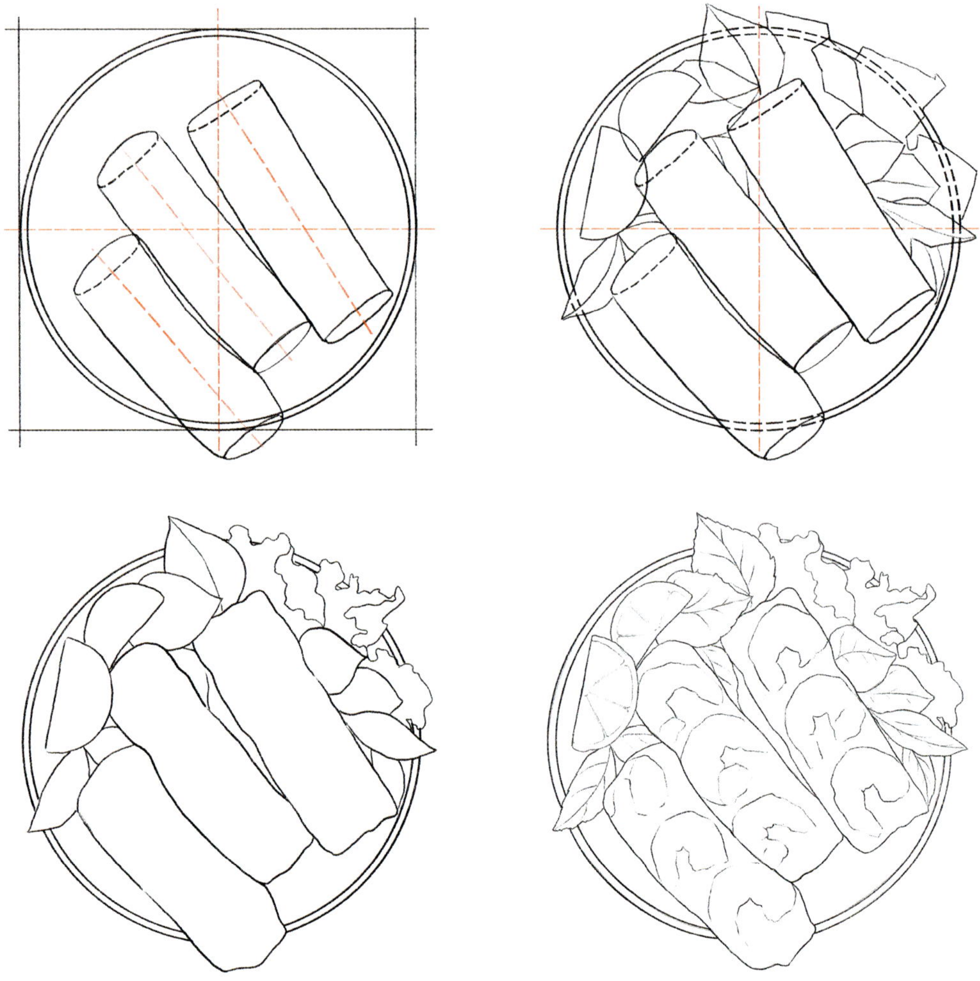

Let's Paint!

First Layer

Spring Rolls: Create an overall shadow area by using a filbert brush #4 to apply the first wash of light-gray mixture to the left side, following basic shading rules for cylinder shapes. Also, add some finer strokes of the same solution to the shadow side of the shrimps to make them stand out.

Lettuce and Herbs: Specifically choose a large brush size such as a filbert brush #4 or round brush #4 to ensure it can hold enough solution for easy blending or dragging of colors while the paper is still damp. For the lettuce, especially the leaves on top, begin by outlining the edges and then pull the color to the remaining area to define the boundary of each leaf.

For the herbs, after applying the initial wash, lightly dab a touch of the Herb Shadow mixture onto areas close to the rolls while the first layer is still damp to indicate they are positioned underneath.

For the perilla leaves, apply the green mixture to the top of the leaf and add a hint of purple mixture to the bottom, blending it upward along the veins.

Lime: Use round brush #1 to apply the Herb Shadow mixture to the half-circle. Instead of drawing an even line, lightly dampen the brush with clean water and create a "bumpy" movement to capture the texture of the peel. Apply the yellow-green mixture to the wedges by stroking short, thin lines toward the center of each slice.

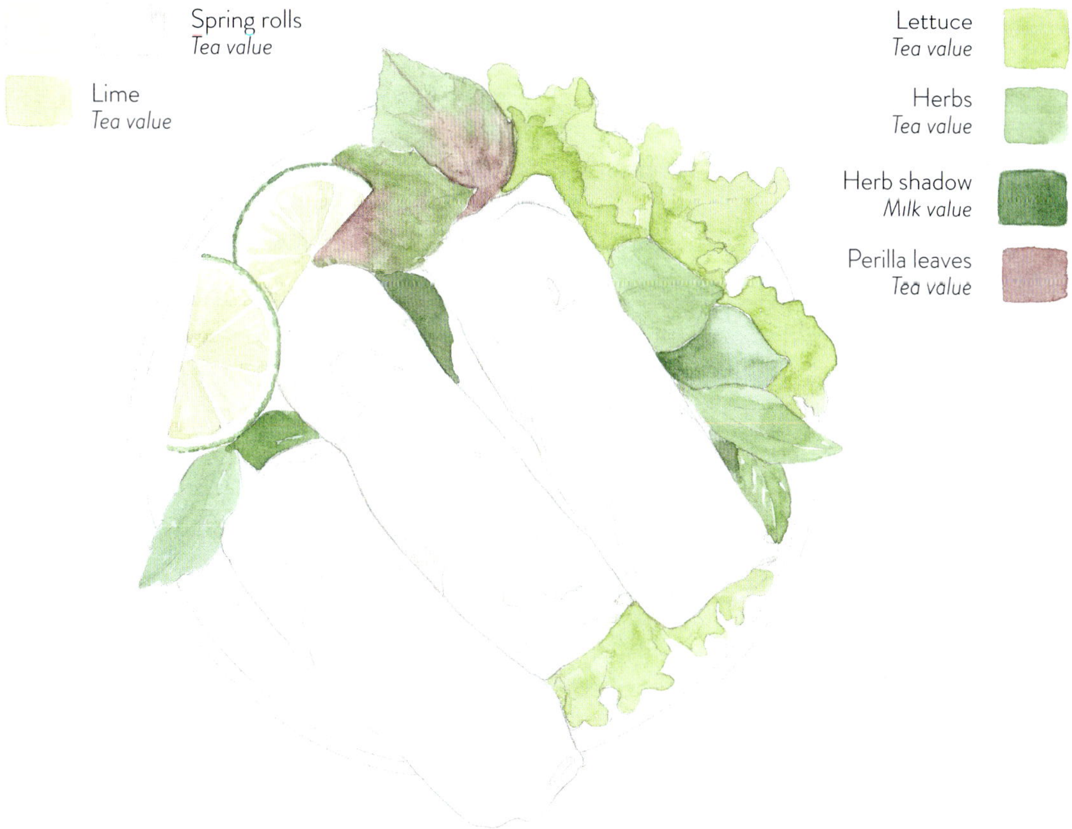

Second Layer

Spring Rolls: Select round brush #1 and add a "Tea" value of the orange mixture to the shrimps. Begin with a random, curvy line extending from the larger arc of the shrimp to the smaller arc, then immediately blend it into a triangle shape with one edge softly fading out.

Dilute the Herb Shadow mixture to "Tea" value and apply it around and underneath the shrimps, envisioning a leaf shape as you paint. After the first layer, add another layer of the same value to gradually deepen the shade. Next, dab the "Milk" value onto one section of the leaf to create the effect of it sticking to the rice paper and appearing clearer.

Lettuce and Herbs: Continue using round brush #4 (or filbert brush #4) to apply a "Milk" value to the lettuce, enhancing depth especially near the rolls. Due to the leaves' wavy nature, areas positioned lower will receive less light and appear darker.

Apply a layer of Herbs mixture (and purple mixture for perilla leaves) in a "Milk" value to deepen all the herbs. Remember to leave narrow gaps between the strokes to depict the midribs and veins of the leaves. Note that those positioned beneath others will naturally appear darker in shade. Feel free to add a bit of the "Cream" value of the Herb Shadow mixture to achieve the dark shade for these areas.

Lime: Repeat the same technique from the first layer using a "Milk" value this time.

Bowl: Use round brush #1 or #2 to add another layer of the black mixture to the bowl. Use the "Milk" value for the left side and "Cream" value for the right side. To make sure the lip of the bowl stands out, leave it white in this step and apply color to it later.

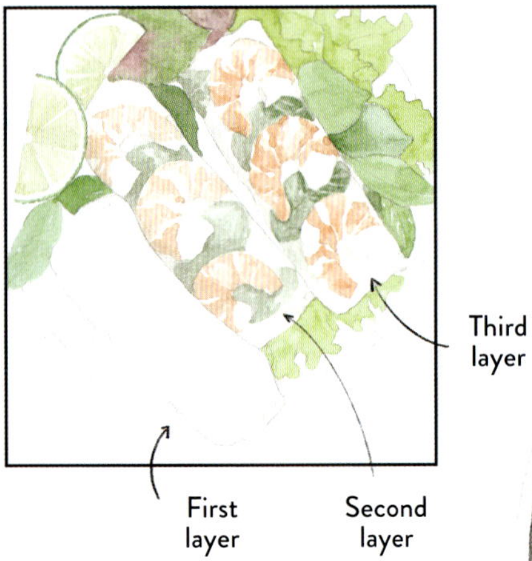

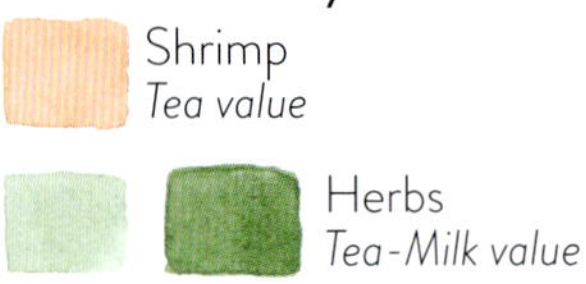

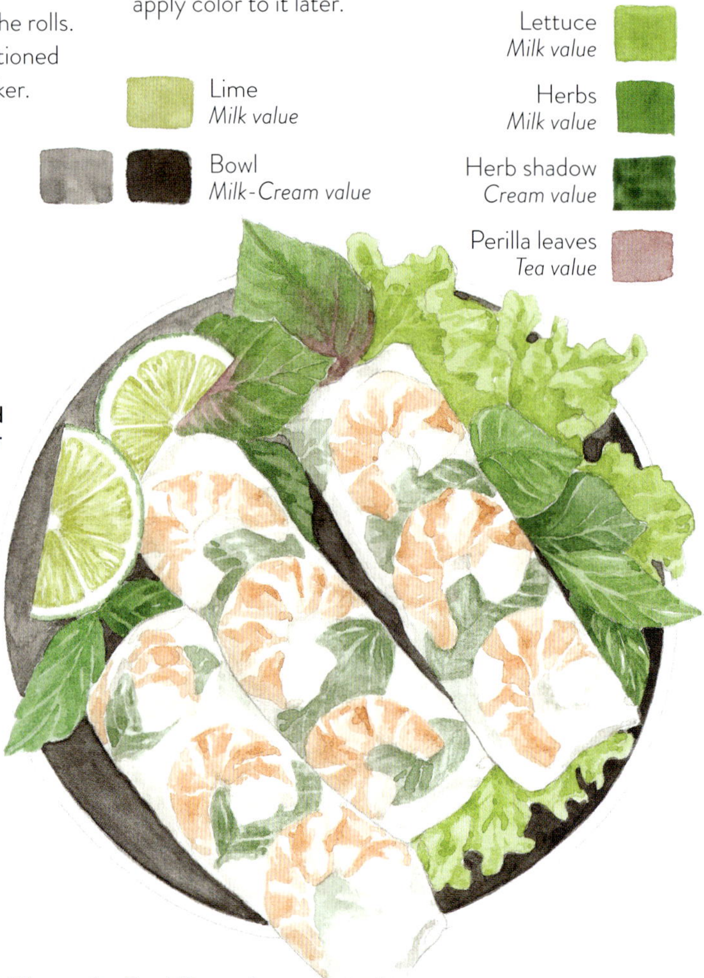

Third Layer

Spring Rolls: Select a filbert brush #4 to apply a "Tea" value of Herb Shadow mixture on the rolls, except the highlight areas (refer to the Light Source Shading Sketch on page 89). Alternatively, you can opt for light gray, though a hint of green will enhance the subtle blending with the herbs inside.

Lettuce and Herbs: Apply the "Cream" value of Lettuce Shadow mixture to the lettuce. Ensure precise brush control and apply this solution only when the paper is fully dry to maintain accuracy, as wet paper may lead to undesired bleeding and soften the contrast.

Deepen the herbs with corresponding "Cream" values.

Pick a spotter brush #3/0 to meticulously outline the midribs and veins of the perilla leaves using a rich, warm purple mixture.

Bowl: Load round brush #1 with a light-brown mixture to draw a thin line around the bowl's lip. The darker and thicker value will be placed mainly on the right side to enhance contrast with the highlight areas.

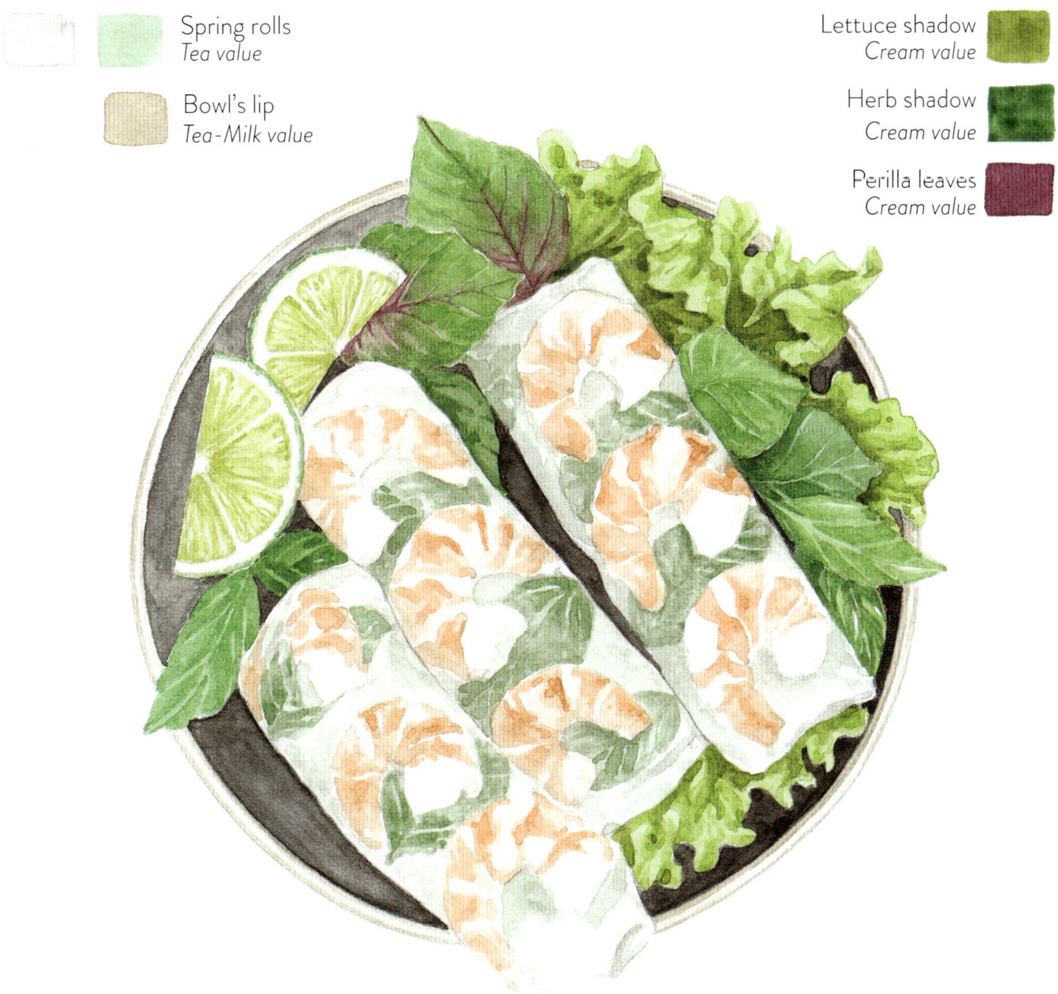

Finishing Touches

Apply a "Milk" value of orange mixture to the areas of the shrimp that touch the rice paper to enhance their appeal. Squint your eyes to assess if the rolls appear too bright compared to the overall composition. If they do, tone them down entirely with a flat wash of light-gray mixture. Additionally, add another layer of light gray to the shadowed side to accentuate the highlights.

Deepen the parts of the herbs that are tucked under the rolls by applying an additional layer of the Herb Shadow solution. This will intensify the contrast and further complement our main subject.

Based on the light source, add a cast shadow on the left side with a gray mixture in "Coffee" value.

Shrimp
Tea-Milk value

Spring rolls
Tea value

Herb shadow
Milk value

Cast shadow
Coffee value

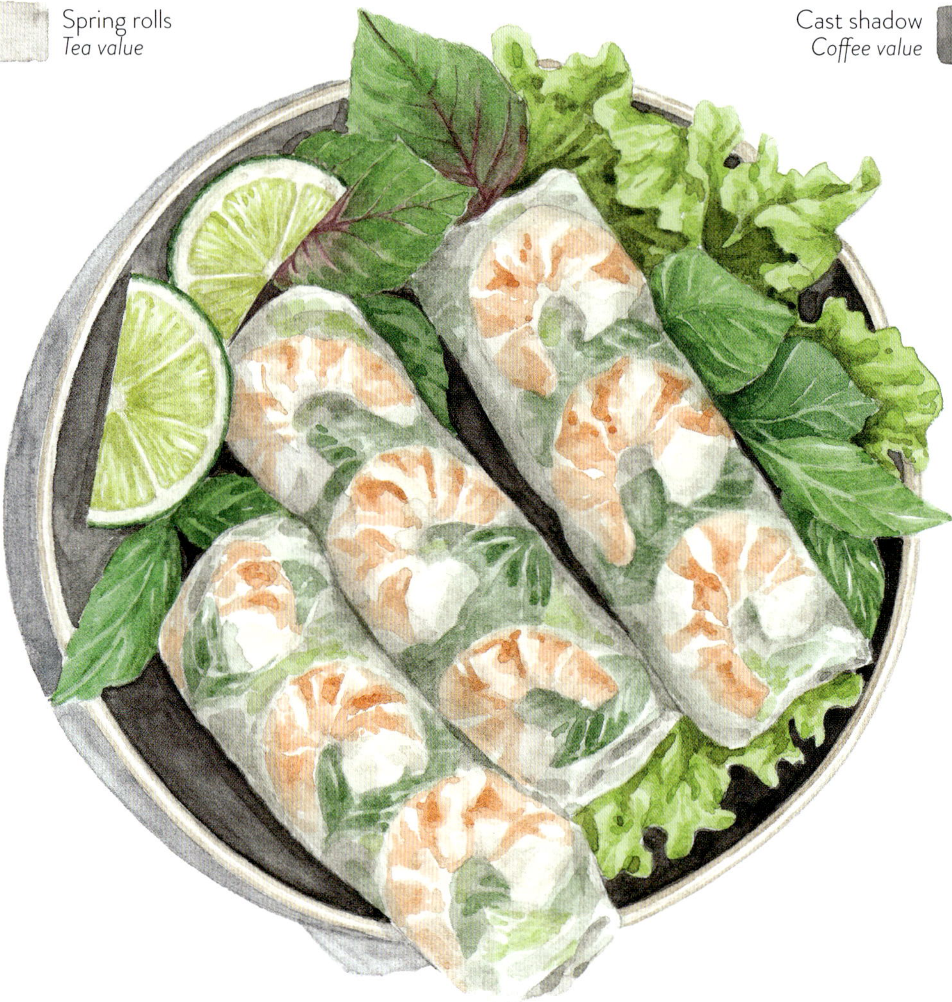

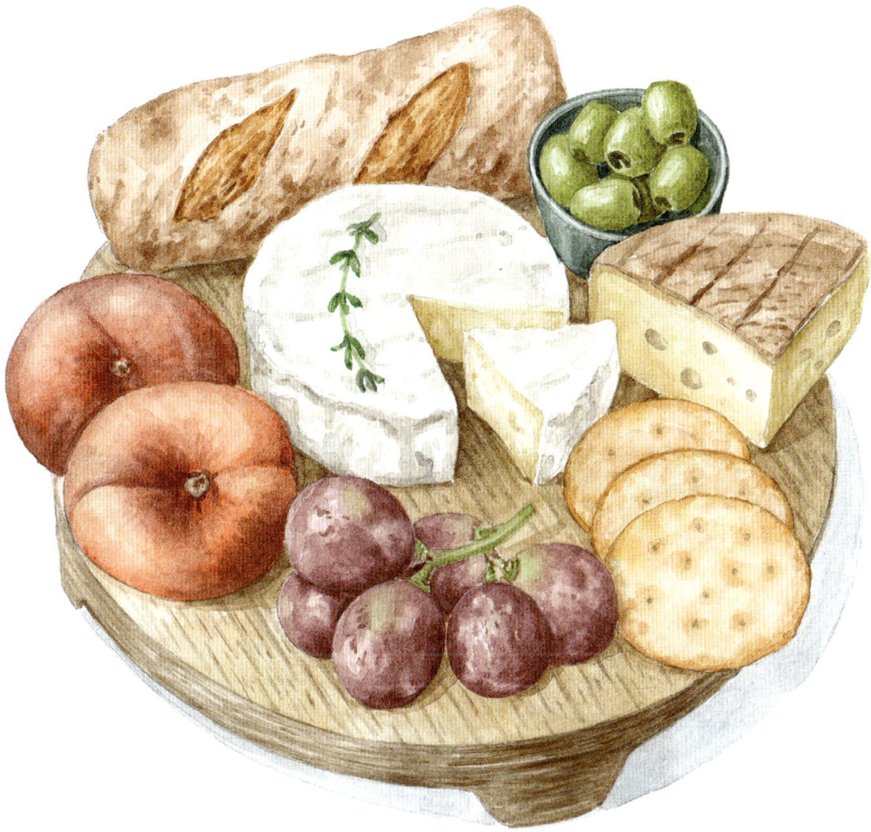

Project 09

Charcuterie Board

(Dimensions: W 6" x H 5¾" / W 15.3 cm x H 14 cm)

This is my way of paying tribute to any aficionado of French cuisine! Handling objects of varying sizes can initially seem daunting, often leading to hesitation when trying to organize them into a cohesive composition, maintain color harmony and ensure each element stands out appropriately. However, mastering these principles through this project will boost your confidence and equip you to apply them effectively in your future endeavors. Furthermore, I'll guide you through depicting grapes, typically clustered and featuring a mildly powdery skin texture.

Brushes

Round brushes: sizes 1, 2 and 4

Filbert brushes: sizes 4 and 8

Color Palette

OBJECT	COLOR NAME	COLOR VALUES		
		Tea/Coffee	Milk	Cream
Olive	Sap Green Quinacridone Gold Raw Umber			
Olive bowl	Phthalo Green Burnt Umber			
Grape stem	Sap Green Quinacridone Gold			
Grape Peach	Quinacridone Rose Raw Umber Permanent Alizarin Crimson			
Peach	Cadmium Red Quinacridone Magenta Permanent Orange			
Wooden board Peach Cheese (inside)	New Gamboge Hansa Yellow Burnt Sienna Raw Umber			
Camembert (outside)	Raw Umber Ivory Black			
Cheese (outside) Baguette	Burnt Umber			
Cracker Baguette	Quinacridone Gold Burnt Sienna			
Wooden board	Hansa Yellow Gothite Raw Umber			

Stick with me here! As your palette expands, you'll have more opportunities to blend colors, adding a touch of warmth or coolness, or incorporating hints of surrounding colors. The possibilities for experimentation will increase dramatically. Remember, the colors I've suggested are just starting points—let your creativity shine and explore beyond them.

Viewpoint & Light Source

Since the objects vary in height, selecting a sitting eye-level viewpoint would be ideal. This perspective allows for a comprehensive view of the entire setup, distinguishing between foreground and background elements. The light source originates from the left side at a low angle, emphasizing the vibrant colors of the peaches and grapes.

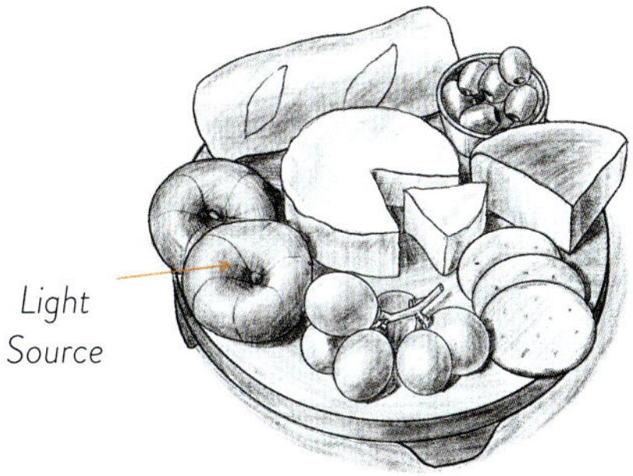

Composition

A charcuterie board usually includes layers of ingredients such as cheese, fruits, crackers and deli meats. In this illustration, I've chosen fundamental items in various colors to achieve a balanced composition. The grapes and peaches are placed at the front and nearer to the light source to draw the viewer's gaze, while larger, neutral-colored items are positioned toward the back.

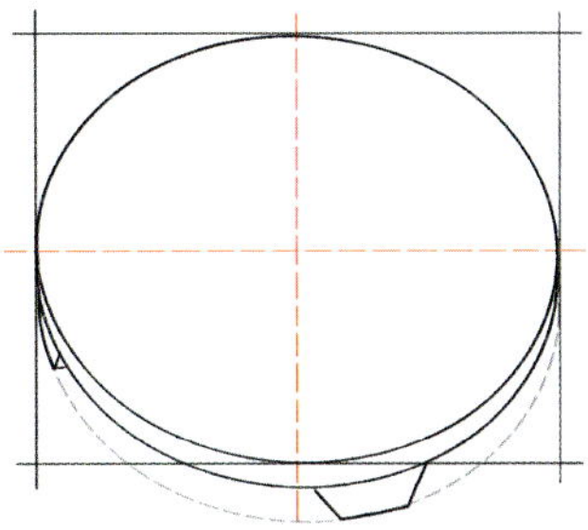

Let's Sketch!

As usual, start by drawing the frame for the ellipse that represents the wooden board. Notice that the little "legs" must adhere to the principles of three-dimensional perspective.

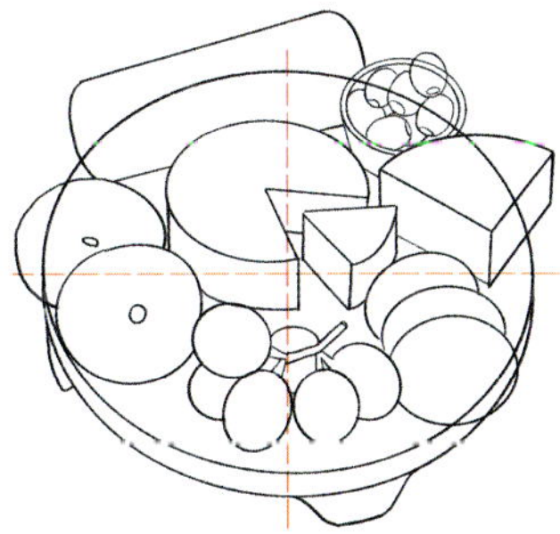

Next, place all the items on the board. Most objects, like the cheese, baguette and crackers, are cylindrical in shape. The peach has a rounded, donut-like form, while the grapes and olives are spherical. Remember to refer to the central lines while sketching the elements to ensure the correct proportions.

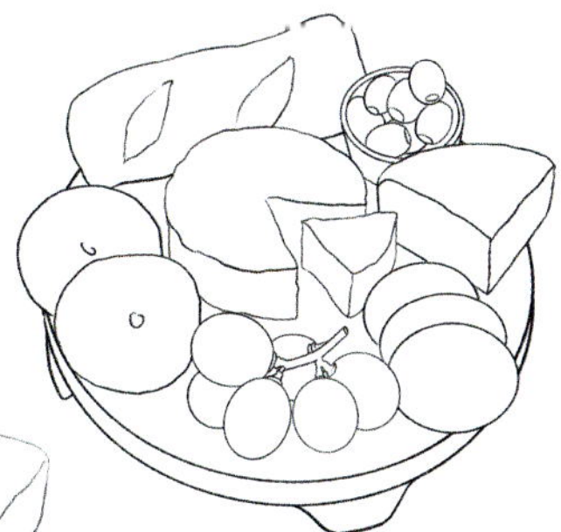

Once you are satisfied with the placement, add necessary details. Finally, lightly erase the pencil lines to prepare the sketch for painting.

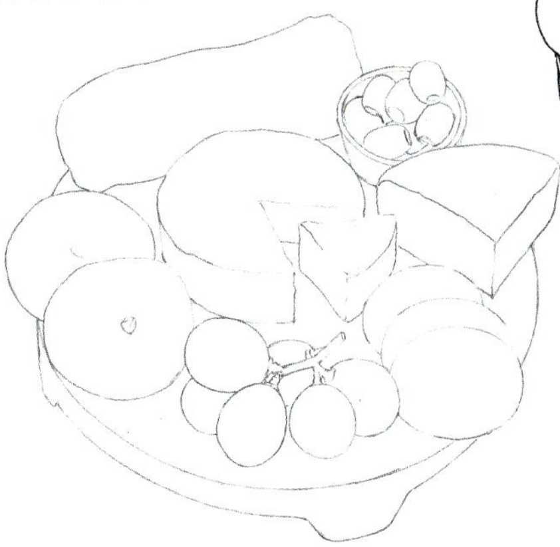

Let's Paint!

First Layer

Olives: Select round brush #1 and wash the "Tea" value on all the olives, leaving the highlight areas on the left side of each one according to the light source. Use the same brush size to apply the "Tea" value of the Bowl mixture on the bowl. While the paper is still wet, add "Milk" value to the inside wall of the bowl to create depth.

Grapes: Work on one grape at a time. Using a filbert brush #4, apply a layer of water to one grape and then immediately apply the "Tea" value of purple, allowing the color to bleed naturally. While the paper is still wet, switch to round brush #1 and gently dab a bit of the green Grape Stem mixture on the grape, allowing it to blend in. These greenish spots can be placed randomly on the grape's body or near the stem base. Repeat this process for all the grapes. Make sure to apply more pigment to the shadow areas and to grapes that are behind others.

Peach Slices: Use round brush #4 to apply a watery layer of a yellow mixture on the slice at the front. While the paper is still wet, switch to round brush #2 and blend the Peach mixture in "Milk" value to the left side of the stem and right side of the fruit, using the gradient wash technique (page 25). Because the peach slice has a donut-like shape, the area around the stem will recede, creating a shadow to its left. Use the "Tea" value of the same color to darken the area around the edge, as it's a midtone area.

Repeat this step for the peach at the back, but apply a touch of purple Grape mixture to the shadow areas to give it a cooler and less vibrant appearance compared to the one in the foreground.

Cheese: For the Camembert cheese, choose a filbert brush #4 and apply a warm gray mixture to its bloomy rind. Use only the flat side of the brush to create a fluffy texture while applying color. Keep the top surface brighter than the sides.

Next, apply the light-yellow mixture in "Tea" value to the interior walls of both cheese wheels. Use a thicker solution on the right side to indicate the shadowed area.

For the Swiss cheese wedge, select round brush #4 to apply the dark-brown mixture on it, dragging the color while it's wet to create a cloud-like effect.

> **Artist's Tip:** Premix colors in "Milk–Cream" value and keep them nearby. If you run out of the "Tea" mixture, you can easily create more by dipping your brush into the thicker mixture, transferring it to an empty area on the palette, and diluting it generously with clean water.

Crackers: Paint one cracker at a time. Start with a watery light-yellow wash as the initial base. While it's still wet, use round brush #1 to apply an orange-brown mixture in "Milk" value to the rim of the cracker, and randomly dab the "Tea" value to depict the bumpy texture. Repeat this process for the other two crackers.

Baguette: Use a filbert brush #4 to apply a watery layer of light brown onto the baguette, avoiding the scored areas. While it's still wet, add the "Milk" value mainly to the lower areas by lightly dabbing the brush on the paper. Repeat the process for the scored areas, using the same orange-brown mixture that was used for the crackers.

Wooden Board: Use a filbert brush #8 to apply the "Milk" value to the side of the board, ensuring it's darker on the right side, in accordance with the light source.

Baguette
Tea-Milk value

Olive / Bowl
Tea-Milk value

Camembert
Tea value

Cheese
Tea value

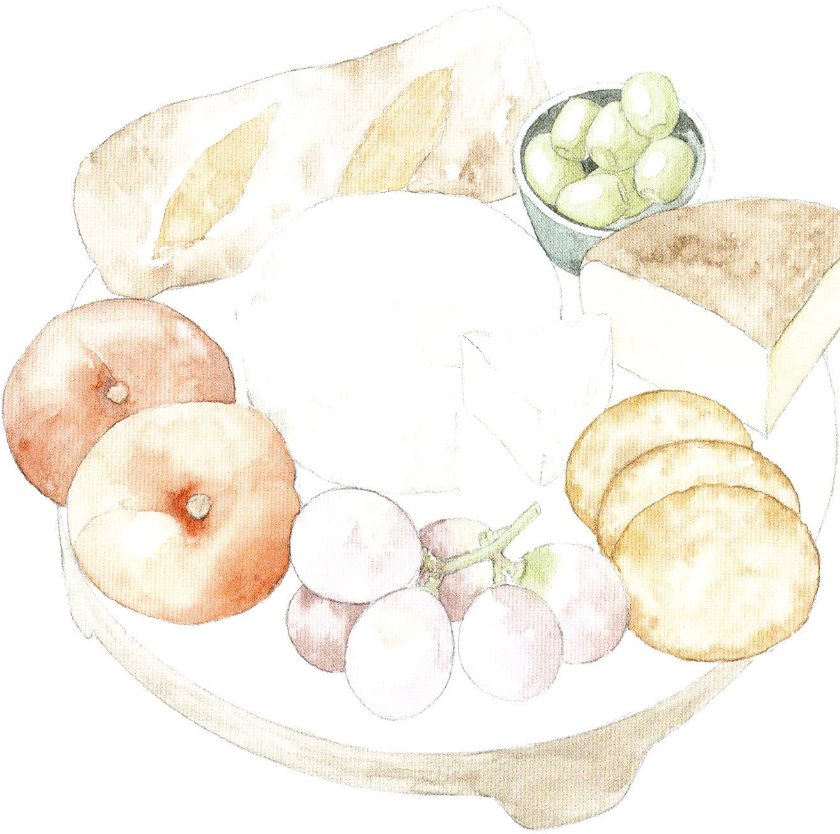

Peach
Tea-Milk value

Cracker
Tea-Milk value

Wooden board
Milk value

Grape
Tea value

Second Layer

For the peaches, crackers, Camembert cheese wheel and baguette, repeat what you did in the previous step but apply the thicker values this time.

Olives: Keep using the round brush #1 and apply the "Milk" value to the right side of each fruit and blend it toward the highlights with a clean, damp brush, following the basic shading rules for spherical shapes. Use the "Cream" value to depict the shadowed side of the holes in the fruit. Additionally, deepen the interior wall of the bowl to enhance its depth.

Grapes: Add the "Tea" value of the purple to each one, this time excluding the highlights (refer to the Light Source Shading Sketch on page 97). While the paint is still wet, use a smaller brush to apply the "Cream" value around the edges of the grapes so that the darker mixture can spread out nicely. Alternatively, you can use a clean, damp brush to blend it out. Continue to use the "Milk" value of the Grape Stem mixture to enrich the stem, keeping the upper part of the long stem a brighter color to depict its highlight.

Swiss Cheese Wedge: Repeat the process done in the first layer with a thicker value, then use round brush #1 to add the parallel lines on the top with a "Milk" value mixture.

Wooden Board: Use a filbert brush #4 to apply the yellow-brown mixture with a "Milk" value to the top. Ensure the area in front of the peaches is the brightest. Add another layer of dark brown to the side by using the flat side of the filbert brush to hatch along the curve, creating a wooden texture.

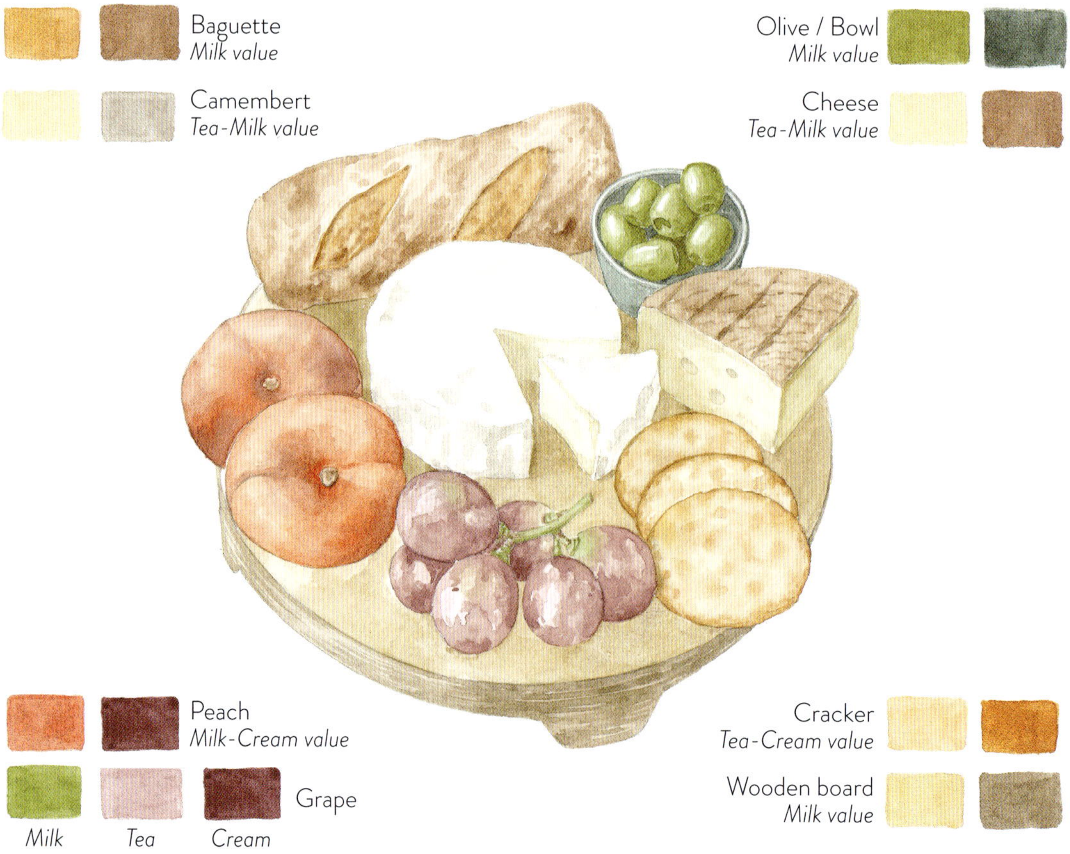

Third Layer

Employ more "Milk–Cream" value for the third layer to deepen the shadow areas of each object. While applying new layers, be careful not to overdo the highlights to maintain their brightness.

Repeat the process in the second layer for the olives and grapes.

Peach Slices: Blend a new mixture of Grape and the orange-red color and use it for the shadow areas.

Cheese: For the Camembert, continue adding an additional layer for shadow areas around the rim and along its height. Additionally, apply parallel uneven lines on the top. Note that the peach slices also cast shadows onto the left side of the rind. Incorporate a hint of Raw Umber into the yellow mixture and use it for the shadow of the cut sides.

For the Swiss cheese wedge, depict some typical oval-shaped holes with a darker value.

Crackers: Apply a darker shade only to the rim of the crackers, keeping the rest in the lighter hue. Additionally, use a bit of "Milk" value to add the holes for each of them.

Baguette: In this stage, only work with a dry surface. Use the side of a filbert brush #4 to create the texture of the bread primarily through scumbling strokes. Begin by applying a "Cream" value to the shadow and midtone areas, blending it toward the upper middle of the bread. While blending, instead of using clean water, dip your brush into the "Tea" value of the same mixture to maintain a thick and rich color.

Wooden Board: After applying an additional layer to both the top and the side, depict the items' cast shadows using the darker brown mixture.

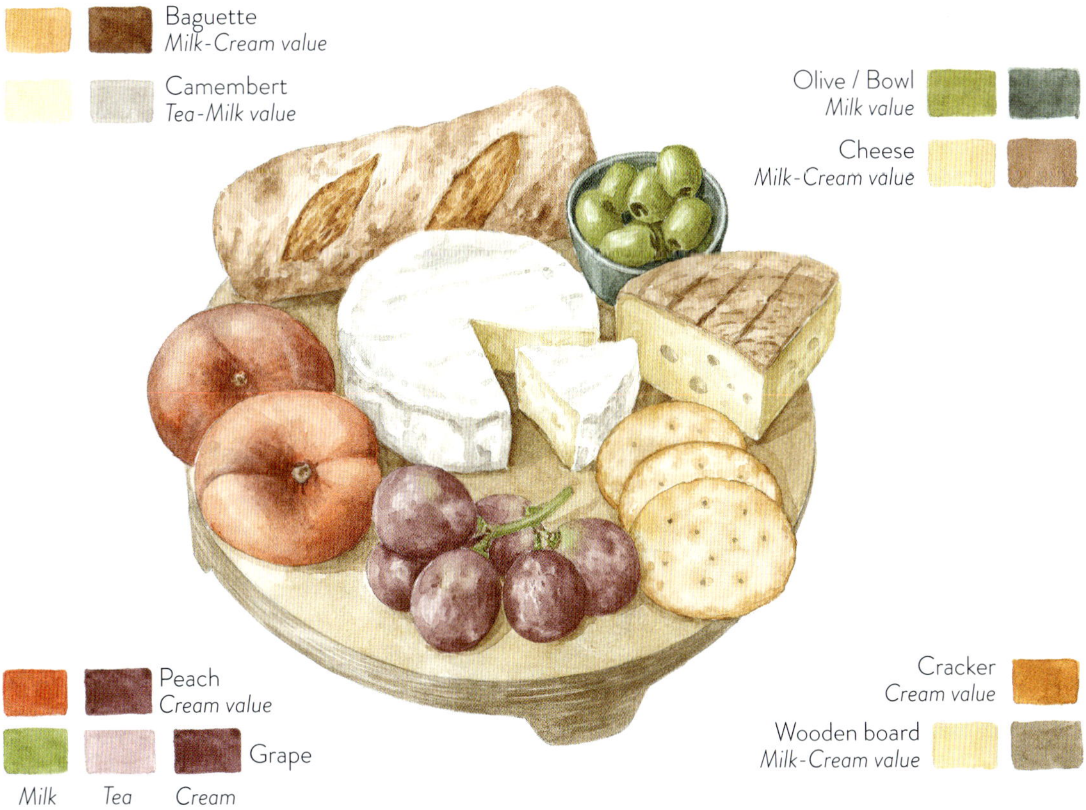

Finishing Touches

Squint your eyes or step away from your painting to assess the overall contrast. If you observe any areas that appear flattened, consider intensifying the shadow with a darker value.

Here, I apply more of the "Cream" value to the darker sides of the grapes and add small details to the stems. The same approach is taken for the peaches.

The entire Camembert cheese is washed with a delicate light gray to prevent it from appearing too bright. A small sprig of thyme is garnished on top. The new green mixture for the leaves consists of Sap Green and Hooker's Green, in "Milk" value. You can reuse the Olive or Grape Stem mixture for the sprig.

Turn to the thin side of filbert brush #4 to hatch thin lines for the wooden texture on the top surface of the board. Keep alternating between long lines, short lines and dots to enhance its natural appearance. Ensure that the lines are more distinct at the front and gradually fade out toward the farther areas.

Lastly, create a cast shadow beneath the board using a cool gray mixture to offset its warm prominence. Given the intricate items on it, use a lighter shade (like "Tea" or "Coffee" value) for the shadow to maintain balance in the composition.

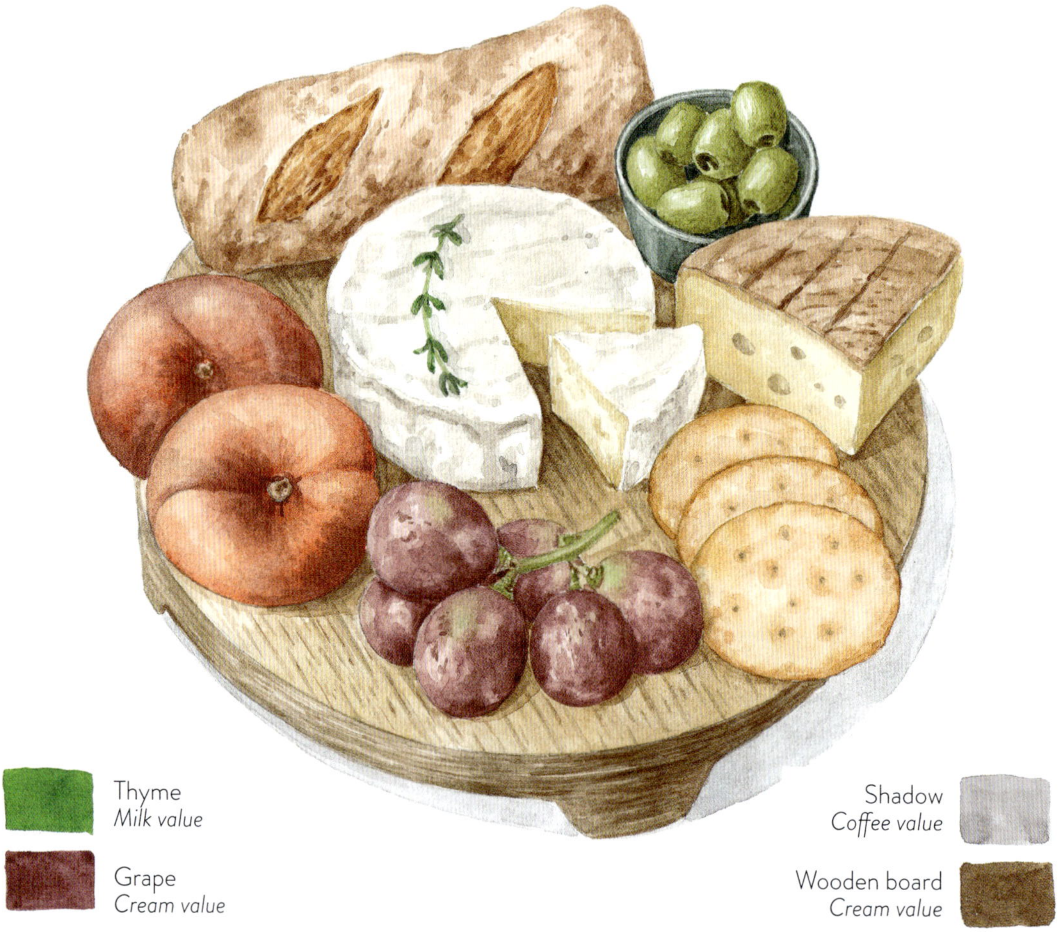

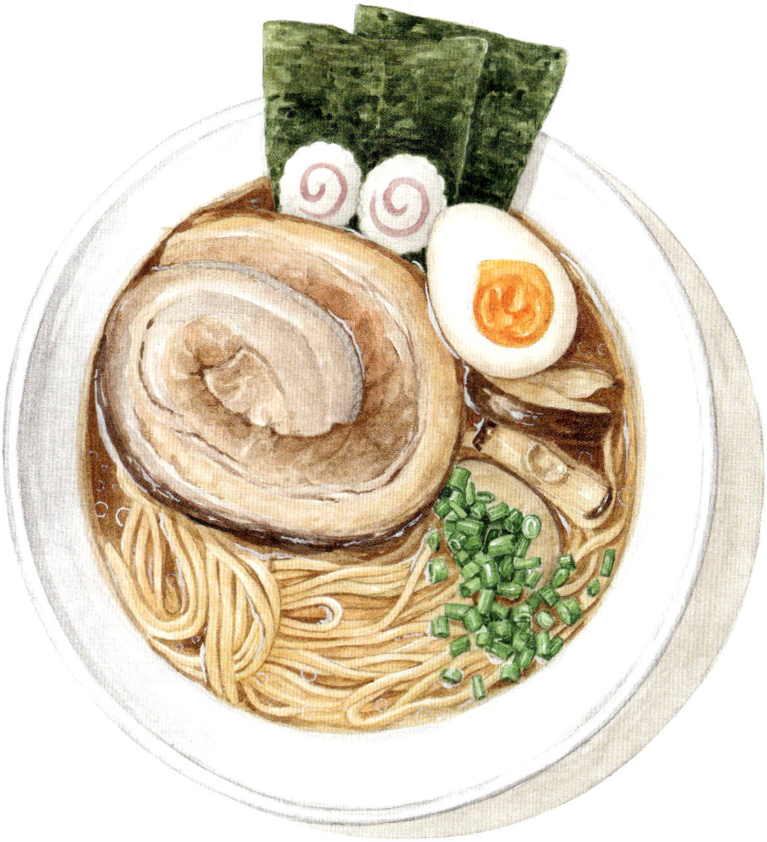

Project 10

Ramen Bowl

(Dimensions: W 5⅞" x H 6½" / W 15 cm x H 16.5 cm)

There's simply no excuse to resist the allure of a steaming bowl of chashu pork ramen, especially for lovers of Asian cuisine. The meticulous attention to detail in crafting this dish elevates it to a level of true excellence, much like the artistry involved in depicting it with watercolors. Through this project, you'll learn how to capture the delicate tenderness of the rolled chashu pork, the coarse texture of nori and the glistening strands of noodles submerged in a pristine broth.

Brushes

Round brushes: sizes 1, 2 and 4
Filbert brushes: sizes 4 and 8
Spotter brush: size 3/0

Color Palette

OBJECT		COLOR NAME	COLOR VALUES		
			Tea/Coffee	Milk	Cream
Seaweed nori	*Mixture 1*	Sap Green Raw Umber			
	Mixture 2	Raw Umber Phthalo Green			
Green onion		Sap Green Hooker's Green Burnt Umber (Cream value)			
Noodle		New Gamboge Burnt Umber Pyrrol Orange			
Mushroom / Broth*	*Mixture 1*	Quinacridone Gold Pyrrol Orange Burnt Umber			
	Mixture 2				
Chashu pork	*Mixture 1*	Raw Umber Pyrrol Orange			
	Mixture 2	Pyrrol Scarlet Raw Umber Ultramarine Blue (Cream value)			
Egg		New Gamboge Pyrrol Orange			
Bowl		Jane's Grey			

**The Mushroom and Broth mixtures exhibit different shades of brown, despite using the same pigments. That is because the first has more Quinacridone pigment, while the latter has more Burnt Umber pigment.*

Viewpoint & Light Source

To best capture the beauty of this delicate dish with predominantly flat items, a top-down perspective is ideal for showcasing all the toppings without focusing heavily on depicting the bowl itself. Despite the noodles appearing flat, their haphazard arrangement and the play of light create dynamic shifts between highlights and shadows, adding visual interest. Remember that each noodle strand behaves like a cylindrical object, so the side not illuminated by the light will naturally appear darker.

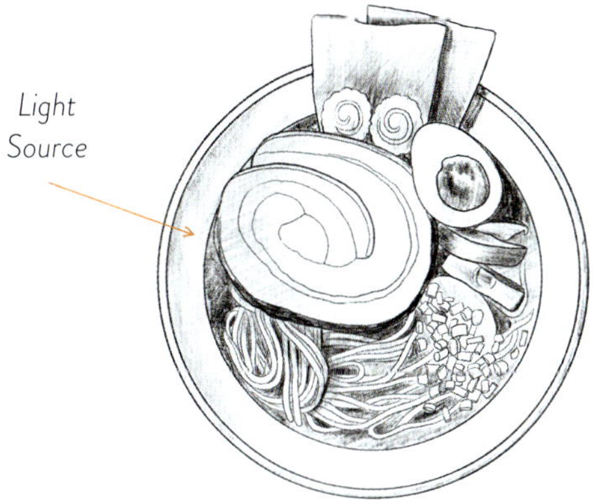

Artist's Tip: As you progress, consider adjusting the height of the light source to enhance the allure of your painting. Here, I position it lower so that the left inner wall of the bowl casts shadows on the toppings, adding depth to the dish while ensuring the highlight accentuates its most appealing features.

Composition

A standard Japanese ramen bowl features nori (seaweed), chashu pork, halved marinated soft-boiled eggs and noodles. In this particular composition, mushrooms, green onions and fish cake (Narutomaki) are included to bring additional color to the bowl. The placement of the nori against the bowl contributes significantly to creating depth alongside the shadows.

Let's Sketch!

Begin with a square frame to outline a full circle symbolizing the bowl. When sketching any noodle bowl, it's crucial to utilize the central lines of the frame as a guide for maintaining proportional elements within it. Here, I draw the chashu pork slab in one corner, extending beyond the central lines in all directions to serve as a focal point. Slices of fish cake, halved egg and mushroom pieces are predominantly placed within the adjacent quarter of the frame. By carefully noting their positions and sizes relative to the central lines, you can ensure balanced ratios.

Add as many details to each item as you prefer, then use an eraser to lighten the entire sketch, especially on areas where light colors will be applied, such as the pork and noodles.

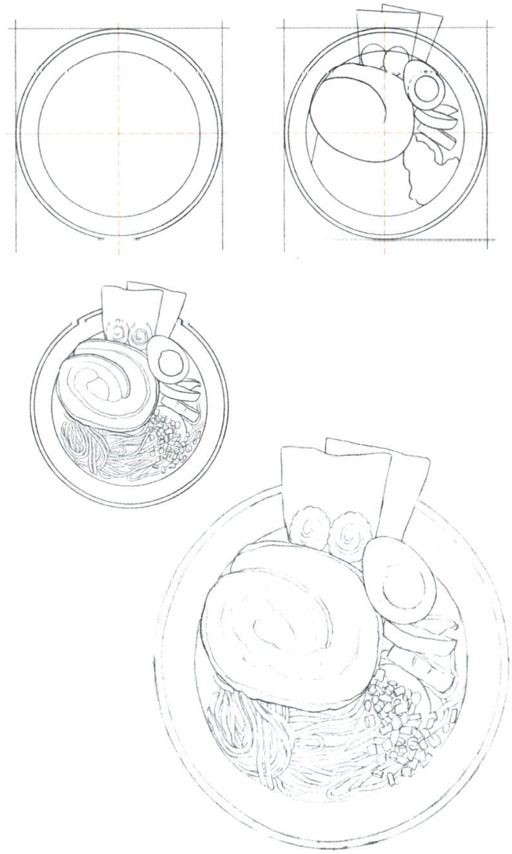

Let's Paint!

First Layer

Noodles: Use round brush #4 to apply the "Tea" value to both the broth and the noodles. The "Tea" value for these two items is quite similar in my color palette, so you can use either one to cover the entire area. Leave the highlight areas with a lighter wash.

Chashu Pork: Pick up a filbert brush #8 to apply a diluted wash of "Tea" value, trying to pull more color to the shadow areas. Use the thin side of the brush to add the "Milk" value to the side of the pork, creating depth. Ensure that the pencil lines remain visible after this initial wash, as they will act as guidelines for the next layer of paint.

Nori: Apply the "Coffee" value mixture to the front piece of pork with round brush #2, using scumbling strokes. Ensure your strokes have larger gaps at this stage to prevent the color from bleeding too closely together.

Repeat this process for the pork piece behind the first. While the "Coffee" layer is still damp, lightly dab some "Milk" value around the edges of the front piece to illustrate the gap between them, enhancing the sense of depth.

Mushroom: Note that there are three parts of the shiitake mushroom that we need to depict (hang with me!), each with a different color at this stage: the underside (gills), the cap and the sides (where they are sliced). Use round brush #1 to apply the yellowish "Tea" value mixture to the gills, and use the reddish mixture for the sides, stems and caps. Afterward, add a layer of dark brown in "Cream" value to the caps. Be sure to leave some white space for the highlights, which will depict shiny spots later. For the mushroom with the most visible cap, depict texture by drawing thin lines along it using the tip of the brush.

Egg: Use round brush #2 to apply a light "Tea" value layer of Chashu Pork mixture on the egg white. Use the same brush to apply Egg Yolk mixture in "Tea" value to the yolk. While it's still wet, add some "Milk" value mixture to the left side and paint a random shape in the center, preparing it for the texture depiction in the next step. I simply blend a bit of Pyrrol Orange to this solution to create a deeper shade of orange for the yolk.

Green Onion: Pick up round brush #1, apply the "Tea" value to most of the pieces and occasionally dip the brush into the "Milk" value to paint some of them. Depending on your reference, you can also mix a touch of warm yellow into your "Tea" value to paint certain pieces, achieving a natural range of colors for the green onion.

Fish Cakes: Use round brush #2 to add a very diluted layer of gray (I use the Bowl mixture) to the fish cakes. When it dries, add a swirl in the center. Here, I use the "Tea" value of Ultramarine Rose.

Bowl: Use a filbert brush #8 to wash a layer of "Tea" value, starting from the left wall and blending it out gradually. Always leave the right wall brighter since it faces the light source.

Mushroom (Mixture 1)
Tea value

Nori (Mixture 1)
Coffee-Milk value

Mushroom (Mixture 2)
Tea-Cream value

Chashu pork
(Mixture 1)
Tea-Milk value

Broth (Mixture 1)
Tea value

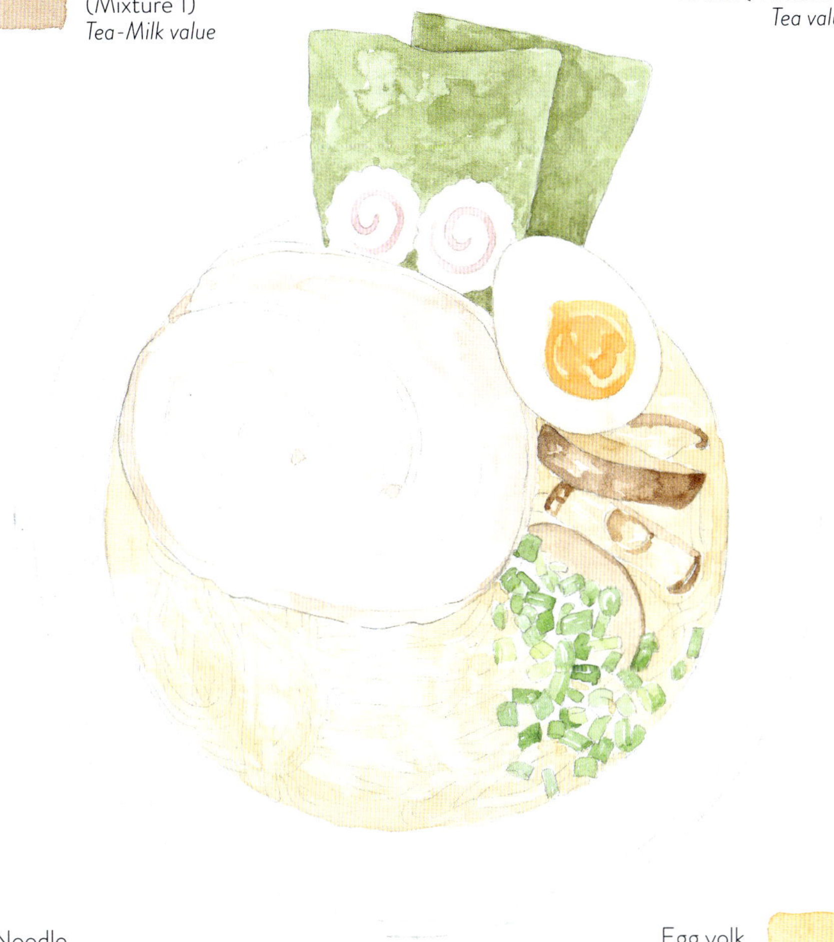

Noodle
Tea value

Egg yolk
Tea-Milk value

Bowl
Tea value

Green onion
Tea-Milk value

Second Layer

Noodle and Broth: Use the round brush #2 to apply the darker Broth mixture in "Milk" value to the corners near the Chashu Pork and Egg. Then, switch to the round brush #1 to apply the bright Noodle mixture in "Milk" value to the negative spaces of the noodles.

Chashu Pork: Choose the filbert brush #4 to apply the colder mixture in "Tea" value to the fat, and the warmer mixture in "Milk" value to the lean meat. Make gentle, short strokes following the roll's curvature to create mild texture on the slab, avoiding the more pronounced texture that comes with scumbling brushstrokes. To highlight the slab's spiral, use the brush tip to add more "Milk" mixture along the seam between the fat and lean meat, enhancing their distinction. Additionally, add a touch of Broth mixture to the edge near the egg and blend it toward the front to depict the midtone area and enhance color harmony.

Nori: Use filbert brush #4 to wet the whole sheet in the front with clean water. While the surface remains wet, alternatively dip the brush into either the "Milk" or "Cream" value, then apply this mixture onto the paper, gently sweeping it from side to side using the thin edge of the brush. This wet-on-wet technique (page 23) allows the green mixtures to spread out softly, generating a textured effect. Ensure the paper is damp enough to blend the solution but not overly watery. Use the darker green mixture for the sheet behind and the area close to the egg.

Mushroom: Repeat the process done in the first layer with thicker mixtures.

Egg: Use the round brush #2 to apply the Broth mixture in "Tea" value to the outer edge of the egg. Then, apply the orange in "Milk" value to the left edge of the yolk. Deepen the darker spots that were created in the first layer.

Green Onion: Prepare a "Milk" value mixture, load it onto round brush #1, and apply it to the onion pieces. Following the basic shading rules for cylindrical shapes, make sure to move the brush along the edges of each piece and leave the highlight areas with a much lighter shade (refer to Chapter 1, Shading, page 15).

Fish Cakes: Add a light wash of Chashu Pork mixture in "Tea" value to dim the white paper down.

Nori (Mixture 1)
Milk value

Nori (Mixture 2)
Cream value

Chashu pork
(Mixtures 1 and 2)
Tea-Milk value

Mushroom (Mixture 1)
Milk value

Mushroom (Mixture 2)
Cream value

Broth (Mixture 2)
Milk value

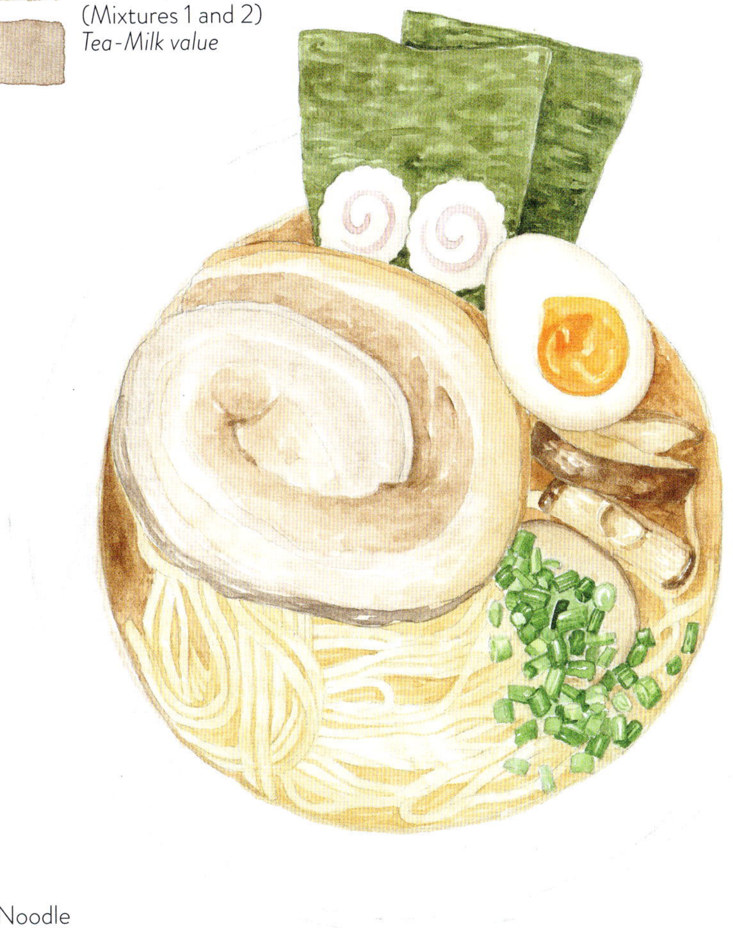

Noodle
Tea-Milk value

Egg Yolk
Milk value

Green onion
Milk value

Third Layer

Noodles and Broth: Add a layer of "Cream" value to the two corners near the pork and egg using round brush #2. Leave the outer edge a bit lighter to create the transparent effect of the broth. When blending the mixture toward the noodles, dip your brush into "Milk" value instead of "Cream" value. Switch to a spotter brush #3/0 and use the same "Milk" value to deepen the negative space between the noodles.

Use the round brush #2 to apply Noodle mixture in "Milk" value to the noodles, particularly focusing on where the strings overlap each other. In this stage, emphasize the contrast between highlights and shadows in broader sections rather than detailing each individual noodle. Once the shadow areas are sufficiently darkened, the string shapes will naturally form.

Chashu Pork: Repeat the process in the previous layer, using "Milk" values this time. The right texture will only be achieved after multiple layers, giving the semi-transparent look for the braised pork slab, especially the fat. Feel free to add a touch of the warm brown Broth mixture to the lean meat to enhance color harmony with other elements.

Switch to round brush #1 to add the dark-brown mixture to the edge of the slab, leaving some white lines, if possible, to depict its glossiness. Alternatively, you can also use white pigment in the final step.

Nori: Use round brush #2 to apply the "Cream" value, employing the same technique as in the previous layer. Keep the gaps between the strokes closer near the bottom of the sheets and gradually widen them toward the top edge. While pulling the brush from side to side, press down firmly at one end for a thicker application and lift gently toward the other end.

Mushroom: Repeat the same process as in the previous layer. This time, integrate some of the cold dark brown of the Chashu Pork mixture to paint the darkest corners of the mushrooms. Keep the sides a warm light brown to distinguish them from the much darker cap.

Egg: Deepen the shadow area with another layer of "Milk" value. Be mindful to leave some parts lighter at this stage, ensuring a clear contrast between the highlight and shadow areas on the paper.

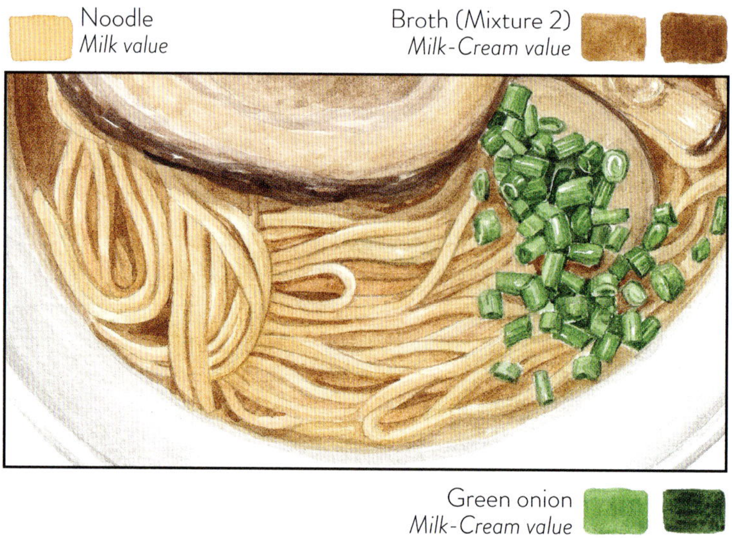

Green Onion: Use round brush #2 to apply another layer of "Milk" value to the pieces. Keep darkening the long edge of each piece, following the shading rule. Add "Cream" value to the space between the pieces to create a darker background. Repeat this negative painting method across the entire area until the top layer pops out when you squint your eyes.

Bowl: Select filbert brush #8 to add another layer of "Tea" value on the right wall. Repeat this step one to two times until there is a clear distinction in shade between the left and right wall. The reason for applying multiple layers of "Tea" value is its thin consistency, making it easy to blend out to the highlight area. However, using a thicker mixture at this stage is also feasible and may achieve the desired shade more quickly, provided the paper is adequately wetted beforehand to prevent uneven marks.

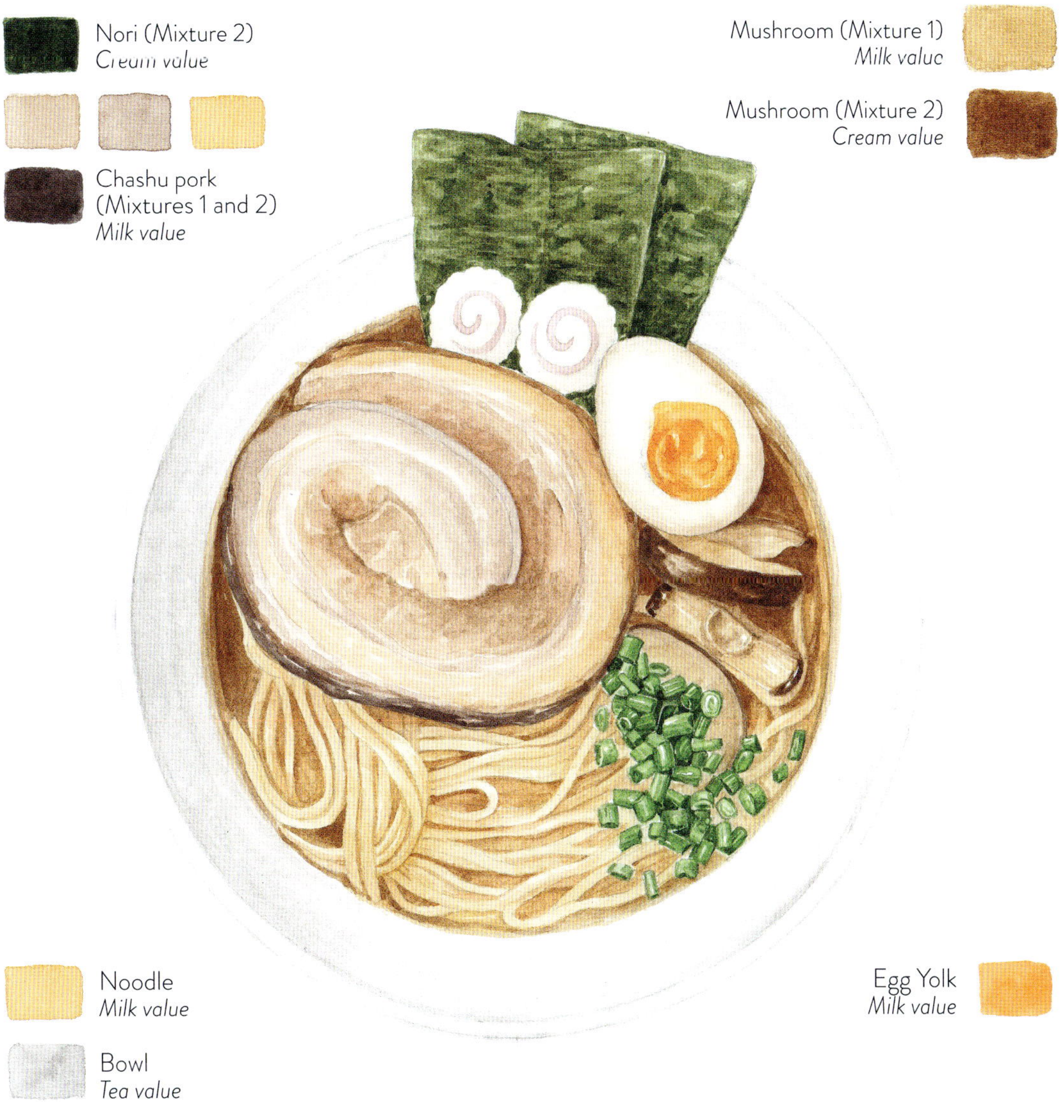

Finishing Touches

Noodles and Broth: Use round brush #1 to apply the "Cream" value to the corners around the pork slab, egg, mushrooms and nori sheets. I also add this mixture to certain shadow areas of the noodles using a spotter brush. Avoid excessive use of this thick solution on the noodles. If your paint looks like dark even lines along the strings, you've added too much. Instead, add the "Milk" value of the Broth mixture bit by bit to negative spaces for a more natural look.

Chashu Pork: Use a thin brush to apply Broth mixture in "Cream" value to the skin near the egg and dark, cooler brown to the opposite end of the slab. If your mushrooms are not dark enough, you can use a bit of this mixture to darken the caps.

Pick up a spotter brush to depict more delicate details, drawing some thin lines in darker brown "Milk" value along the curvature of the lean meat and some more at the center of the spiral.

Nori: Add some dark-green mixture to the bottom and around the edge of the nori using the same brushstrokes and mixture as in the third layer.

Squint your eyes to check if the egg white is too bright. If so, dim it with a layer of Chashu Pork mixture in "Tea" value.

Fish Cakes: Add another layer for the pink swirl in "Tea" value.

Bowl: Use round brush #1 to add a thin line around the bowl's lip with "Milk" value. To enhance the highlight on the bowl's lip, add some strokes of the same mixture to the left wall.

Add a cast shadow for the bowl with the "Coffee" value of Raw Umber.

Use the spotter brush #3/0 to apply some white pigment in "Butter" value to the left borders of certain objects to depict liquid reflections.

Nori (Mixture 2)
Cream value

Chashu Pork
(Mixtures 1 and 2)
Milk-Cream value

Broth (Mixture 2)
Cream value

Mushroom
Cream value

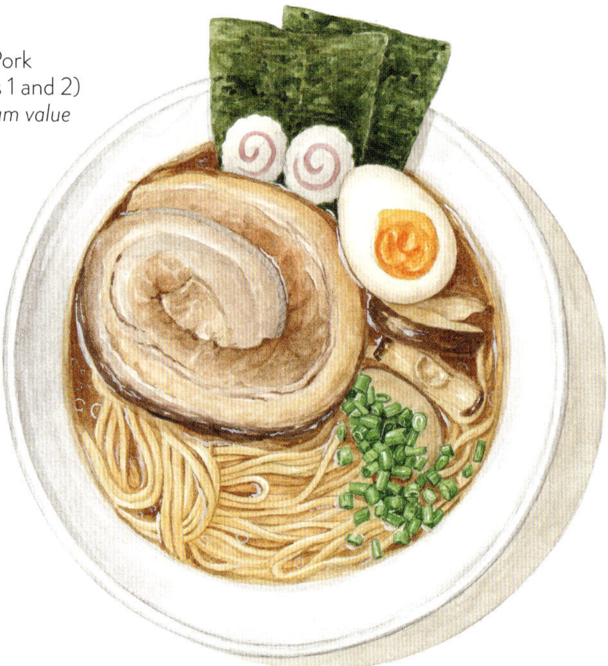

Bowl
Milk value

Egg Yolk
Cream value

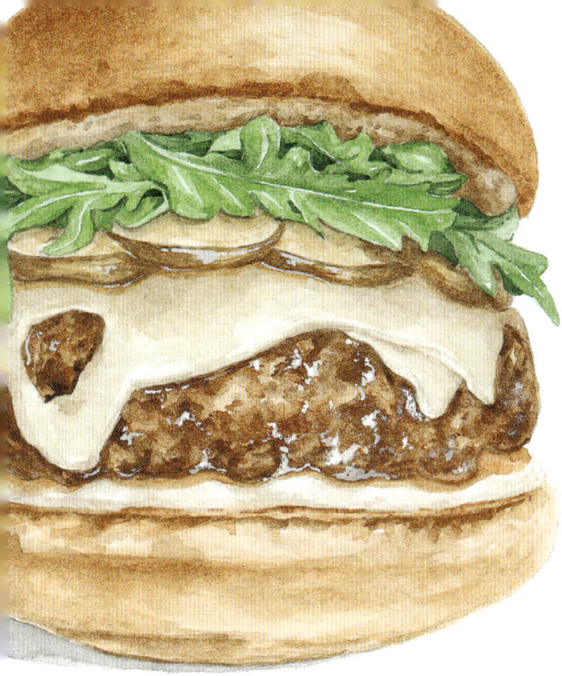

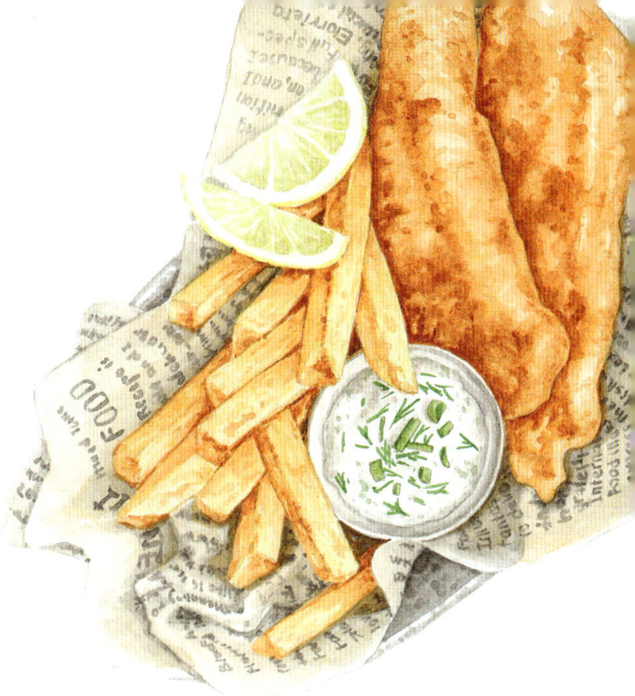

Lunch & Dinner Entrees

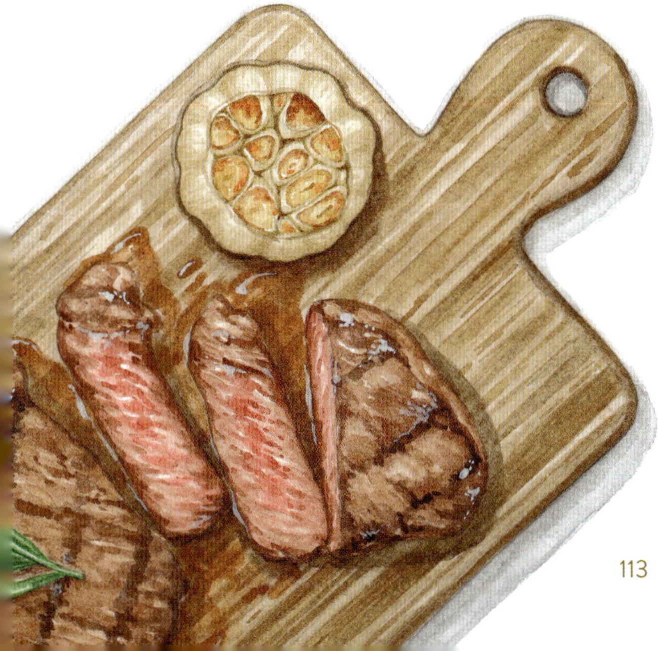

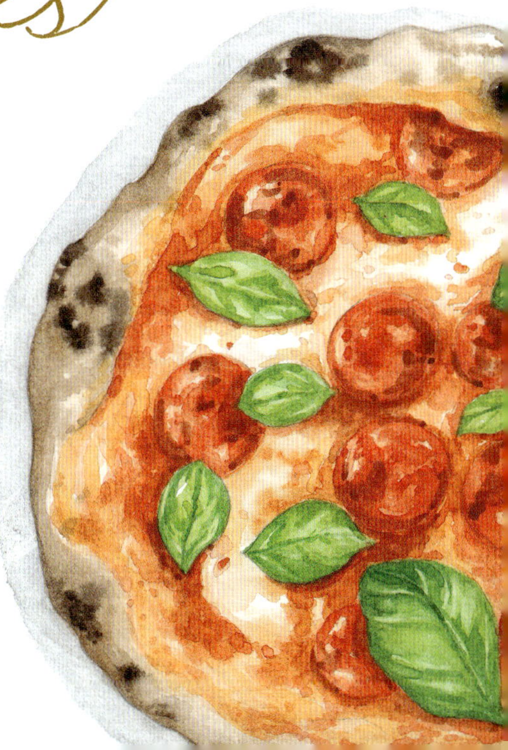

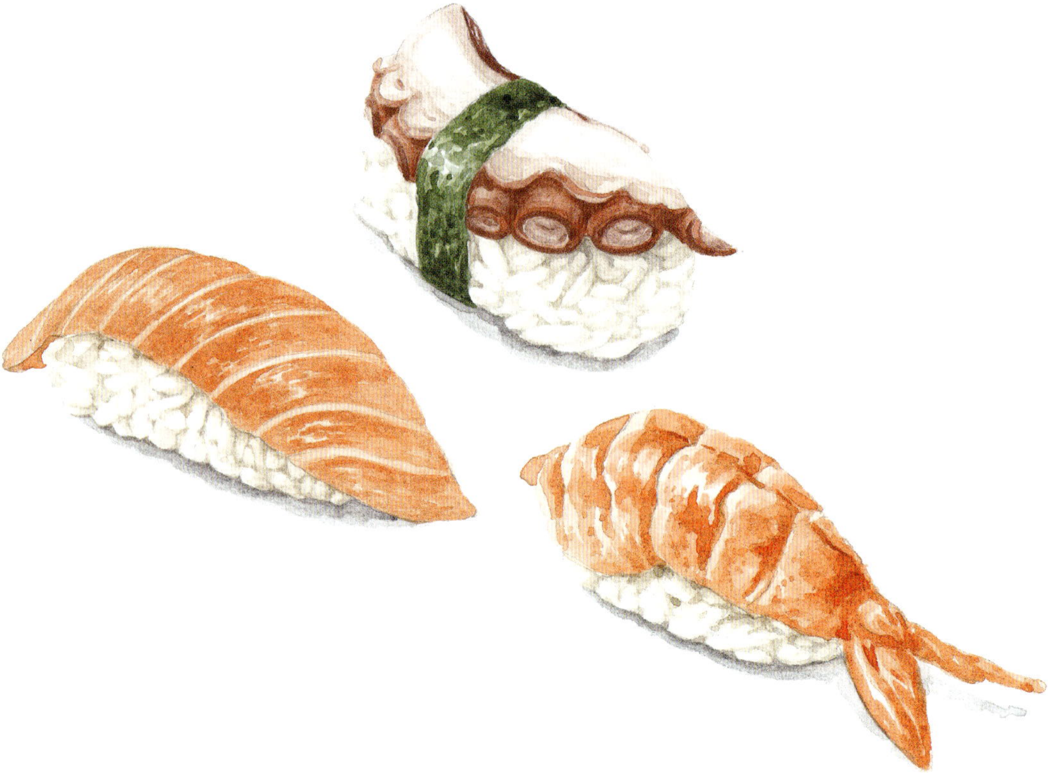

Project 11

Nigiri Sushi

(Dimensions: Salmon: W 3¼" x H 1¾" / W 8 cm x H 4.5 cm
Octopus: W 2½" x H 2¼" / W 6.5 cm x H 5.8 cm
Shrimp: W 3¼" x H 2" / W 8 cm x H 5 cm)

Let's continue our exploration of Japanese delicacies by diving into the art of illustrating three nigiri sushi pieces, each adorned with unique toppings. This exercise shifts away from the complexity of our recent projects, but it promises to be both enjoyable and educational, introducing new techniques to enhance your watercolor skills. You'll learn how to depict rice without painstakingly painting each grain, as well as the steps required to convincingly portray the meltingly soft texture of a salmon slice and other raw seafood toppings.

Brushes

Round brushes: sizes 1, 2 and 4
Spotter brush: size 3/0

Color Palette

OBJECT	COLOR NAME	COLOR VALUES		
		Tea/Coffee	Milk	Cream
Seaweed Nori	Sap Green Raw Umber			
	Phthalo Green Raw Umber			
Salmon	Permanent Orange Pyrrol Orange Pyrrol Scarlet			
Shrimp	Pyrrol Orange Pyrrol Scarlet Burnt Sienna			
Octopus *(Mixture 1)*	Permanent Alizarin Crimson Pyrrol Scarlet Burnt Sienna			
Octopus *(Mixture 2)*	Mixture 1 Permanent Violet			
Rice	Raw Umber			

Viewpoint & Light Source

The chosen viewpoint is at sitting eye-level, emphasizing the side view of the rice balls, a crucial and attractive component of nigiri sushi. The light source originates from the upper left corner, casting highlights along the center-left edges and creating thin shadows directly beneath the rice.

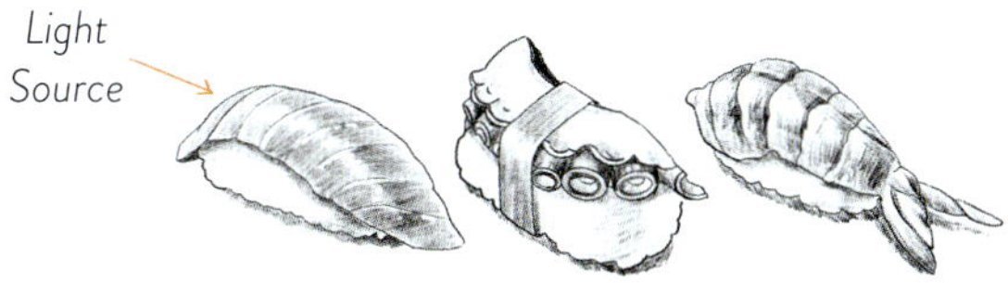

Composition

In this project, we'll depict three types of nigiri sushi lined up in a row: salmon, octopus and tiger prawn. The salmon, with its soft texture, covers the rice like a blanket. The octopus, firmer in structure, features the intricate details of its suckers. Lastly, the tiger prawn will be neatly laid out, covering a substantial portion of the rice ball. While they may share a similar form, the unique nature of each topping and the handmade pressing of each rice ball will impart distinct characteristics that we'll observe and sketch.

Let's Sketch!

The rice base may vary in shape but can generally be framed as a cuboid. Let's begin by outlining a basic framework to ensure each piece's stability on an imaginary surface. Next, proceed to refine each sushi piece according to your reference, focusing on chamfering the corners and smoothing them out. For the tiger prawn specifically, draw a central guideline along the piece to ensure its midline follows 3-D principles accurately.

To sketch and shade the rice grains, begin with the outline (see 1 in the image). Then, sketch the grains on the front layer that are not covered by any other grains (see 2 in the image); this layer will be the brightest. Next, sketch the grains that lie behind the first layer, ensuring some ends are covered by the grains in front (see 3 in the image); this layer will have a darker shade (see 4 in the image). The small spaces between these grains will be the darkest (see 5 in the image). Finally, lightly shade the shaded side of the grains in the front layer to create a 3-D effect (see 6 in the image).

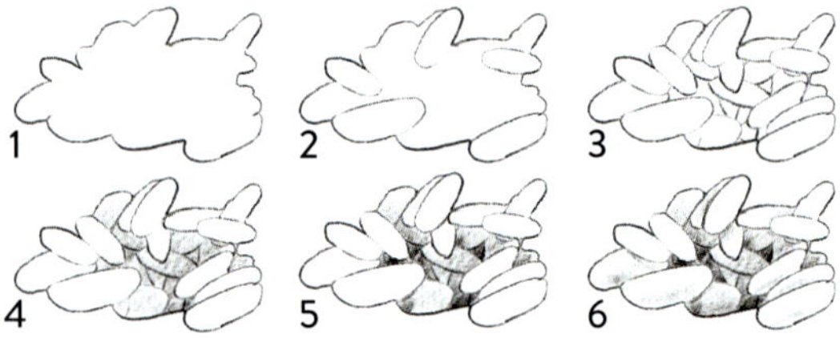

Artist's Tip: When painting rice, it's not necessary to sketch each grain in advance. This theory is meant to help you grasp the underlying principles so you can paint with more confidence. For such intricate details, a spotter brush will be optimal for controlling strokes and achieving effective color application.

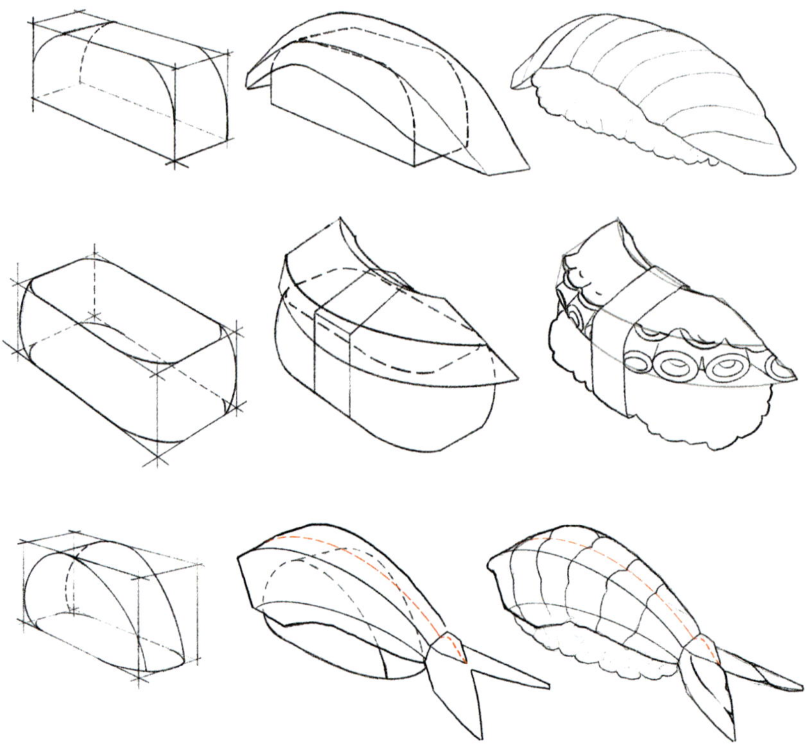

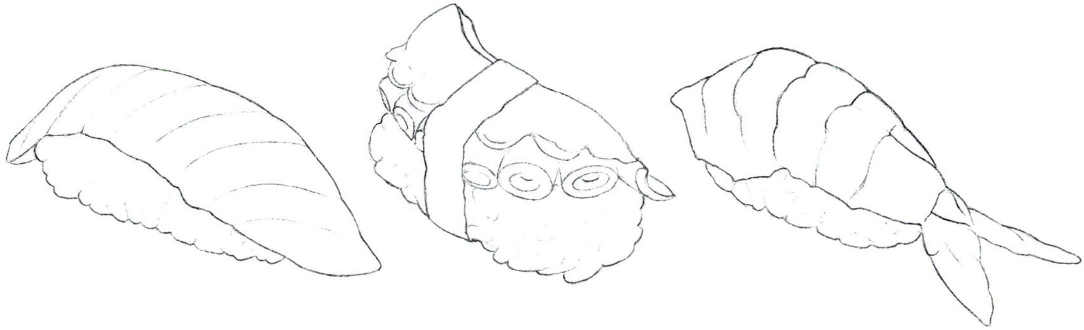

Let's Paint!

First Layer

Salmon: Use round brush #4 to apply the "Tea" value mixture, making sure to leave less pigment on the highlight areas. Pull a bit more mixture at the tail end where it curves downward to indicate a darker shade.

Octopus: With round brush #4, apply a light wash of "Tea" value of Mixture 2 to the entire section. Then, switch to round brush #1 to apply the bright-green mixture to the nori, using the scumbling brushstroke to create a textured base. Leave some white space on the upper left edge while scumbling to depict the shiny effect.

Tiger Prawn: Use round brush #4 to apply the "Tea" value mixture, following the Light Source Shading Sketch (page 115), and leave the highlight areas a bit lighter than the others.

Rice: Use round brush #1 to apply the "Tea" value of Raw Umber to the rice balls. Leave the sides facing the light source brighter, and make the shadow areas slightly darker, especially focusing on the underside of the topping to create a sense of layering.

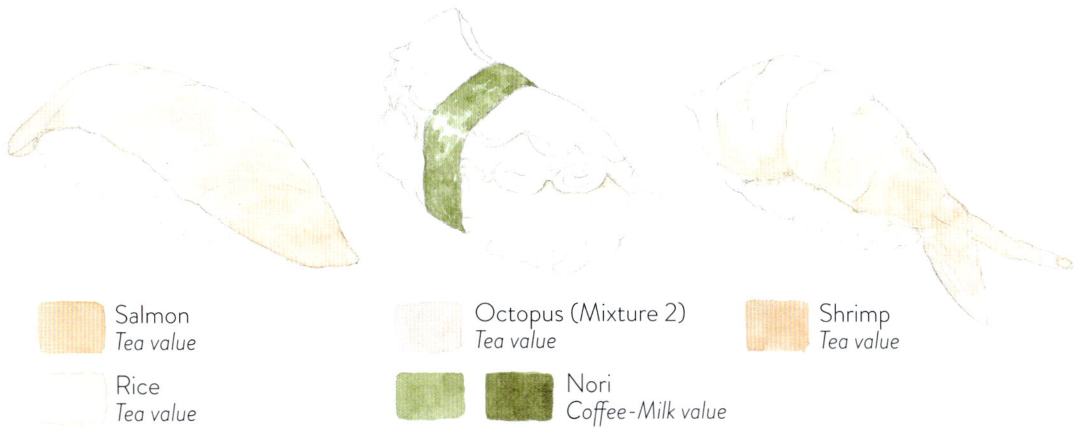

Second Layer

Salmon: Use round brush #1 and prepare the "Coffee" value mixture. When applying the solution, move your brush gently along the cross lines. Lift the brush up as it approaches highlight areas. Compared to the farther end of the slice, the highlight toward the "tail" has higher contrast because it's closer to your viewpoint. Therefore, apply a thicker mixture to paint the flesh in this area. Remember to leave some very light stripes to indicate the salmon's distinctive albumin.

Octopus: Use round brush #1 to apply the "Coffee" value of Mixture 1 to the suckers. Notice that each sucker is derived from a cylindrical shape adhering to a vertical surface, so shading should follow this rule accordingly. Apply the mixture in the shadow areas and blend it out toward the top where the light hits.

Nori: Repeat the process in the first layer, using "Cream" value this time, to deepen the texture. The gaps between your scumbling strokes are closer in the shadow areas and gradually widen as they approach the highlights, which enhances the texture, especially when closer to your viewpoint.

Tiger Prawn: Begin by applying the solution along the right vertical curved line that marks each abdominal segment, using round brush #1. Press the brush and drag the color up and down toward the left to create a smooth blend within each section. Ensure the curved line has the thickest and sharpest shade of color, which gradually thins and blurs toward the left. Repeat this process for all segments.

Rice: Pick up a spotter brush to add "Tea" value mixture to the gaps between the grains, using the negative painting technique (page 63). Focus specifically on the shadowed areas.

Third Layer

Salmon: Pick up round brush #1 to repeat the process done in the second layer, using thicker values this time. The "Milk" value is mainly applied to the farther end, while the "Cream" value is for the middle and the closer end, increasing the sense of depth for the painting. If you are confused about where to put the highlights, refer to the curve determined in the sketching phase. Once the layer is completely dry, use the "Tea" value mixture to dim the white stripes to enhance the natural appearance.

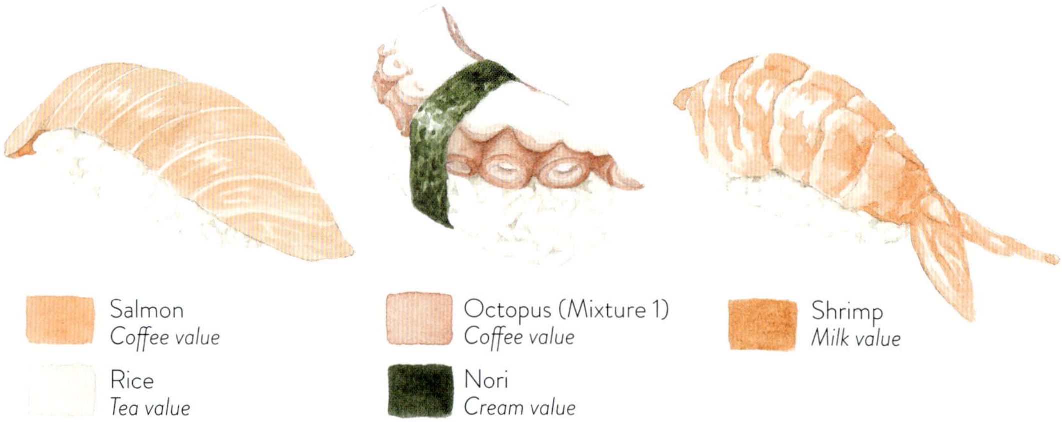

Octopus: Use round brush #2 to add "Tea" value of Mixture 2 to the white flesh. Then, switch to round brush #1 to add the "Cream" value of both mixtures to the suckers. Start from the deep corners and blend outward using a clean, damp brush. Leave the hollow parts in a brighter shade, avoiding them becoming too dark, by applying the "Tea" value of Mixture 2.

Tiger Prawn: Repeat the steps in the second layer with round brush #1 and "Cream" value this time. Because this hue is vibrant, use it sparingly; apply it mainly along the main curved lines and the tail, which are closer to the viewpoint. Add random tiny dots on its body and intermittent strokes along the midline.

Rice: Add another "Milk" value layer to the areas beneath the toppings to depict their shadows cast on the rice balls. Deepen some gaps between the grains but refrain from painting around all the grains.

Finishing Touches

Add a subtle shadow beneath the rice balls, defining their uneven edges to enhance their presence without excessive painting.

Squint your eyes to assess the contrast between highlight and shadow areas on each object. Here, I add another layer of "Cream" value to the octopus's suckers and "Tea" value for its white flesh.

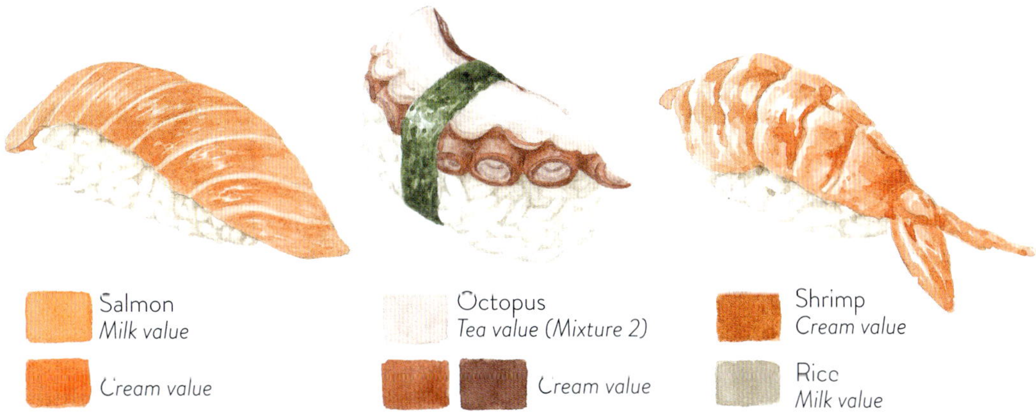

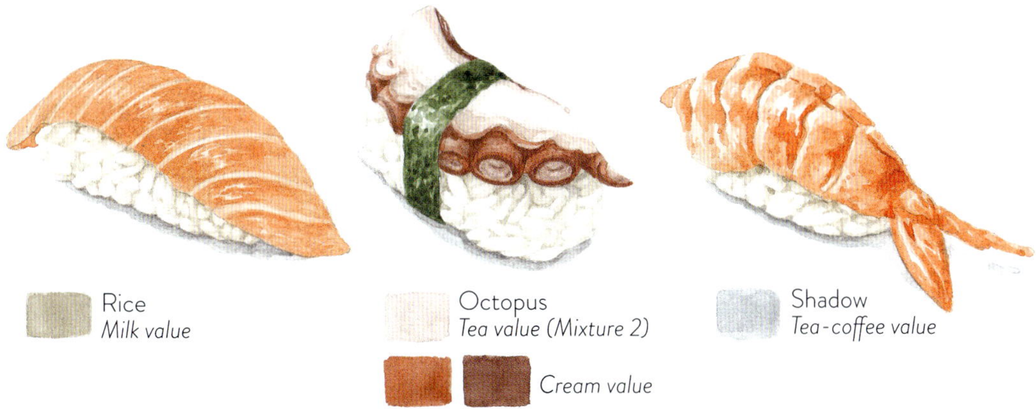

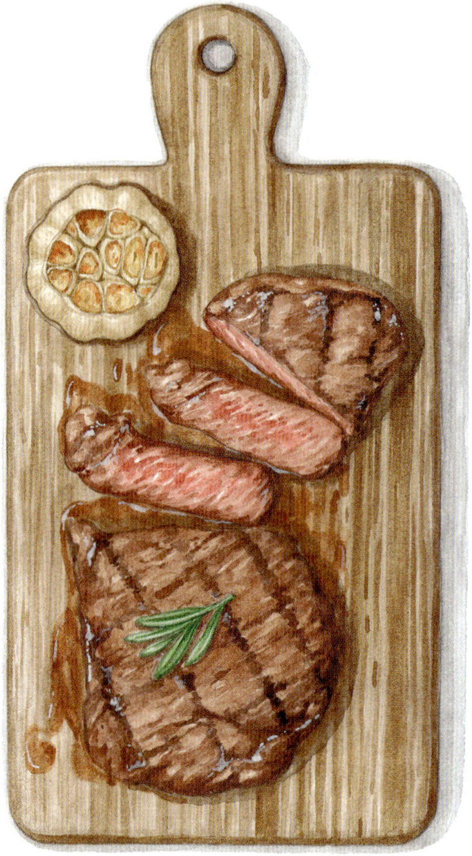

Project 12

Beef Steak

(Dimensions: W 4" x H 7½" / W 10 cm x H 19 cm)

You are in for a treat, red meat lovers! Presented on an attractive wooden board, this dish features a straightforward layout from above. The centerpiece is a drool-worthy steak adorned with a sprig of rosemary, accompanied by a grilled garlic bulb. We'll learn how to depict the steak's outer firmness and the juicy, fibrous texture inside and also apply and build upon skills from Project 06: Tomato Caprese (page 74) and Project 09: Charcuterie Board (page 95) to showcase the complete wood grain on a display board.

Brushes

Round brushes: sizes 1, 2 and 8
Filbert brushes: sizes 4 and 8
Spotter brush: size 3/0

Color Palette

OBJECT	COLOR NAME	COLOR VALUES		
		Tea/Coffee	Milk	Cream
	Permanent Alizarin Crimson Pyrrol Scarlet			
Steak	Burnt Umber Burnt Sienna Permanent Alizarin Crimson			
	Burnt Umber Ivory Black Permanent Alizarin Crimson			
Garlic *(Skin)*	Quinacridone Gold Raw Umber			
Garlic *(Flesh)*	Quinacridone Gold Burnt Sienna Pyrrol Orange			
Rosemary	Sap Green Phthalo Blue GS			
Wooden board	Raw Umber Burnt Umber			
Shadow	Jane's Grey			

Viewpoint & Light Source

This time, we can experiment with a bird's-eye viewpoint and a layout in which all the objects neatly fit inside the entire display. This approach is effective because the wooden board itself is visually appealing. The light source originates from the left at a considerable height, causing cast shadows to fall to the right side, though not extending too far out to distract from the main subject.

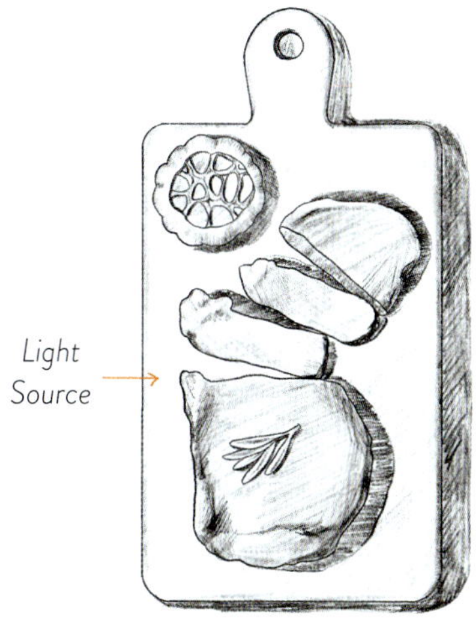

Composition

I intentionally "dissect" the steak into some thin slices to reveal its inner texture, while larger chunks display grill marks on their exteriors. Placing a grilled garlic bulb at the upper left corner of the board ensures visual balance throughout the layout. The board's distinct straight grains provide noticeable contrast, so I maintain a simple composition to highlight its natural beauty.

Let's Sketch!

The steps to sketch this project are straightforward and mainly conveyed through the images themselves.

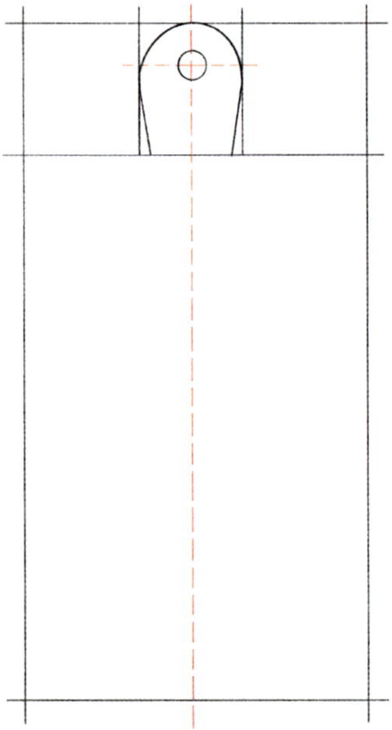

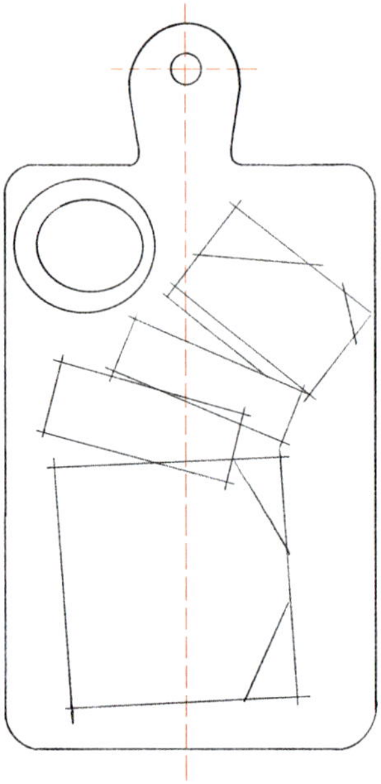

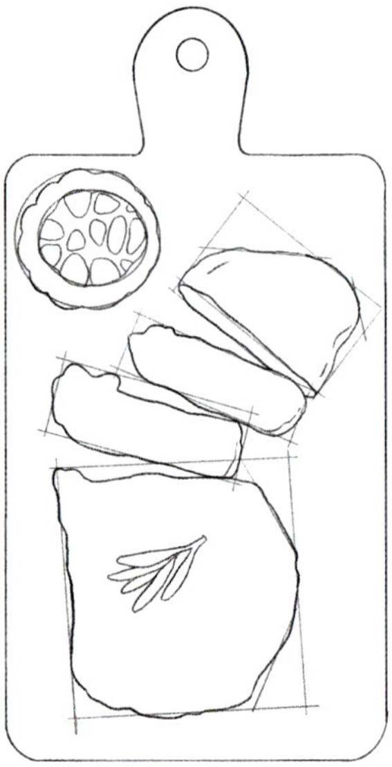

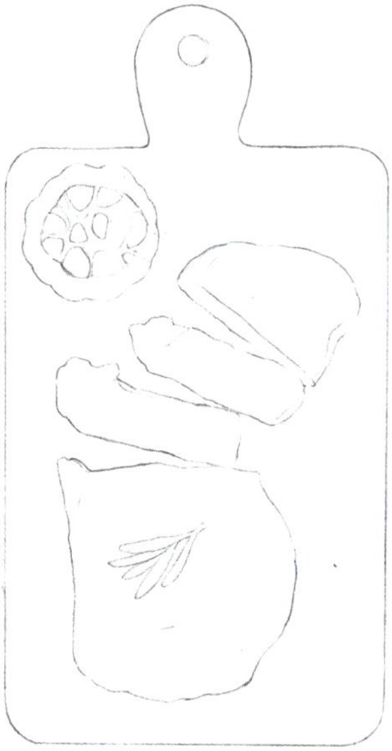

Let's Paint!

First Layer

Steak Slices: Select round brush #2 to apply the "Tea" value of the most vibrant red mixture to the two thin slices, employing thick-and-thin strokes in a diagonal direction across each slice to establish an initial base for the fibrous texture.

Steak Chunks: Use round brush #4 to apply the "Milk" value of the warmer brown mixture to the two chunks and the ends of the slices. While applying the mixture, periodically dip your brush into clean water to blend it on the paper, creating a bleeding effect and an uneven base. I also intentionally add more mixture to the right side of the objects to define the shadow areas.

Garlic Bulb: Use round brush #2 to wash a layer of "Tea" value onto the whole bulb and wait for it to dry. Then, switch to round brush #1 and apply the "Milk" value to the gaps between the cloves.

Rosemary: Apply the "Tea" value to the sprig, using round brush #1.

Wooden Board: Use round brush #8 to apply a thin layer of clear water evenly across the board, then apply the "Tea" value of the brown mixture onto the wet surface. For large areas such as this one, applying a layer of water beforehand will help you to control and blend the solution more easily.

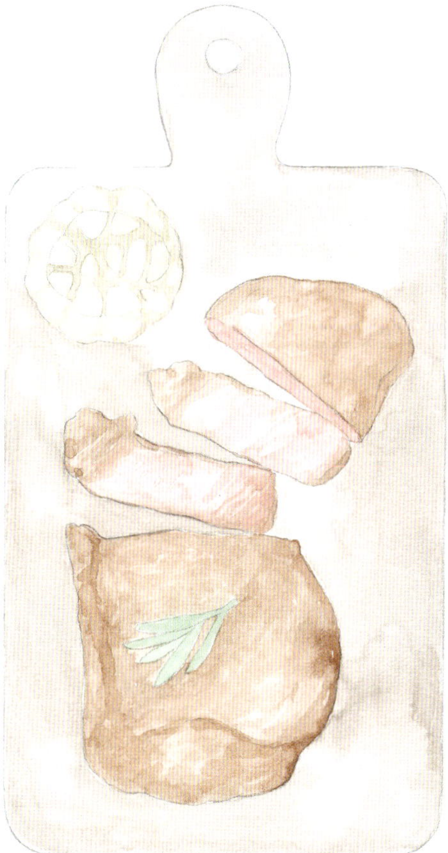

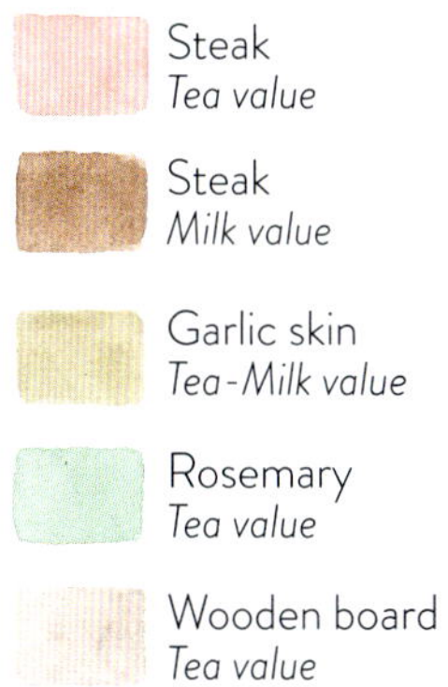

Second Layer

Steak Slices: Use round brush #2 to apply the red mixture in "Milk" value to the interior of the meat, following the same diagonal direction as in the first layer. Press the brush and pull the solution toward the other side, leaving some space between the strokes. Occasionally vary the direction slightly to create natural curves (see Detail 1 in the image on the next page). Use the same brush to apply the "Milk" value of the brown mixture to the ends and outline of the slices, employing the same technique but avoiding pulling the brush all the way across (see Detail 2 in the image on the next page).

Smaller Chunk: Use round brush #4 to apply a layer of clear water across the whole surface. Then, switch to round brush #2 to add the "Cream" value of brown mixture. Start from the right edge and gently pull the color inward diagonally, using the tip of the brush, to create a soft blend. Define the boundaries for the top surface to indicate its thickness, then employ the same technique around its edge.

Next, apply more of the "Cream" brown mixture to the top surface. Continue using the dab-and-pull movement, moving left to right (or vice versa) as you did for the steak slices to depict the grain of the meat. While doing this, think about where the grill marks are going to be and add more solution there, leaving some lighter areas to create a contrast (as seen in the third layer).

Finally, add some "Milk" value of the red mixture to the cut section using the dab-and-pull technique, starting from the bottom upward.

Big Chunk: Follow the first step done for the Smaller Chunk with the same "Cream" value and round brush #2. Due to the larger surface area, the paper might dry before the entire chunk is covered. If this occurs, rewet the areas, including some of the previous strokes, then continue applying the solution. When this entire layer is about 70 percent dry, apply additional strokes (using the technique from Detail 1) primarily along the right edge, leaving some space between the strokes to enhance the appearance of the meat grain.

Garlic Bulb: Use round brush #1 to apply the "Tea" value of the Garlic Flesh mixture and darken the edges of the flesh with the "Milk" value. For the skin, use round brush #2 to deepen the valleys between the cloves with the "Milk" value, focusing more on the right side as this is the shadow area. Change to the "Cream" value of Garlic Skin mixture and use a spotter brush to paint fine lines that depict the gaps between the cloves on the inside.

Rosemary: Repeat the step in the first layer. Then, use the "Cream" value to depict their midribs and stem.

Wooden Board: Start creating the wood grain with round brush #2 and a "Milk" value mixture. Orient the paper so that the length of the board is facing you, allowing for easy movement of your hand and brush from left to right. Load a good amount of the mixture on the brush and apply horizontal lines across the board. Aim to vary their thickness and length, occasionally overlapping them. Once finished, add a thin, even line of the same value to the right border of the board to depict its chamfered side.

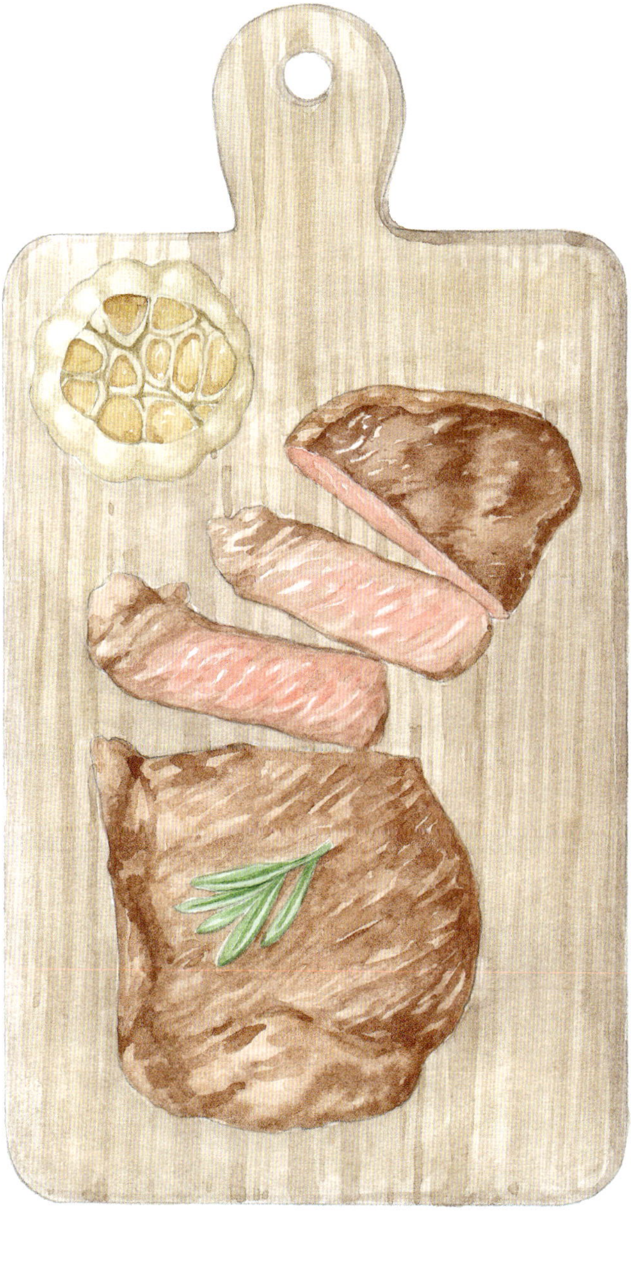

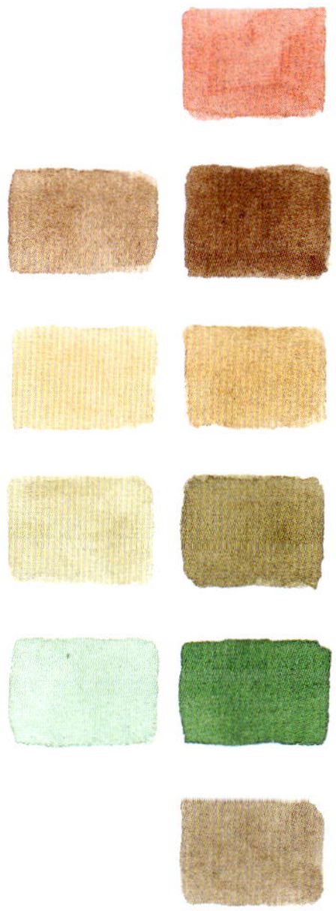
Steak
Milk value
Steak
Milk-Cream value
Garlic flesh
Tea-Milk value
Garlic skin
Milk-Cream value
Rosemary
Tea-Cream value
Wooden board
Milk value

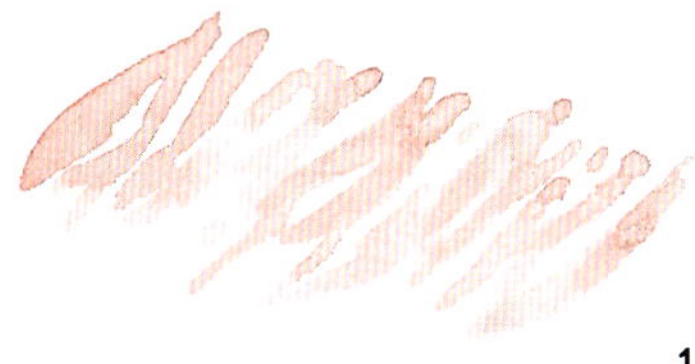

1

2

Third Layer

Steak Slices: Add a bit of the brown mixture to the red mixture to give it a warm undertone, then apply this in "Cream" value to the center by repeating the technique used in the second layer. For the edges, use the "Cream" value of the brown mixture, focusing on applying more pigment to the right edges.

Steak Chunks: Repeat the technique from the second layer to deepen the brown shade of the top surfaces of both chunks, using round brush #2 and maintaining the diagonal direction. Add more solution to the shadow areas on the right. Next, use the same brush to paint the grill marks with the darkest brown mixture in "Cream" value. While painting, gently shake your wrist in a zigzag motion with varying pressure points to create uneven lines that follow the diagonal direction of the meat grain.

Garlic Bulb: For the flesh, repeat the steps from the second layer. Choose a spotter brush to deepen the edges of each clove with the "Cream" value. To enhance the burnt effect in certain spots, add more Pyrrol Orange to the original mixture to achieve a warmer brown, then apply this solution to those spots. You can add a touch of dark brown from the Steak mixture to fill in the gaps between the cloves and the outlining on top.

For the skin, use the same brush and the "Cream" value of Garlic Skin mixture to depict texture by hatching thin lines from the edge inward. To paint the cast shadow, add a bit of dark brown into the current mixture. Ensure that the shadow follows the curvy shape of the bulb accurately.

Rosemary: Use the spotter brush to apply the "Cream" value to the edges and midribs of the leaves.

Wooden Board: Deepen the wood grain with the same technique as the previous layer, using filbert brush #8 and alternating between the "Milk" and "Cream" values. Use the flat side of the brush for broader stripes and the thin side for sharper, more defined stripes. Add the Garlic Skin mixture to some parts to diversify the shades of brown.

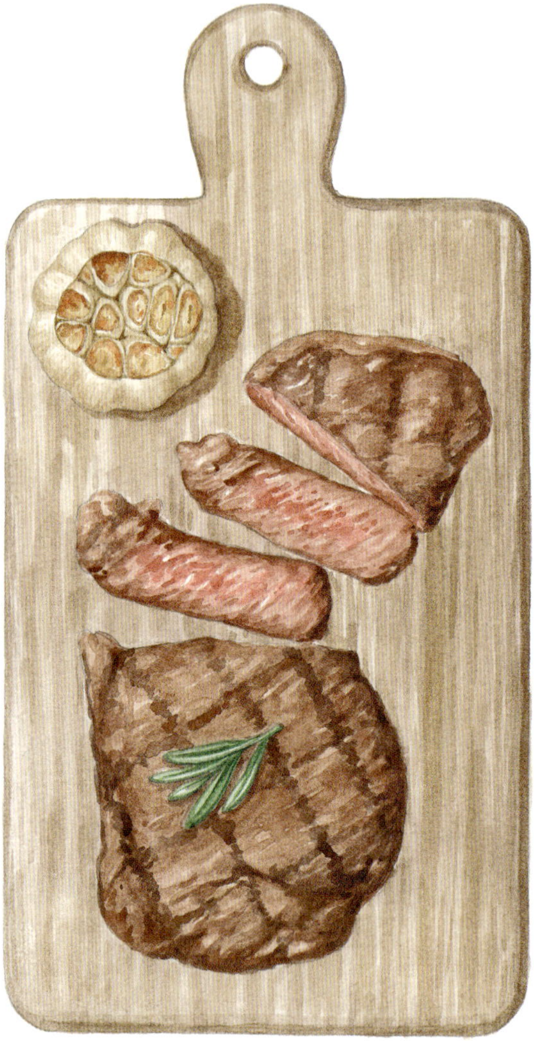

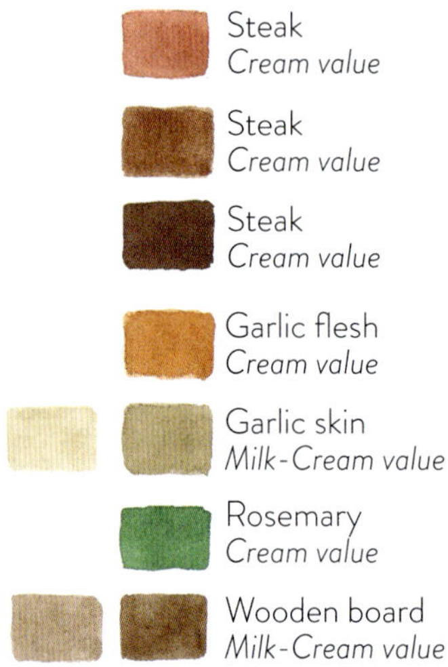

Finishing Touches

Steak Chunks: Randomly apply dark-brown mixture to some parts of the grill marks to enhance the burnt and realistic appearance.

Use filbert brush #4 to deepen the stripes for the wooden board with "Milk" and "Cream" values, focusing more on the right side where it's further from the light source. Add a touch of the Steak dark brown to the "Cream" value, then add a layer of this solution to the chamfered edge on the right and the left side of the hole. Use this same solution to deepen the cast shadow for the garlic bulb and add new ones for all the steak pieces.

Use the warm brown Garlic Flesh mixture to paint the juice around the steak. This will connect the steak as the focal point to its background, the board, and enhance the liveliness of the painting.

When the painting is completely dry, use a spotter brush to add some Chinese White pigment on the steak and juice to depict reflections.

Lastly, add a cast shadow for the board, using a filbert brush #8 and the "Milk" value of Jane's Grey.

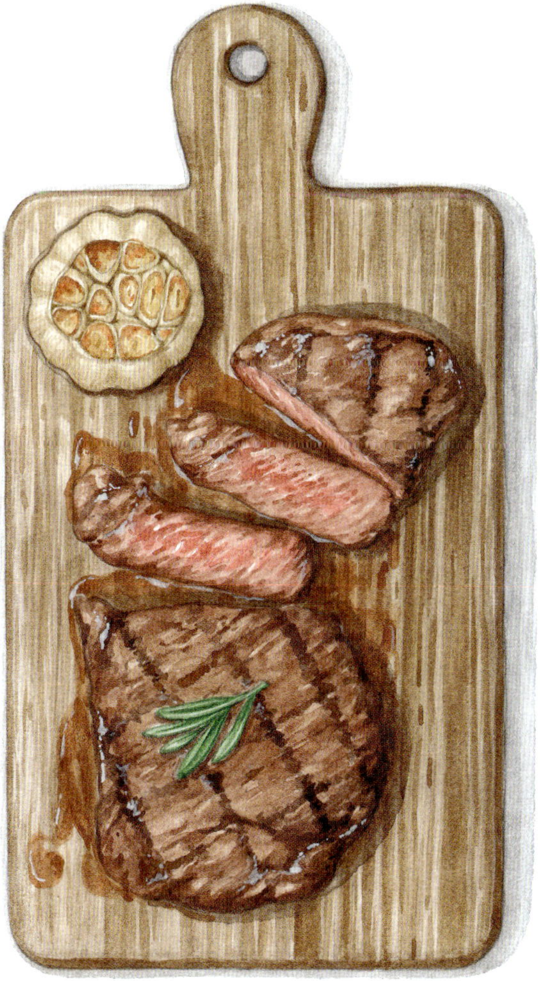

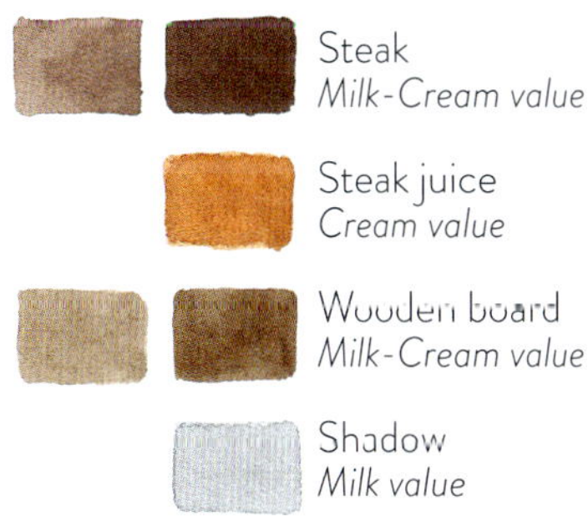

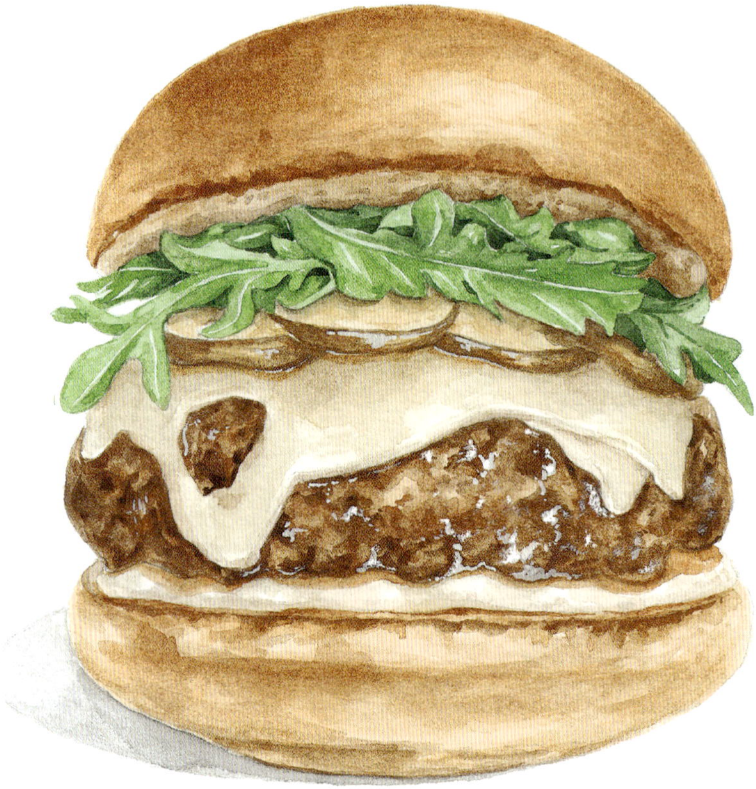

Project 13

Cheeseburger

(Dimensions: W 3¾" x H 4" / W 9.5 cm x H 10 cm)

This is the very first complete side-view project in this book thus far, and it could be a turning point in your food illustration journey as you grasp the principles behind the sketching phase, which have broad applications. I selected a dish familiar to nearly everyone across the globe, representing the epitome of layered food art with a simple color palette. The skills acquired in depicting green leaves in various dishes and the glossy skin of soft bread, such as on the bagel in Project 01: New York Bagel (page 39), can be significantly refined through this exercise. Let's dive in!

Brushes

Round brushes: sizes 1, 2, 4 and 8

Filbert brush: size 4

Spotter brush: size 3/0

Color Palette

OBJECT	COLOR NAME	COLOR VALUES		
		Tea/Coffee	Milk	Cream
Rocket leaves	Hooker's Green Sap Green (Milk value) Ivory Black (Cream value)			
Burger bun	Pyrrol Orange Quinacridone Gold Burnt Umber			
Cheese	Raw Umber Quinacridone Gold			
Grilled beef	Burnt Sienna Burnt Umber Quinacridone Gold			
Grilled beef Mushroom	Burnt Sienna Burnt Umber Ivory Black			
Shadow	Jane's Grey			

Viewpoint & Light Source

Side viewpoints, as discussed in Chapter 1, Composition (page 16), are ideal for illustrating dishes with multiple layers. Imagine the cheese-burger as a domed cylinder: The higher the viewpoint, the fewer fillings are visible, and the buns resemble flatter circles. Opting for this side view allows us to appreciate each layer's beauty and the appealing curvature of the bun. The light source is positioned at the front right and at a lower angle to shed light on all the ingredients.

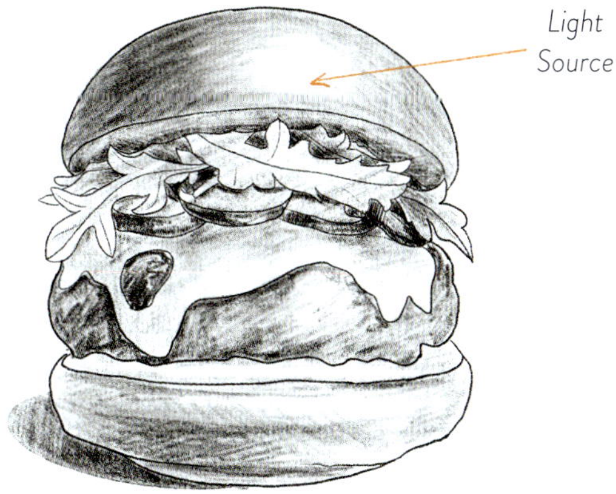

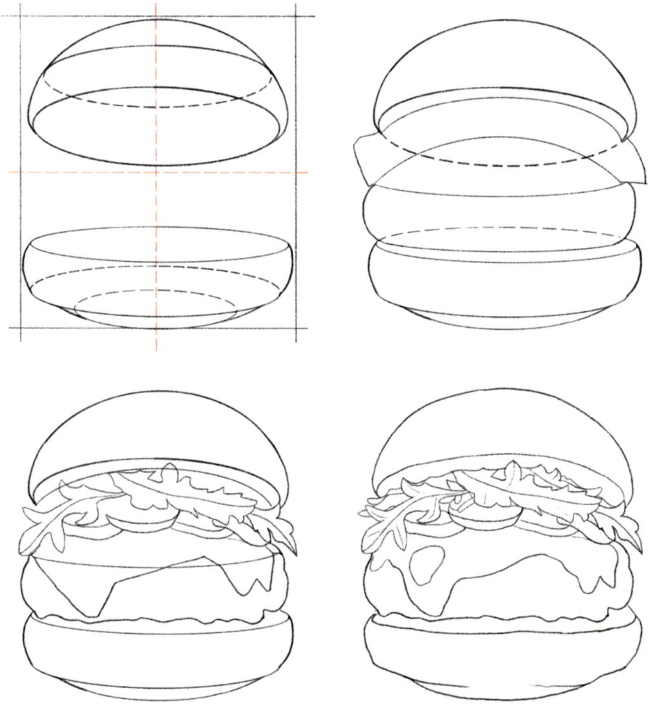

Composition

Since there are no other subjects besides the burger, our focus will solely be on how to arrange the layers to achieve color and layout balance. Starting from the base, there's a thin layer of sauce, followed by a thick and juicy grilled beef patty, then melted cheese and mushrooms and finally, rocket leaves to introduce some green to the composition, which prominently features warm tones. Consider "fluffing up" the layers to clearly see each one, similar to the technique used in food commercials.

Let's Sketch!

Define a rectangular frame and its central lines. Understanding the general shape as a domed cylinder is a good approach here, and you can start drawing the ovals adhering to 3-D rules. Given that our viewpoint is a bit lower than the center of the frame, we'll see more of the under surface of the top-half bun. Once you are happy with the buns, add the layers in between them, starting with the outlines for all of them to check the layout balance, then add more details later.

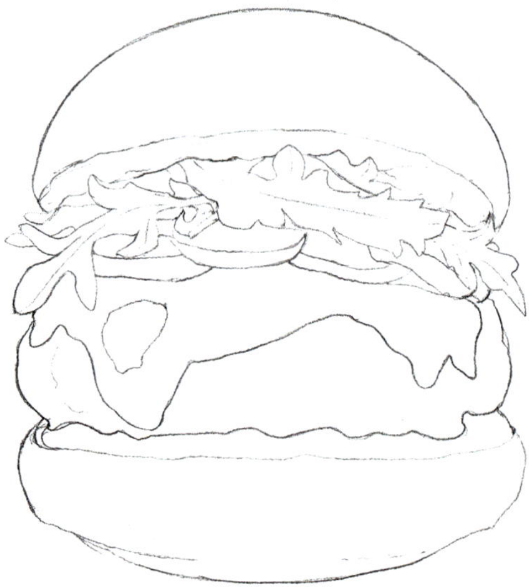

Let's Paint!

First Layer

Rocket Leaves: Choose round brush #2 to apply a layer of "Tea" value to the whole area.

Burger Bun: Use round brush #8 to wash a thin layer of clear water on the top half, then add the "Coffee" value of the orange-brown mixture to it. Try to pull more solution to the left so the highlight area has a lighter shade. Do the same for the bottom half. Next, add a layer of the dark brown from the Beef mixture to the underside of the top half.

Mushroom: Use the same mixture for the bun, applying it with round brush #2. After that, switch to round brush #1 to add the dark-brown mixture in "Milk" value to the mushroom's cap. Move the brush along the curve and randomly leave some gaps between the strokes.

Cheese: Use a filbert brush #4 to wash a layer of "Tea" value to the whole area. Even though it's very light at this stage, purposely pull more solution to the shadow areas while keeping the highlight brighter. (Refer to the Light Source Shading Sketch on page 129 for clearer guidance.)

Grilled Beef Patty: Wash a layer of water across the entire area, using round brush #4. Immediately switch to round brush #2 to add both "Milk" values of warm brown and dark-brown mixture. Gently apply the solutions onto the wet paper using a scumbling brushstroke motion, allowing the water to blend the colors naturally. Since the light is coming from the right side, I give more warm brown to the front of the patty and darker brown to its left side. Take your time at this stage and observe how the colors blend, and only interfere by pulling the color with your brush to create bleeds of varying sizes.

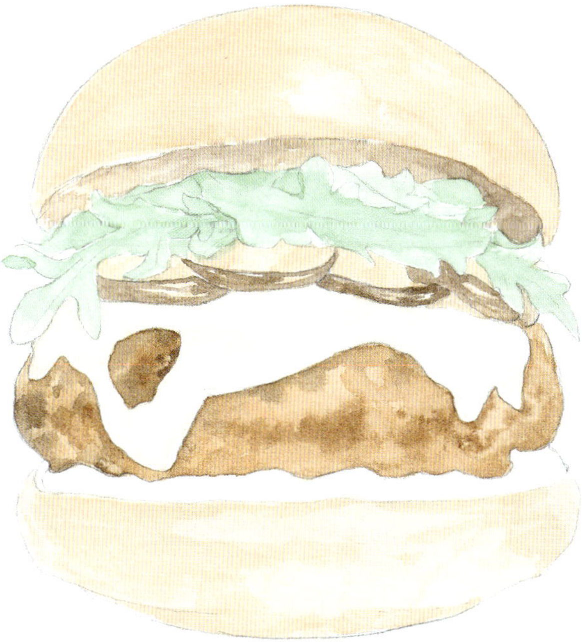

Rocket leaves
Tea value

Burger bun / Mushroom
Coffee value

Cheese
Tea value

Grilled beef
Milk value

Grilled beef / Mushroom
Milk value

Second Layer

Rocket Leaves: Use round brush #1 to apply the "Milk" value. Start from the midrib and blend it out to the rear, following the direction of the veins. Remember to keep the midribs and some veins in a lighter shade. Add more of the mixture where the front leaves overlap with those in the back to enhance depth.

Burger Bun: Repeat the steps from the first layer, with "Milk" value this time. Then, add another layer of dark brown from the Beef mixture to the underside of the top half, focusing more on the areas surrounding the leaves. Choose round brush #2 to add a darker shade to the rim of the bottom half, where the bun is cut in half. Note that the texture of this part is not as glossy and vibrant as the top one, so your color blending does not need to be as smooth.

Mushroom: Repeat the steps from the first layer, using "Cream" value to deepen the shades for all areas. Besides the dark-brown tone for the caps, I add a touch of Quinacridone Gold for a more vibrant look.

Cheese: Repeat the steps from the first layer, with a "Coffee" value this time. Since the cheese is melted, its shape follows the beef patty's shape. Therefore, the vertical surfaces and areas close to the mushroom will be a darker shade. Use the same mixture to dim the white paper of the sauce down.

Grilled Beef Patty: Use round brush #1 and both warm brown and dark-brown mixture in "Cream" value in this layer. The texture of the patty is quite bumpy, necessitating sharper contrast in shades to depict it effectively, with bright and dark spots placed next to each other. The areas closest to the light source will have the sharpest contrast, while contrast diminishes farther away from the light. Use short scumbling brushstrokes to apply the thick solutions. Remember to dedicate more dark-brown mixture to the bottom and the left side. Occasionally wet your brush with clear water to gently blend out the color in some areas.

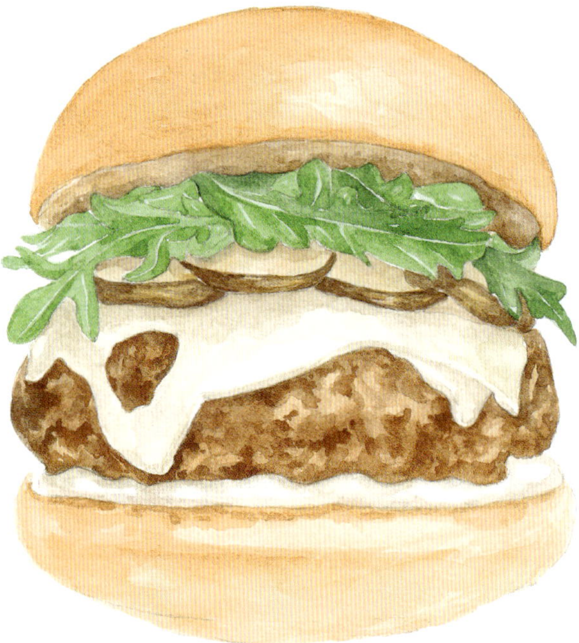

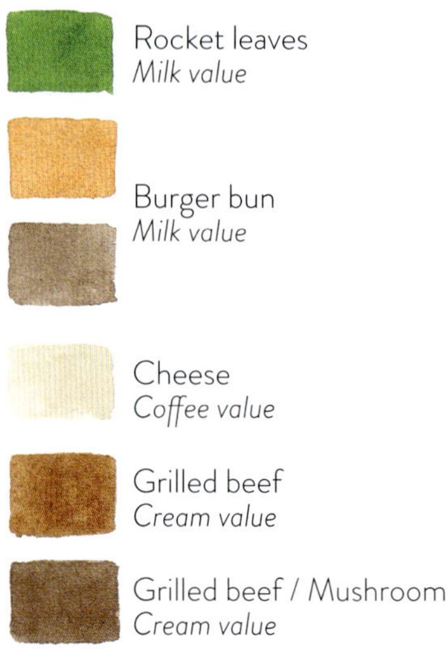

Third Layer

Rocket Leaves: Pick up a spotter brush to add the "Cream" value to the leaves in the back, employing the negative painting technique (page 63): Focus on the corners surrounding the ones in the front rather than painting each leaf meticulously. Here, I also add a touch of Ivory Black to the mixture to create a deeper green shade. Simultaneously, apply another layer of "Milk" value to some parts to enhance contrast.

Burger Bun: Repeat the previous steps, using a "Cream" value this time. Keep in mind that the bottom half should always have a lighter shade, as it does not receive direct heat when baked. To intensify the burnt rim effect for both halves, I add a bit of dark brown to this current mixture and apply it unevenly.

Cheese: Continue deepening the shadow areas with the "Milk" value, making the highlight stand out even more. Load the mixture onto round brush #1 and paint a thin line along the edges of the cheese to dedicate the thickness of the slice.

Mushroom: Add the "Milk" value of the Cheese mixture to indicate some shadows of the rocket leaves on the mushrooms.

Grilled Beef Patty: Repeat the steps from the second layer, but be more selective about where you put the mixture. Deepen the darker areas and leave some lighter spots where the highlight is to maintain the contrast.

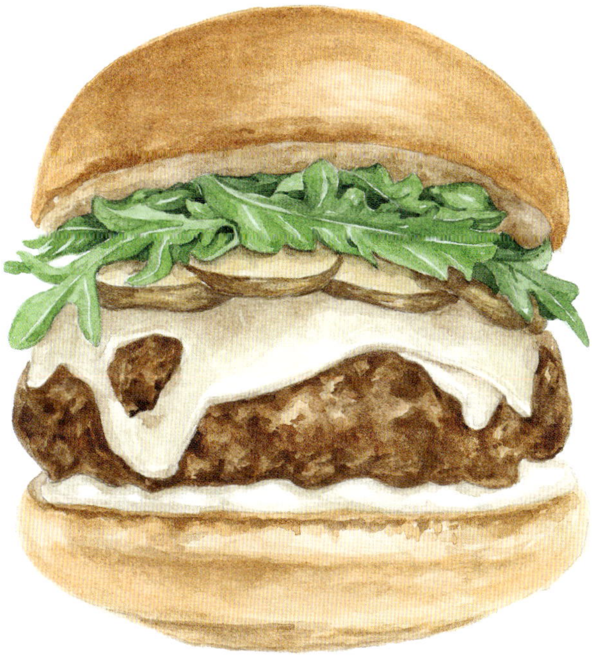

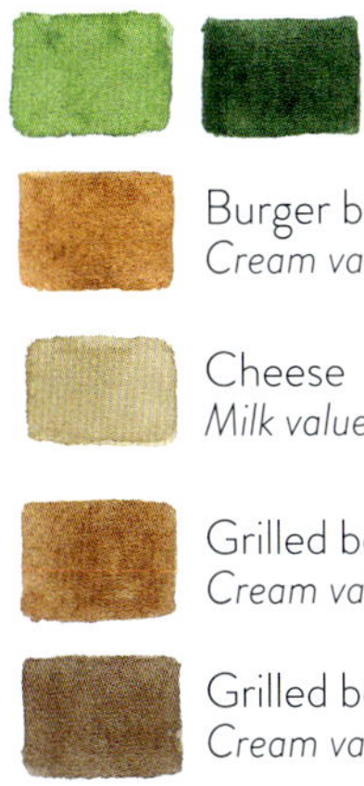

Rocket leaves
Milk-Cream value

Burger bun
Cream value

Cheese
Milk value

Grilled beef
Cream value

Grilled beef
Cream value

Finishing Touches

Burger Bun: Reuse the warm brown mixture for Grilled Beef to deepen shadow areas and the rim for the top half. Apply color on the left side first, then blend it out using the gradient wash technique (page 25). Add this solution to the burnt rim as well. For the underside, load a small amount of solution and start scumbling the tip of the brush to create a bit of texture.

For the bottom half, dilute the solution, ideally to "Milk" value, then add it mainly to the left side and the rim. Lastly, squint your eyes to check the contrast of the whole bun. If the highlights appear too bright, feel free to add a thin diluted layer of warm brown to dim them down.

Cheese: Prepare a new warmer solution with the "Tea" value of Cheese mixture and a touch of Hansa Yellow. Apply it to the whole cheese to tone it down.

Use round brush #1 and the warm brown Grilled Beef mixture to add an uneven line along the bottom of the patty to depict its juice.

Use a spotter brush to add some white reflections on the beef patty and on the mushrooms.

Add cast shadow on the left using round brush #2 and the "Coffee" value of Jane's Grey.

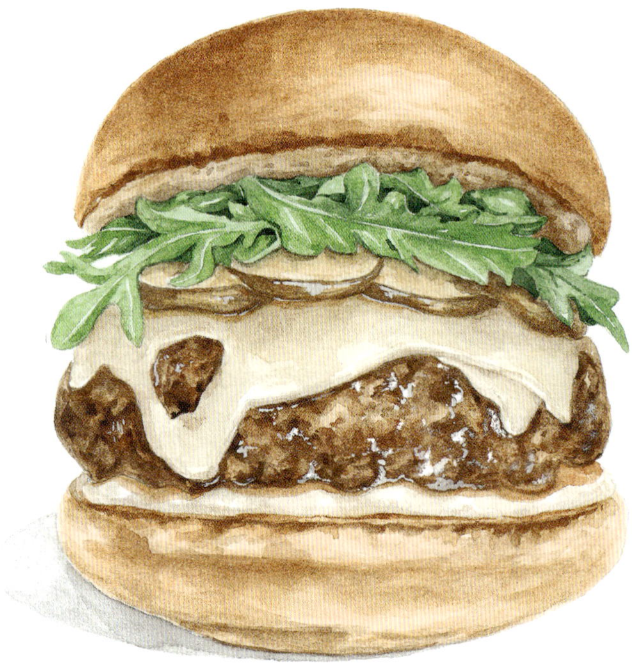

Burger bun
Cream value

Cheese
Tea value

Shadow
Coffee value

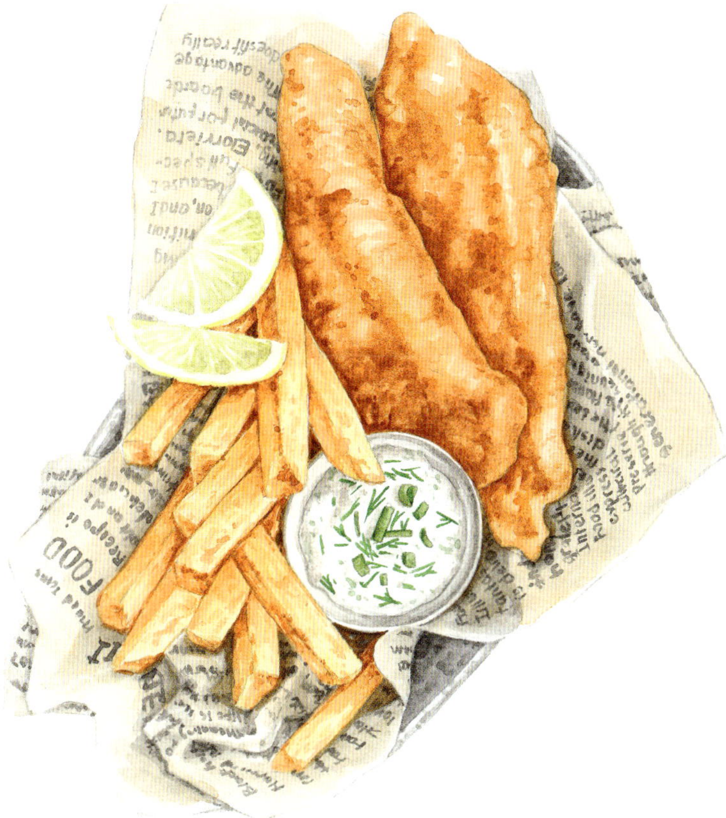

Project 14

Fish & Chips

(Dimensions: W 5¾" x H 6¼" / W 14 cm x H 15.8 cm)

You might have wondered whether I would feature a deep-fried dish in this book. The answer is an obvious yes. I love them as much as many of you do! Fish and chips, considered a national dish of Britain, has captured the attention and affection of many countries worldwide. Since the ingredients for this meal are straightforward, I want to introduce a bit of a challenge by presenting them wrapped in paper (with printed words) instead of just on a tray or plate. By completing this project, you'll gain the principles of painting any deep-fried dish, whether battered or not, and develop a solid approach to observing and depicting a surface that appears to move and fold randomly.

Brushes

Round brushes: sizes 1, 2, 4 and 8
Spotter brush: size 3/0

Color Palette

OBJECT	COLOR NAME	COLOR VALUES		
		Tea/Coffee	Milk	Cream
Chips (*Highlight*) Lemon peel	**Hansa Yellow Medium**			
Chips (*Shadow*) Battered fish	**New Gamboge**			
Battered fish mixture	**Quinacridone Gold** **Pyrrol Orange** **Burnt Sienna**			
Lemon pulp	**Hansa Yellow** **Raw Umber**			
Herbs	**Sap Green** **Hooker's Green (Cream value)**			
Tartar sauce	**Raw Umber**			
Metal tray / Cup / Wrapping paper	**Ivory Black**			
Wrapping paper	**Battered fish mixture** **New Gamboge**			

Viewpoint & Light Source

A top-down viewpoint will be ideal to present a holistic arrangement of all the objects inside the wrapping paper. The light source comes from the right side, so the inner right wall of the metal tray and wrapping paper will be sharper and darker on the right.

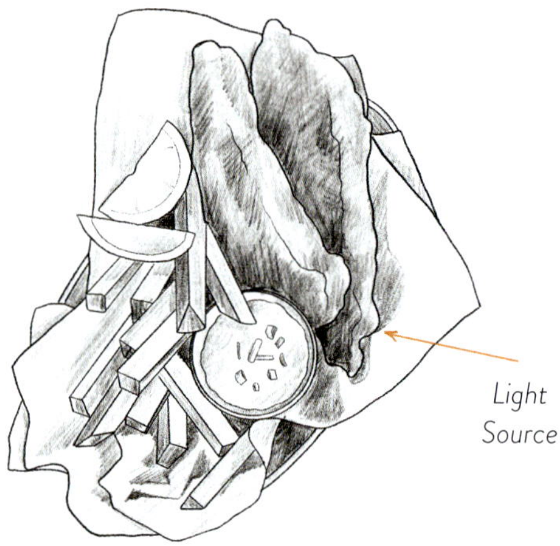

Composition

This dish consists of only three main items: deep-fried fish in beer batter, chips and tartar dipping sauce. Their varying sizes and shapes naturally create a pleasing combination, with the fish sticks occupying a significant portion of the overall layout. We only need to place them strategically to ensure balance. Despite the egg-shaped tray being positioned diagonally, all elements are arranged in a way that counteracts this orientation.

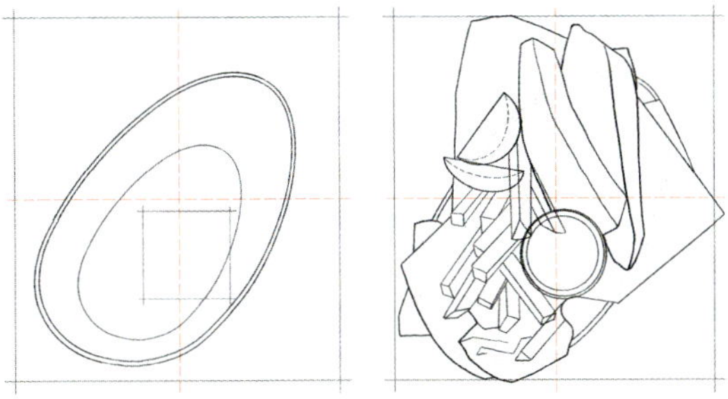

Let's Sketch!

The chips clustered on printed wrapping paper may pose a challenge in deciding where to begin sketching. It's always helpful to start with a general framework, such as the metal tray, which confines our focal points. The bigger rectangular frame surrounding it defines the outer limits of the entire dish. Then, proceed to sketch the smaller elements, beginning with those closest to your viewpoint: the dipping sauce in a small round bowl, lemon wedges, the fried fish and chips and finally, the wrapping paper beneath them all. Ensure the chips are sketched in various directions to capture their randomness. For the battered fish strips, though their shapes appear spontaneous, start by outlining them within a chamfered elongated cuboid to accurately depict their thickness.

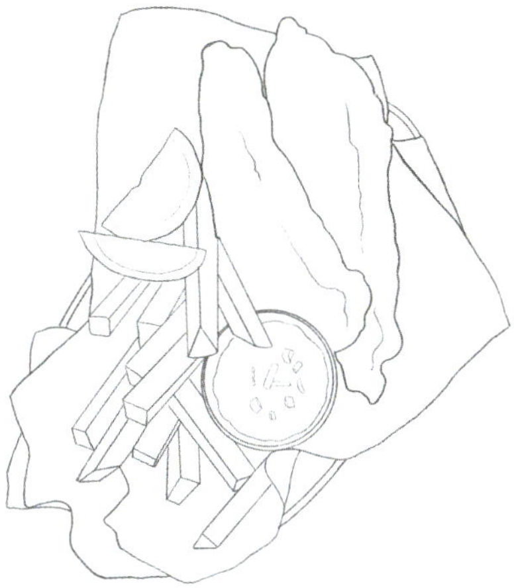

Since the folds of the wrapping paper do not adhere to specific rules, we must observe how it interacts with each object and how far each corner extends from the nearest elements. That's why saving it for last is ideal, ensuring the overall composition follows the contours of the tray. With the tray mostly obscured by the paper, I just need to leave the visible lines after sketching everything else. Lastly, lighten the whole sketch to prepare for the painting phase.

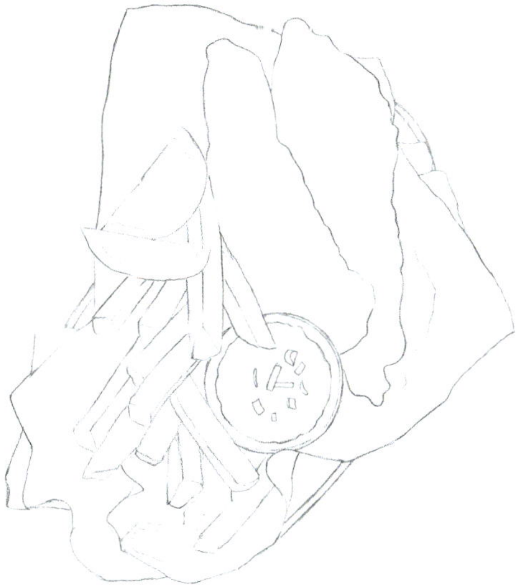

Let's Paint!

First Layer

Battered Fish: Work on one strip at a time. Use round brush #8 to wash a generous amount of water across one strip, then switch to round brush #4 to apply the "Tea" value of the yellow mixture on it. When the paper is still damp or wet, use the tip of the brush to dab the brown mixture in "Cream" value onto the shadow area, which is mainly on the left side. Unlike a smooth surface, fried batter has a bumpy texture. Hence, instead of pulling the brush back and forth gradually on the damp paper, employ a short dab-and-pull motion, so the thicker and deeper solution is clearly marked and has a certain bleed to the background. Look closely at your reference to identify where else the darker shades are needed and apply the solution accordingly. Leave the right side of the strip light yellow to depict the contrast of the highlight and shadow areas.

Chips: Use round brush #2 to apply a layer of yellow color in "Tea" value to all the chips. Once completed, keep using the same brush to add the "Tea" value of New Gamboge color to the shadowed sides of the sticks.

Lemon: With round brush #1 and the same "Tea" value of Hansa Yellow that was used for the chips, paint a thin line along the lemon peel. Wash the brush thoroughly, then apply the Lemon Pulp mixture by making some thin lines from the outer edge toward the center of the wedge to establish the texture base. Make sure to leave some white space between the pulps.

Tartar Sauce: Use round brush #4 to wet the entire area with clear water. Immediately switch to round brush #2 and apply the "Tea" value of Raw Umber using a scumbling brushstroke. This will create a soft bleed effect once dry. Aim to place more color on the left side and leave some areas white.

Paper: Use round brush #4 to apply the "Tea" value of Ivory Black to the shadow areas of the paper.

Tray: Use the "Milk" value of Ivory Black to paint the inner wall of the tray.

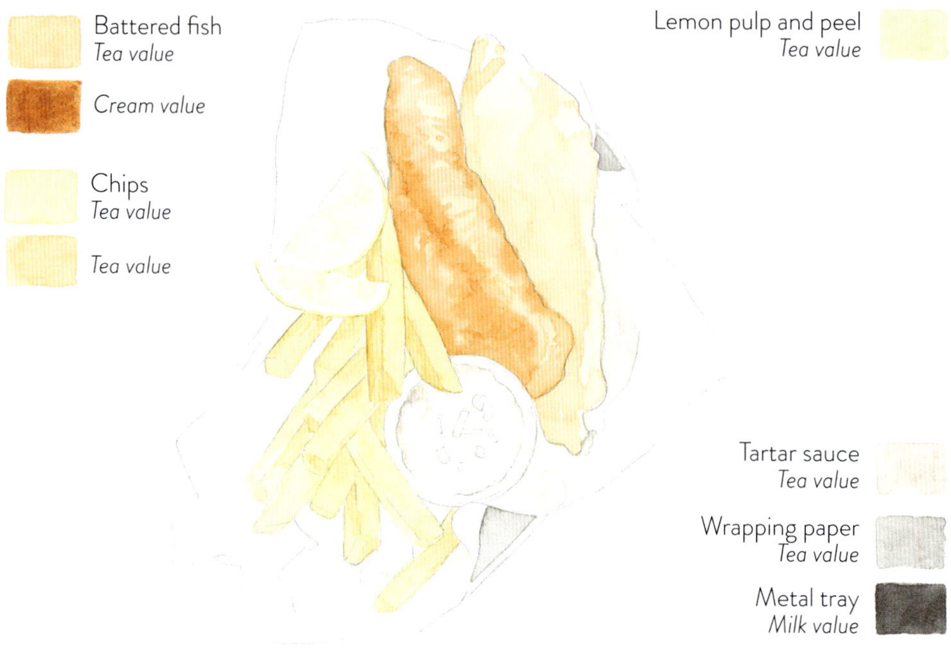

Second Layer

Battered Fish: Repeat all the steps for the other strip when the first one is dry. Keep in mind that this one is not as well lit, resulting in a darker shade overall. Add a bit more "Cream" value of the brown mixture along the boundary line of the two strips to make the front one stand out.

Artist's Tip: If your paper is retaining excess water, causing the solution to be pushed to the edges of the object, simply wait a bit longer or use a clean, dry brush to absorb some water before applying the mixture. The ideal moisture level for achieving this texture is when the paper is damp enough to hold the mixture where it's applied so that you can blend the edges softly.

Chips: Use round brush #2 to apply the "Milk" value of New Gamboge to the shadow sides of the sticks to enhance their 3-D shape. Add a bit of brown Battered Fish mixture to the negative gaps between the chips.

Lemon: Repeat the steps from the first layer to deepen the shade of the lemon pulps, leaving some lighter gaps to depict their glossiness.

Tartar Sauce: Use round brush #1 to apply the green mixture in "Coffee" value to the herbs. Wash your brush thoroughly, then apply a thin layer of gray to the right wall of the bowl. Again, this side is not receiving light, so it should be darker.

Paper and Tray: Repeat the steps from the first layer to deepen the shadow areas of both objects. Pay attention to how the light casts shadows of the items onto the wrapping paper. The ones closer to the light source should appear darker and sharper.

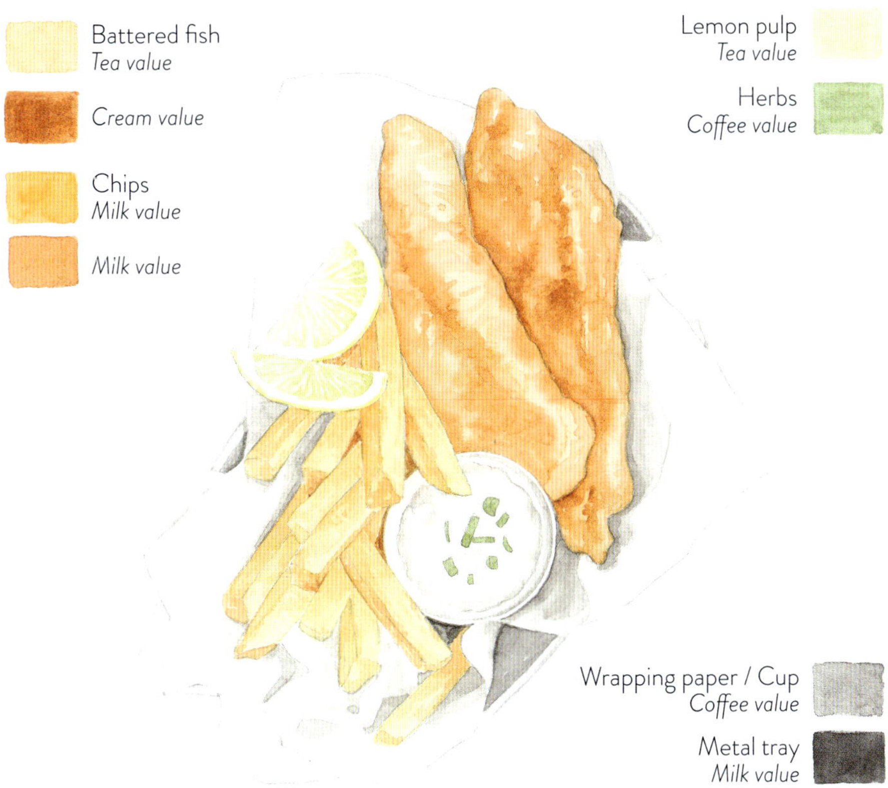

Third Layer

Battered Fish: Use round brush #2 to apply the "Cream" value of the brown mixture to some areas on the shadow sides and along the boundaries where objects overlap. This helps deepen the brown shade along the edge to help make the highlight more pronounced. At this step, you can paint on dry paper in order to leave sharper brushstrokes that enhance the bumpy character.

Chips: Keep using the "Milk" value of the brown Battered Fish mixture to deepen the shadow sides of all the sticks.

Lemon: Apply another layer of "Tea" value to the lemon pulps, focusing specifically on the arcs closer to the peel. Add the "Milk" value of the Lemon Peel mixture to highlight the bright yellow of the peel, using a spotter brush to maintain thin lines in this area.

Tartar Sauce: Add another layer of gray to the shadow areas that were indicated from the second layer. Then, use round brush #1 to add the green mixture in "Milk" value to the herbs. Switch to a spotter brush to draw some chopped dill using "Cream" value. As the sauce is white, the herbs can be added later without changing the color.

Paper and Tray: Apply the "Milk" value to the shadow areas of the paper and some diluted strokes to the bright areas. As we keep deepening the darker shades for other objects, the white paper might become too bright for the overall setting.

For the tray, use round brush #2 to apply the more concentrated black to the deep corners and blend it toward the lip to indicate depth.

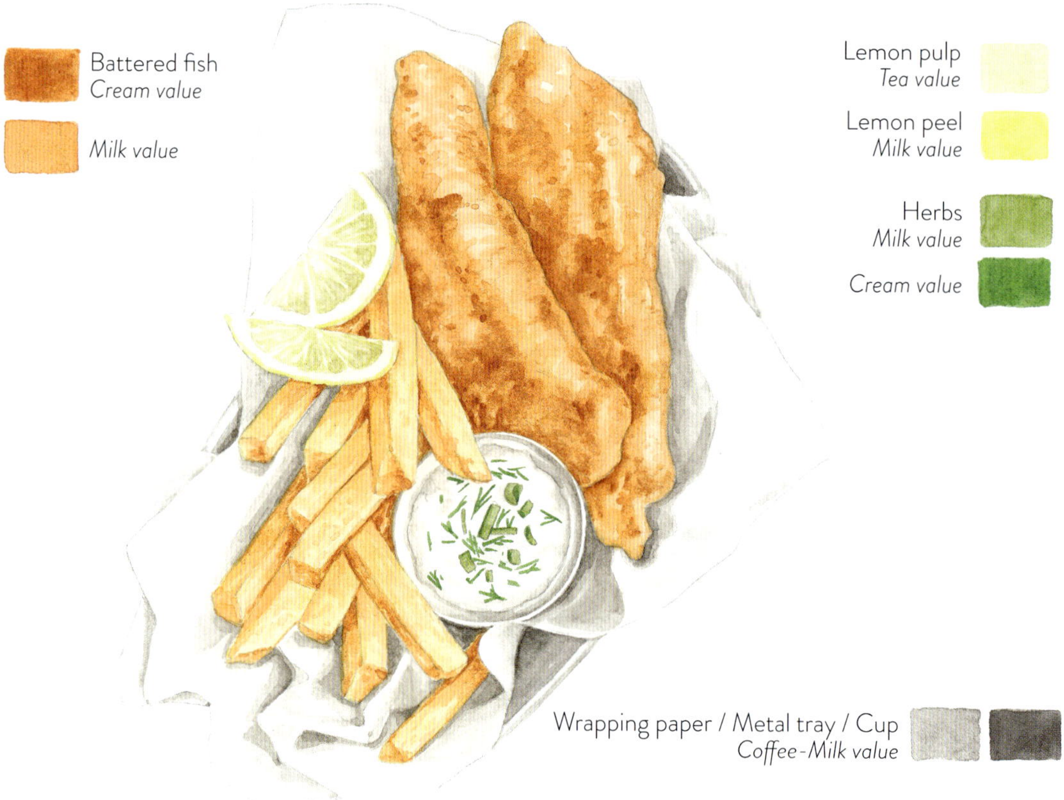

Fourth Layer

Battered Fish: Add "Cream" value one last time to the areas where the strips overlap each other or other objects to intensify the sense of layering.

Apply some "Milk" value of the same mixture to the shaded parts of the chips. Make some scumbling strokes on the highlight areas to further depict the texture. Feel free to reuse the Battered Fish "Cream" value for slightly burnt edges on some sticks or where they touch the paper.

Use the "Tea" value of the Herbs mixture to depict the pieces that lay underneath the Tartar sauce.

Paper: Prepare a new mixture for the vintage paper color by combining the "Tea" value of Battered Fish solution with a touch of New Gamboge. Pick up round brush #8 to wash a layer of it to the entire paper, including the highlights.

Once the paper is completely dry, use a pencil to draw the lines on the paper, following the "peaks and valleys" of the folds.

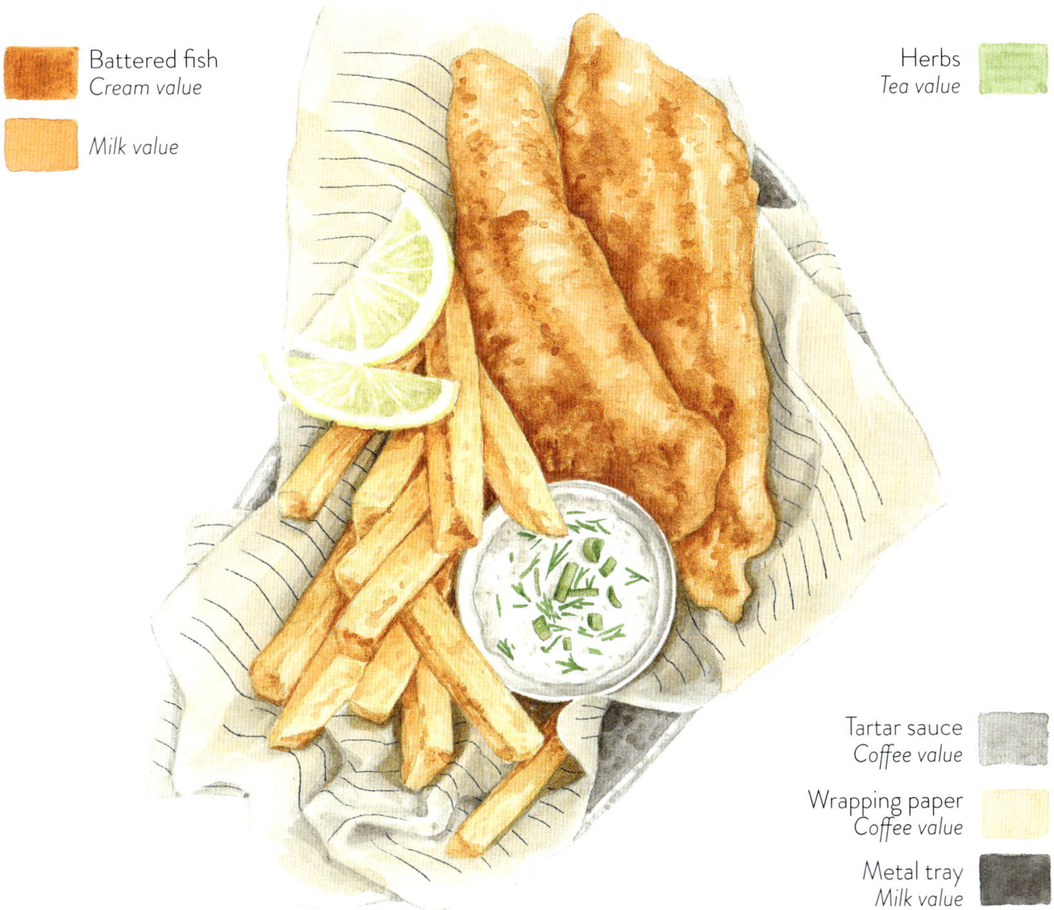

Finishing Touches

Use a thin brush, such as spotter brush #3/0, and Ivory Black color in "Coffee" and "Milk" values to write characters along these pencil lines. The text is very small, so coherence is not necessary. I write random existing words where they're clear, but elsewhere, I move the brush up and down to mimic letters. After the paint dries completely, gently erase the pencil lines.

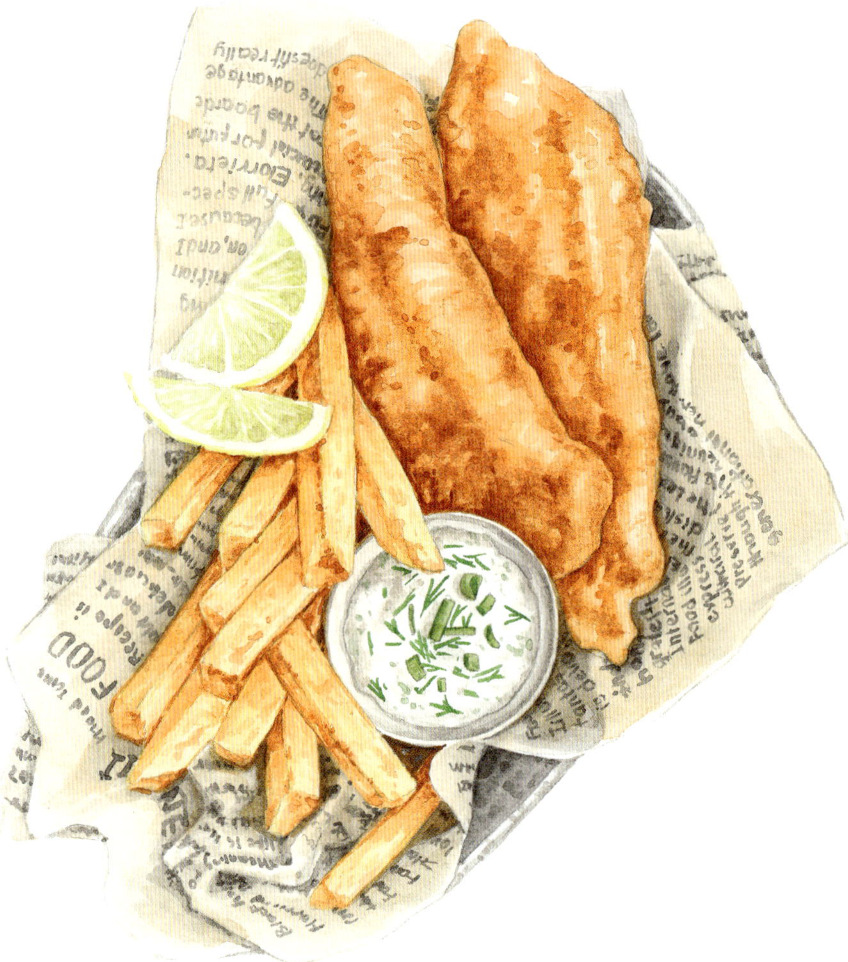

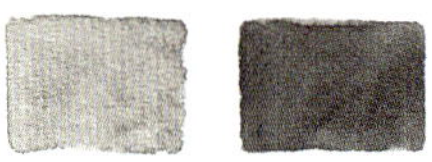

Text
Coffee-Milk value

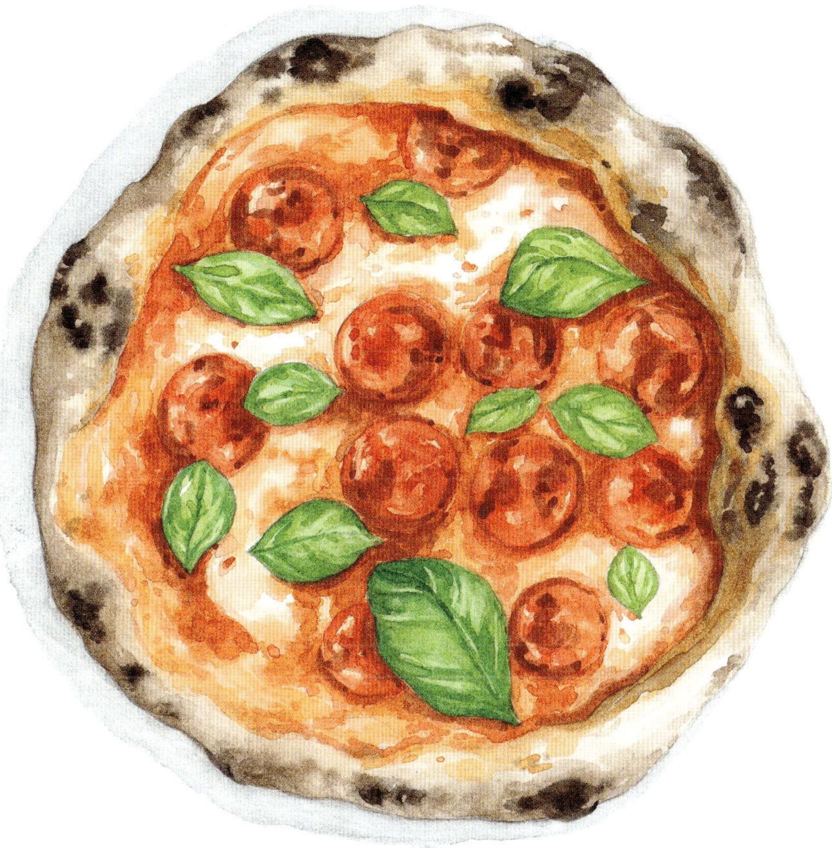

Project 15

Salami Pizza

(Dimensions: W 5¼" x H 5¼" / W 13.5 cm x H 13.5 cm)

Not only is this a starting point for you to paint different types of pizzas you'll encounter later on, but it also provides a foundation for depicting baked dishes that have tempting burnt parts that always make our mouths water. This will be the final project in the entree category, and I want the process to be enjoyable without being overly ambitious or introducing too many new challenges. Instead, it should feel like a review and playful exploration of what you have learned so far, focusing on the wet-on-wet technique, which is specifically advantageous in food illustration. I hope that just as pizza is a reliable choice for many of us, this delightful exercise will be a source of wonder for you.

Brushes

Round brushes: sizes 1, 2, 4 and 8

Color Palette

OBJECT	COLOR NAME	COLOR VALUES		
		Tea/Coffee	Milk	Cream
Pizza crust	Raw Umber Burnt Umber			
Burnt pizza crust	Burnt Umber Ivory Black			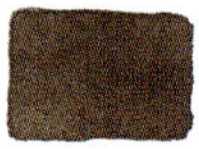
Finishing touch pizza crust	Hansa Yellow New Gamboge Quinacridone Gold			
	Pyrrol Orange Quinacridone Gold Burnt Sienna			
Salami Tomato sauce	Pyrrol Scarlet Pyrrol Orange Burnt Sienna			
	Pyrrol Scarlet Burnt Umber			
Basil	Hansa Yellow New Gamboge Phthalo Blue GS	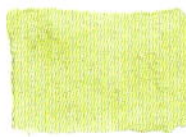	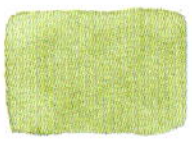	
	Hooker's Green Burnt Umber		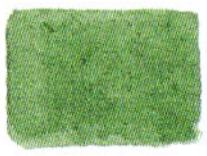	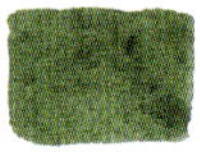

Viewpoint & Light Source

As you might have guessed, we'll go for the top-down viewpoint to ensure all toppings are fully visible. The light source comes from the right side, creating a shadow cast by the inner right wall onto the topping (as seen in the side view).

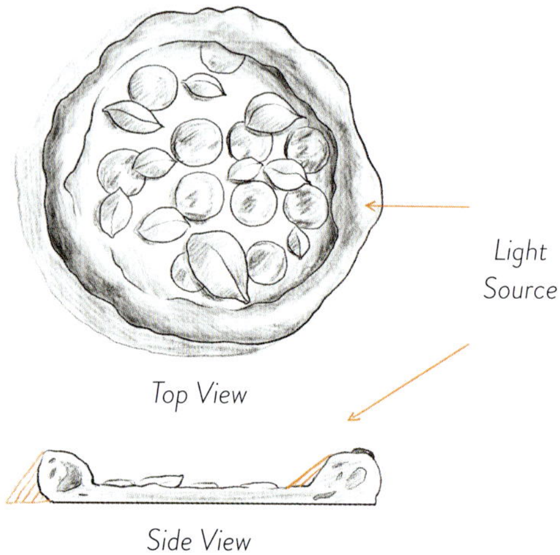

Composition

It can't get simpler or more fun than this: All you need to do is place the toppings to create color harmony and layout coherence. There is no need to follow exactly what I sketch here; let your creative mind fly.

Let's Sketch!

This simple sketch will be quite a relief after the complexity of the last project. Start with a circle, and another smaller one that doesn't necessarily share the same center as the first. Homemade or sourdough pizzas typically have irregular thickness, as is the case here. All toppings will stay within the smaller circle. As you arrange the elements, remember to allow some to overlap others to create a sense of layering and randomness.

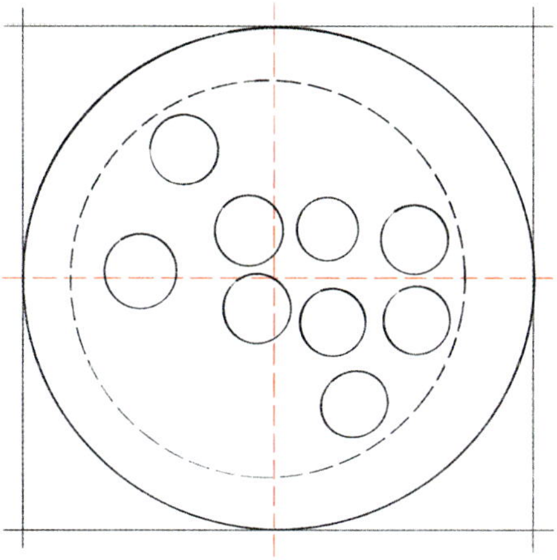

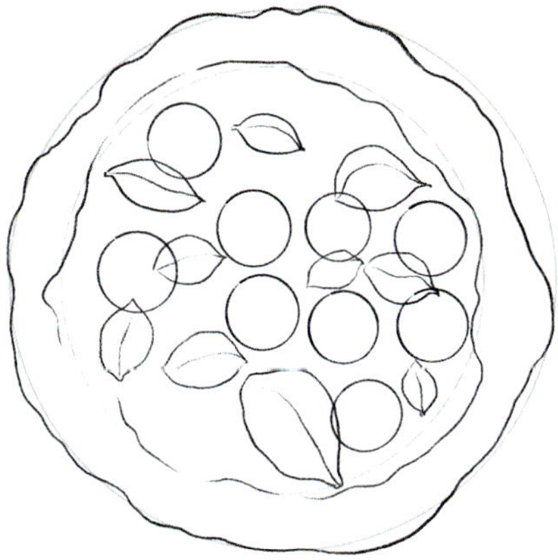

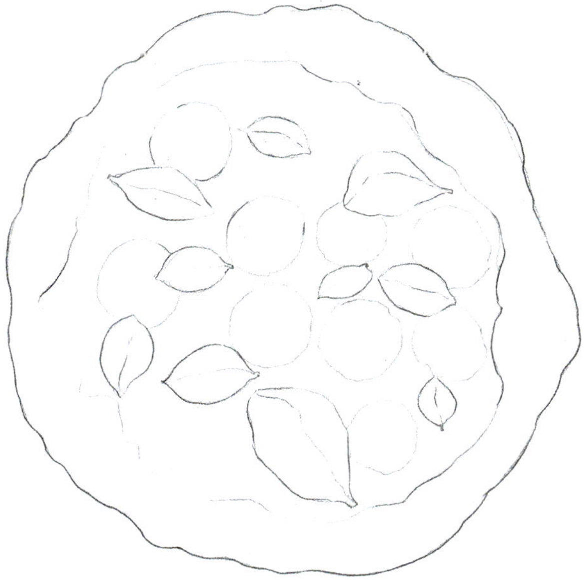

Let's Paint!

First Layer

Pizza Crust: Use round brush #8 to apply a layer of water to the entire area, then immediately add the "Tea" value mixture. The damp paper will ensure a soft bleed effect without exposing any sharp strokes. At this stage, you can add a bit more color to the shadow areas to establish an initial sense of depth.

Tomato Sauce and Salami: Use a clean round brush #8 to apply a layer of water on paper, excluding the basils and the crust. While the paper is still wet, use round brush #4 to apply the "Coffee" value of the orange mixture where the sauce and salami will be. If the mixture doesn't spread out on paper, that means your paper isn't wet enough. In this case, use the round brush #8 to apply more water on paper then proceed to add color. Keep some areas in white to depict the cheese later.

> **Artist's Tip:** To effectively use the wet-on-wet technique (page 23) over a large area, keep two brushes at hand: one for applying water and the other for applying colors. Rather than trying to cover the entire large area at once, which could lead to it drying too quickly before you can add color, divide it into smaller sections and execute the process one after another.

Basil Leaves: Use round brush #2 to apply the "Milk" value of the warmer green mixture to all the leaves.

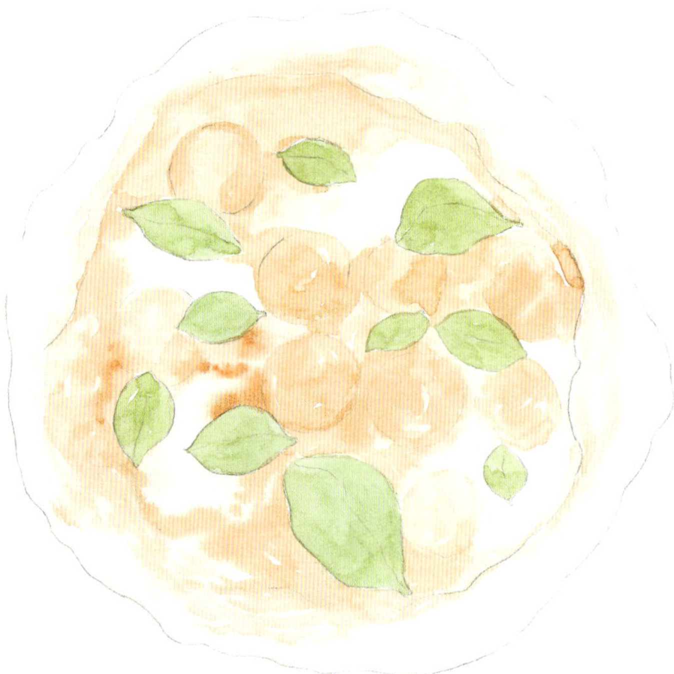

Second Layer

Pizza Crust: Repeat the process done in the first layer, with the "Milk" value this time. Provide more mixture to the shadow side on the left and a part of the right inner wall to increase contrast. Essentially, the shading rule here can be a combination of a bent cylinder and sphere (where the dough puffs up).

Salami: Use round brush #2 to apply the reddish mixture in "Milk" value to the salami slices. Employ the scumbling brushstroke here, generally in an arc motion, and leave some dry gaps in between. While the color is still wet, use the tip of the brush to pick some "Cream" value and add it randomly on the slices to depict texture.

Basil Leaves: Use round brush #2 to apply the yellow-green mixture along the margins. Right after that, dip the brush into clear water to blend it inward, using a technique similar to gradient wash (page 25). While the paper is still wet, pick some colder green in "Milk" value and apply mostly to the base and shadow areas. Keep moving the brush following the direction of the veins, leaving thin gaps to depict them.

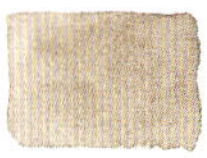

Pizza crust
Milk value

Basil
Milk value

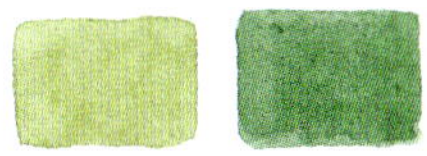

Salami
Milk-Cream value

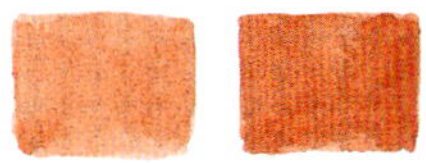

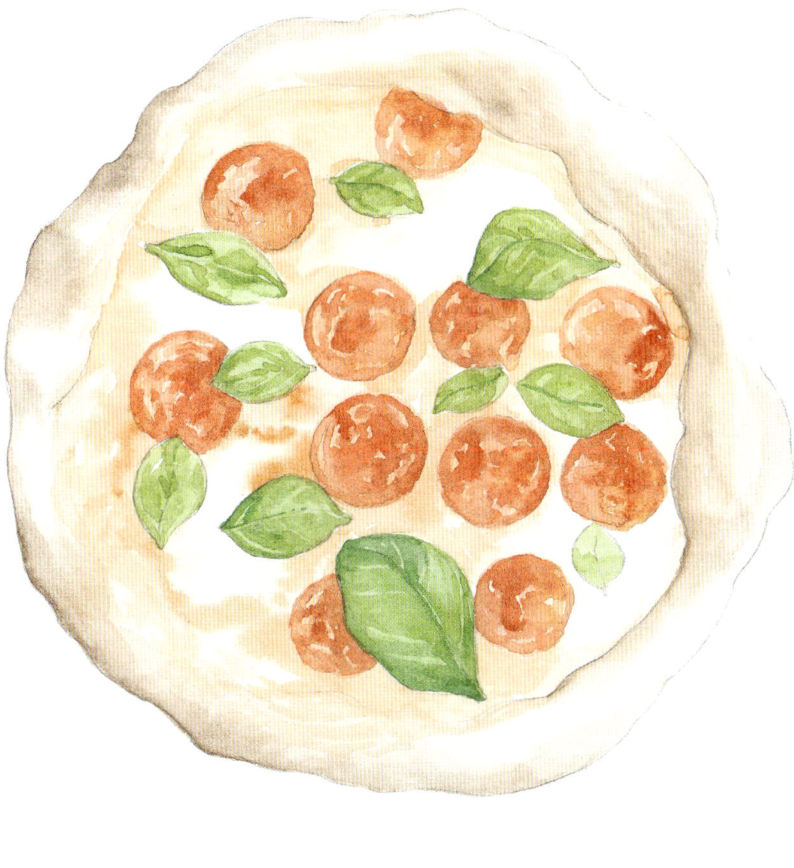

Third Layer

Pizza Crust: Again, keep employing the wet-on-wet technique as in the previous two layers, this time with the "Cream" value to depict the burnt areas. Without the soft bleeding effect achieved through the process I introduced, the crust might appear overly rough and harsh. Scatter small dots randomly to enhance realism.

Tomato Sauce: Repeat the wet-on-wet technique from the first layer, now using the "Milk" value in order to deepen the orange shade. Leave more solution on the right edge in order to represent the shadow cast by the crust.

Salami: Pick up round brush #2 and scumble the "Cream" value of the red mixture to all the slices. Be careful not to over-apply this mixture; leave some lighter areas to maintain the texture.

Basil Leaves: Simultaneously use "Milk" and "Cream" value for the midribs and the edges that are not facing direct light.

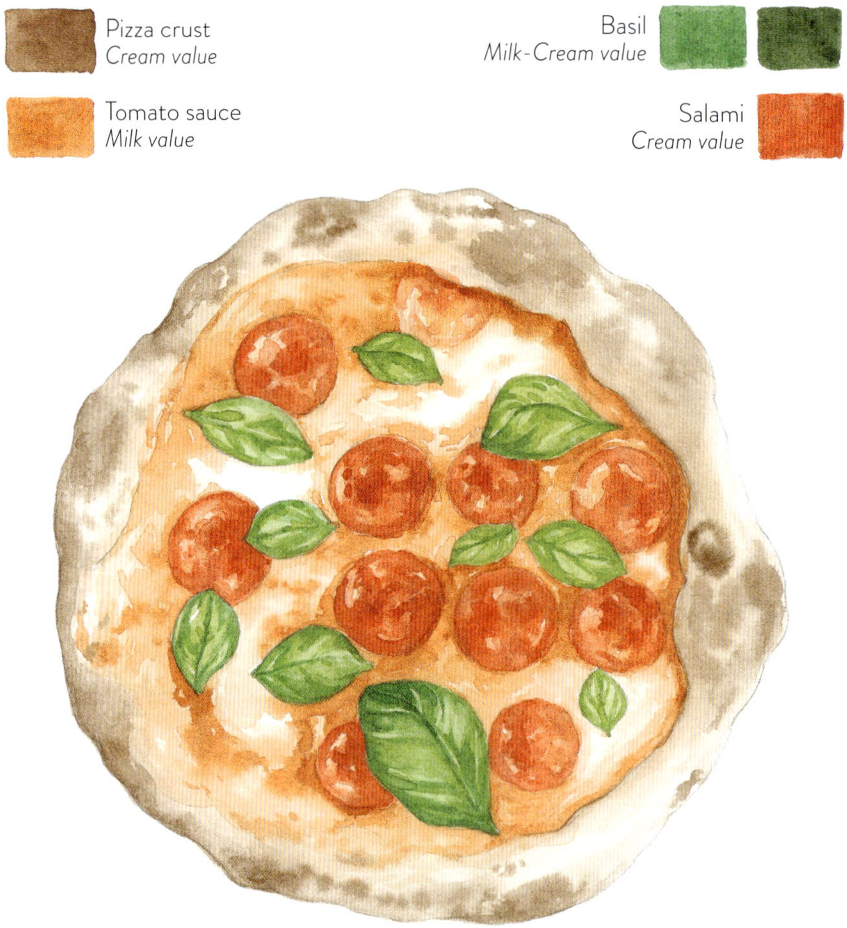

Finishing Touches

Pizza Crust: Apply a thin layer of water where you want to deepen the burnt effect, then start dabbing the dark-brown mixture in "Cream" value on it, using round brush #2. At this stage, the paper moisture should be lessened so it can hold the color mixture right where you apply it. Try to dapple the brush with different pressures to achieve a realistic burnt effect. Finally, apply the orange-brown mixture around the inner wall to illustrate the tomato sauce smearing on it, and to create color coherence.

Tomato Sauce: Use round brush #2 to apply the Salami red mixture to certain surface areas, particularly focusing on the left side of the basil leaves to depict their shadows, and around the salami slices.

Pick up round brush #1 and apply some touch of red-brown mixture to the salami slices. Since this solution is highly concentrated, use caution regarding the amount applied. Use the same mixture to deepen the shadow cast by the right inner wall of the crust onto the sauce.

Add a cast shadow for the whole pizza using round brush #8 and a gray mixture in "Coffee" value.

Burnt pizza crust
Cream value

Pizza crust
Milk value

Tomato sauce
Cream value

Salami
Cream value

Shadow
Coffee value

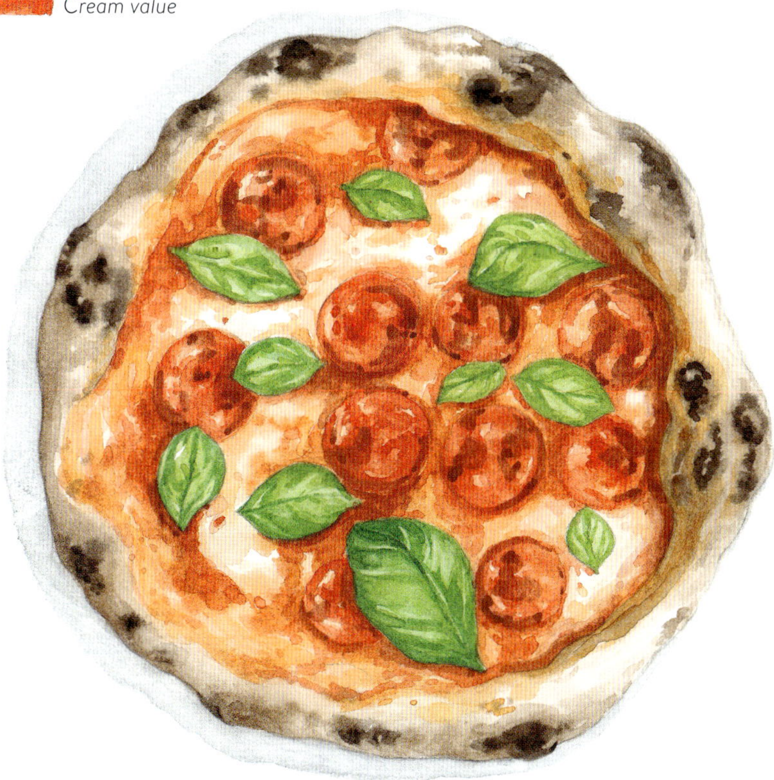

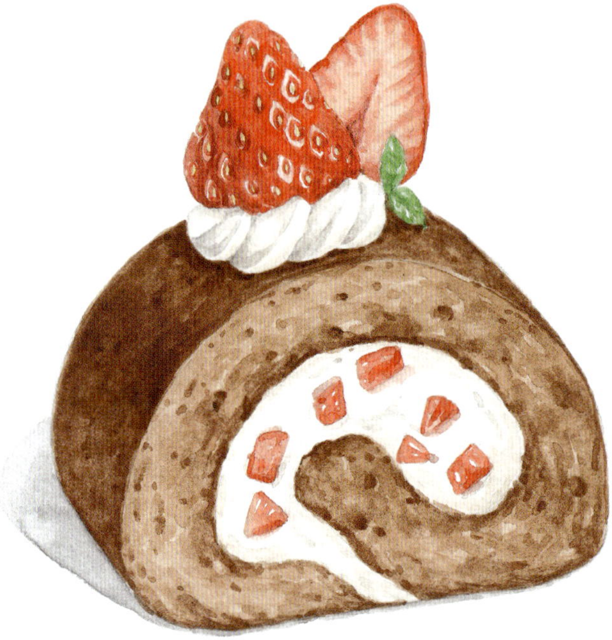

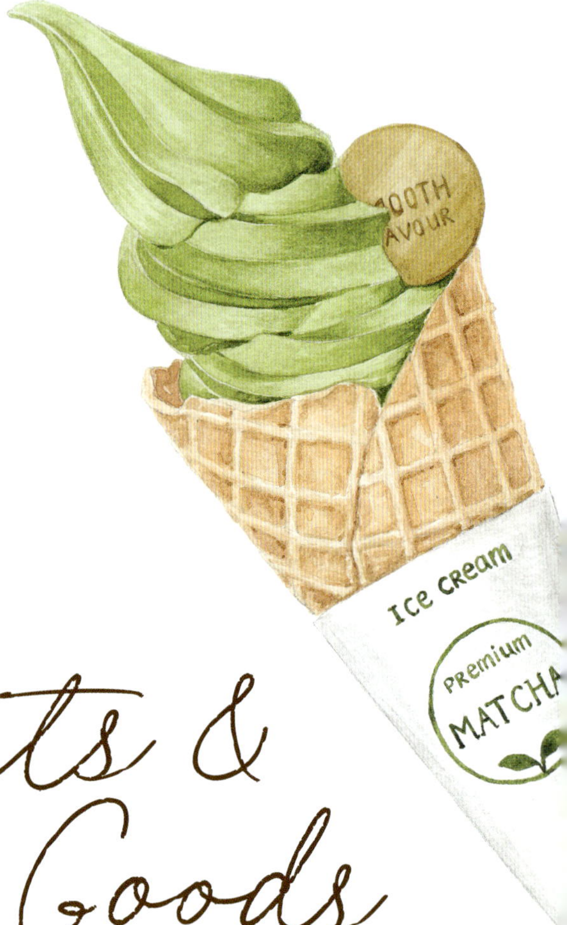

Desserts & Baked Goods

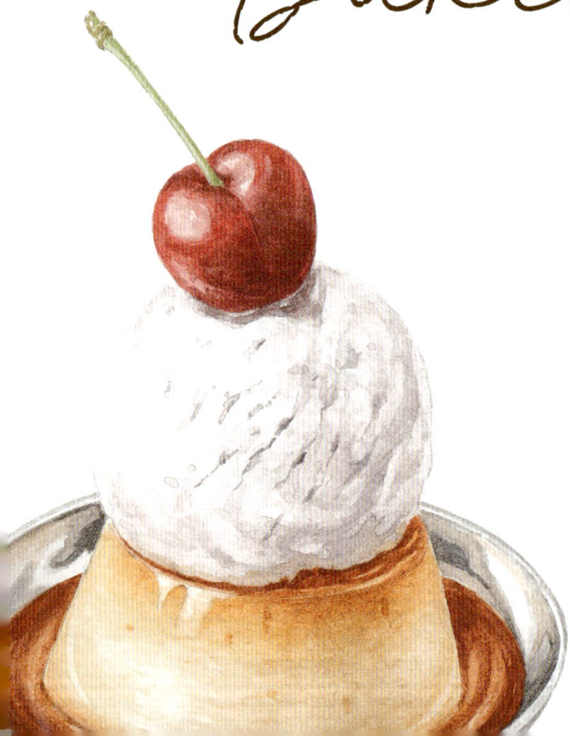

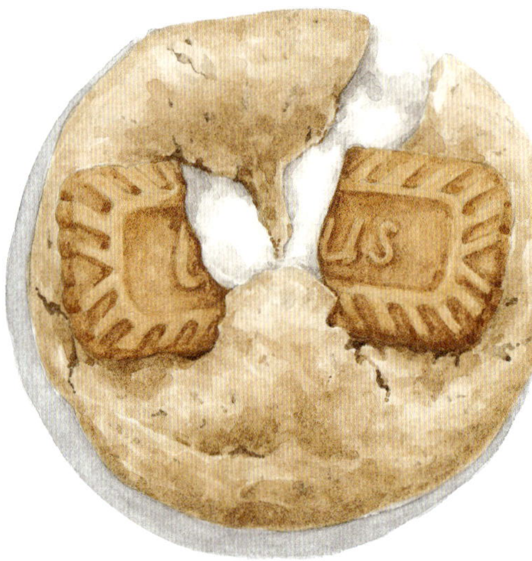

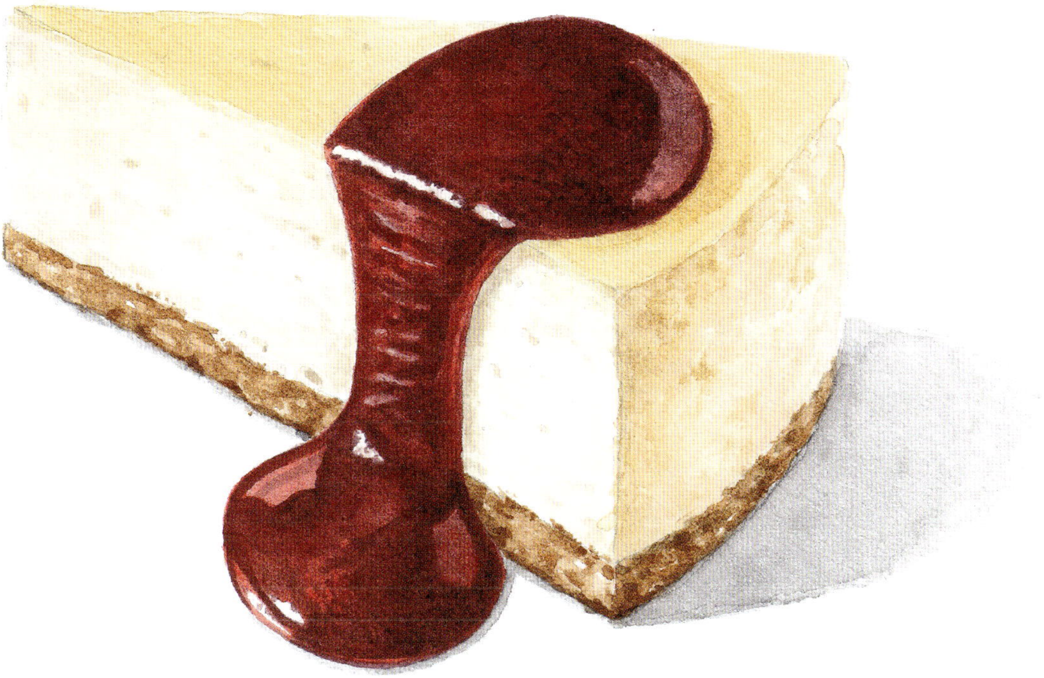

Project 16

Cheesecake

(Dimensions: W 3¾" x H 2¾" / W 9.5 cm x H 7 cm)

As we transition to a new section tailored for those with a sweet tooth, I want to provide an almost effortless beginning in terms of technicality. All phases for this illustration, from sketching and shading to painting, require only basic skills, yet the results are breathtaking and can serve as an inspiring step for beginners. For cheesecake enthusiasts, this exercise will enable you to paint numerous variations with different toppings and sauces, or any type of chilled cake with a creamy, cheesy filling, satisfying your creative exploration.

Brushes

Round brushes: sizes 1, 2 and 4

Color Palette

OBJECT	COLOR NAME	COLOR VALUES		
		Tea/Coffee	Milk	Cream
Cheesecake *(Filling)*	Hansa Yellow Quinacridone Gold			
	Hansa Yellow Quinacridone Gold Raw Umber			
Cheesecake *(Crust)*	Quinacridone Gold Burnt Sienna Raw Umber			
Berry sauce	Permanent Alizarin Crimson Permanent Violet			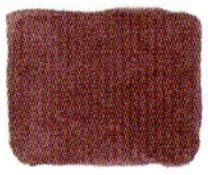
	Pyrrol Scarlet Permanent Alizarin Crimson			
Shadow	Jane's Grey			

For the filling, we only use "Tea" and "Coffee" values, as the color of the cream cheese mixture is delicate and subtle.

Viewpoint & Light Source

From my experience, the optimal viewpoint for a cake slice (wedge) is at eye level, as it captures three facets simultaneously: the top, the cut section and the curved side. This perspective effectively brings out the realistic appearance of our main subject and is sure to stimulate anyone's cravings. Here, I choose a light source coming from the left at a low angle to complement the dripping berry sauce, adding a sense of motion to an otherwise still cheesecake painting.

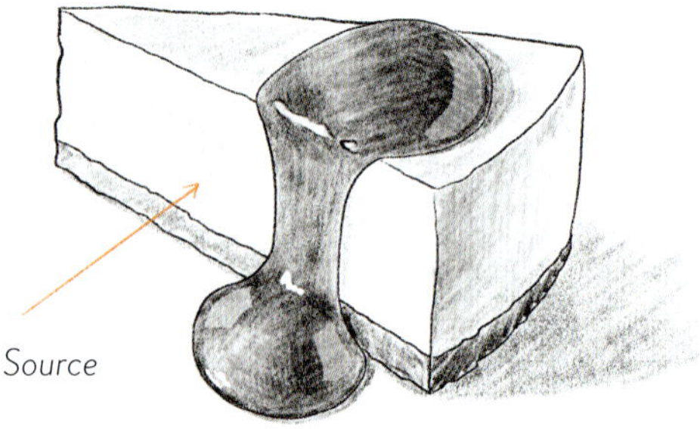

Light Source

Composition

This is perhaps the simplest composition in my series (besides Project 01: New York Bagel, page 39). True to my promise of simplicity, I've omitted any display plate or additional utensils, presenting just a wedge of cheesecake on an imaginary surface. It's a testament to the principle that less can be more. I allow the sauce to slightly extend beyond the edge to add visual interest, though it can also remain completely within the slice's boundary.

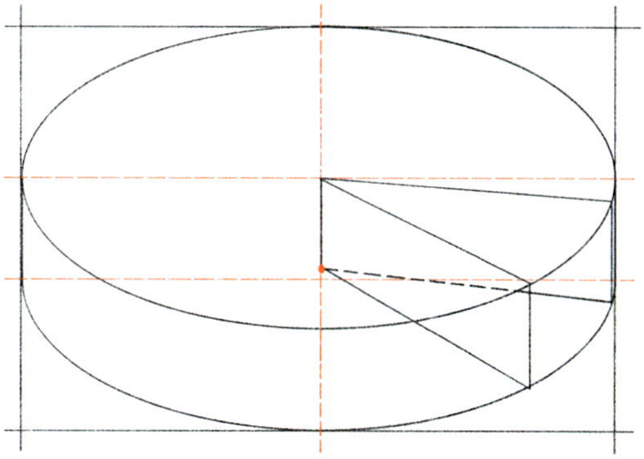

Let's Sketch!

A cheesecake slice is part of a larger log typically derived from a short cylinder shape. Here, I draw the entire log to illustrate the approach, but this step isn't necessary for you, as long as you can ensure your sketch adheres to the principles of sketching cylinder shapes that we learned in Chapter 1. By visualizing it within a cylindrical frame, you can select the optimal position for any cake slice to emphasize its beautiful toppings and layers.

Add some irregularities to the edges as you wish. Be mindful about where the sauce touches the imaginary surface, ensuring that both it and the cast shadow of the slice are on the same plane. Finally, use the eraser to lighten the sketch.

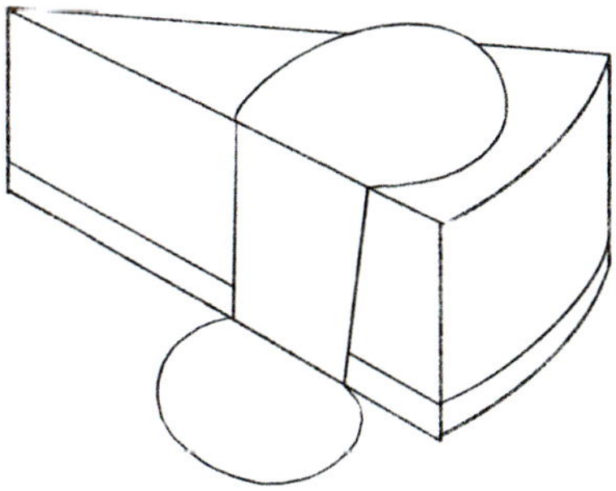

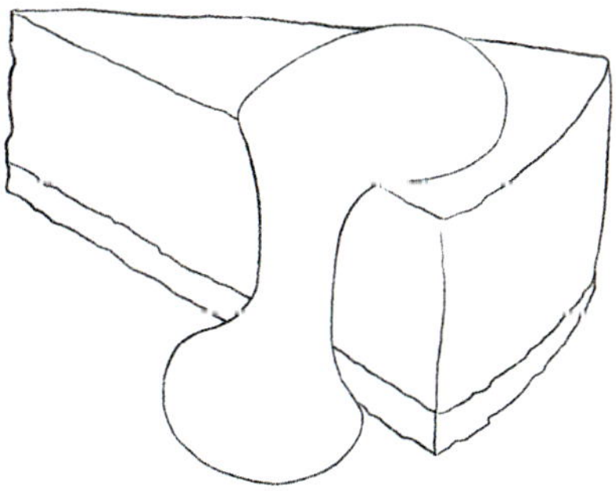

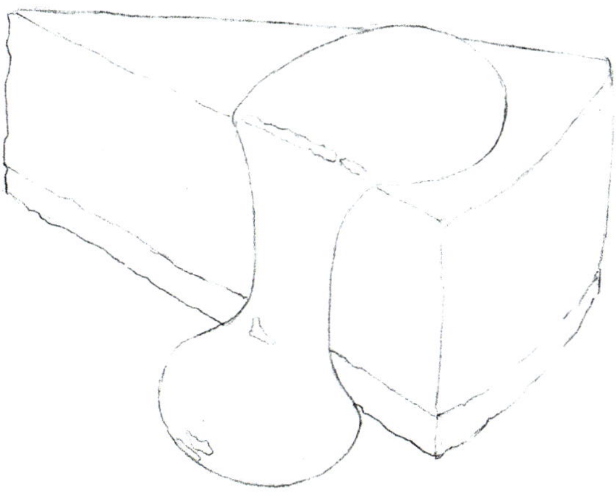

Let's Paint!

First Layer

Filling: Use round brush #4 to apply the "Tea" value across the entire filling area. As it's not facing the light source, give the right side a darker shade by adding a touch of Raw Umber to the current mixture. Dab the brush to leave more mixture on the edges that are close to the top and the cut section to create a sharp contrast between the highlight and shadow areas.

Crust: Select round brush #2 to apply the "Milk" value, employing the scumbling brushstroke to give an initial impression of its rough texture. Add more mixture to the right side to indicate the shadow area.

Berry Sauce: Apply the "Tea" value of the more purple mixture to the whole area, using round brush #4. Make sure to identify and leave empty spots to depict the glossy effect later. These reflections typically occur when the liquid faces a light source and changes direction as it drips downward from the top face, then spreads across an imaginary flat surface.

Berry sauce
Tea value

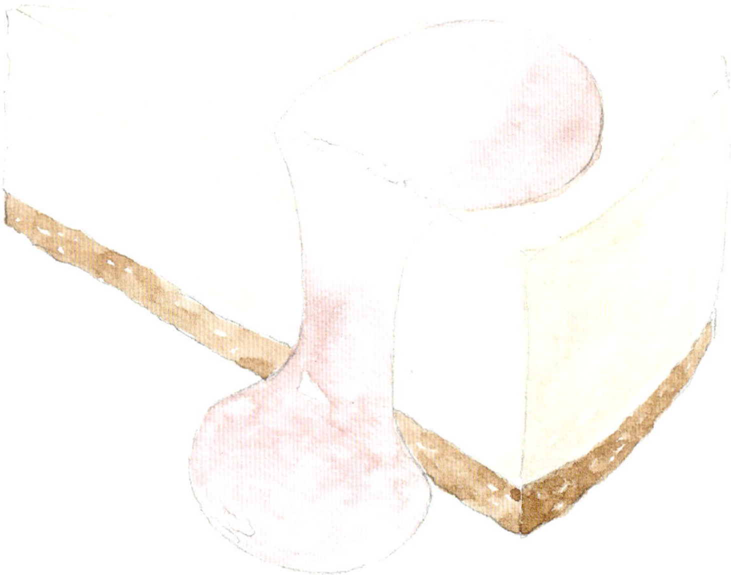

Cheesecake filling
Tea value

Cheesecake crust
Milk value

Second Layer

Filling: Continue using round brush #4 and the "Tea" value, applying it only to the cut section on the left. We need to maintain this side as the brightest (with the least pigment) since it faces the light source. Then, switch to the "Coffee" value and apply it to the top surface to enhance the sense of depth in the painting. Next, add a touch of Raw Umber into the current "Coffee" mixture to paint the shadowed side on the right, ensuring it's the darkest shade among the three surfaces. Slightly draw a vertical line on the right of the dripping sauce to indicate its shadow onto the cut section.

Artist's Tip: Be patient while painting light-colored objects. Avoid adding too much pigment at once, as it may alter the true color of the object. Instead, apply "Tea" value mixtures multiple times along the boundary between the highlight and shadow areas to gradually and effectively define the 3-D shape.

Crust: Repeat the steps in the first layer, with "Cream" value this time to enhance the texture. Instead of covering the whole area, focus on the darker strokes that have been created in the first layer to deepen their shade further. Leave the lighter strokes as they are for now to maintain a fitting contrast with the filling.

Berry Sauce: Use round brush #4 to apply a thin layer of water to the sauce, preparing for the wet-on-wet technique (page 23). Immediately afterward, apply the "Milk" value from the Berry mixture to it, referring to the Light Source Shading Sketch (page 152) if uncertain. At the upper section, ensure a slightly smooth transition toward the light-purple shade painted from the first layer. This part will be a midtone reflection that helps emphasize the thickness of the sauce. For the vertical section, move your brush from side to side, skipping some strokes in between to form some small lighter gaps that mimic light reflections on the sauce.

Berry sauce
Milk value

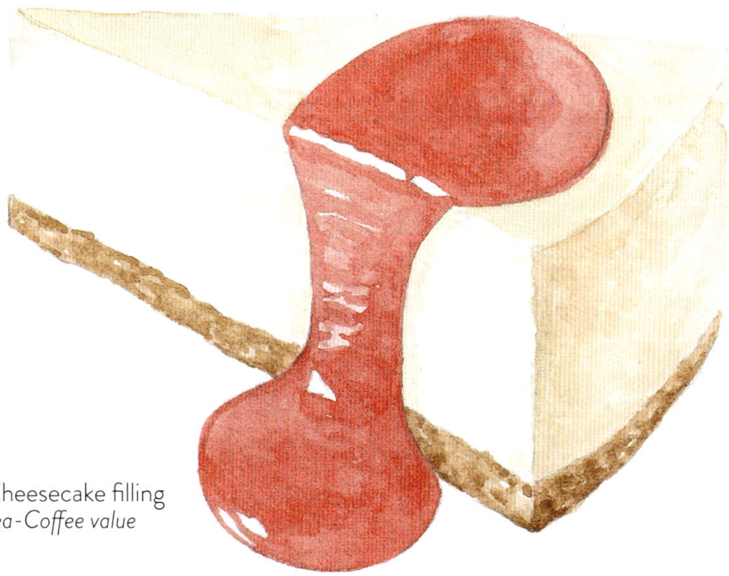

Cheesecake filling
Tea-Coffee value

Cheesecake crust
Cream value

Third Layer

Filling: Now that its 3-D shape has been adequately formed in the second layer, we'll focus on depicting finer details on its surfaces. Use round brush #1 and "Coffee" value mixture to add random brushstrokes on the left and right sides to indicate the texture. Alternate between dab-and-pull strokes, short strokes and dots to enhance the realistic feel. Pick up round brush #4 to add another flat wash layer on the top surface to bring out the yellowish cheese color. Note that the top face is fairly smooth compared to the sides. Finally, deepen the shadow of the dripping sauce on the cut section.

Crust: Repeat the process from the second layer to deepen the brown shade a bit more.

Berry Sauce: Use the tip of round brush #2 to draw thin lines around the brightest reflection areas with the "Cream" value of the more purple mixture to create sharper boundaries. Next, apply the same mixture to remaining areas that should be in the darkest shade (refer to the Light Source Shading Sketch). For a smooth transition toward the midtone, dip your brush into the "Milk" value of the same mixture instead of using clear water, and blend it out. This gradient wash technique (page 25) gives the sauce a vibrant undertone.

Berry sauce
Milk value

Berry sauce
Cream value

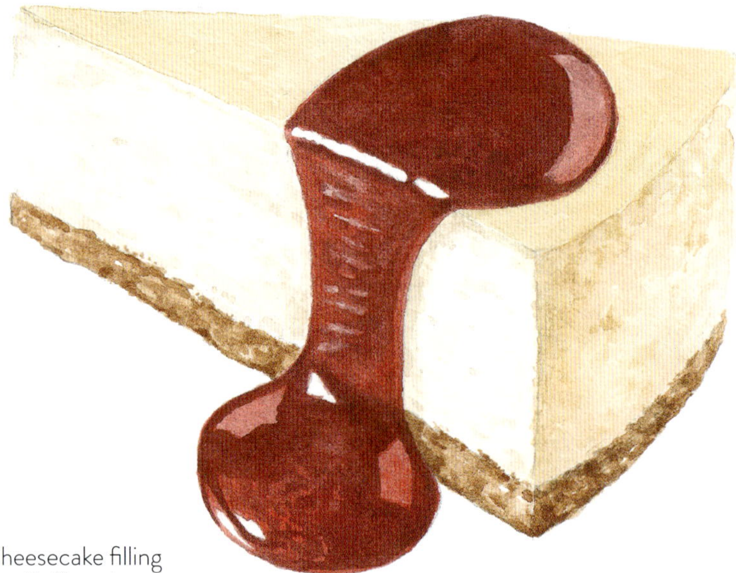

Cheesecake filling
Tea-Coffee value

Cheesecake crust
Cream value

Finishing Touches

Filling: Use the tip of round brush #1 to deepen some details with the "Coffee" value mixture on the two vertical sides. For specific spots, use a mixture that includes a hint of Raw Umber, but be cautious not to overdo it to maintain a variety of shades for a realistic effect.

Here, I also add another layer of "Coffee" value to the top surface to enhance the yellow tone. When this layer dries, add shadow for the sauce using the same solution.

Crust: Deepen the bottom of the crust to anchor it more firmly to our imaginary table. Continue painting with uneven brushstrokes with round brush #1 and "Cream" value.

Berry Sauce: Use round brush #2 and the gradient wash technique to apply another "Cream" value layer to the shadow areas, which are usually darker around the reflection areas. Squint your eyes to check if the reflection spots are too bright; if so, you can add a layer of "Tea" value to dim them down.

Add cast shadow for the side, using round brush #4 and "Coffee" value of a gray mixture. Begin at the edge where the left and right sides intersect and blend out toward the upper right. Employ the gradient wash technique to lighten the shadow the farther it extends from the object. Finally, switch to round brush #1 to draw a thin line of the same mixture along the bottom of the left side and around the sauce to depict their shadows.

Berry sauce
Tea-Cream value

Shadow
Coffee value

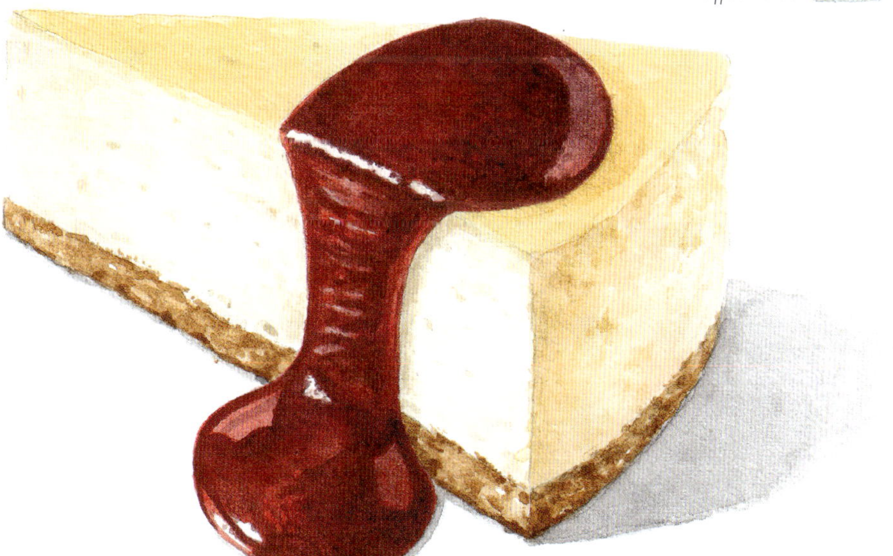

Cheesecake filling
Coffee value

Cheesecake crust
Cream value

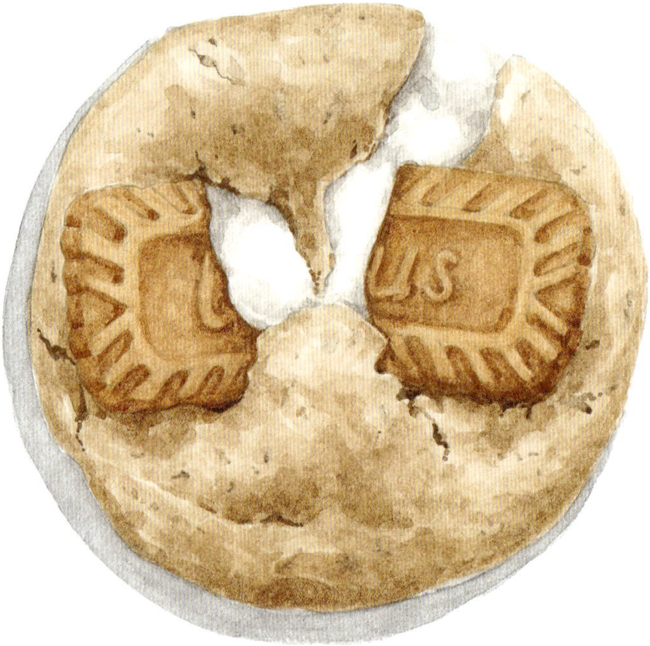

Project 17

S'mores Cookie

(Dimensions: W 3¼" x H 3¼" / W 8 cm x H 8 cm)

You don't have to be a Boy or Girl Scout to appreciate the diverse flavors and textures of this treat! Nor do you need to be an expert or even an intermediate food illustrator to complete this project with a bang! After this non-complex project, I bet you'll want s'more of this soothing meditation for your soul. But do not underestimate the broad applications of the skills you'll learn here, as I'll walk you through the process of depicting three different textures: the gooey marshmallow, the cracked cookie and the crunchy, fine-grained Biscoff®.

Brushes

Round brushes: sizes 1, 2 and 4

Spotter brush: size 3/0

Color Palette

OBJECT	COLOR NAME	COLOR VALUES		
		Tea/Coffee	Milk	Cream
Cookie	Raw Umber Quinacridone Gold Pyrrol Orange			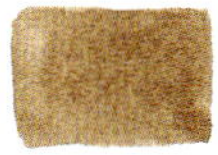
	Raw Umber			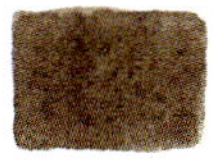
Biscoff	Quinacridone Gold Burnt Umber Pyrrol Orange		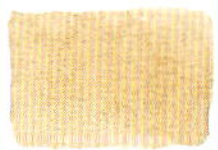	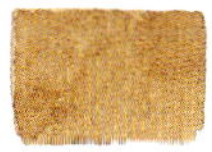
Marshmallow	Raw Umber Jane's Grey			
Shadow	Jane's Grey			

Viewpoint & Light Source

As the cookie is relatively flat, I opt for the top-down view to fully see the details on top of it. A sitting eye-level viewpoint might also work here, but you must select the angle carefully to capture the marshmallow spillover. The light source is from the upper right corner, casting shadows toward the lower left, including the shadow of the Biscoff onto the cookie surface. Note that the light source should be placed high enough to prevent overly elongated shadows, causing distraction from the main subject.

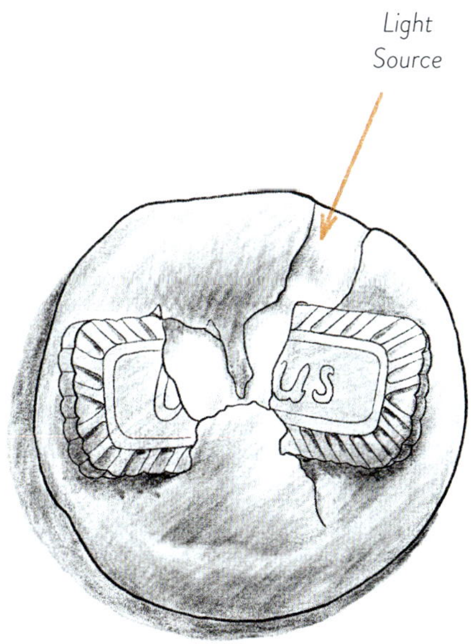

Composition

Since we only have one food item here, the focus will be placing the three elements within it to achieve visual coherence. The melty marshmallow leaks out in a random way, and two Biscoff pieces jammed down boldly bring life and appeal to the whole layout.

Let's Sketch!

With this viewpoint, our cookie looks almost round. As usual, start with a frame for the main circle, then determine where the Biscoff pieces will be by drawing a 3-D flat box. Only add details after indicating where the cracks will be for the marshmallow to leak out, ensuring you're satisfied with the overall composition. The Biscoff involves intricate features that may require patience but will make the painting phase much easier.

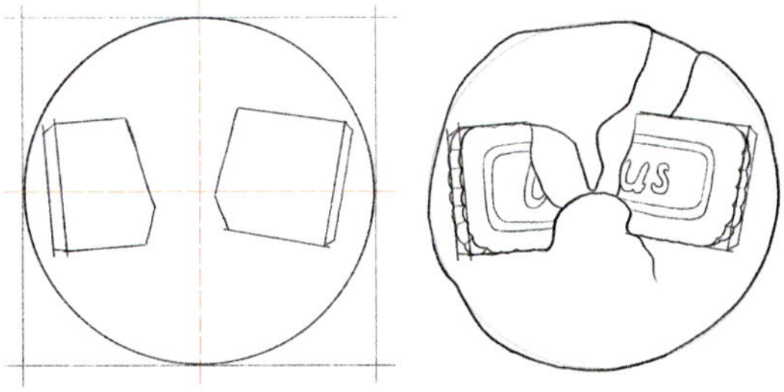

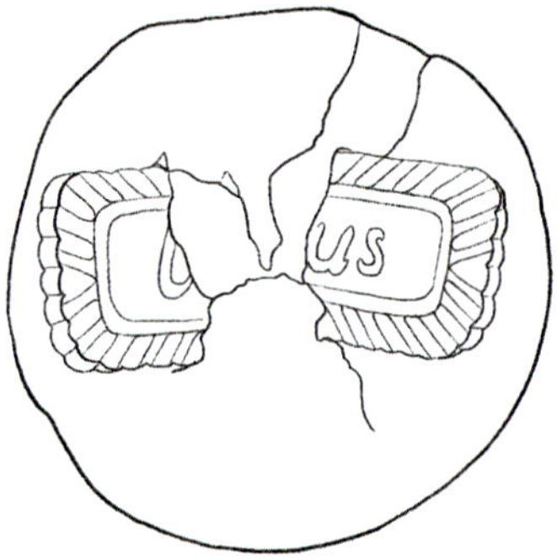

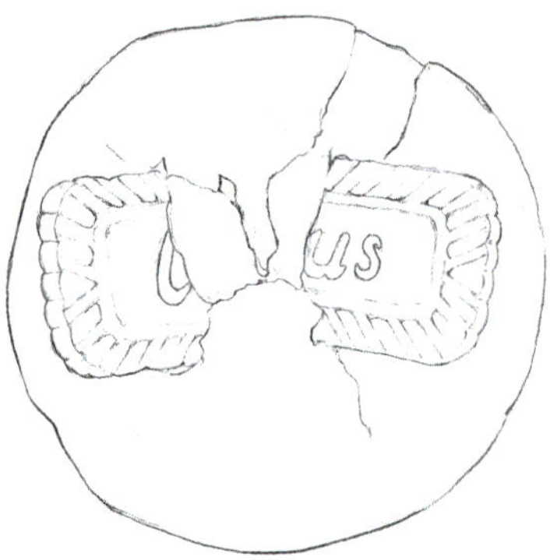

Let's Paint!

First Layer

Biscoff: Apply a flat wash of the "Milk" value mixture, using round brush #4.

Cookie: Keep using round brush #4 to apply the "Tea" value mixture across the whole area. Since the cookie has a lovely golden-brown color and a crispy exterior, there will naturally be some slightly darker areas. Therefore, letting your brush create some uneven bleed on the paper is absolutely fine and can assist in depicting texture later on.

Marshmallow: Select round brush #2 to apply the "Tea" value solution around the edges of the leak next to the cookie dough. On one hand, most of it lies underneath the cookie, so there will be a bit of shadow cast on it. On the other hand, it's pressed down by the Biscoff pieces, causing it to bulge and have a lighter shade in those parts.

Keep this notion in mind and repeat this step multiple times for the second and third layer until you achieve the desired shade.

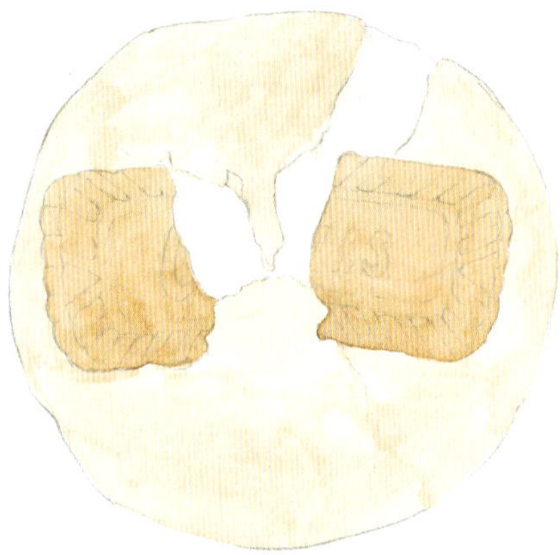

Biscoff
Milk value

Marshmallow
Tea value

Cookie
Tea value

Second Layer

Biscoff: Use round brush #2 to apply the "Cream" value to the "teeth" around the perimeter and the inner edge of the center rectangle. Give the thickness a bit more solution as it's not facing the light.

Cookie: Use round brush #4 to add a layer of the "Milk" value mixture. Focus on adding more mixture to the shadow areas, using scumbling brushstrokes to gradually create texture.

Third Layer

Biscoff: Add another layer of "Cream" value to the same areas as in the second layer, using round brush #1 to enrich the golden-brown color. Concentrate the pigment more heavily on the sides, gradually lightening it in an upward direction, following the light source. However, note that the center rectangle is indented, so its shadow area will be in the upper right corner. You can also begin adding shadows for the letters.

Cookie: Use round brush #2 to add the "Cream" value mixture to the shadow areas, using scumbling brushstrokes strictly for application and blending. Instead of dipping the brush in water while doing the scumbling brushstroke, add the "Milk" value when blending to keep the brush moist but still retain the rich color of the mixture. Add a darker shade to the area under the Biscoff to indicate its shadow onto the cookie and along the cracks that are not facing the light source.

Artist's Tip: The blending process here should be done only when the previous layer is dry or slightly damp, depending on how crispy you want your cookie to appear. After applying the thick mixture on paper, dip your brush in clear water or the "Tea" value of the same mixture to dilute the solution on your brush. Use this diluted solution to blend out the thick application. This approach makes the process easier to manage and prevents sharp brushstrokes on dry paper.

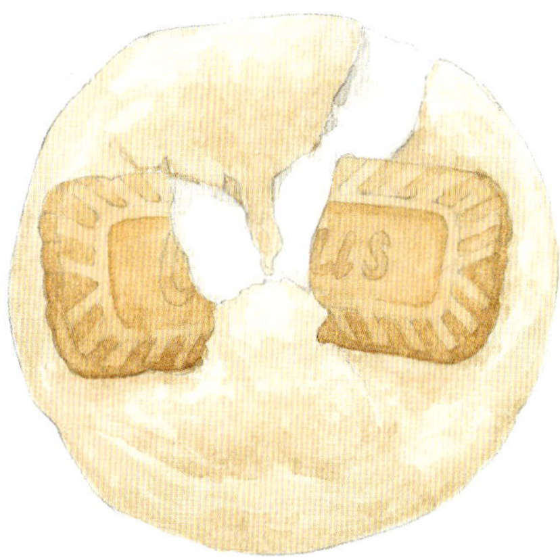

Biscoff
Cream value

Marshmallow
Tea value

Cookie
Milk value

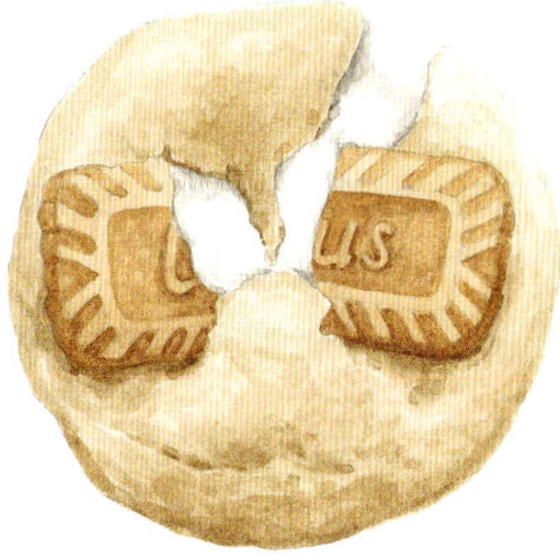

Biscoff
Cream value

Marshmallow
Tea value

Cookie
Milk-Cream value

Finishing Touches

Biscoff: Continue using the "Cream" value to further deepen the details, particularly focusing on intensifying the darkest corners. Depict the areas where the Biscoff pieces meet the marshmallow with a darker shade compared to the rest to emphasize how they were pressed into the cookie.

Cookie: Apply the "Cream" value of the warm brown mixture to shadow areas. Squint your eyes to compare the contrast between the highlights and shadows. The cookie's texture has a low contrast between these areas, so the highlights should not stand out too much; if they do, add a layer of "Tea" value to dim them down.

Use a spotter brush to add the dark-brown mixture in "Cream" value to the lower edges of the Biscoff to depict its shadow on the cookie. Additionally, use the brush tip to draw tiny cracks and random spots on the surface.

Marshmallow: Besides the "Tea" value, you can add a gray mixture in "Coffee" value to darken the shadow around the edges.

Add the cast shadow of the cookie on the paper using round brush #2 and gray mixture in "Coffee" value.

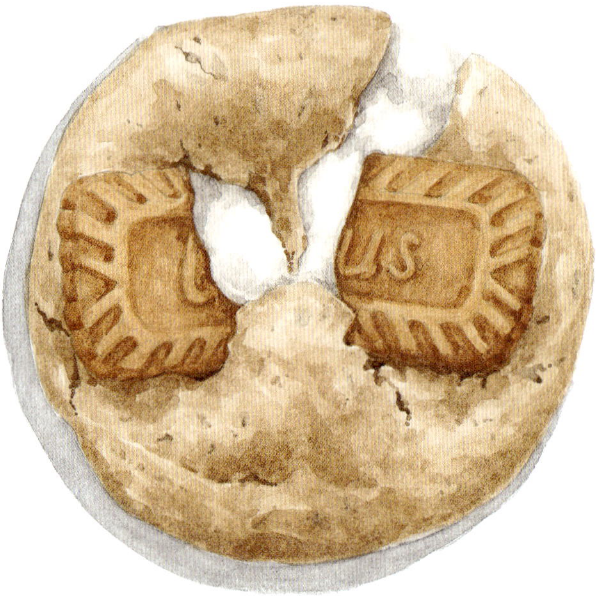

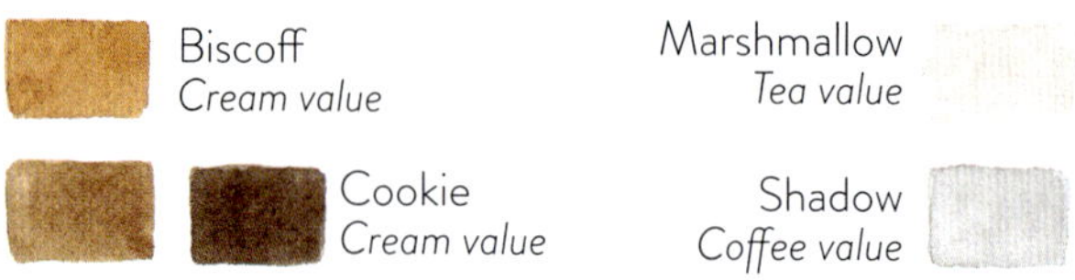

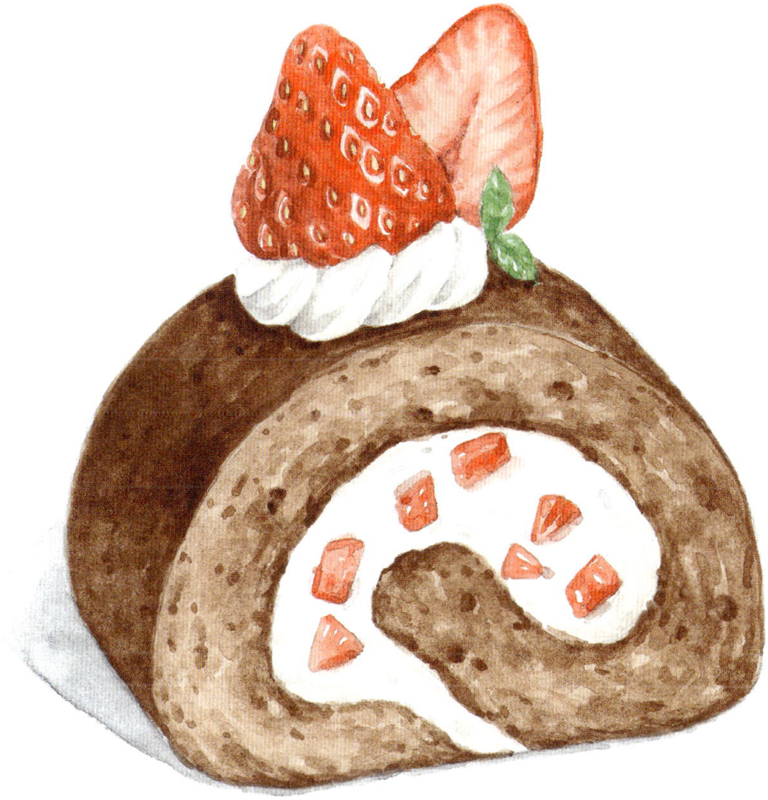

Project 18

Strawberry Chocolate Roll Cake

(Dimensions: W 3⅞" x H 4⅛" / W 9.8 cm x H 10.5 cm)

Our desserts collection would not be complete without a chocolate treat. I choose the roll cake to maintain a variety of shapes in the food illustration world. It's also an opportunity to widen your skills in depicting textures, as sponge cake differs from toast (Project 02: Toasted Bread with Fruits & Cream, page 45) or baguettes (Project 05: Shakshuka, page 66) with its softer and more foamy appearance, as the name suggests. Presumably, the challenge in this project will be painting the outer skin of the strawberry with all the seeds (achenes, to be precise) included. As I have emphasized many times in this book, there is nothing too difficult to illustrate if you refine your ability to translate elements into basic shapes—and this delight will serve as another example of just that.

Brushes

Round brushes: sizes 1, 2 and 4

Spotter brush: size 3/0

Color Palette

OBJECT	COLOR NAME	COLOR VALUES		
		Tea/Coffee	Milk	Cream
Strawberry	Pyrrol Scarlet			
	Permanent Alizarin Crimson			
Mint leaves	Hooker's Green Sap Green (Cream value)			
Chocolate cake	Burnt Umber Burnt Sienna Pyrrol Orange Permanent Violet			
Cream Shadow	Jane's Grey			

Viewpoint & Light Source

To showcase the appealing cross-section of the slice, its thickness and the toppings, there is no better viewpoint than eye level. The light source will be positioned on the right, slightly tilted toward the front, casting the cake's shadow to the left and backward.

Composition

Creating a nice composition here is not a difficult task, as the slice and toppings themselves are already contained and pleasing to the eye. The only consideration might be the height of the toppings in relation to the cake and the overall layout.

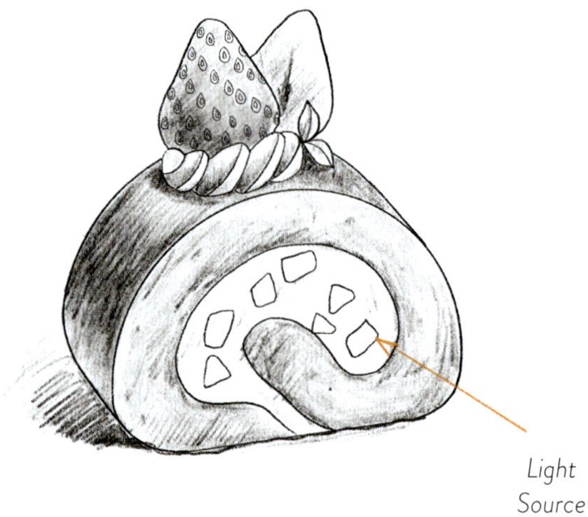

Let's Sketch!

Firstly, a slice from this type of cake is derived from a long cylinder pressed against a surface underneath, giving its bottom a relatively flat appearance. Another way to visualize it is as a box with a curved top. With either approach, you can begin with a frame and then add rounded corners and layers of cream in a loose spiral.

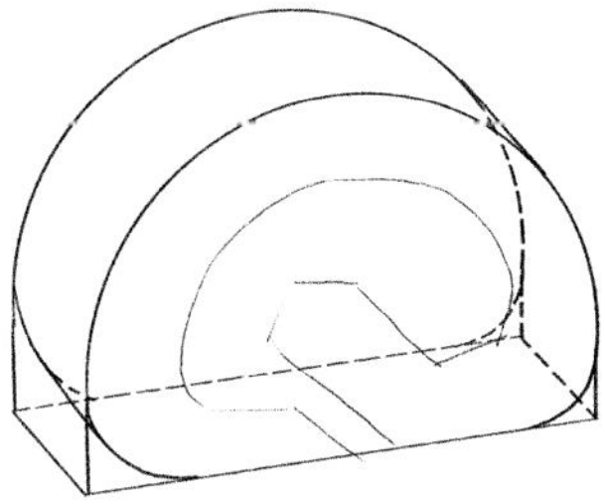

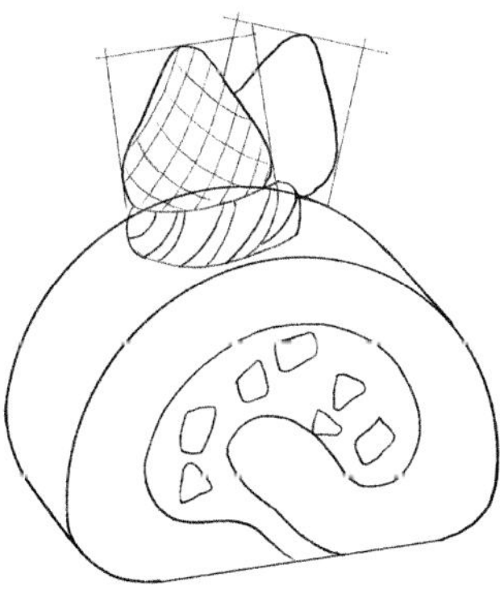

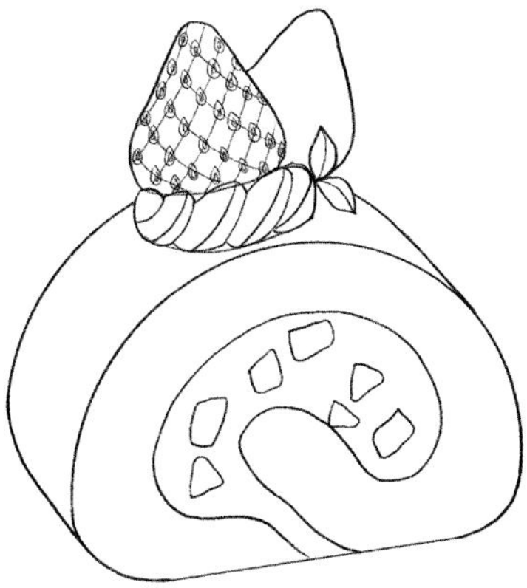

Inside the cream, there will be strawberry chunks added to introduce color and visual interest to the front surface. As for the half-cut strawberry piece on top, its little seeds are placed at the points of a lattice. Note that the gaps between them should decrease in size as they move further away from your viewpoint.

Here is a magnified view of the seeds: You can observe that they are situated within small indentations (pockets, to simplify between us), where shading rules will be applied accordingly. And finally, lighten the whole sketch to prepare for the painting phase.

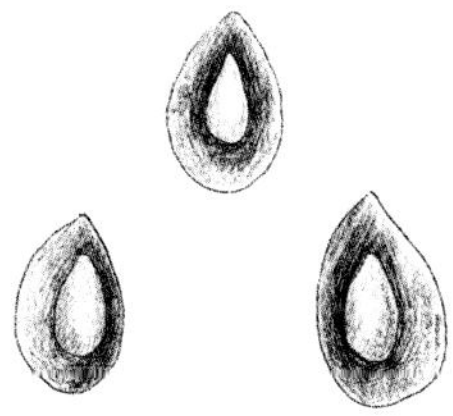

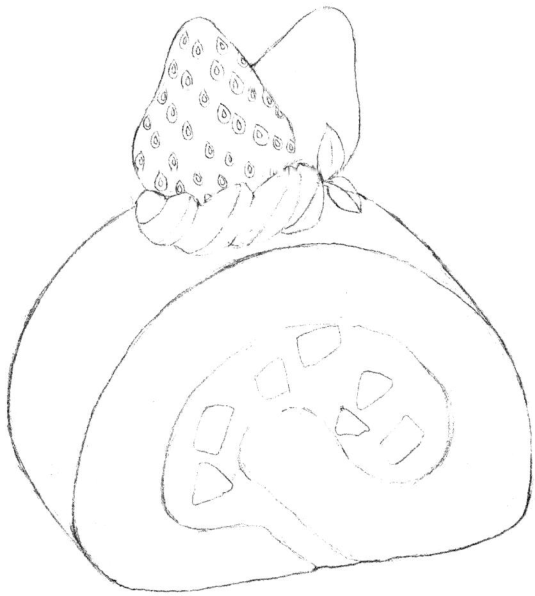

Let's Paint!

First Layer

Chocolate Cake: Select round brush #4 and apply a generous amount of the "Tea" value mixture to the whole cake surface, using the scumbling brushstroke. Don't leave any white space on the paper: it's chocolate sponge cake, so even the brightest highlight will be in a brown tone.

Strawberry: For the front half, use a spotter brush to first cover the tiny seeds with a light-yellow mixture; I choose Hansa Yellow in "Coffee" value here. Once it dries, use the same brush to paint the red mixture in "Milk" value around each seed.

For the half at the back, pick up round brush #2 to wash a thin layer of water on paper first. Then, apply the "Coffee" mixture to the rim, pulling the tip of the brush toward the center of the strawberry. Apply the same mixture to the center along the height of the strawberry as well, starting from the base and lifting the brush upward. The process should be done quickly enough before the paper dries to create the desired bleeding effect.

For the chunks, use round brush #1 and the "Coffee" mixture to paint the base layer. Then, add the "Milk" value solution to one edge of each piece and drag the color out to the opposite edge, leaving some small gaps in between.

Whipped Cream: Apply a thin layer of gray mixture to the shadow sides of the little swirls on top with round brush #2, which are mainly on the left.

Mint Leaves: Use round brush #1 to apply the "Tea" value, employing the scumbling brushstroke. Make sure to leave some white space.

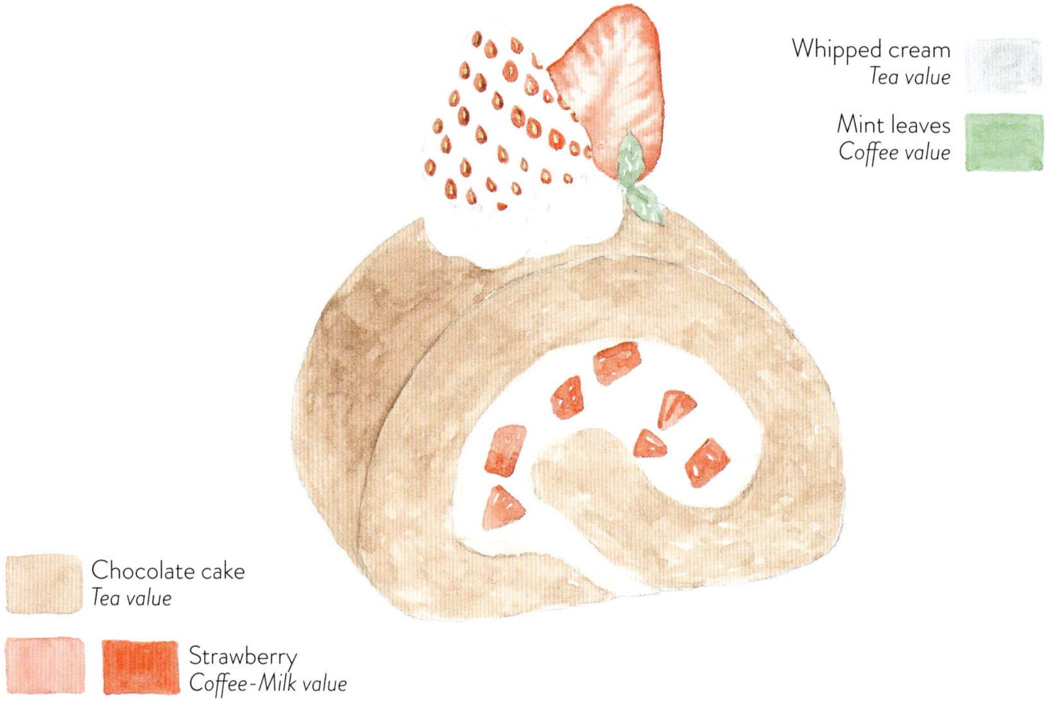

Second Layer

Chocolate Cake: When the first layer is completely dry, keep using round brush #4 to scumble the "Milk" value to the front side to enhance the texture. For its top surface, switch to the "Cream" value, ensuring a smoother texture by reducing the gaps between your scumbling strokes.

Strawberry: For the front half, apply the "Cream" value of Pyrrol Scarlet to the entire white space with round brush #1. Drop the mixture first on the right side and then spread it toward the left, leaving a thin white space around some seeds in the middle-right side to depict the reflection of light. As you approach the left rear, dip your brush into clear water to slightly dilute the mixture, creating a gradient wash at this end. While some seeds may fuse into this layer of red mixture, keep in mind that each yellow seed is surrounded by a narrow pocket. This notion will help you execute the next layer.

> **Artist's Tip:** When painting the strawberry, just focus on the area you are working on so as not to be confused by the other details. After the primary layers, the strawberry shape and texture will appear.

For the half at the back, use round brush #1 to apply a thin line of "Milk" value around the rim.

Whipped Cream: For the swirls, use round brush #1 to apply another layer of gray in "Tea" value to the lower left sections.

For the spiral, with the same solution, add more details by applying gentle strokes along the curve and around the strawberry chunks.

Mint Leaves: Deepen the green shade of the mint leaves with the "Cream" value mixture.

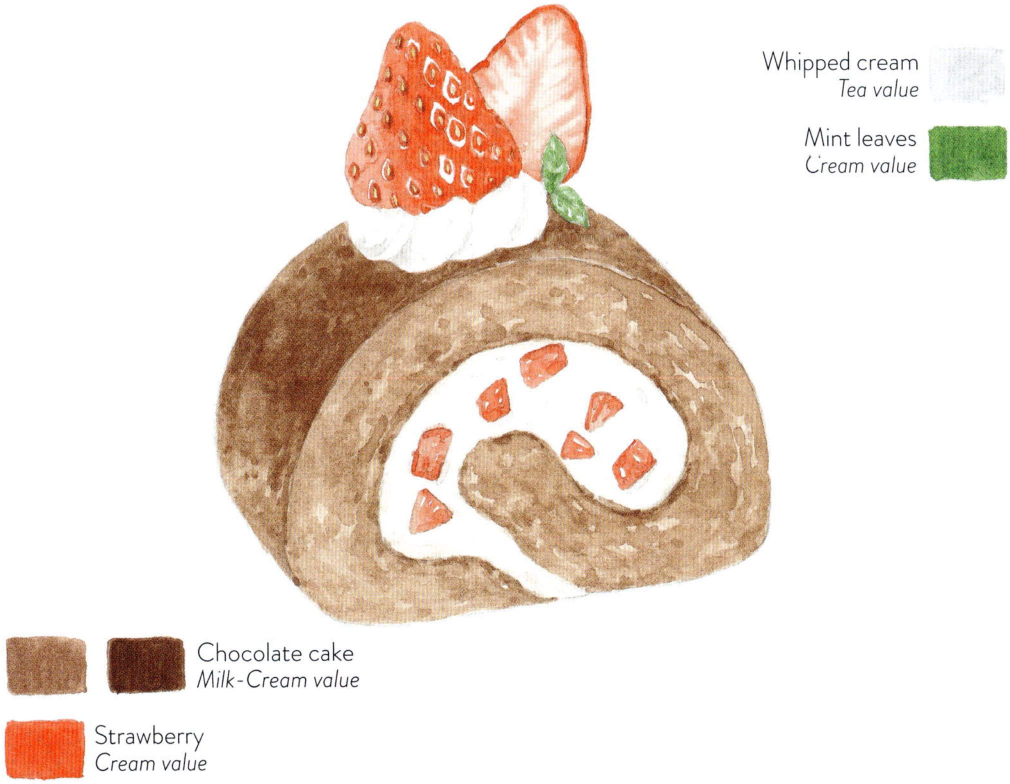

Third Layer

Chocolate Cake: For the front side, use round brush #2 to scumble the "Cream" value along the edges where it meets the white cream. This will highlight the cream and reveal the cake's texture depth. On the outer arc, use the brush tip to apply darker strokes to illustrate air pockets, enhancing the soft and fluffy texture.

For the top surface, use round brush #4 and the same "Cream" value. Apply more mixture for this side to make a deeper brown shade, increasing the contrast between the two facets. The texture here should be slightly less pronounced than on the front to further complement the depth of our object. Always adhere to the basic shading rule for cylinder shapes—the darkest shade should be on the left. Use concentrated scumbling strokes instead of a flat wash to preserve a textured appearance.

Strawberry: For the front half, prepare the "Cream" value of the Permanent Alizarin Crimson color and apply it to the shadow area at the bottom left, using round brush #1. Strictly exclude the pocket lining around each yellow seed. Again, employ gradient wash technique (page 25) to blend this application out toward the top right. After that, deepen the red border around certain seeds in the midtone area using the same mixture.

For the half at the back, add the "Cream" value to the center.

For the chunks, mix a small amount of Strawberry solution into the gray mixture and apply light strokes around them. Be careful not to overdo it to ensure the cream spiral stays white.

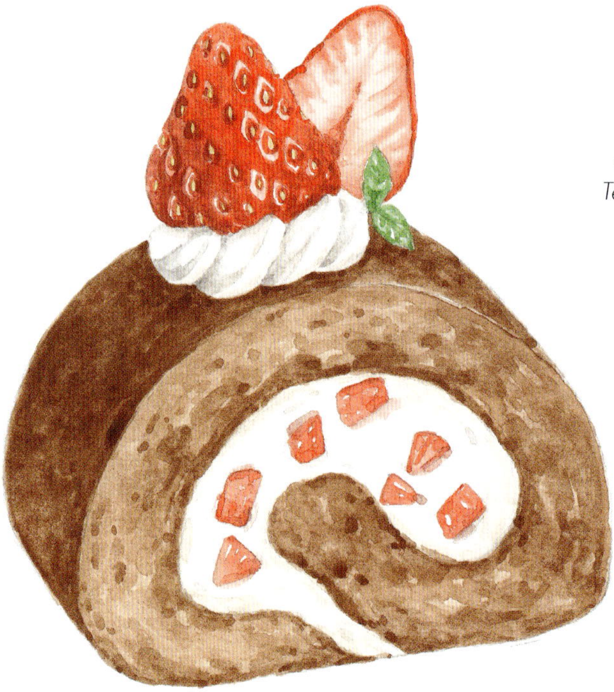

Cream
Tea value

Chocolate cake
Cream value

Strawberry
Cream value

Finishing Touches

Chocolate Cake: For the front side, add another layer of "Cream" value to deepen the areas that we worked on in the third layer, using round brush #1.

For the top surface, switch to round brush #2 and add another "Cream" value layer to the shadow area, particularly around the whipped cream swirls on top to depict their shadows.

Strawberry: For the front half, use the tip of the spotter brush to paint very thin borders around the yellow seeds with the "Cream" value to create more depth.

For the half at the back, wash a thin layer of "Tea" value onto the whole piece to give it a warmer look.

For the chunks, add one to two strokes of "Cream" value to each one to sharpen the details.

Whipped Cream: For the swirls, repeat the steps in the second layer one to two more times to effectively bring out their shapes. As with all light objects, always use "Tea" values and gradually deepen the shadow areas.

For the spiral, mix a touch of brown into the gray mixture for a warmer tone. Then, lightly scumble this mixture onto the designated darker areas to emphasize the spiral's foamy texture.

Use round brush #2 to paint the shadow for the slice, using the "Milk" value of Jane's Grey. The shadow should be most defined closest to the light source and soften as it extends farther away.

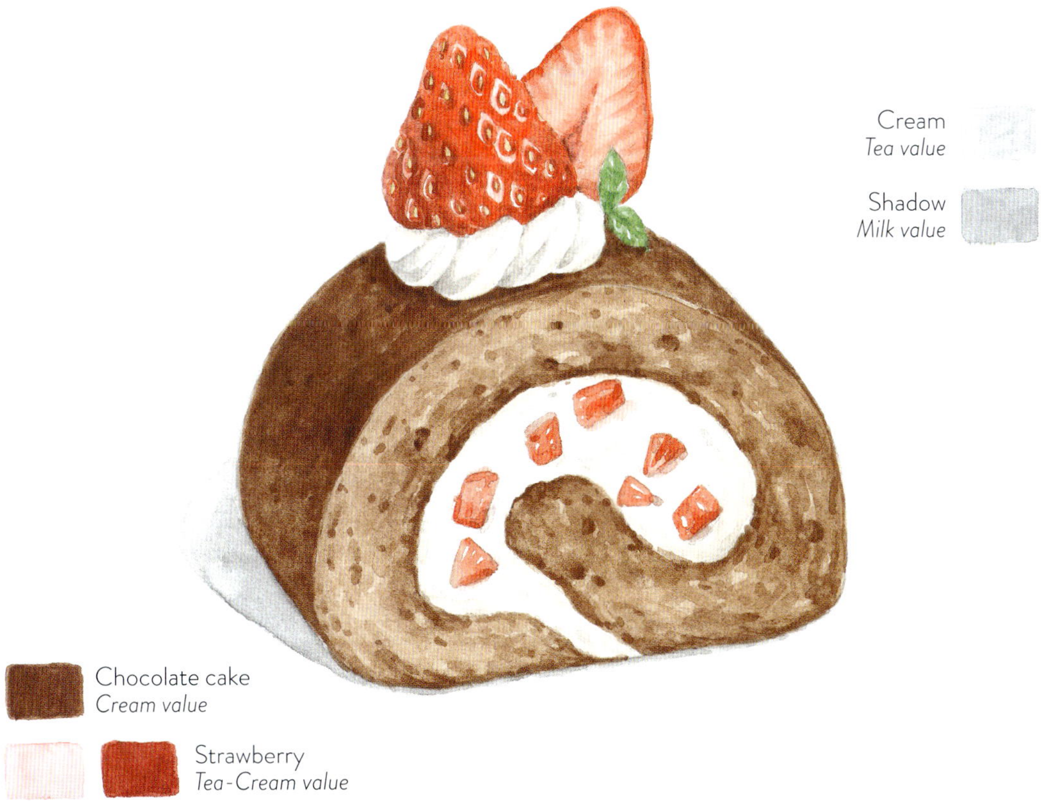

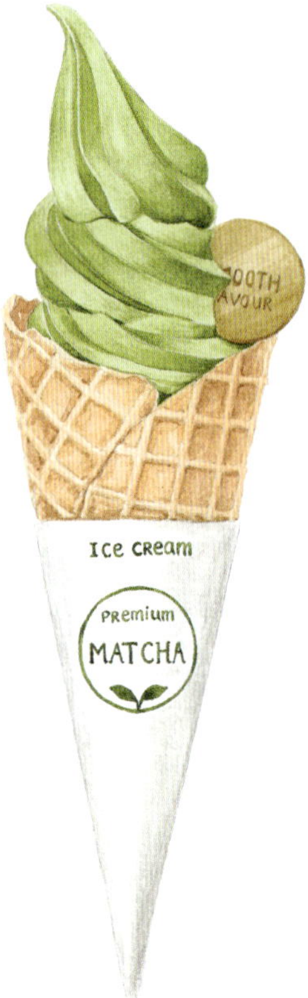

Project 19

Matcha Ice Cream Cone

(Dimensions: W 2¼" x H 7½" / W 5.8 cm x H 19 cm)

If you've ever lived in a hot climate, you'll understand the sheer comfort and relief that a soft-serve ice cream can offer. Among the myriad flavors, matcha is my personal favorite, cherished for its refreshing grassy aroma and delightful nutty undertones. Despite its simpler-than-ever standalone composition, this project presents its own set of challenges: understanding the structure of soft serve and effectively depicting the crisscrossed pattern characteristic of waffle cones. This could still be a walk in the park if you already grasp all the fundamental knowledge and practice introduced in my book. But if you're simply a die-hard fan of matcha ice cream, that alone is reason enough to jump right in!

Brushes

Round brushes: sizes 1, 2 and 4

Spotter brush: size 3/0

Color Palette

OBJECT	COLOR NAME	COLOR VALUES		
		Tea/Coffee	Milk	Cream
Waffle cone *(Mixture 1)*	**Quinacridone Gold Pyrrol Orange New Gamboge**			
Waffle cone *(Mixture 2)*	**Burnt Umber Pyrrol Orange New Gamboge**			
Matcha soft serve	**Sap Green Hansa Yellow**			
Paper tag	**Quinacridone Gold Raw Umber**			
Cone wrapper	**Jane's Grey**			

As you can see, there are two mixtures for the waffle cone. Mixture 1 is more orange and will be the main tone for the highlight area, while Mixture 2 has a tint of red and is more brownish, which will be used for the shadow area and to depict darker details on the cone.

Viewpoint & Light Source

This is the second of only two projects featuring the complete side viewpoint in the entire chapter. That doesn't diminish its usefulness; when used correctly, it works wonders! Even though the cone is placed midair without a surface to cast shadows on, we still need a proper light source for shading. It will be coming from the left, approximately at the height of the middle of the cone.

Composition

Our standalone object consists of four elements: soft serve neatly placed in a waffle cone partially wrapped with white paper featuring printed text, garnished with a small circular paper tag. The wrapping paper serves two purposes: It adds visual interest and offers an opportunity to develop skills in depicting paper and practicing brush writing.

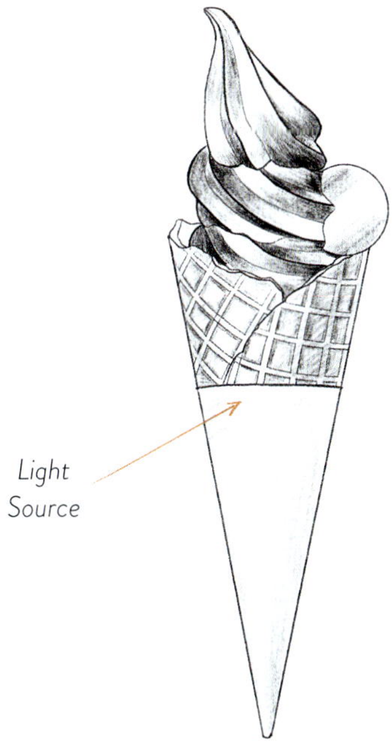

Let's Sketch!

Start with a general frame that defines the width and height for the three primary elements. The waffle cone is conical in shape (refer to Chapter 1, Sketching, page 14). Its opening slopes downward, exposing a portion of the soft serve. When creating the crisscrossed pattern, remember to narrow the gaps between the lines gradually as they move away from your viewpoint.

The soft serve swirls into three spirals, beginning larger at the base, positioned below the cone's opening, and narrowing to a point at the top, resembling the shape of the cone. In my sketch, the red lines correspond to the red dots on the star-shape nozzle (in top view) and the black lines align with the black dots. The red lines are further from your viewpoint, while the black lines are closer.

After that, draw the circle for the tag, partially pressed into the soft serve. Once you are satisfied with your sketch, use an eraser to lighten it and get ready for the next phase: painting.

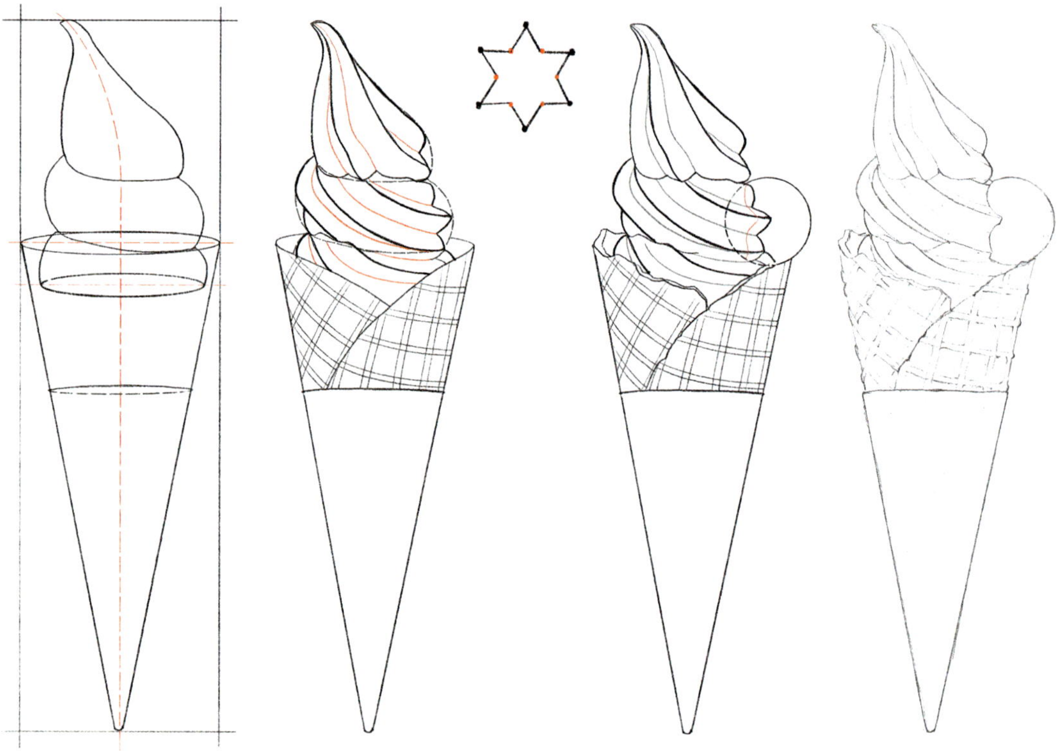

Let's Paint!

First Layer

Soft Serve: Use round brush #4 to apply a flat wash on the paper, using the "Coffee" value of the green mixture.

Waffle Cone: Use round brush #4 to apply the "Tea" value of Mixture 1, leaving a bit more solution on the midtone and shadow areas.

Wrapper: Use round brush #4 to apply the "Tea" value of the gray mixture on the left and right edges of the cone (midtone and shadow areas). Then, smoothly blend it out toward the highlight by using gradient wash technique (page 25).

Paper Tag: Use round brush #2 to wash a layer of the "Coffee" value across the whole surface.

Second Layer

Soft Serve: I include a chart demonstrating orange strips where you'll apply the solution. Use round brush #1 to add the "Milk" value to them, starting from the bottom right of each segment, then blend it upward and to the left using gradient wash technique.

Waffle Cone: With round brush #1, add a flat wash of the "Milk" value of Mixture 2 to the square units on the shadow and midtone sides. For those within the highlight area, apply another layer of Mixture 1 in "Tea" value. The crisscrossed pattern will become more apparent after these steps.

Wrapper: Repeat the previous steps in the first layer to gradually deepen the shadow and midtone areas.

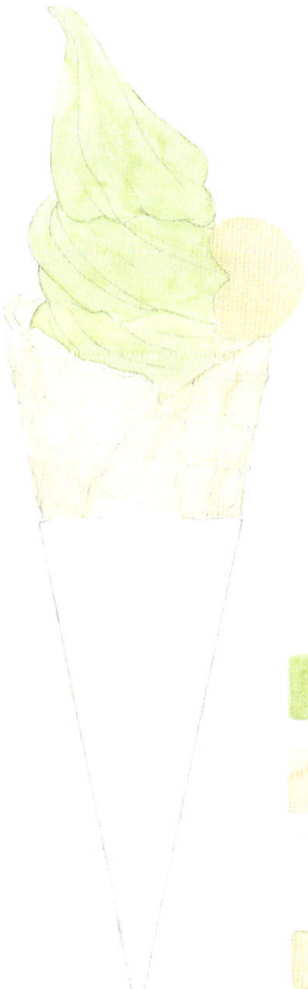

Matcha soft serve
Coffee value

Waffle cone
Tea value (Mixture 1)

Cone wrapper
Tea value

Paper tag
Coffee value

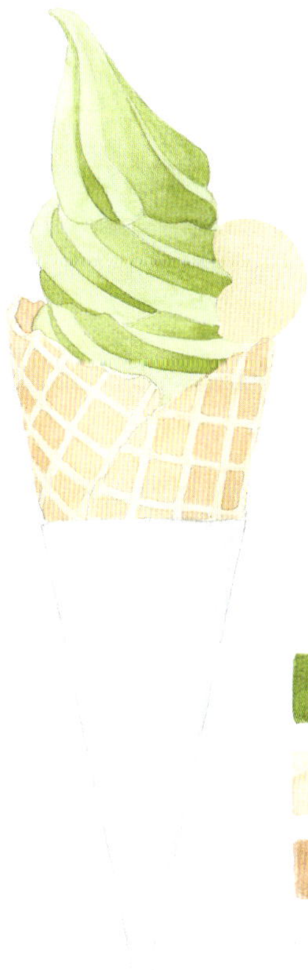

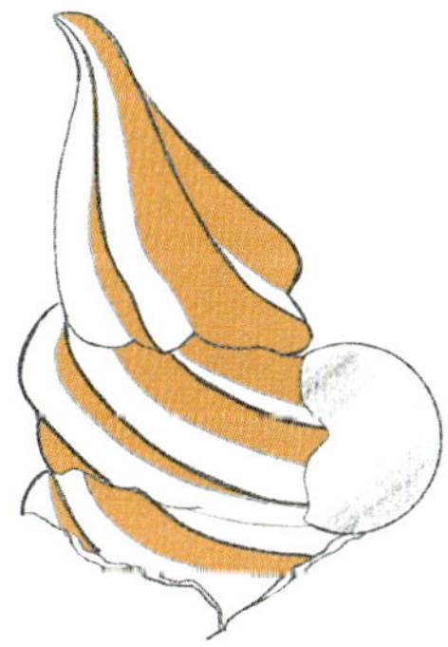

Matcha soft serve
Milk value

Waffle cone
Tea value (Mixture 1)

Waffle cone
Milk value (Mixture 2)

Cone wrapper
Tea value

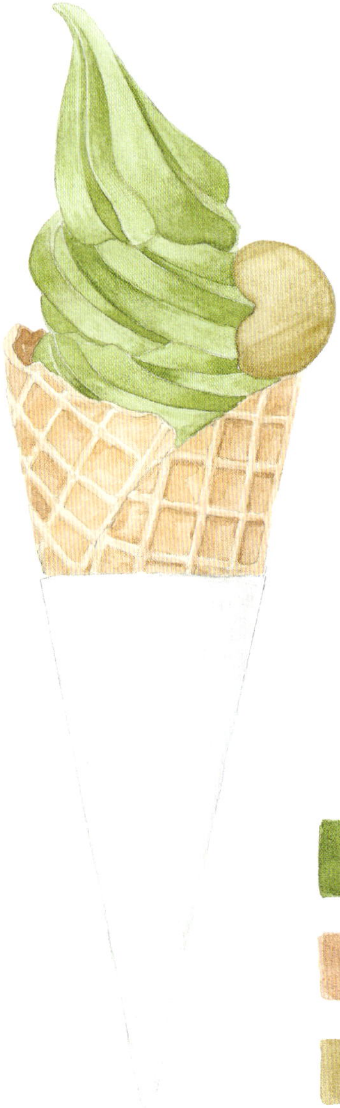

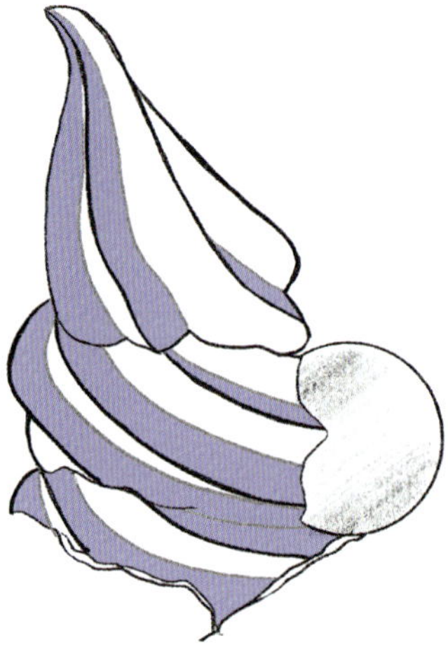

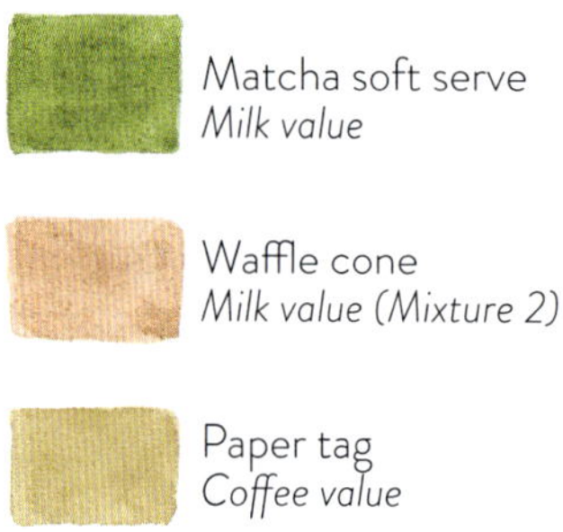

Third Layer

Soft Serve: Refer to the explanatory chart. The purple strips are where you should apply the color. Continue using round brush #1 and the "Milk" value, but reverse the direction—start from the top left and blend downwards toward the right. Since these strips are not directly facing the light source, they inherit less contrast between darker and lighter tones. Therefore, I dilute the solution slightly compared to the orange-marked strips to create a milder transition for them.

Waffle Cone: Use round brush #1 and the "Milk" value of Mixture 2 to apply on the left edges of each square unit on the shadow side. Since the light source is from the left and these squares are lower than the ridges, their left edges should be darker. Gently drag your brush along them, but avoid blending the mixture out. Instead, let them dry naturally, creating a beautiful watercolor effect. After that, use the tip of the brush to wash a thin layer of "Tea" value onto the whole grid to dim it down, ensuring the highlight area remains the brightest.

Paper Tag: Apply the "Coffee" value mixture with round brush #1 to the outline of the tag. Then add parallel diagonal strokes to its lower and upper thirds, leaving the middle part in a brighter shade. This technique will create a golden effect for the tag.

Finishing Touches

Soft Serve: Deepen the orange-marked strips with "Cream" value, repeating the same steps from the second layer. After that, switch to a spotter brush to add some dark-green mixture to the bottom right of these strips to increase the depth.

Waffle Cone: Use round brush #1 to apply Mixture 1 in "Milk" value to the squares in the highlight area and Mixture 2 in "Cream" value to those in the shadow area. Paint the overlapping edge on the front with the same "Cream" value to emphasize the layering. Finally, squint your eyes to assess the contrast. If the highlight is not prominent enough, gradually add more brown mixture to the shadow side until you achieve the desired tones.

Wrapper: Add one to two more layers of gray color to the shadow and midtone areas to create the pointy tip effect (refer to Chapter 1, Shading, page 15). When the paper is completely dry, pick up a pencil to lightly draw the logo on the wrapper. Then, use a spotter brush and the "Cream" value to trace over the pencil sketch.

Paper Tag: Repeat the steps in the third layer to deepen the golden shade. Next, use a spotter brush to write on the tag. As a matcha fan, I chose "smooth flavour" for my painting, but feel free to include your own message. Just remember that parts of the letters will be hidden when the tag is pressed into the soft serve.

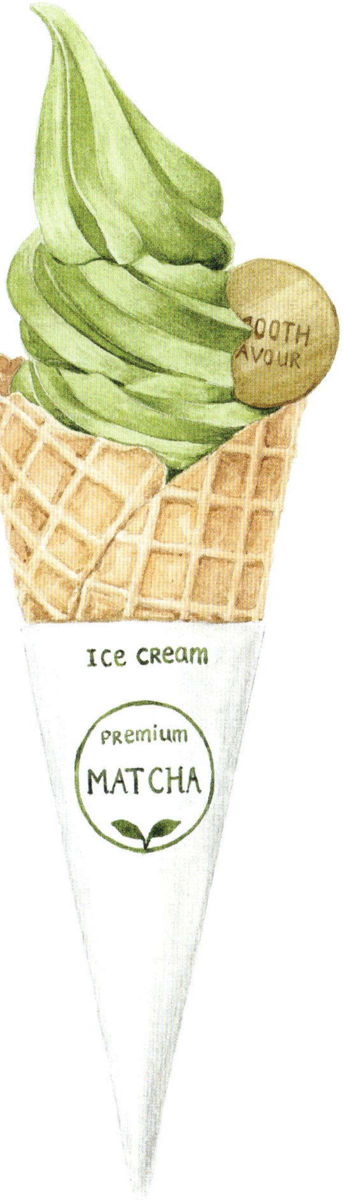

Logo /
Matcha soft serve
Cream value

Waffle cone
Milk value (Mixture 1)

Paper tag
Cream value

Waffle cone
Cream value (Mixture 2)

Cone wrapper
Tea value

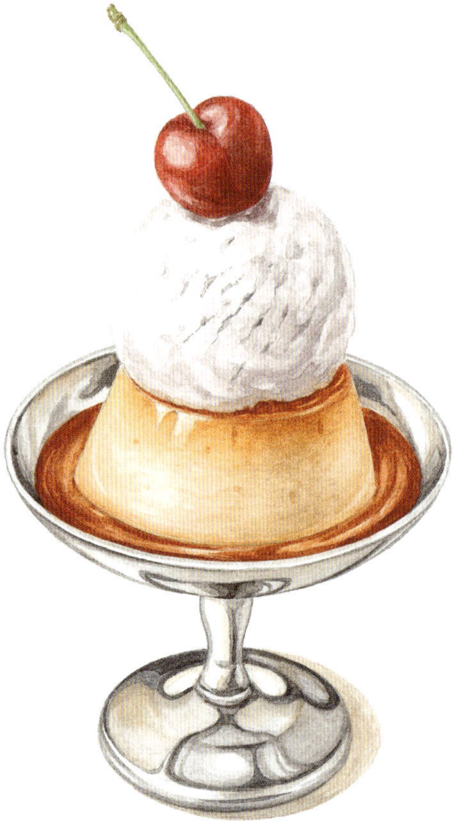

Project 20

Flan & Vanilla Ice Cream

(Dimensions: W 3½" x H 6⅛" / W 9 cm x H 15.5 cm)

We have come a long way to the final project of Chapter 2, with a significant learning curve. Upon completing this final illustration, you are a deserving winner worthy of celebration, having successfully tackled three challenging tasks in one project: depicting highly reflective metal, a soft and creamy ice cream scoop and glossy, silky flan. I sincerely appreciate your effort in every project you have undertaken so far. The next chapter awaits with even more excitement and exploration, expanding your skills beyond painting, and it's just a few pages away.

Brushes

Round brushes: sizes 1, 2 and 4

Spotter brush: size 3/0

Color Palette

OBJECT	COLOR NAME	COLOR VALUES		
		Tea/Coffee	Milk	Cream
Cherry Mixture 1	Pyrrol Scarlet Permanent Alizarin Crimson			
Cherry Mixture 2	Pyrrol Scarlet Permanent Alizarin Crimson Permanent Violet			
Cherry stem	Sap Green			
Ice cream	Cherry Mixture 2 Jane's Grey			
Flan	New Gamboge Pyrrol Orange Burnt Umber			
Caramel sauce	Pyrrol Orange Pyrrol Scarlet Burnt Umber Burnt Sienna Raw Umber (Tea Value)			
Stainless steel cup	Jane's Grey			
	Ivory Black			

Viewpoint & Light Source

With five components on hand, it's best to employ an eye-level viewpoint to highlight their appeal. Position the light source on the left, around the midpoint of the dish's height. It's crucial to carefully consider the shading for the cup. Due to its high reflectivity, the glossy stainless steel may not follow the object's original shape in shading. Reflections will appear in the shadow areas, typically darker than those in the highlighted areas. Moreover, in specific spots, the brightest and darkest shades will be adjacent to each other.

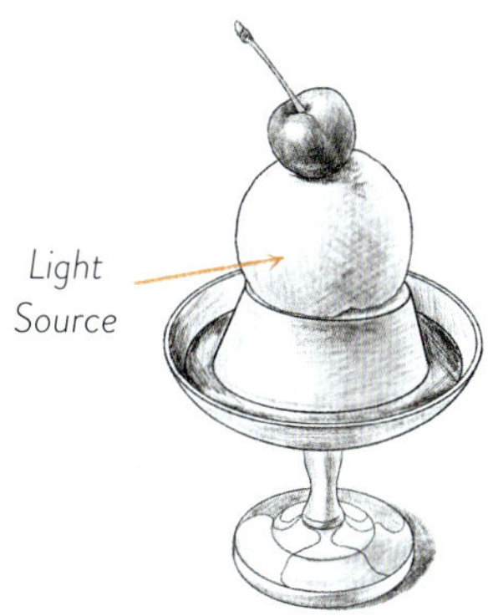

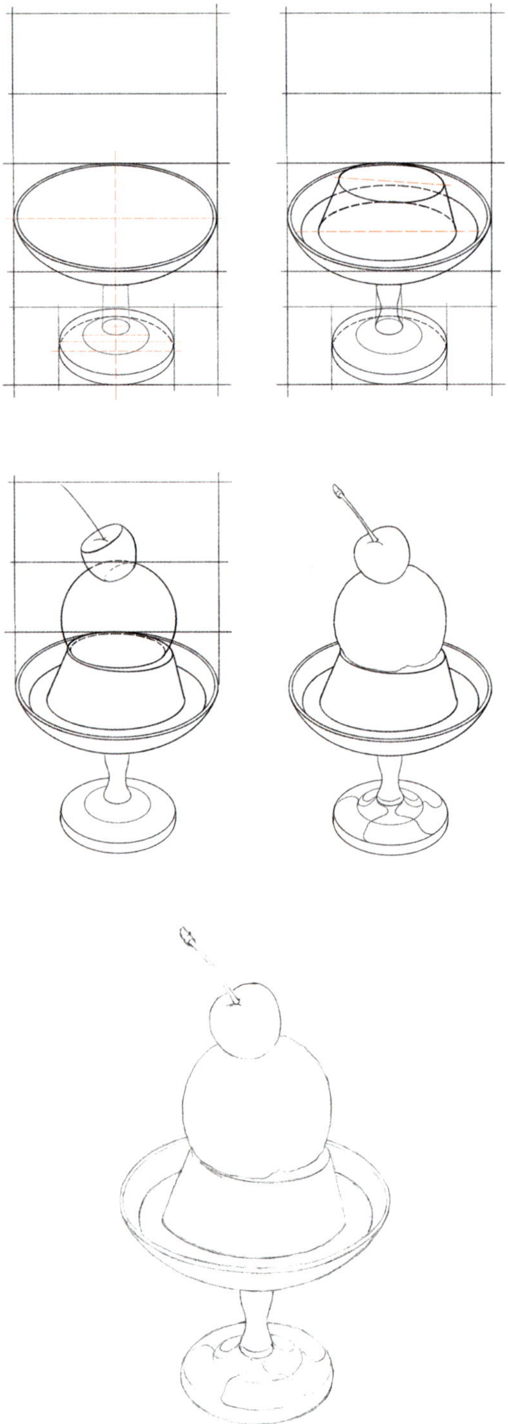

Composition

Rather than using a flat serving plate, I opt for a tall pedestal cup to give the dish a vintage aesthetic and elevate its appearance. This arrangement is most suitable for presentation on paper in portrait orientation, given its greater height compared to its width. The components from top to bottom include a cherry, ice cream and flan submerged in caramel sauce.

Let's Sketch!

Begin by outlining a general frame and establishing the height of the main components. Then, sketch the cup, considering its body as a hollow sphere with an elliptical rim and very small thickness, its stem as a tall curved cylinder, and its base as a short cylinder.

Afterwards, begin sketching the other components. Here's their breakdown of basic shapes: The flan resembles a short cylinder with a wider bottom, while the ice cream and cherry can be likened to spheres. Pay attention to placing the diameter of the ice cream scoop slightly diagonally, and do the same for the cherry, instead of stacking them straight on top of each other. This small tip adds movement to the overall layout. Also, indicate the wavy reflections of the cup's body and stem on its base, as they are crucial for the painting phase. Finally, erase any unnecessary lines and lighten the entire sketch.

Let's Paint!

First Layer

Cherry: Use round brush #2 to apply a base layer with the "Tea" value of Mixture 2. For the stem, switch to a spotter brush and the "Coffee" value of the green mixture. Next, mix Quinacridone and Raw Umber in "Milk" value to add a brown tint to the head of the stem.

Ice Cream: Use round brush #4 to wash a layer of light-gray mixture across the whole area. Here, I use the "Tea" value of Jane's Grey, mixed with a touch of Mixture 2 (for Cherry), to introduce a pinkish tint. This is because pure gray pigment may make food appear dull and plain.

Flan: Pick up round brush #4 and apply the "Tea" value, leaving more solution on the shadow and midtone area and blending it out toward the highlight by employing gradient wash technique (page 25)—which will be the key process for this object throughout. Next, add some "Tea" value of Caramel Sauce mixture to the shadow side to deepen it.

Caramel Sauce: Use round brush #2 and apply the "Cream" value to provide a warmer undertone for the sauce.

Cup: Use round brush #2 to apply a layer of gray in "Tea" value to most areas, excluding the lip of the cup. You can also start to pull more pigment to the areas that will be in darker shades.

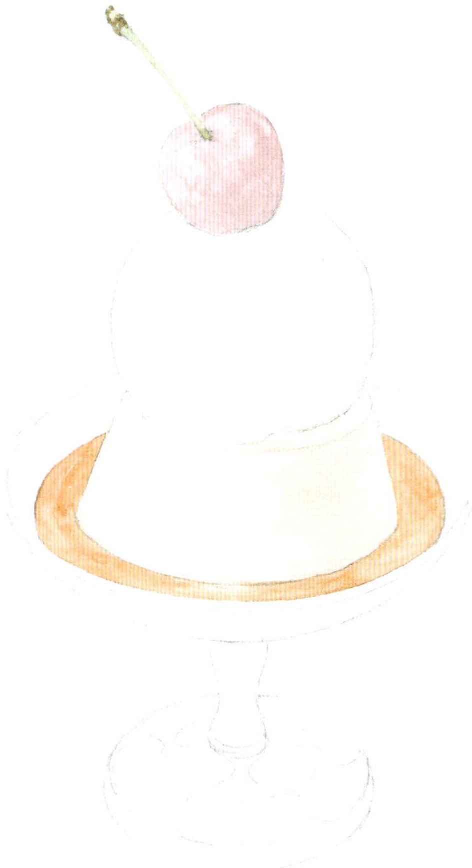

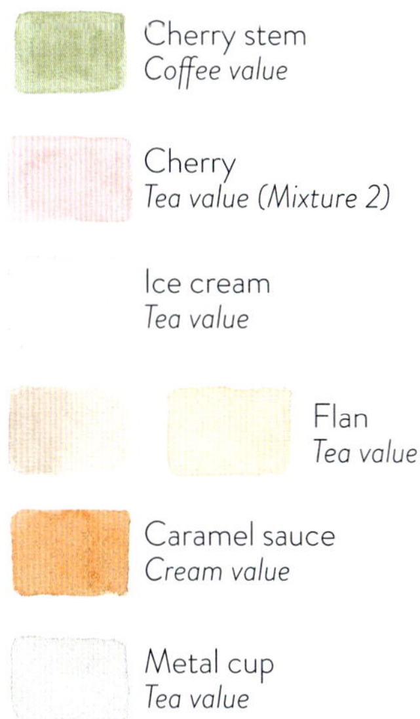

Second Layer

Cherry: Apply the "Milk" shade of Mixture 1 to the cherry using round brush #1, excluding the highlights. Employ a concentrated scumbling motion to blend the mixture around the brightest spots, as explained in Chapter 1, Depicting Texture, Glossy & Semi-Glossy Surfaces (page 27). Note that this cherry has a long dent along its body, which will be best depicted by placing a lighter area on the left and a much darker shade on the right. If you're unsure, please refer to the Light Source Shading Sketch (page 177).

For the stem, following the cylinder shading rule and with the light source coming from the left, add the "Milk" value to the right side and keep the left side brighter to create a 3-D shape.

Ice Cream: Use round brush #4 and the same "Tea" value as used in the first layer, adhering to the shading rule of a sphere. Apply the solution by employing a dab-and-pull movement, pressing the brush down firmly to create wide strokes, with some overlapping each other. This will serve as the base layer to establish the texture of the ice cream.

Flan: Use round brush #2 to apply the "Milk" value to the top and about one-third down the height of the flan, then create a gradient wash toward the bottom. Remember to exclude bright reflection spots on the highlight side, possibly by applying masking fluid. Next, combine the "Tea" value of the Caramel Sauce mixture with a touch of Raw Umber, then apply it to the shadow side and midtone areas. Dimming them gradually over several layers will enhance the prominence of the highlight. Make sure that each new layer has a smooth transition into adjacent sections using the gradient wash technique, maintaining the flan's silky texture.

Caramel Sauce: Add the "Cream" value using round brush #1 with long, slightly wavy strokes along the ellipse shape. Leave more pigment on the left side and the upper right corner. Additionally, apply this mixture to the top surface of the flan directly below the ice cream scoop to indicate its shadow.

Cup: Use round brush #1 to paint reflections on the exterior wall of the cup with the "Coffee" value from the cooler gray mixture (Jane's Grey). For the interior wall, use the warmer gray (Ivory Black) in the "Milk" value to paint the reflection, as the warm color of the flan influences the cup's color.

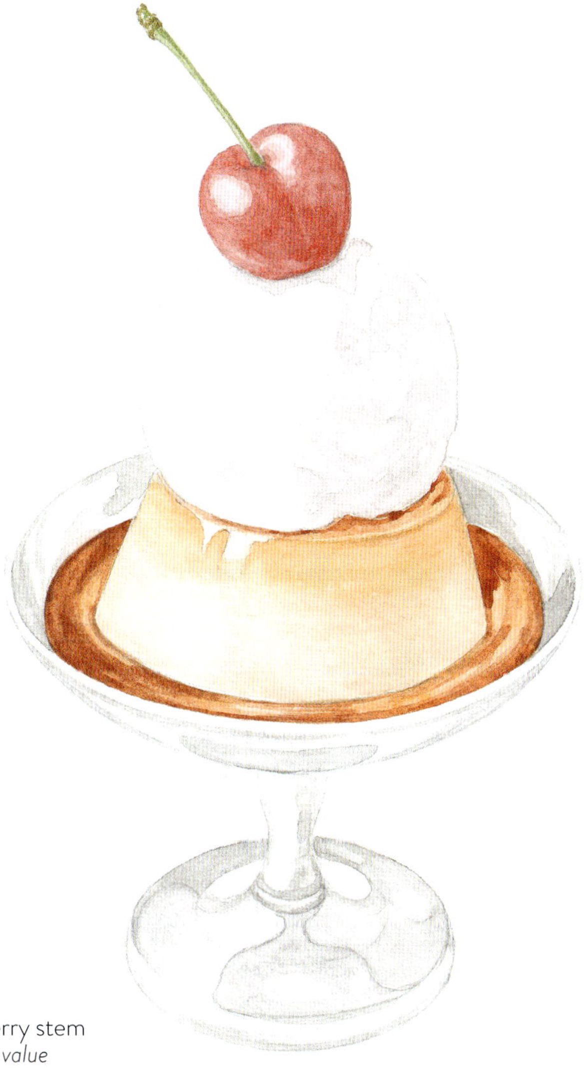

Cherry stem
Milk value

Cherry
Milk value (Mixture 1)

Ice cream
Tea value

Flan
Tea-Milk value

Caramel sauce
Cream value

Metal cup
Coffee value (Mixture 1)

Metal cup
Milk value (Mixture 2)

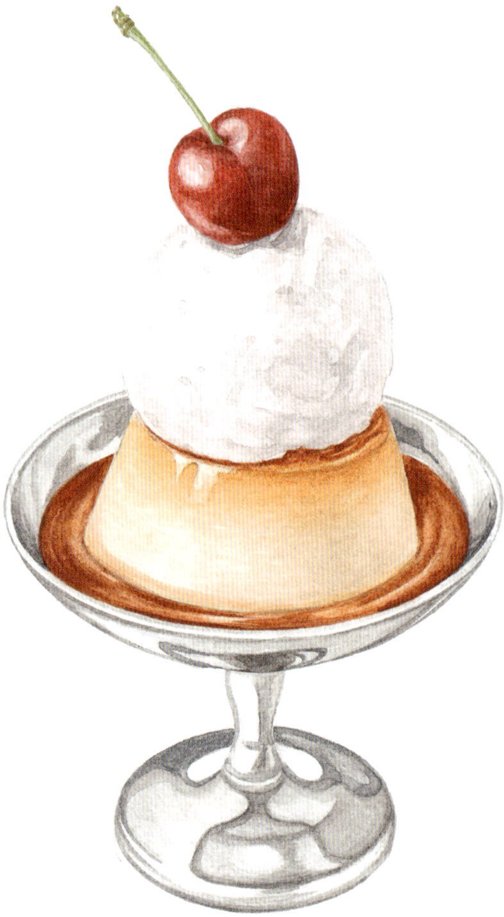

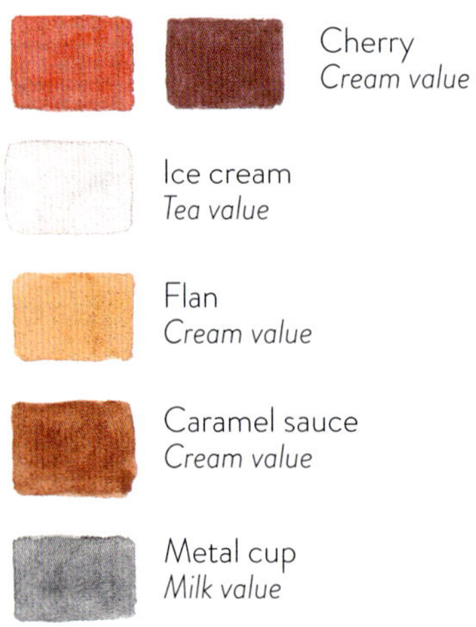

Third Layer

Cherry: Use round brush #1 to add the "Cream" value of the bright-red mixture around the reflections and darker red for the shadow area. Implement short and concentrated scumbling strokes to apply and blend the mixture to keep the smooth and glossy texture for the cherry. Dragging the brush too much may lead to inaccuracies in mixture application and texture depiction, probably resulting in a rough appearance of the cherry's skin.

Ice Cream: Repeat the steps in the second layer to increase the contrast between the highlight and shadow areas. Add some small and subtle strokes on the highlight to improve its texture.

Flan: Prepare the "Cream" value and use round brush #2 to apply it first to the top third of the shadow side, ensuring a smooth transition downward. Repeat this process for the remainder of the top third, using a more diluted mixture as you approach the highlight.

Caramel Sauce: Add another layer of "Cream" value, following the rule mentioned in the second layer. Leave some lighter-brown streaks amidst the rich reddish-brown to achieve the desired sauce consistency. Apply another layer to the top surface of the flan to deepen the ice cream's shadow.

Cup: Add sharper details for the reflections with the "Milk" value of Jane's Grey, using round brush #1.

Finishing Touches

Cherry: Add the "Cream" value of Mixture 2 to the shadow area. Deepen the valley on top that is not facing the light by painting a thin line around the stem with the same solution.

Ice Cream: Repeat the previous steps in the third layer until the ice cream's 3-D shape is apparent when squinting your eyes. As more layers are added, use smaller brushstrokes to focus on detailing. Use a spotter brush to depict some cracking lines on the surface, using the "Milk" value. Lastly, add this mixture right below the cherry to depict its shadow on the ice cream.

Flan: Add another layer of the "Cream" value to the flan, following the instructions from the third layer. But this time, you can extend the application slightly to the bottom as well. Use the tip of the brush to add some small dots on the flan with "Coffee-Milk" value of the Caramel mixture to depict the air bubbles.

Caramel: Using a spotter brush, add the "Cream" value around the outer edge of the caramel to further deepen the red-brown shade. Work in small sections to avoid darkening the entire area and achieve the contrast seen in this image.

Cup: Pick up round brush #1 to deepen the dark areas of the exterior walls with sharper lines, using the "Cream" value of Ivory Black. Then, return to the "Milk" value, add a touch of Flan mixture and apply it to the interior wall, as well as some spots on the stem and base. Use the same mixture to paint the shadow for the whole dessert cup.

Artist's Tip: To show a connection between the food object and the surface they're sitting on, you can add a little of the color of the food to the surface. Here, I've added a little bit of the flan color in "Milk" value to the cup to give it some warmth.

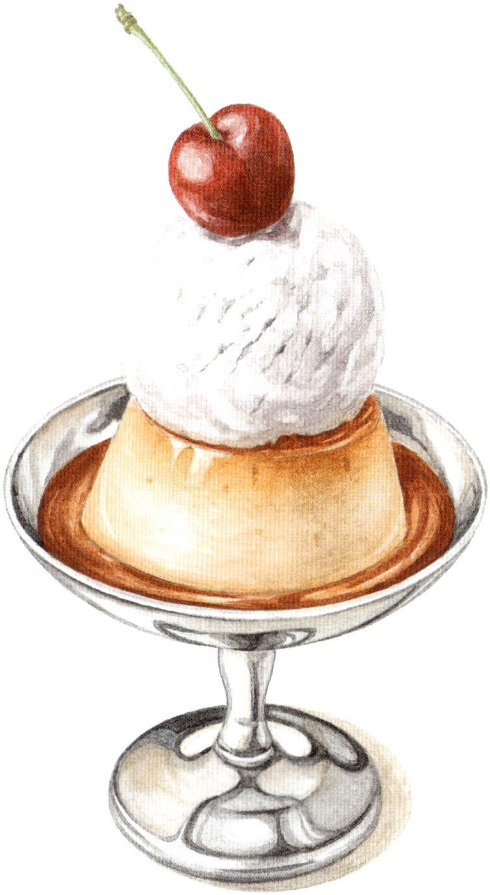

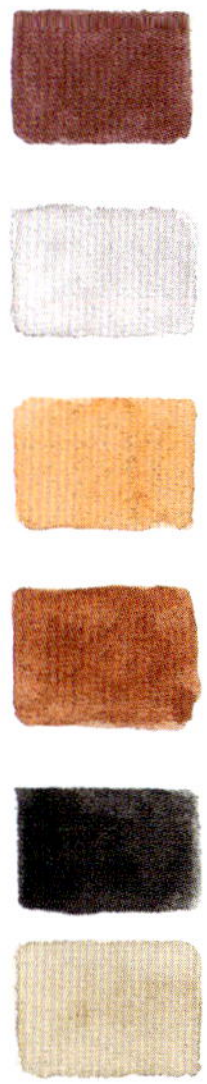

Cherry (Mixture 2)
Cream value

Ice cream
Milk value

Flan
Cream value

Caramel sauce
Cream value

Metal cup
Cream value

Metal cup
Milk value

Chapter III

Recipe Layouts

Good to see you again! Get ready because in this chapter, I'm going to show you how to jazz up your recipe cards with your own flair! Whether you're using them for your own kitchen endeavors or giving them away as thoughtful gifts, we'll explore various placement ideas and I will provide you all the tips you will need to create recipe cards that are nothing short of stunning. So, let's get this creative cooking party started!

Four Key Steps To Perfect Layouts

The following steps have wide applicability: You can create recipe cards, incorporate them into journal sketchbooks or simply decorate any layout featuring food illustrations and text components.

Step 1 - Mapping the Composition

Visualize or sketch the primary framework on paper. Decide on the overall flow for your layout. The illustration of the main dish might dictate how you arrange the text and smaller illustrations surrounding it. I'll delve into these details in the next part as we explore each layout in more depth.

Step 2 - Refining the Layout with Harmony & Balance

Once you have a rough idea of how and where to place each element in your layout, begin outlining the main dish and each ingredient to ensure they harmonize well. Take into account the amount of text you intend to include in your recipe and ensure there is adequate space for it. I recommend carrying out this step on regular paper (not watercolor paper) because it allows you to freely experiment with different arrangements until you are satisfied; this sketch will serve as a preliminary draft for your more refined version on watercolor paper.

Step 3 - Watercolor Sketching & Painting

The third step involves sketching on watercolor paper, starting with the largest illustration and progressing to smaller ones to ensure adequate space for ingredients and text. Next comes the painting phase. Aim to echo the main dish's color in the ingredients or their containers for overall harmony. If your layout contains numerous similar or neutral colors, strategically introducing varied colors (using triadic or complementary color scheme, for example) for containers or displaying ingredients can help spice up the design while maintaining a balanced look.

Step 4 - Adding Text

Always reserve space near your main illustration for the dish's name or title, as they will harmonize effectively. You can experiment with different fonts directly on paper using a pencil. Alternatively, you can type the text on your computer and transfer it onto paper with a pencil. Once satisfied with the text sketch, enhance it using a fine brush with watercolor or a pen for a charming finish.

> **Artist's Tip:** Before writing, draw guidelines for the text to ensure your letters align neatly within straight lines. Practice consistent letter spacing to adopt a slower and more deliberate writing pace, avoiding unnecessary mistakes.

On the right are some hand-writing examples.

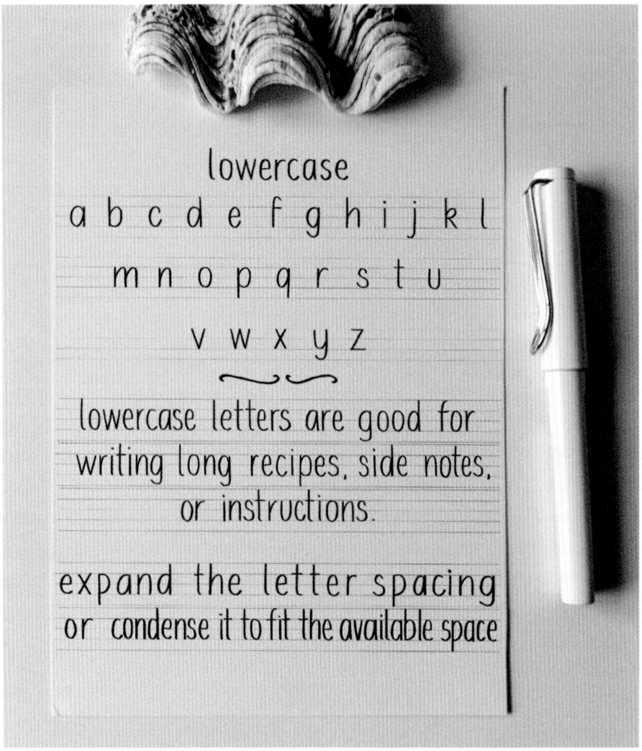

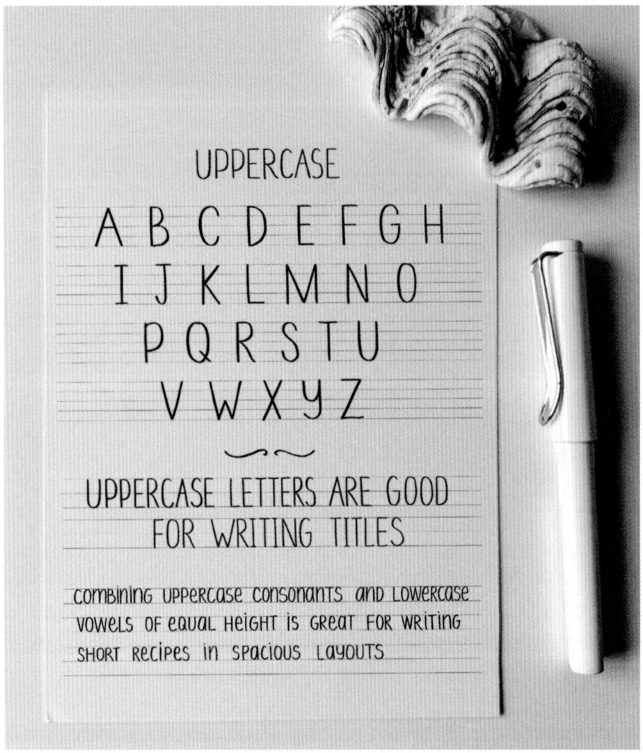

Personally, when combining uppercase and lowercase letters, I prefer to write vowels and the letters "m" and "n" in lowercase while keeping the remaining consonants in uppercase style.

Nine Essential Recipe Layouts

The design of recipe cards changes based on the type of food and its presentation. We tailor the layout to complement the food's specific characteristics: Typically, landscape layouts suit visibly tall or wide illustrations, whereas portrait layouts are ideal for rounder dishes or those with a 1:1 width-to-height ratio, allowing for a more creative distribution of ingredient illustrations around the featured food item.

We will examine nine layouts—six portrait and three landscape—using foods from the 20 projects showcased in Chapter 2, with the aim of bridging the thought processes and actions across the two chapters. In this part of the book, our emphasis will shift from detailed step-by-step instructions on watercoloring food textures (the focus of Chapter 2) to integrating a multitude of visual elements beyond mere illustrations. If you need assistance, check out the Library of Ingredients, Chapter 4 (page 212) for additional methods for how to illustrate different elements.

In the diagrams below, the **red circles** depict the main dish illustration on your recipe card, while the **blue paths** indicate the movement or sequence of elements around it.

Landscape Layouts

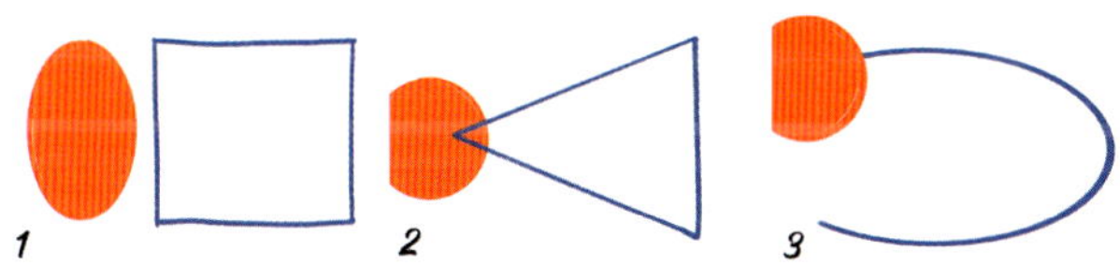

Portrait Layouts

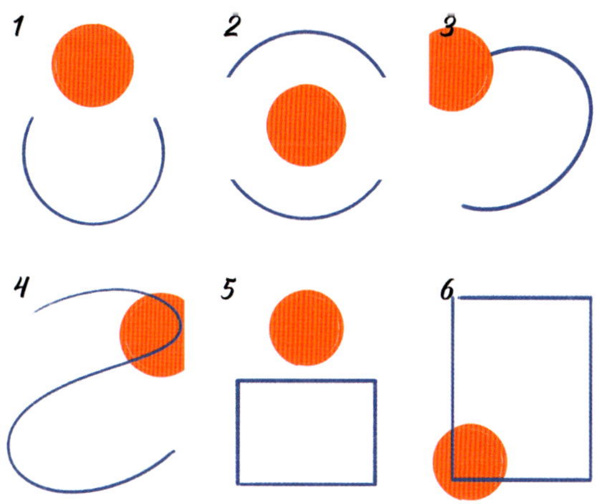

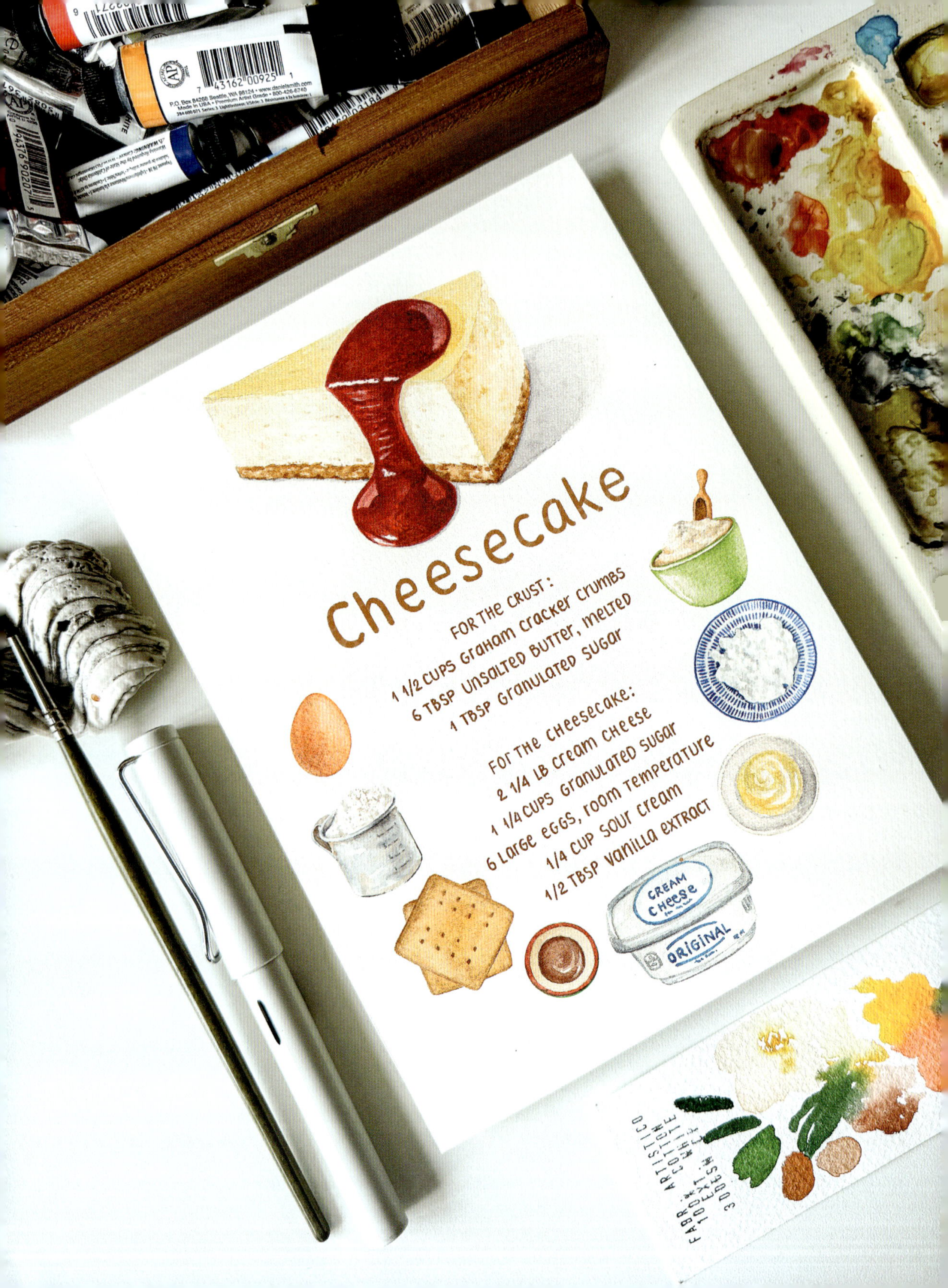
Cheesecake
FOR THE CRUST:
1 1/2 CUPS Graham cracker crumbs
6 TBSP UNSALTED BUTTER, MELTED
1 TBSP Granulated SUGAR
FOR THE CHEESECAKE:
2 1/4 LB cream cheese
1 1/4 CUPS Granulated SUGAR
6 Large EGGS, room temperature
1/4 CUP SOUR cream
1/2 TBSP Vanilla extract
CREAM Cheese
ORIGINAL

Portrait Layout 1

Cheesecake

This layout works well when you want to highlight illustrations within uniform, contained frames, ensuring balanced arrangements. It's advisable to choose a featured dish with a predominantly light color, like Project 16: Cheesecake (page 151), to maintain a harmonious composition without overwhelming the top section. The flow is guided by smaller ingredient paintings arranged in a curved line, leading toward the main illustration.

Step 1 - Mapping

Make sure that your main illustration does not exceed one-third of the paper's total height. After positioning it and placing the main title just below, list and mark the ingredients you plan to paint along the curved line at the bottom two-thirds of the paper. Refrain from including all the ingredients from your recipe reference; instead, focus on selecting items that are similar in size to ensure they fit well within the composition.

Step 2 - Refining the Layout

Following the principle of keeping elements within tidy frames, select viewpoints for each so they maintain a near 1:1 width-height ratio, avoiding extra details that extend too far beyond or leave excessive empty space. Additionally, begin planning the colors for depicting the ingredients and arrange them roughly to achieve harmony. When centering the text, carefully draft the line lengths to ensure they contribute to an aesthetically pleasing layout.

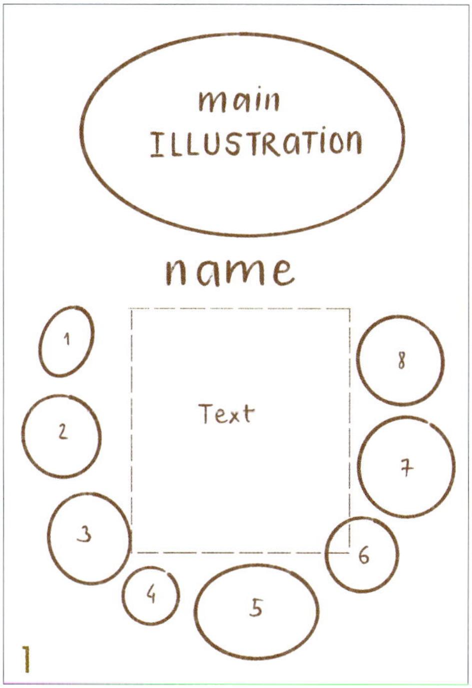

1

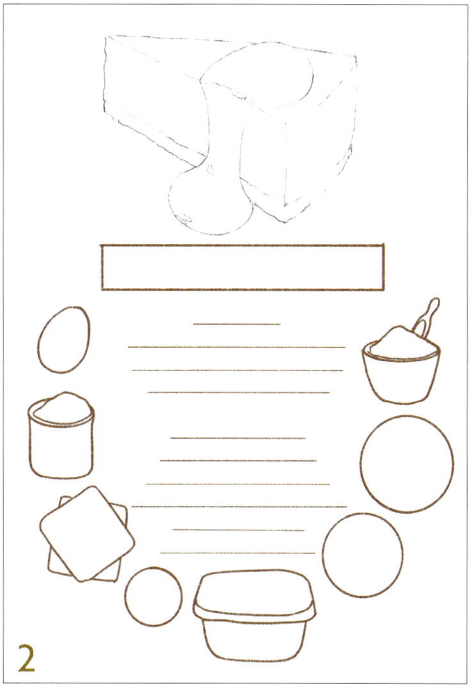

2

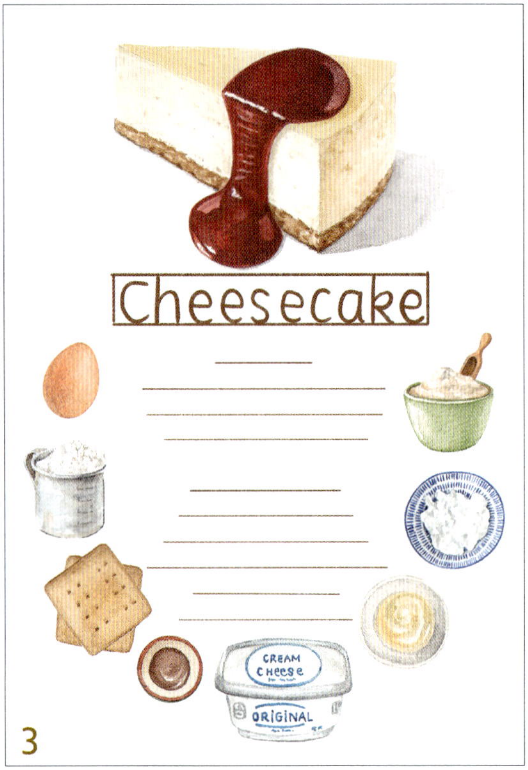

Step 3 - Painting

Implement the envisioned color harmony from the previous step. Here, I intentionally intersperse white or light-colored objects (such as cream cheese, sour cream and a cup of granulated sugar) among colorful items (like crackers, vanilla and melted butter). Avoid clustering vibrant colors on one side and neutrals on the other, as this layout is centrally focused. Ensure shapes, arrangements, colors and shades are balanced both vertically and horizontally for a cohesive composition.

Step 4 - Adding Text

For the title, I opt for a simple yet bold rounded font, which resonates with the rich and smooth flavor of this delightful dessert.

The ingredient list is divided into two sections: "For the crust" and "For the cheesecake." I use uppercase letters but stylize all vowels in lowercase, ensuring they maintain consistent height. This approach gives the text a more casual and relaxed feel.

Portrait Layout 2

S'mores Cookie

When considering dishes that are round or oval-shaped, or have a nearly equal width-to-height ratio, center-focused recipe layouts offer an appealing choice for those who appreciate a clean and organized presentation. Food items like cookies, round buns and pastries, or Project 17: S'mores Cookie (page 158), are ideal candidates for this portrait-oriented layout style, prioritizing the beauty of your food illustrations and the well-constructed symmetry of the overall composition.

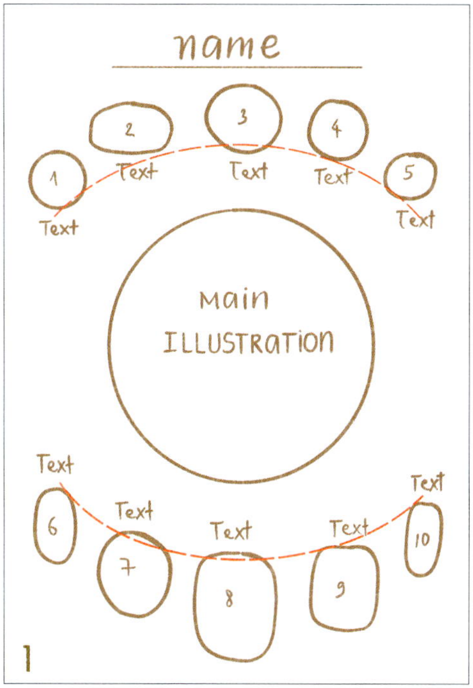

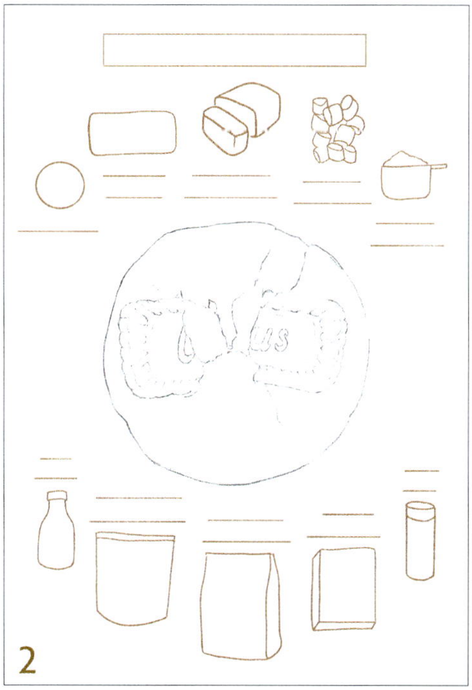

Step 1 - Mapping

Building on the well-balanced principles from Portrait Layout 1 (page 189), the main dish is placed right in the middle, surrounded by ingredient illustrations arranged in two arcs mirrored vertically through the center. The primary painting should occupy approximately one-third of the total layout height, following the effective rule of thirds in composition. Place the main title at the top of the page. Divide ingredients evenly between the upper and lower arcs, with the largest item in the middle and sizes gradually decreasing toward the edges.

Step 2 - Refining the Layout

I opt to sketch the ingredients along the lower arc in their packaging to lend a charming touch to the recipe. On the upper arc, most ingredients will be depicted in their natural forms. It's essential to place the larger, chunkier shapes at the bottom to anchor the layout and provide a grounded feel. Conversely, lighter and smaller shapes will occupy the higher space, promoting a light and airy flow throughout the composition.

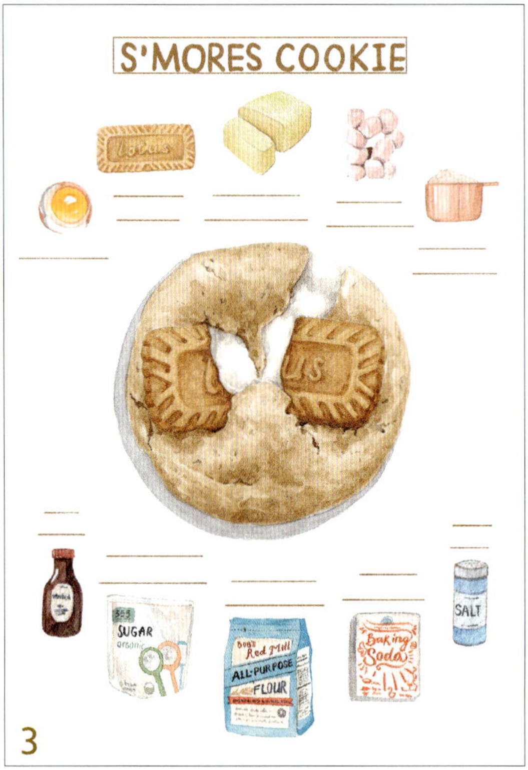

Step 3 - Painting

As we consider how to use colors effectively in a recipe layout—avoiding monotony or confusion—I introduce a triadic color scheme. This scheme blends the golden-brown hue of our complete S'mores Cookie (page 158) with touches of light blue and vintage red for the packaged goods in the lower arc. This approach adds a playful visual appeal while maintaining a cohesive color palette tied to the main subject.

On the other hand, the ingredients displayed above follow a monochromatic scheme with the main dish but showcase their unique qualities through shapes and textures: The cracked egg reveals a vibrant orange yolk, while the Biscoff's crunchy golden-brown texture is highlighted. Similarly, the unwrapped butter and mini marshmallows emphasize their softness without containers or wrappers.

Step 4 - Adding Text

Since this layout primarily showcases watercolor illustrations, the text should be concise enough to sit below or above each piece, ideally in two lines to prevent excessive spread. The main title should feature a rounded, uppercase font to reflect the round shape of the cookie, particularly the "O."

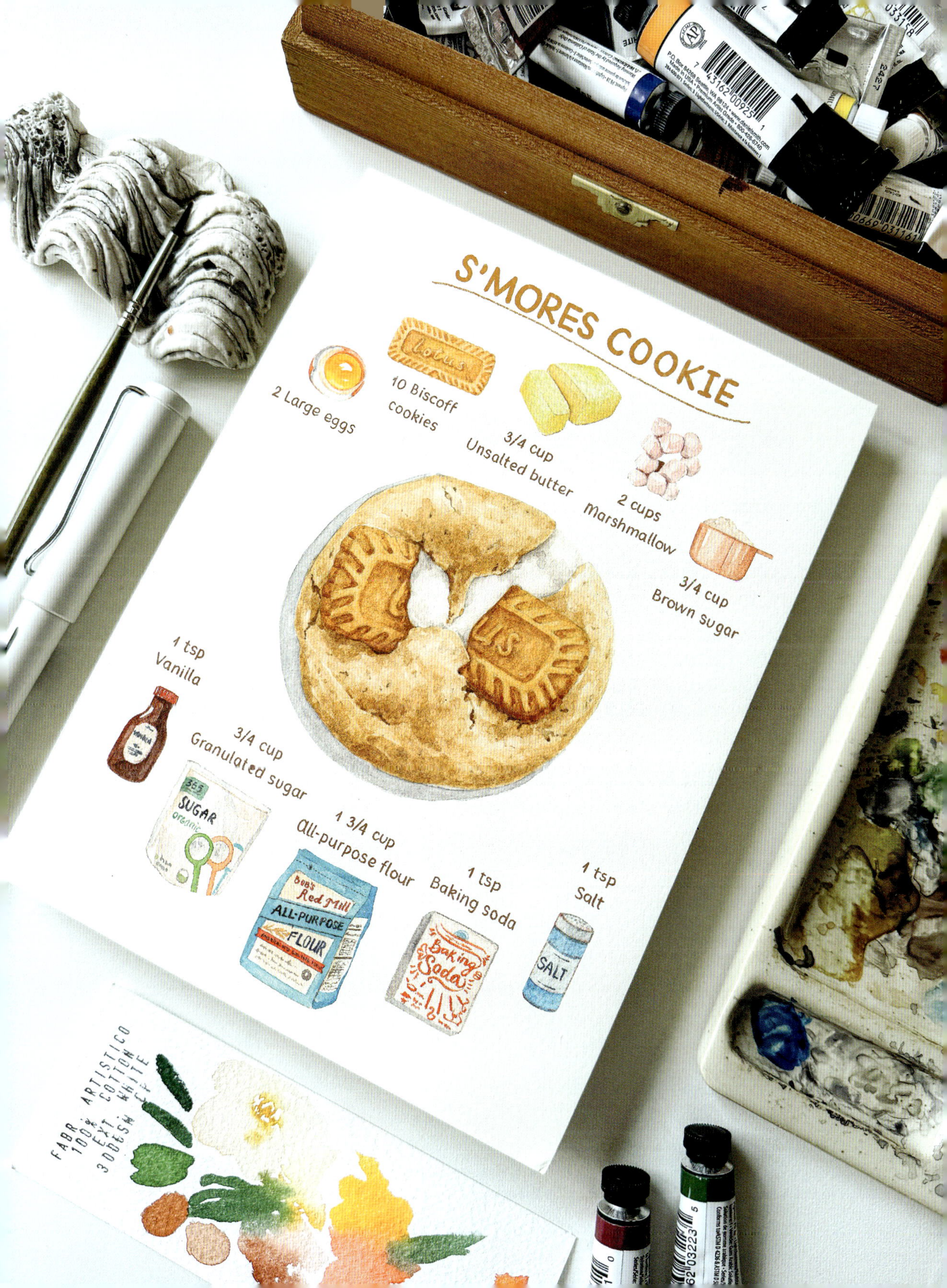
S'MORES COOKIE
2 Large eggs
lotus
10 Biscoff cookies
3/4 cup Unsalted butter
2 cups Marshmallow
3/4 cup Brown sugar
1 tsp Vanilla
3/4 cup Granulated sugar
SUGAR
1 3/4 cup All-purpose flour
Bob's Red Mill
ALL-PURPOSE
FLOUR
1 tsp Baking soda
Baking Soda
1 tsp Salt
SALT
FABR. ARTISTICO
100% COTTON
EXT. WHITE

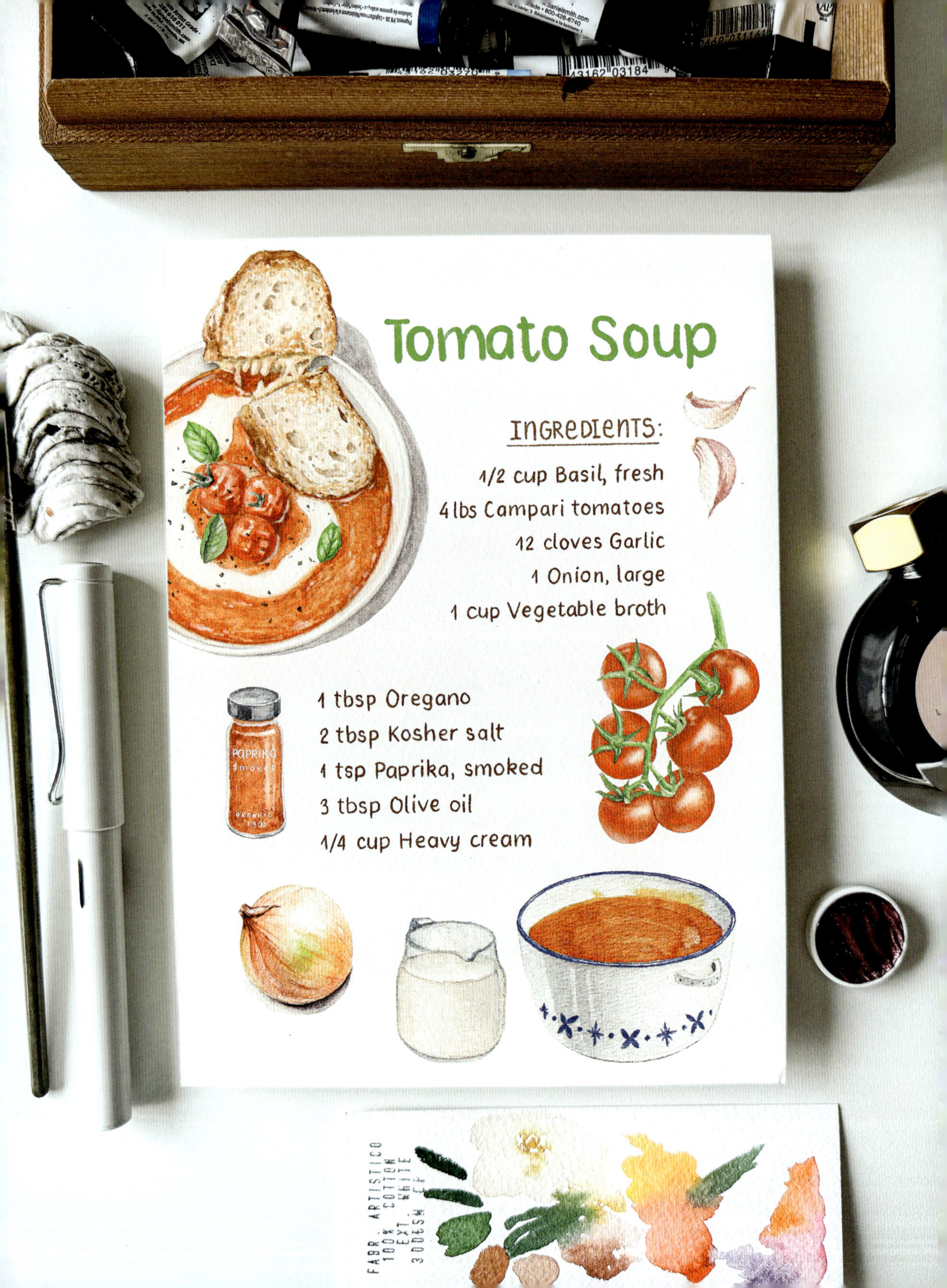
Tomato Soup
INGREDIENTS:
1/2 cup Basil, fresh
4 lbs Campari tomatoes
12 cloves Garlic
1 Onion, large
1 cup Vegetable broth
PAPRIKA
smoked
1 tbsp Oregano
2 tbsp Kosher salt
1 tsp Paprika, smoked
3 tbsp Olive oil
1/4 cup Heavy cream

Portrait Layout 3

Tomato Soup

This layout builds on Landscape Layout 3 (page 210) but is tailored for portrait orientation. It's well-suited for showcasing foods that benefit from tall illustrations rather than wide ones. The main artwork can be positioned in the upper left or right corner, depending on your preference. Smaller illustrations surround the text with diverse sizes and shapes, effectively filling gaps across the composition. Based on these criteria, Project 07: Tomato Soup (page 81) serves as an exemplary choice for this design.

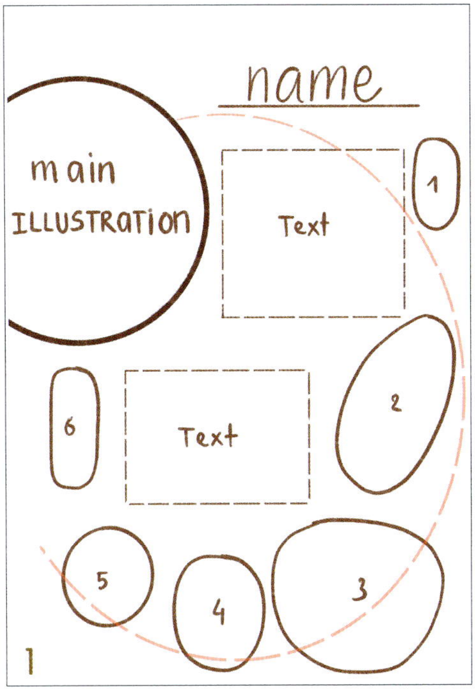

Step 1 - Mapping

Since the main illustration adopts a top-down viewpoint and will be partially cropped, it's important to highlight its most important elements, which in this case are the roasted tomato and the bread. The visual path, similar to Landscape Layout 3 (page 210), forms a circle, which should be filled with items of varying sizes and shapes. I find it best to include just enough items to prevent overcrowding, ensuring that the smaller illustrations also capture viewers' attention.

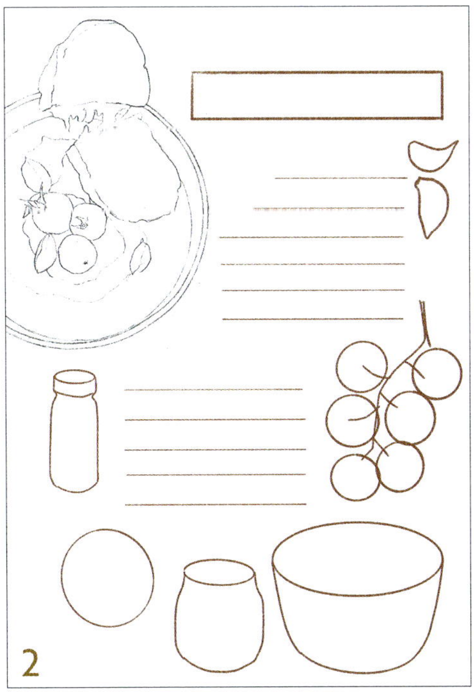

Step 2 - Refining the Layout

Begin sketching the smaller illustrations based on the predefined frames from Step 1. For instance, a bunch of baby tomatoes fits perfectly into Item 2, while two individual cloves of garlic occupy the space for Item 4. The guiding principle is to arrange heavier items (by mass or by color) lower down and lighter ones higher up. Consider different ways to depict these ingredients—whether in their natural state, packaged or in containers. I suggest incorporating a porcelain pot of cooked soup to evoke a home-cooked ambiance for the entire layout.

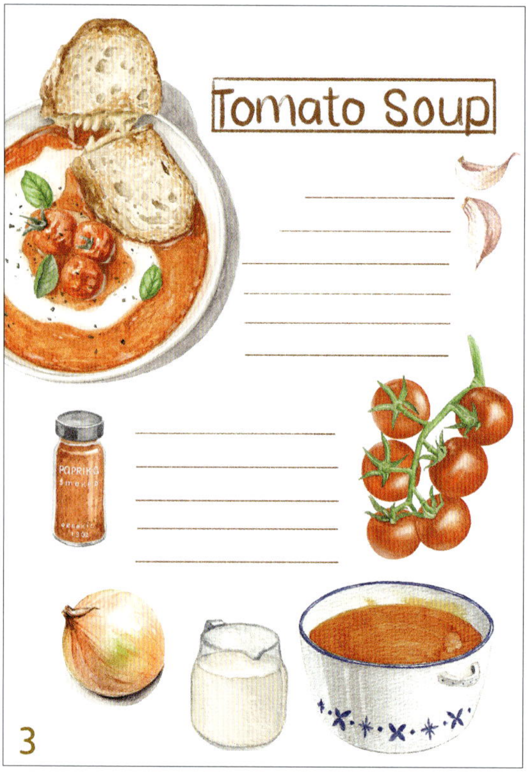

Step 3 - Painting

This is one of the layouts that feature bold and vibrant colors prominently, provided they are distributed in a balanced manner. The deep red appears in the fresh bunch of tomatoes, the soup pot and paprika powder. Other items can be in lighter hues to offset these bold colors. Additionally, I introduce a touch of blue in the decorative pattern of the porcelain cookware to evoke a European vibe to reflect the dish's origin in the south of Spain.

Step 4 - Adding Text

The alignment of your text body depends on available space and content. Experiment with different layouts to find the most suitable. In this example, the first part is aligned to the right and the second to the left. The main title features a clean, rounded sans serif font in a green shade similar to that used for the herb garnishes in the primary illustration and tomato stem.

Portrait Layout 4

Shakshuka

Based on the same principles as the previous layout, this design features secondary illustrations dispersed in varied sizes and shapes, giving it a unique visual path reminiscent of an S shape. Project 05: Shakshuka (page 66), perfectly fits this profile, with the skillet's handle extending beyond the dish's frame, cleverly dividing the text into two parts. Such compositions with an organic flow appeal to individuals seeking spontaneity in their recipe cards, offering greater freedom and opportunities for creativity.

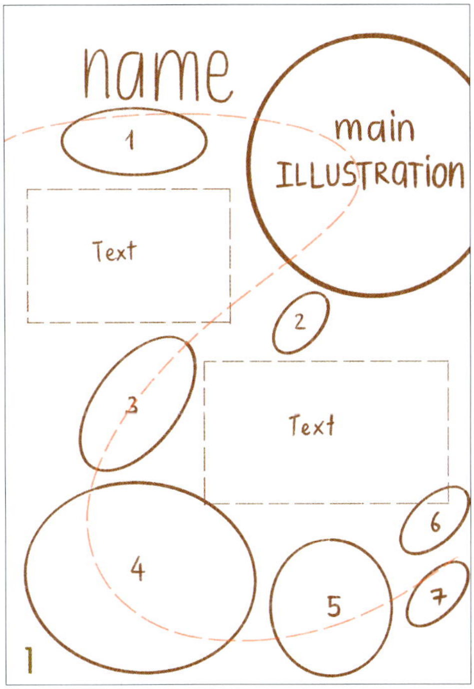

Step 1 - Mapping

Revisiting the effective use of cropped images, the Shakshuka is placed in the upper right corner, with the skillet's handle reaching downward to the left. From there, carefully size smaller illustrations to follow the flowing S arrangement, envisioning how each item will fit into the available space. The largest item, Item 4, balances out the main illustration positioned diagonally across at the lower left corner. If your chosen dish has a short ingredient list, consider adding extra notes or instructions to fill out the available space creatively.

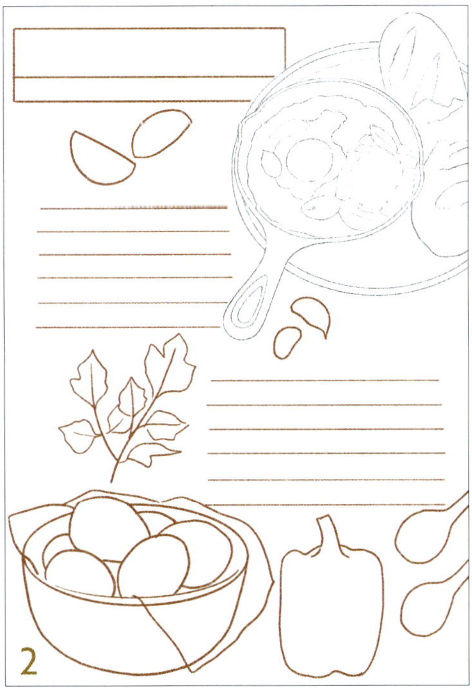

Step 2 - Refining the Layout

Sketch each item with real illustrations. I position the tomato wedges just below the title to effectively underscore it and highlight the key components of the famous Shakshuka simultaneously. The next essential ingredients, eggs, are portrayed in a bowl with a vintage cloth, allowing for creative exploration. Remember, you have full artistic control over how you represent each element. As an example, I opt to showcase the bell pepper by cutting it in half, introducing a playful challenge to the composition.

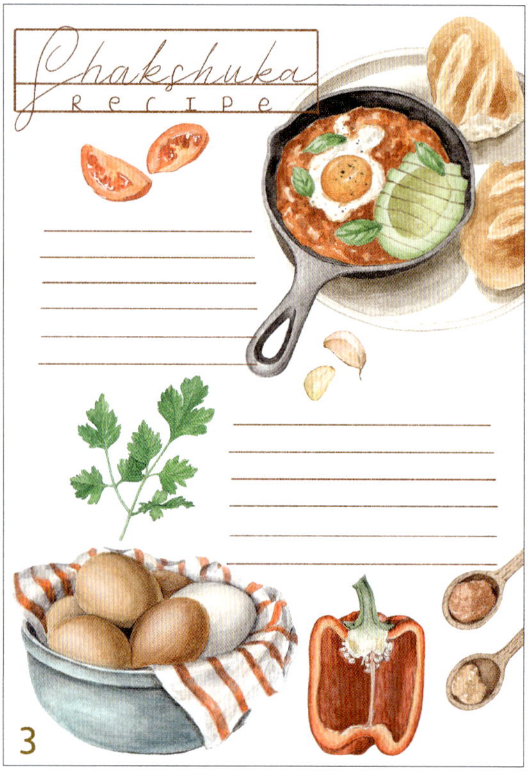

Step 3 - Painting

This layout features a complementary color scheme of deep red and rich green, both balanced out by a golden-brown hue from the bread and eggs. The deep red appears consistently throughout the design, encompassing the main dish, tomato wedges, the striped cloth pattern and the bell pepper. Meanwhile, the rich green accents are found in avocados, a sprig of coriander and small basil leaves, adding vibrancy and freshness to the composition.

Step 4 - Adding Text

With numerous bold and captivating illustrations, the main title should adopt a simple and light handwriting style that reflects our visual journey, mirroring the flow of an S. Below it, I include the word "recipe" in mostly capital letters to give the layout a sense of firmness.

As you populate the text space, assess how the words align visually. You can squint to pinpoint any areas that may need adjustment and rearrange them until the layout feels just right to you.

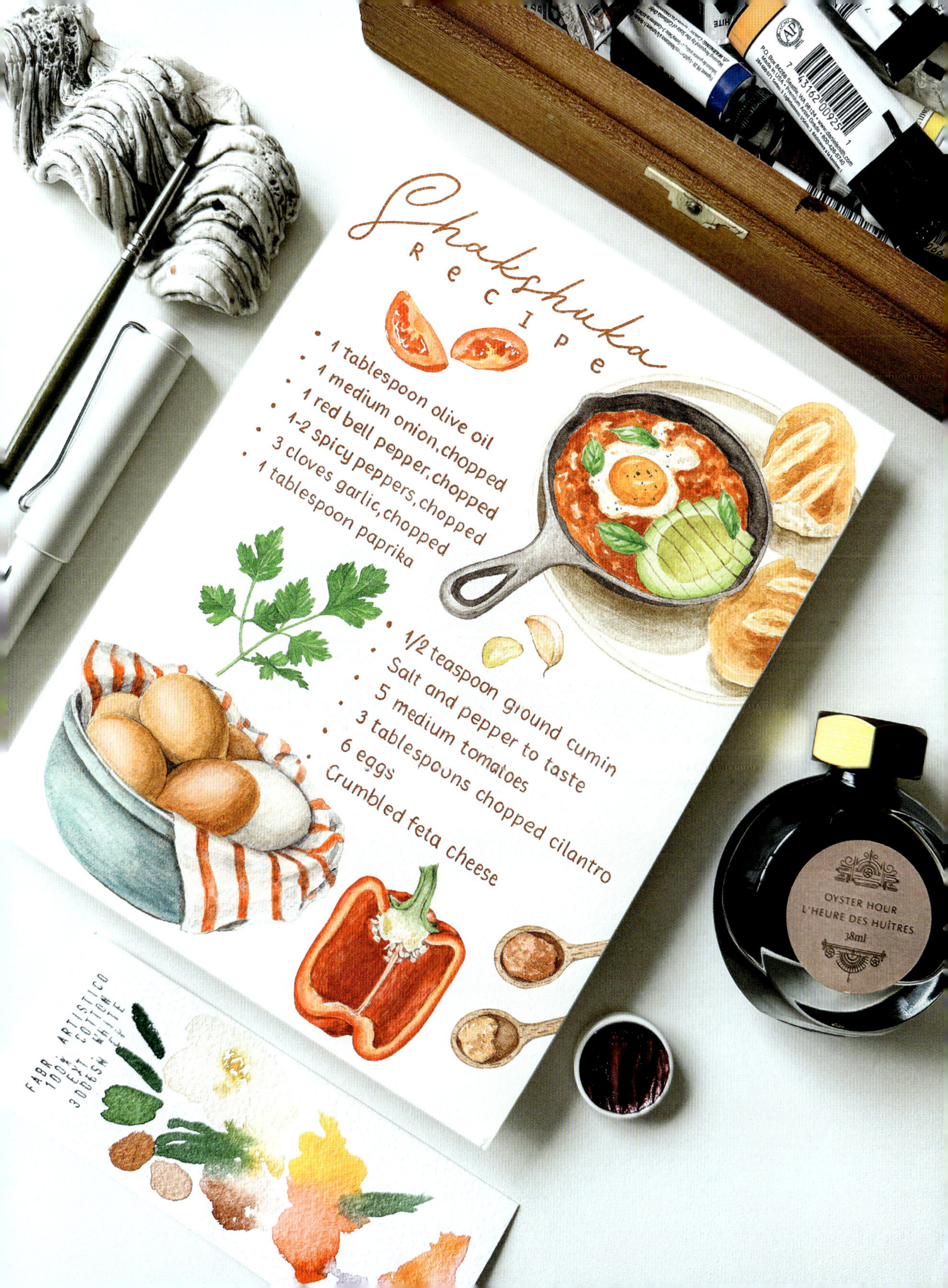
Shakshuka
RECIPE
• 1 tablespoon olive oil
• 1 medium onion, chopped
• 1 red bell pepper, chopped
• 1-2 spicy peppers, chopped
• 3 cloves garlic, chopped
• 1 tablespoon paprika
• 1/2 teaspoon ground cumin
• Salt and pepper to taste
• 5 medium tomatoes
• 3 tablespoons chopped cilantro
• 6 eggs
• Crumbled feta cheese
OYSTER HOUR
L'HEURE DES HUÎTRES
38ml
FABR. ARTISTICO
100% COTTON
EXT. WHITE

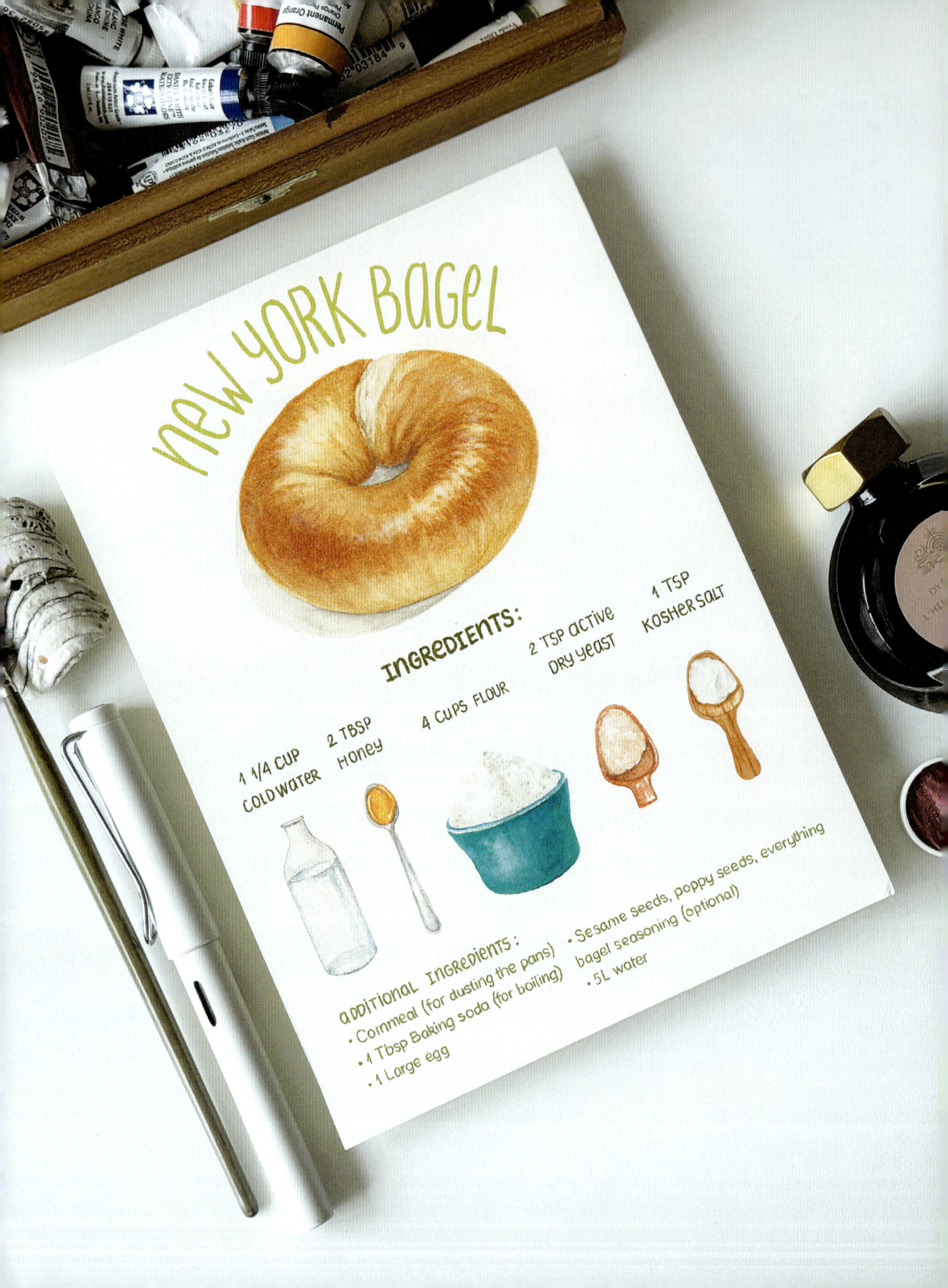
NEW YORK BAGEL
INGREDIENTS:
1 1/4 CUP COLD WATER
2 TBSP HONEY
4 CUPS FLOUR
2 TSP ACTIVE DRY YEAST
1 TSP KOSHER SALT
ADDITIONAL INGREDIENTS:
• Cornmeal (for dusting the pans)
• 1 Tbsp Baking soda (for boiling)
• 1 Large egg
• Sesame seeds, poppy seeds, everything bagel seasoning (optional)
• 5L water

Portrait Layout 5

New York Bagel

This portrait layout is ideal for those who appreciate minimalism and straightforward simplicity. It features a clean composition with a pleasing color palette—just enough, neither too much nor too little. While versatile enough for dishes of various shapes, it particularly shines with those close to a 1:1 width-height ratio. Among the 20 projects in Chapter 2, Project 01: New York Bagel (page 39) stands out as a perfect fit, with its curved title following the round shape of the bagel, making it an excellent choice for this layout.

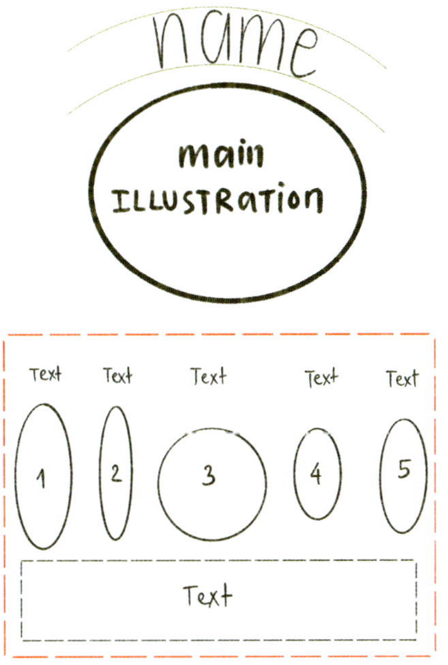

1

Step 1 - Mapping

The structure of this recipe card leaves little room for uncertainty: The title will gracefully follow the curve, and the ingredients will be neatly arranged below. Our primary illustration should not occupy more than one-third of the card's height. Aim to center smaller illustrations or maintain consistency in their sizes and shapes. Embrace minimalism by avoiding the urge to fill all available space—I intentionally empty areas on either side of the bagel to emphasize its aesthetic appeal.

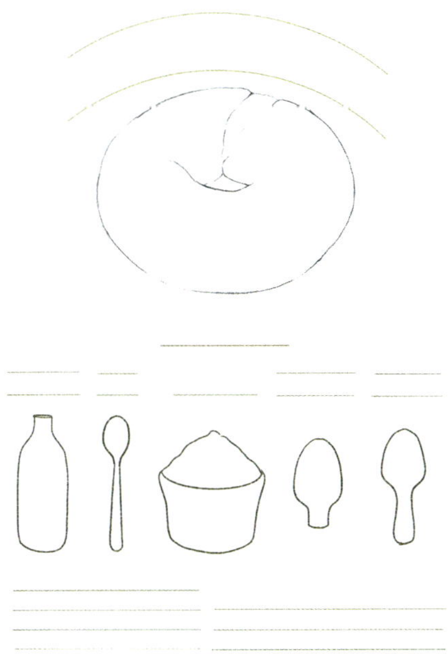

2

Step 2 - Refining the Layout

Create detailed illustrations within each frame, working on the specific shapes of every ingredient. I envision placing the text above each illustration to ensure horizontal alignment and a cohesive overall look. Each spoonful of ingredients should point upward, directing focus toward our main component and serving as visual guidance.

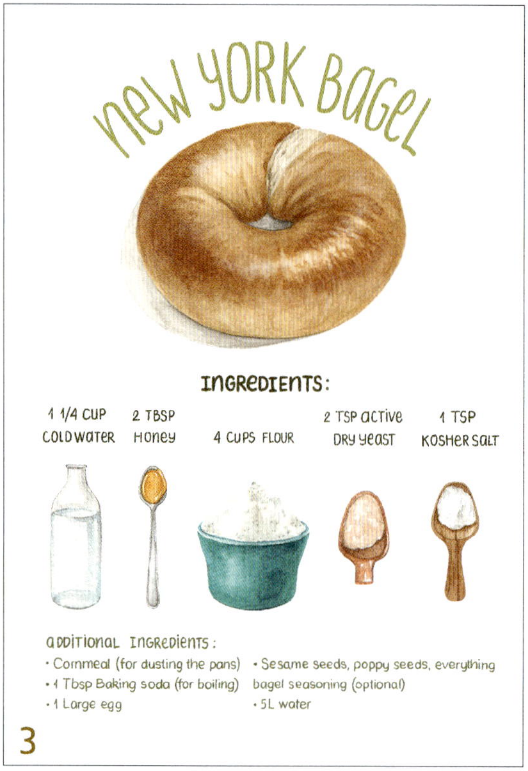

Step 3 - Painting

Since our featured dish consists solely of different shades of golden brown, you have the flexibility to select color schemes. I choose a monochromatic approach, accentuated by a single dark-turquoise element placed strategically in the center of the ingredient list.

Step 4 - Adding Text

I generally stick to the same font throughout this layout, adjusting letter spacing and height as needed. Feel free to experiment with combining uppercase and lowercase letters in the text to find the style that suits you best. Because the ingredients are mostly neutral, I select a green-gold color for the text. It strikes a balance with the turquoise accent and the various shades of brown used in the design.

Portrait Layout 6

Strawberry Chocolate Roll Cake

The key advantage of this last design is its ample space for text, making it perfect for accommodating long lists of ingredients, as is the case with the featured dish from Chapter 2, Project 18: Strawberry Chocolate Roll Cake (page 163). As a result, the illustrations of ingredients become a secondary focus with less prominent display space. Additionally, placing the main title at the bottom—a departure from the usual top placement—adds an intriguing twist. This serves as a valuable case study in understanding composition priorities and leveraging all elements to support those priorities effectively.

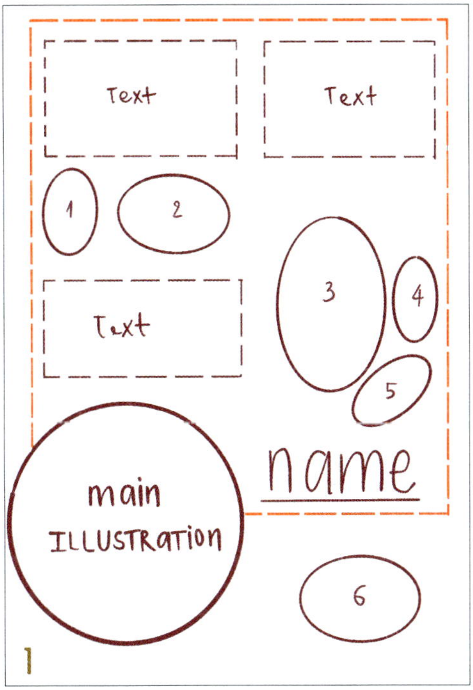

Step 1 - Mapping

With the main dish positioned in the bottom-left corner, the layout follows a visual path along the perimeter of the paper, divided into two sections: two text columns at the top with two small illustrations below, and a separate section dedicated specifically to the Whipped Cream ingredients, featuring a cluster of three illustrations.

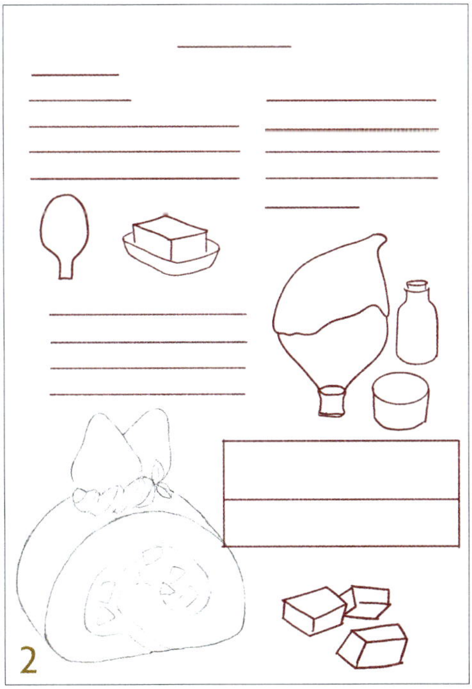

Step 2 - Refining the Layout

At the top, I choose to illustrate two ingredients: cocoa powder and butter. They act as a visual divider between the first and second sections. The Whipped Cream section, which features only three ingredients, is framed on the right edge with a whisk of cream to convey a "freshly made" sense to the recipe. Below the title, I include chunks of dark chocolate to balance out the empty space.

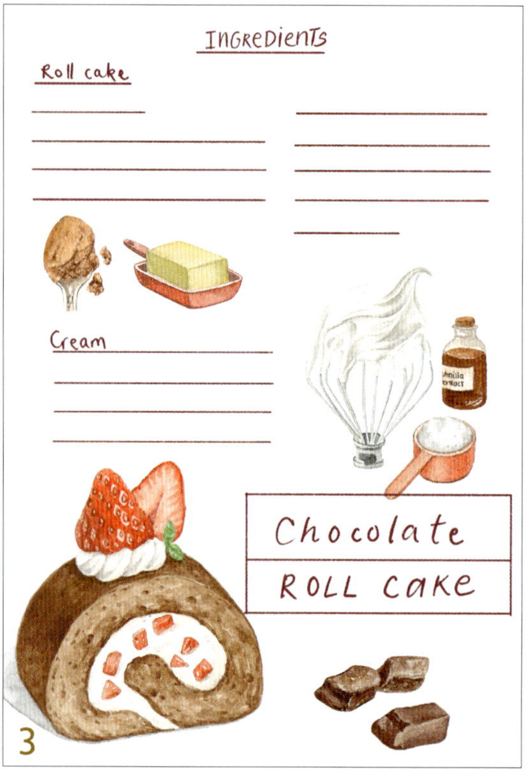

Step 3 - Painting

The rich brown color of the cake gives a substantial presence, so I've carried this color throughout the entire layout to maintain visual harmony. You'll see it reflected in the cocoa powder spoon, chocolate chunks and vanilla bottle. The measuring cup and butter tray also echo the strawberry's color in the design.

I intentionally enlarged the image of the whipped cream whisk to fill the space, while keeping its airy and light appearance intact, ensuring a smooth flow throughout the layout.

Step 4 - Adding Text

The word "Chocolate" in the title is written in a cursive font to impart a romantic visual element to the cake. "Roll cake" is written in uppercase using a simple, round font to reinforce a solid and foundational feel for the entire layout.

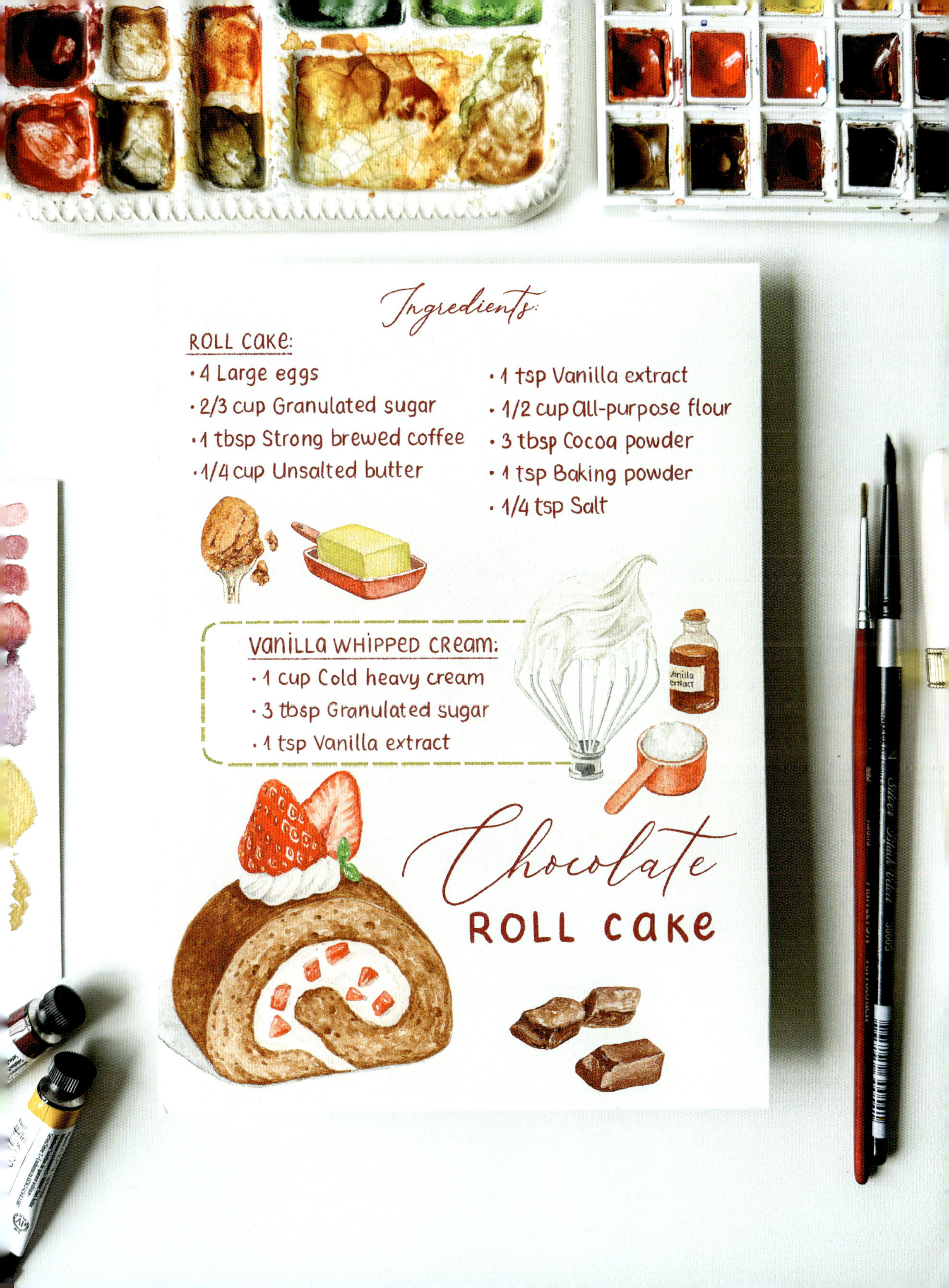
Ingredients:
ROLL CAKE:
• 4 Large eggs
• 2/3 cup Granulated sugar
• 1 tbsp Strong brewed coffee
• 1/4 cup Unsalted butter
• 1 tsp Vanilla extract
• 1/2 cup All-purpose flour
• 3 tbsp Cocoa powder
• 1 tsp Baking powder
• 1/4 tsp Salt
VANILLA WHIPPED CREAM:
• 1 cup Cold heavy cream
• 3 tbsp Granulated sugar
• 1 tsp Vanilla extract
Vanilla extract
Chocolate
ROLL CAKE

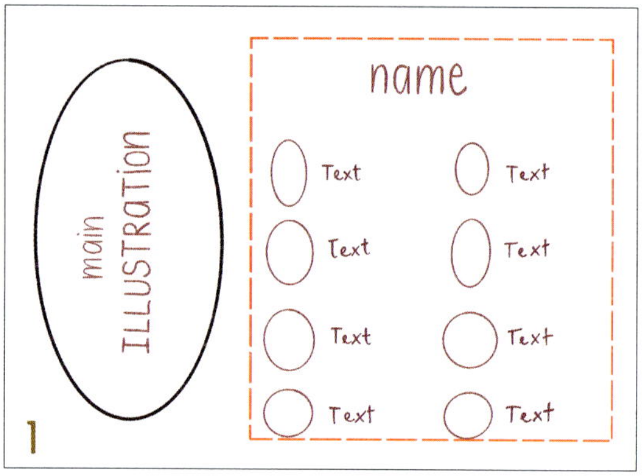

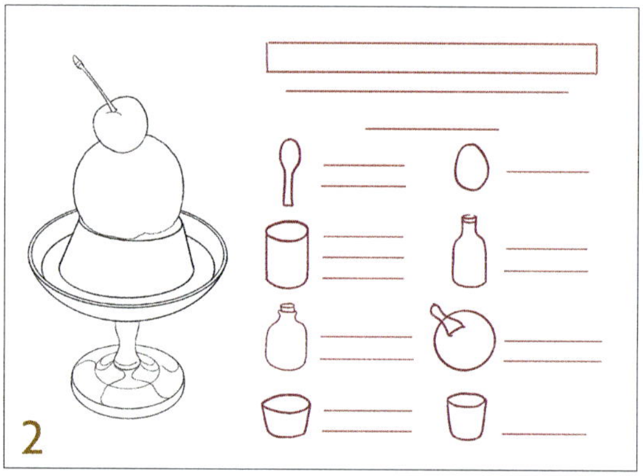

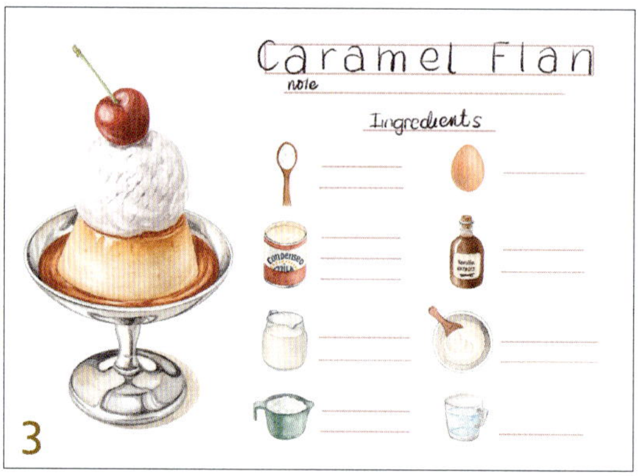

Landscape Layout 1

Flan & Vanilla Ice Cream

This layout is most ideal for dishes that have either significantly greater height than width, or vice versa, and contain fewer than ten ingredients. An excellent example from Chapter 2 is Project 20: Flan & Vanilla Ice Cream (page 176), perfectly suited to this landscape format. The main illustration occupies one side of the layout, while the remaining space is neatly arranged for ingredients and text in straight lines.

Step 1 - Mapping

Draw on paper the sections for the main illustration and the ingredients. If using watercolor paper, lightly mark these areas with dots or thin lines that can be erased later. For this layout, sketch the cup in the center of the left side of the paper, while all eight small illustrations of the ingredients and accompanying text will be on the right side.

Step 2 - Refining the Layout

Outline the shapes of your ingredients. In this layout, I opt for an eye-level viewpoint to sketch most of them, except for the tablespoon and bowl of cream cheese (top-down viewpoint). As they are placed within two columns, we should prioritize angles that showcase their vertical sides to ensure ample space for text.

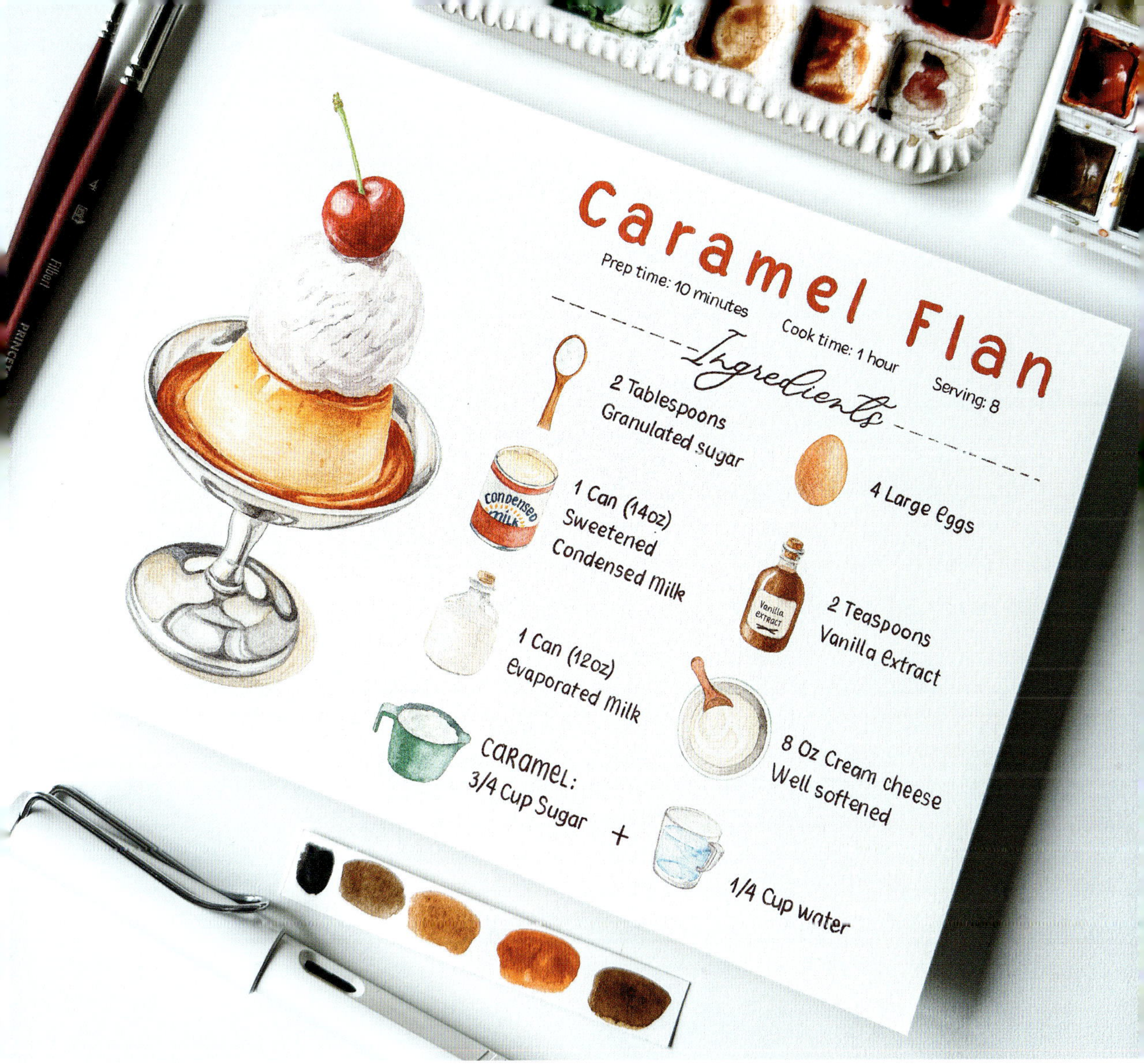

Step 3 - Painting

The main dish features a lovely golden orange color. Hence, to balance out the warm tones for the overall design, I choose a charming vintage green color for the sugar cup and a light-blue hue for the water.

Step 4 - Adding Text

When thinking about caramel flan, we recall its smooth texture and its sweet, creamy flavor. I selected a round and bold font for the title to complement the dessert's character. Once all the ingredient text is filled in, I include a line of notes beneath the main title and the word "Ingredients" to connect the two sections.

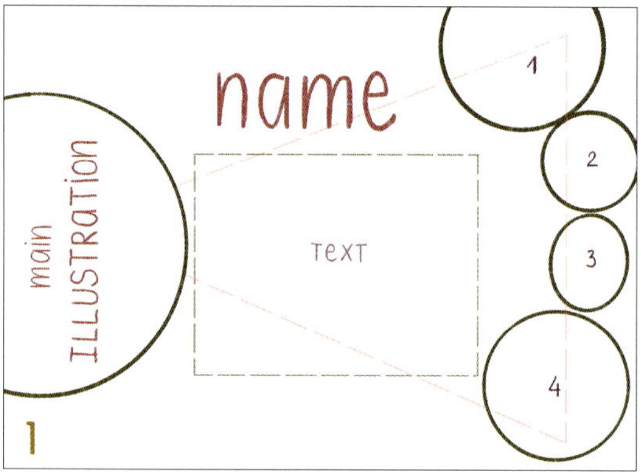

1

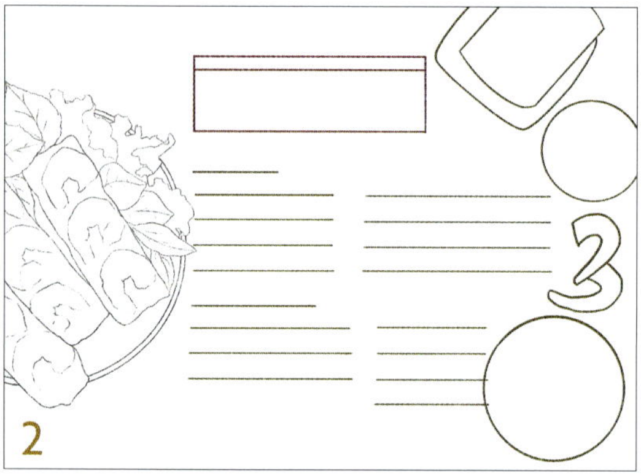

2

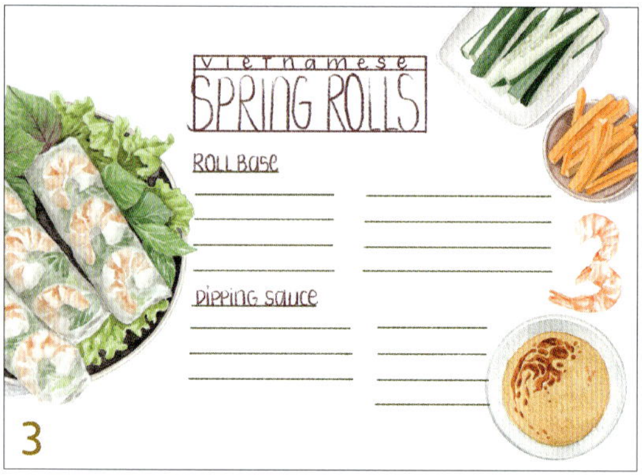

3

Landscape Layout 2

Vietnamese Spring Rolls

Project 08: Vietnamese Spring Rolls (page 88) is a delightful dish that captivates with its abundance of fresh ingredients. If your chosen food item has many ingredients that require larger illustrations for better visibility, consider depicting only the key ones—especially those that immediately bring the dish to mind. This approach helps prevent overcrowding in your layout, which requires practice to perfect. In this dynamic layout, I opt to highlight the dipping sauce and three other ingredients for a more engaging flow.

Step 1 - Mapping

To highlight the enticing details of the rolls, I zoom in to the bowl and crop part of it away. This technique effectively minimizes unused corners and allows you to adjust the orientation of the primary component as desired. To balance the bowl's visual weight on the left, I place the ingredients on the far right with varying sizes, leaving the central space for text. Please observe that the dashed line signifies the visual path and engagement, guiding how your eyes connect these points, forming a triangle in this instance.

Step 2 - Refining the Layout

The main illustration adopts a top-down viewpoint, which I extend to highlight other elements, effectively showcasing the ingredients within plates or bowls. In addition to the notable dipping sauce and standalone prawns, another distinctive feature of this dish is the julienned veggies, displayed in a light-neutral dish to emphasize their presence.

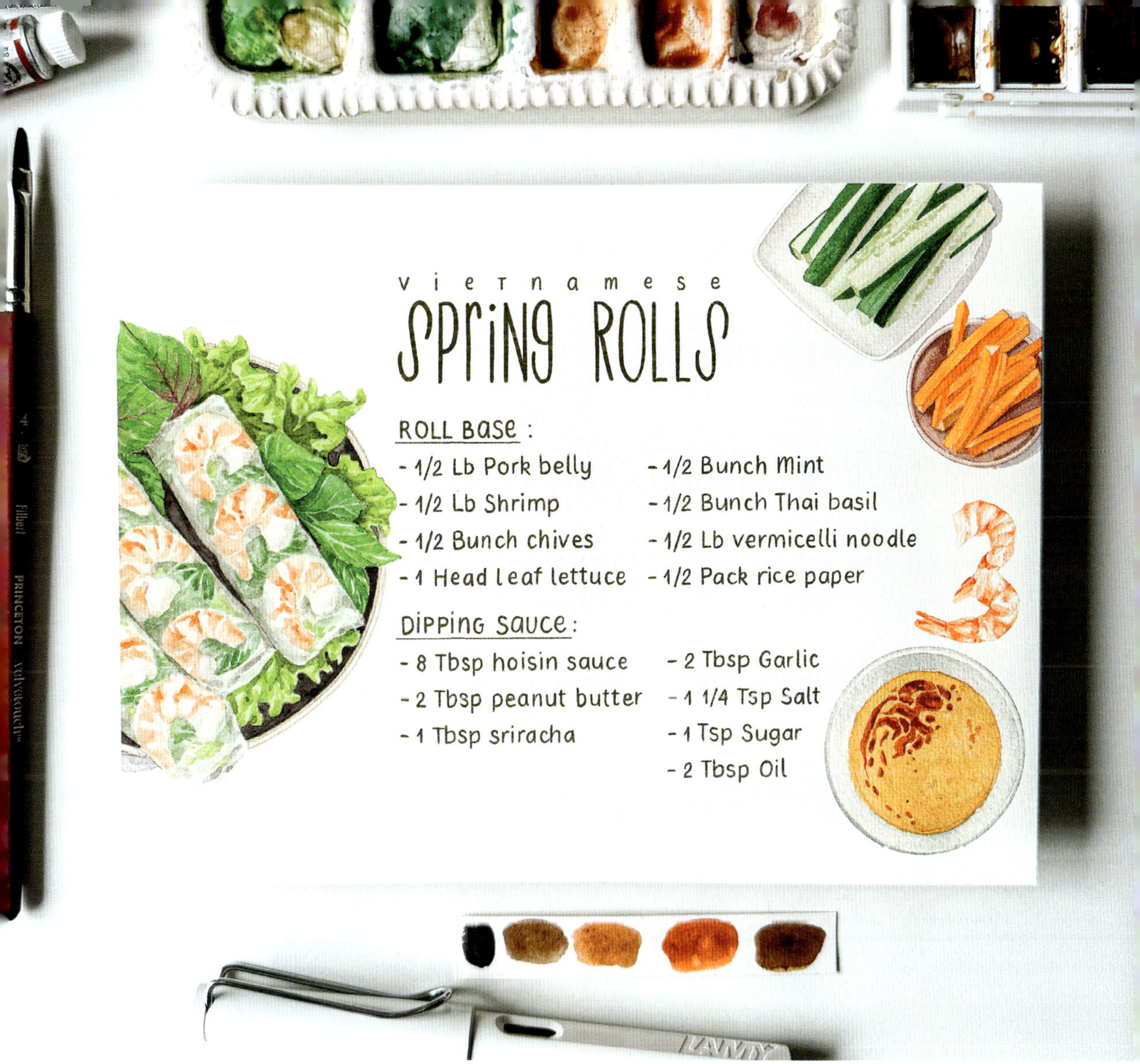

Step 3 - Painting

Since the main colors of our featured dish are predominantly simple, consisting of various shades of green and orange, I opt to replicate these thematic colors with the cucumber, carrot and shrimp to amplify freshness and achieve color harmony.

Step 4 - Adding Text

The text consists of two parts: the roll base and the dipping sauce, with each part organized into two columns to optimize space for all the content. I also add a small line with the word "Vietnamese" expanded to match the length of the main title, underscoring the dish's authenticity.

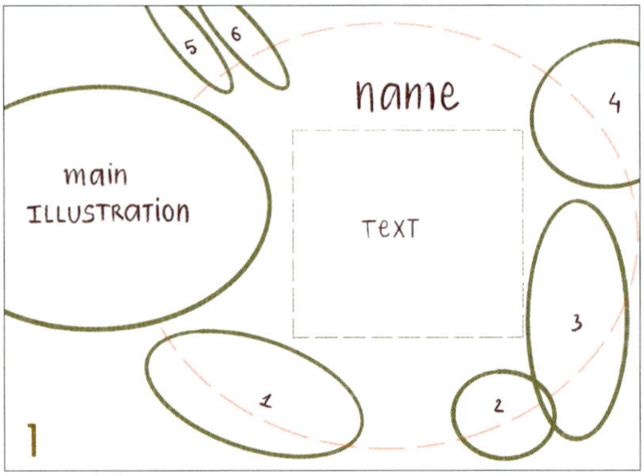

1

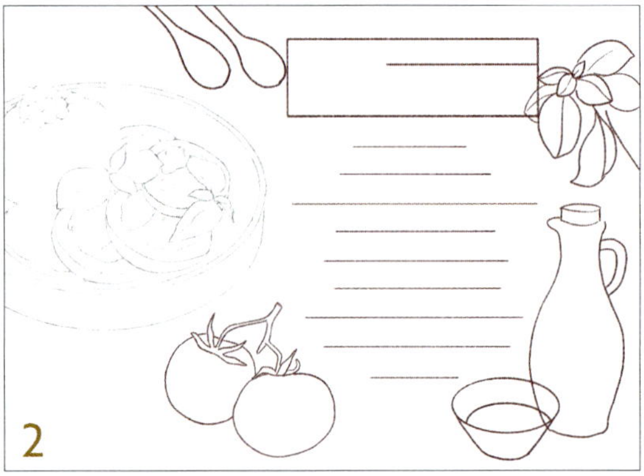

2

3

Landscape Layout 3

Tomato Caprese

This layout is an excellent choice for showcasing slightly wider illustrations and featuring a short, straightforward ingredient list, as seen in Project 06: Tomato Caprese (page 74). The dish's predominantly raw ingredients are irresistible and palate-provoking, prompting us to dedicate the majority of the space to painting them.

Step 1 - Mapping

Like Landscape Layout 2 (page 208), the main illustration will also feature a partial cut. However, in this layout, our visual path will form a closed circle around the text body. This is why I choose to position our main dish slightly higher on the paper, providing enough space for a smaller element. It's important to vary the size and shape of these smaller illustrations to create distinct subfocal points throughout the layout.

Step 2 - Refining the Layout

Here, most of the ingredients adopt the same eye-level viewpoint as the main dish, showcasing their natural forms. The tomatoes, with their solid shape and vibrant color, add weight to the layout, so I position them at the bottom left of the page. In contrast, at the top right are basil leaves, offering a lighter element. The vintage glass bottle of olive oil introduces an Italian touch to the layout. To complete the circular sequence, I include teaspoons of salt and pepper at the top of the layout, positioned between the main illustration and the title.

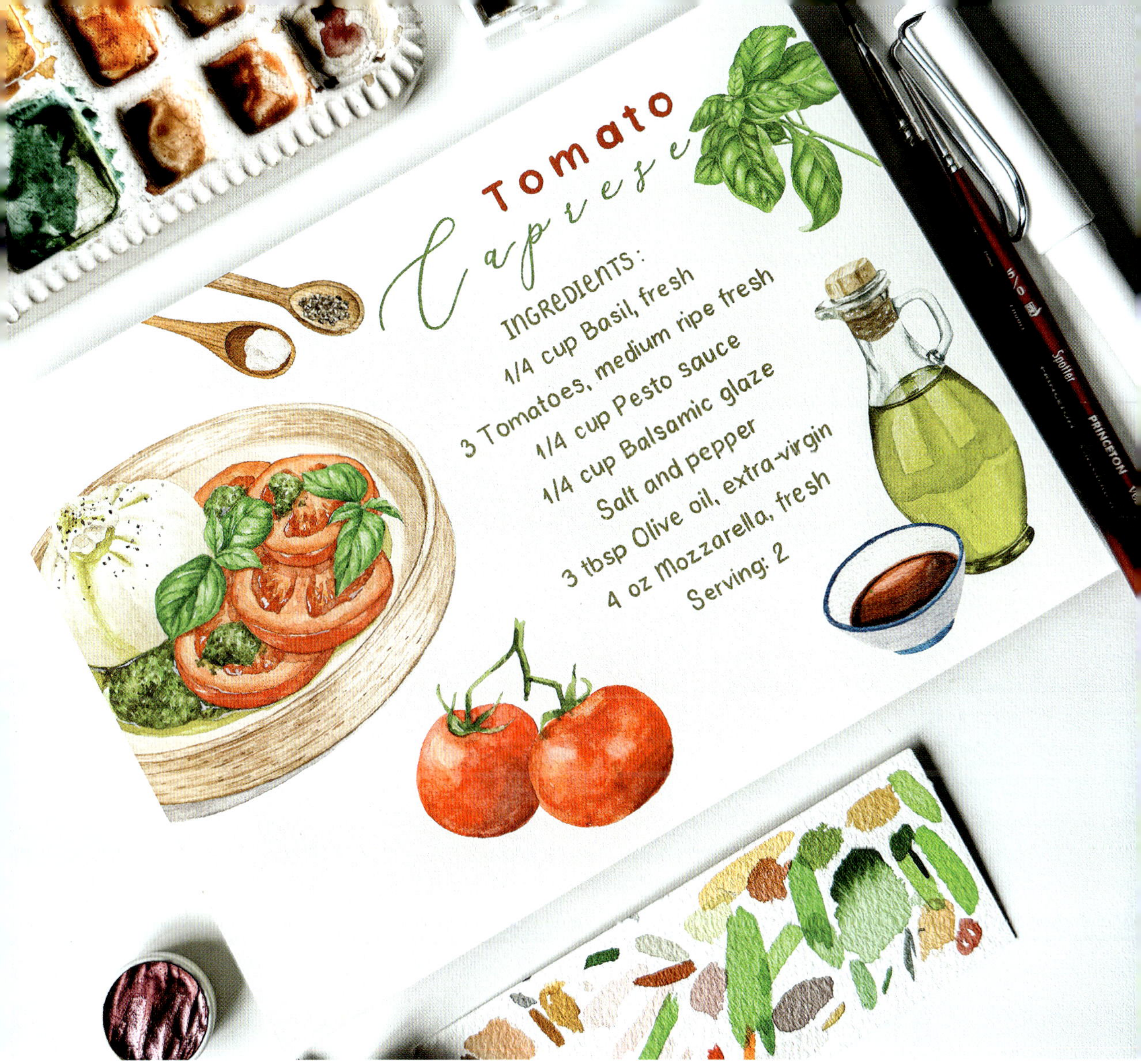

Step 3 - Painting

This layout features a bold color palette combining deep red and bright green, creating a striking contrast. Depicting olive oil in a similar shade of green, as a thick liquid in a glass bottle, contributes to the overall balance of the design. Additionally, I select a wooden texture for the spoon to complement the vintage appearance of the bottle and serving plate.

Step 4 - Adding Text

For this recipe, I selected two distinct fonts: The rounded sans serif font used for "Tomato" complements the round shape of the tomatoes, while "Caprese" is written in a thinner, flowing style to add a lighter touch and elegance to the layout, which is already rich with bold elements. The ingredient text is centered to serve as the focal point around which all the illustrations are arranged.

Chapter IV

Library of Ingredients

Anything in your kitchen can be the perfect subject for your next illustration! Just take a look around—open your pantry and let your kitchen inspire you. It's often easiest to paint things you're already familiar with, like your floral-patterned plate, glass jars or measuring tools.

In this chapter, I share various ingredients and containers you might find in your kitchen. Think of it as a handy library for when you're starting a new design. Whenever you need some inspiration, just refer to this chapter and choose an idea that sparks your creativity.

I've organized the library into four easy-to-navigate categories that you'll commonly find in any kitchen. First, we have Equipment and Utensils (page 214), featuring items like wooden spoons, mixing bowls and spatulas. Next is Packaged Goods (page 215), which includes ingredients like olive oil, vinegar and mustard, all in various containers. The third category is Herbs and Spices (page 217), showcasing a range of small jars with different colors and textures. Finally, we have Baking Ingredients (page 217), covering essentials such as flour, sugar, butter and eggs.

Sketching Common Shapes in the Kitchen

As always, let's start with the sketching phase. At this point, you should be able to easily apply the knowledge from Chapter 1 to break down any items found in the kitchen into basic shapes. I group them based on the fundamental shapes that they derive from, with certain distinctive characteristics. I trust that after these references, you'll be able to sketch any observed objects with this mindset and consistent practice.

Short cylindrical shapes can be found in round baking trays, measuring cups, etc.

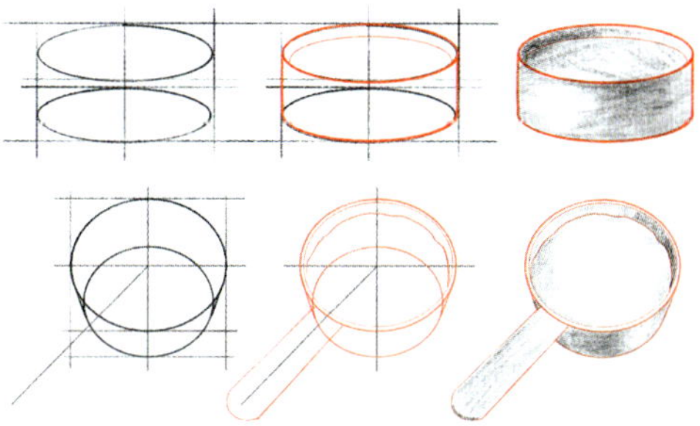

Narrow-necked cylindrical shapes can be found in bottles of vanilla extract, milk, water, etc.

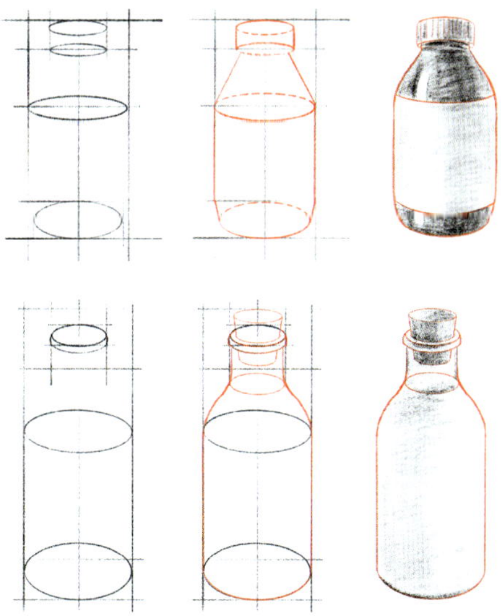

Cylindrical shapes with lids can be found in containers of herbs and spices, etc.

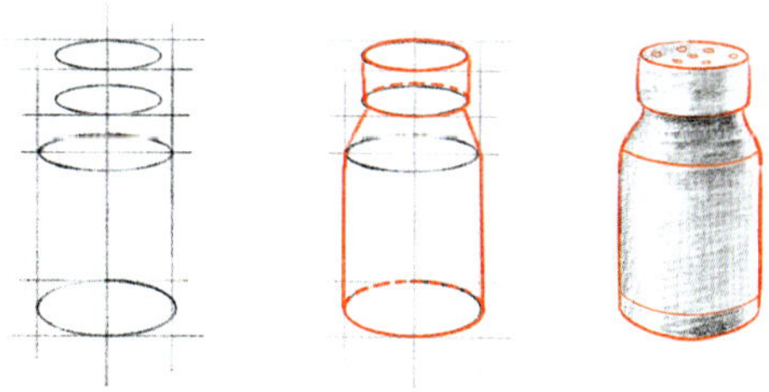

Egg shapes can be found in eggs, avocados, mugs, etc.

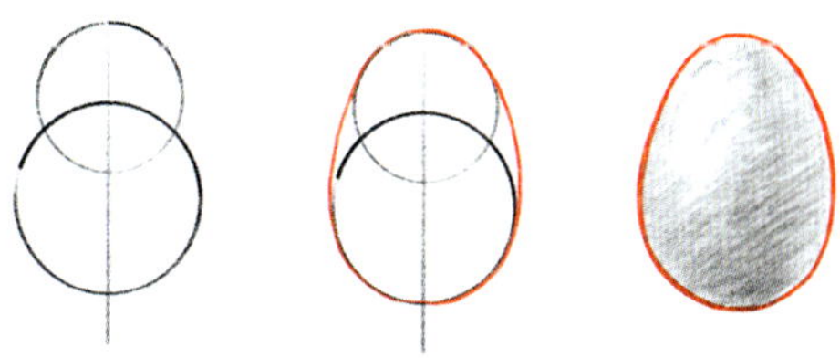

Small-bottomed cylindrical shapes can be found in mixing bowls, coffee mugs, salad bowls, etc.

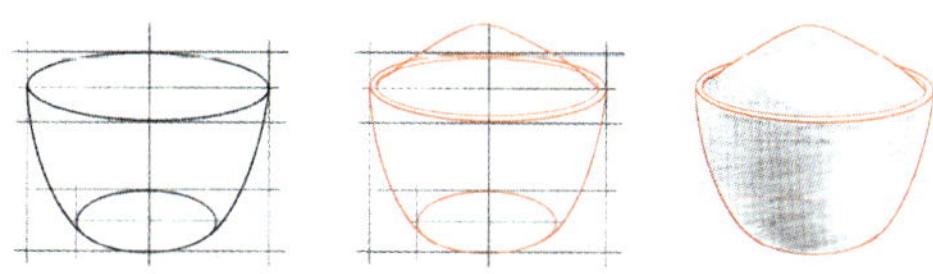

Curved cylindrical shapes can be found in glass jugs, etc.

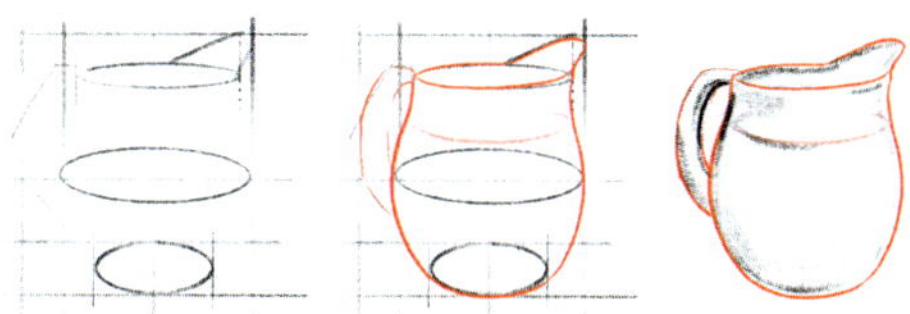

Irregular cylindrical shapes can be found in canvas flour bags, grocery paper bags, etc.

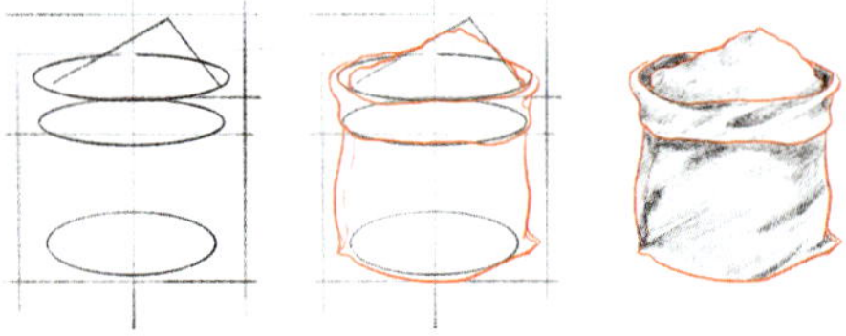

Tube shapes can be found in tubes of wasabi, honey, vanilla paste, etc.

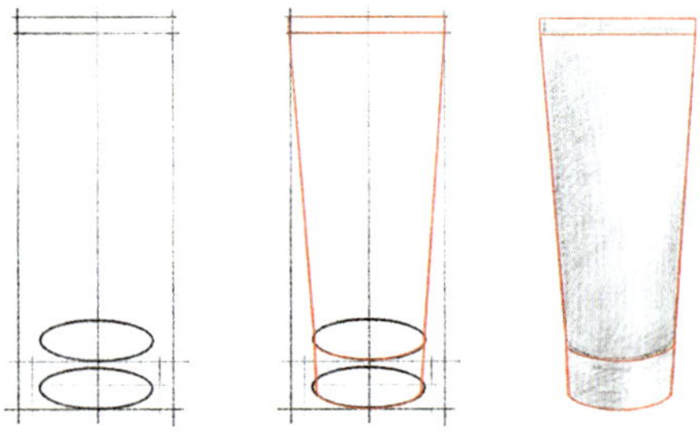

Cuboid shapes can be found in blocks of chocolate, baking pans, milk cartons, packaged flour bags, etc.

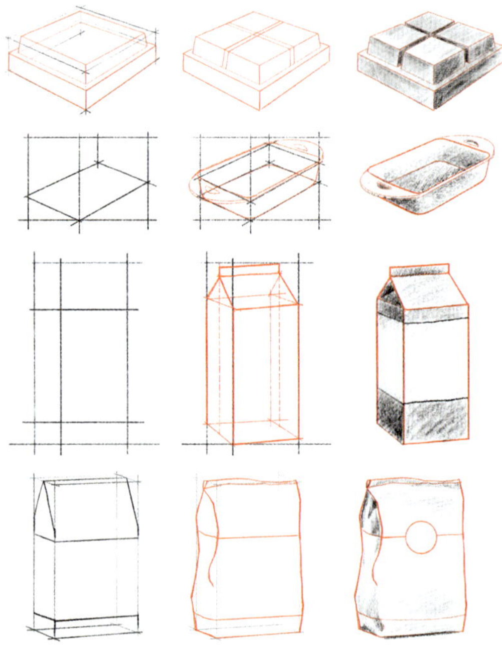

Library of Ingredients

Equipment and Utensils

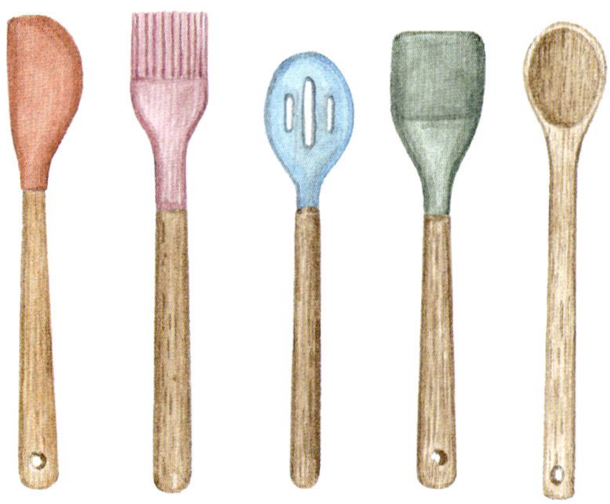

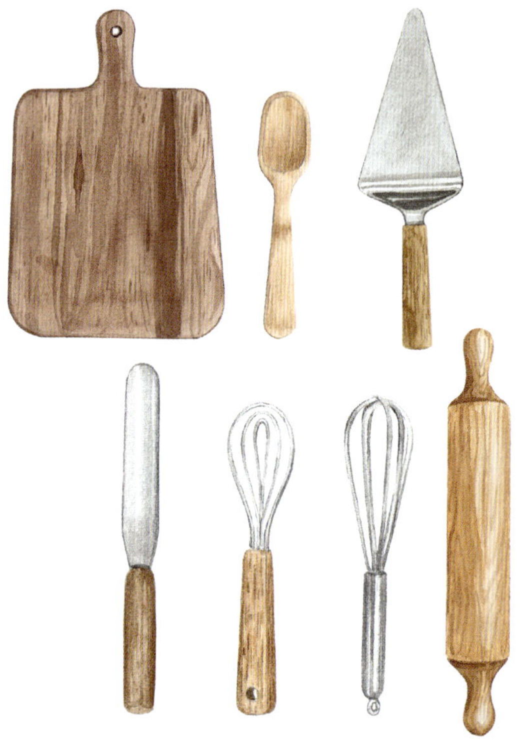

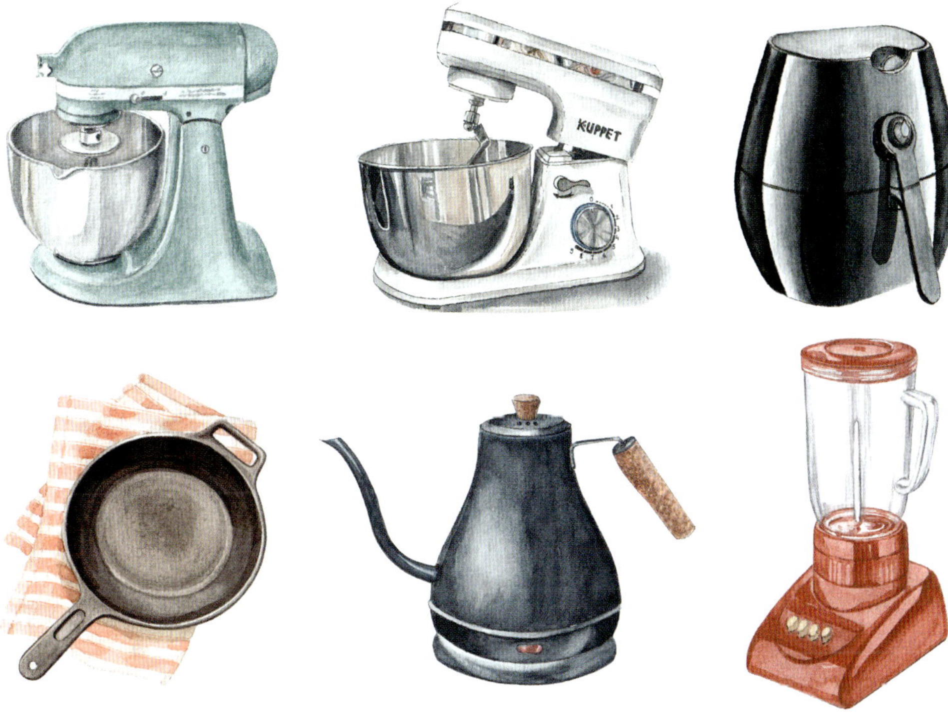

Packaged Goods

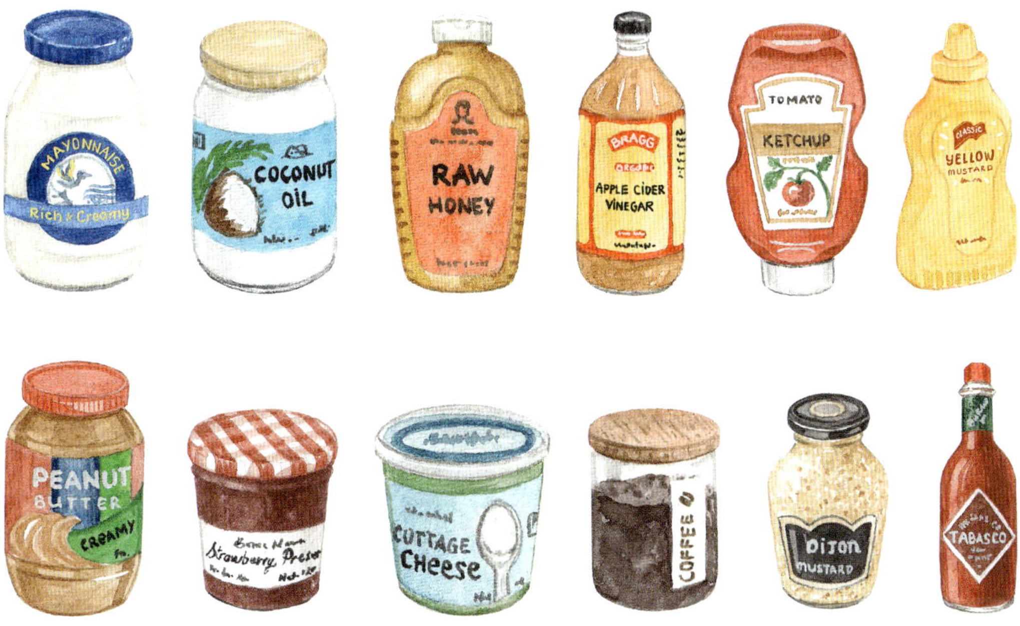

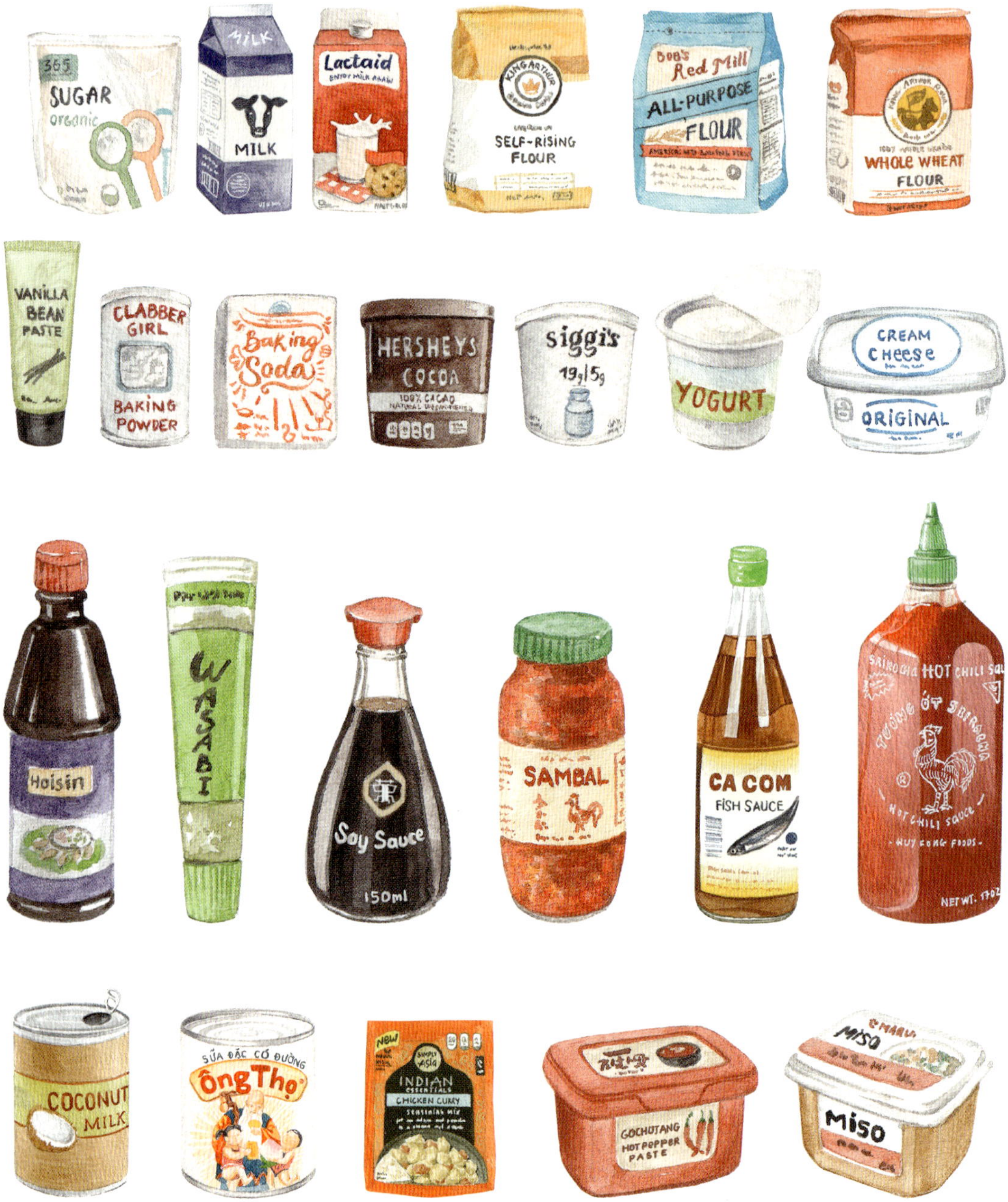
365
SUGAR
organic
MILK
MILK
Lactaid
SELF-RISING
FLOUR
Bob's
Red Mill
ALL-PURPOSE
FLOUR
WHOLE WHEAT
FLOUR
VANILLA
BEAN
PASTE
CLABBER
GIRL
BAKING
POWDER
Baking
Soda
HERSHEY'S
COCOA
100% CACAO
siggi's
YOGURT
CREAM
Cheese
ORIGINAL
Hoisin
WASABI
Soy Sauce
150ml
SAMBAL
CA COM
FISH SAUCE
HOT CHILI SAUCE
HUY FONG FOODS
COCONUT
MILK
SỮA ĐẶC CÓ ĐƯỜNG
Ông Thọ
NEW
INDIAN
ESSENTIALS
CHICKEN CURRY
GOCHUJANG
HOT PEPPER
PASTE
MISO
Miso

Herbs and Spices

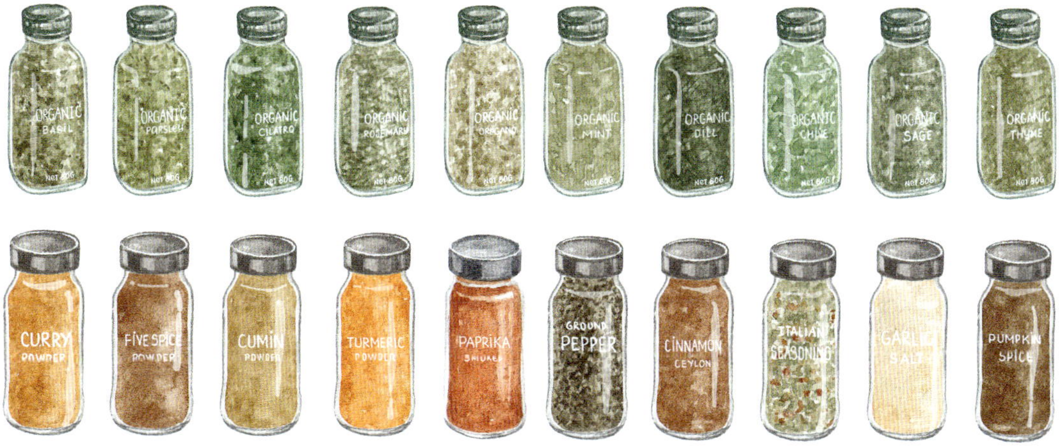

Baking Ingredients

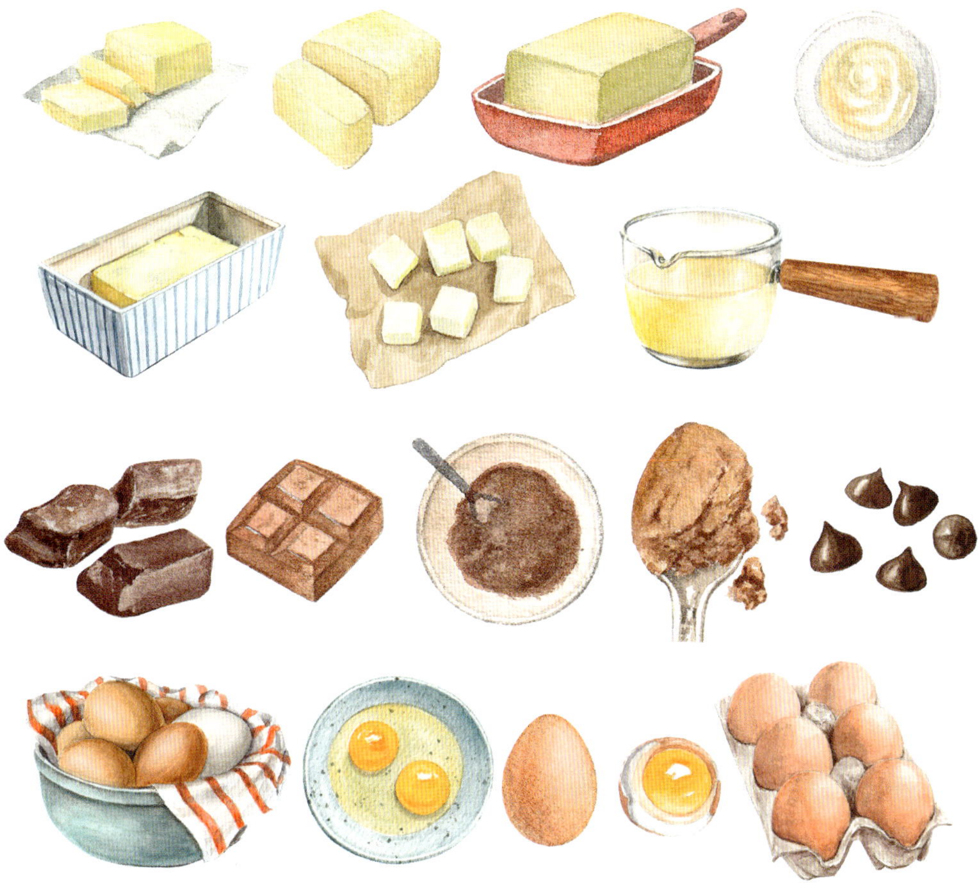

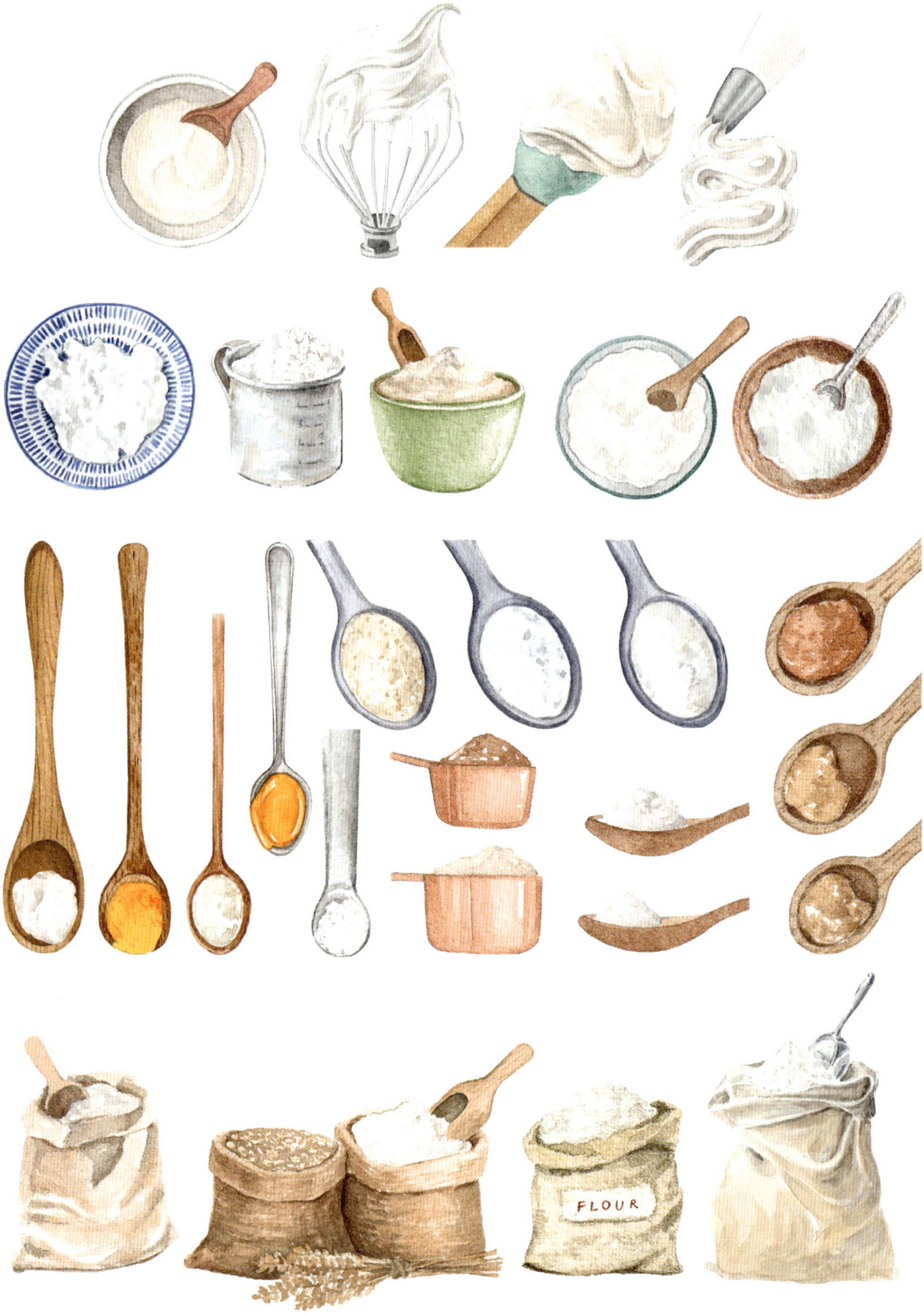
FLOUR

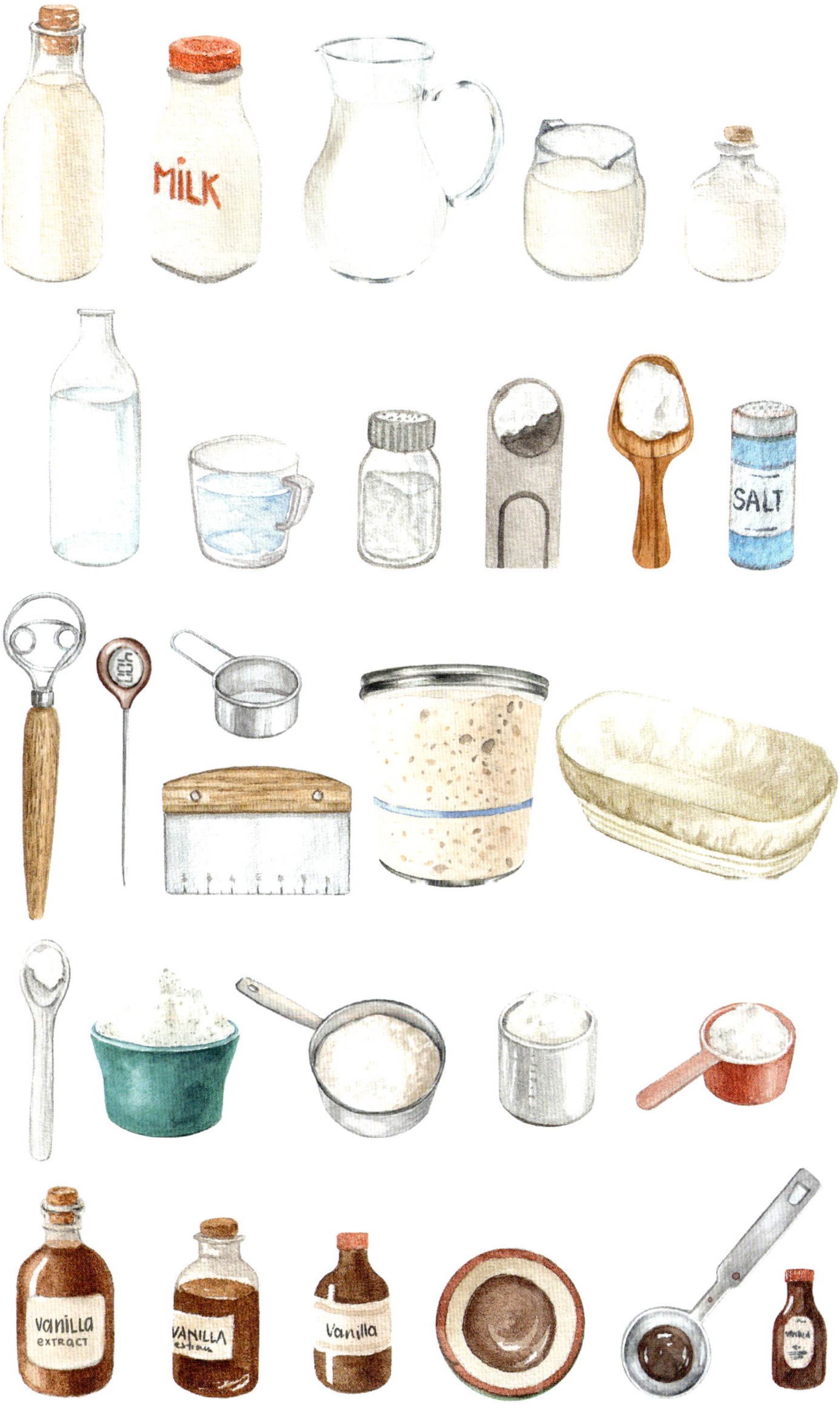
MILK
SALT
vanilla
EXTRACT
VANILLA
Vanilla

Acknowledgments

I extend my heartfelt gratitude to Sarah and the entire team at Page Street Publishing for reaching out to me, supporting me at every step of this challenging first book project and ultimately bringing it to life. Your team's dedication and excellence have been nothing short of amazing!

Special thanks to my dear friend, Boi Quynh, for taking the time to read my first drafts and provide invaluable feedback. This book would not be the same without your insightful contributions.

I must also acknowledge my husband, Jack, who has generously devoted his limited time off work to assist with photographing and organizing the digital elements of this book. His unwavering support and encouragement have been a cornerstone throughout this project.

Lastly, to every reader who picks up this book and embarks on their own artistic journey, thank you!

About the Author

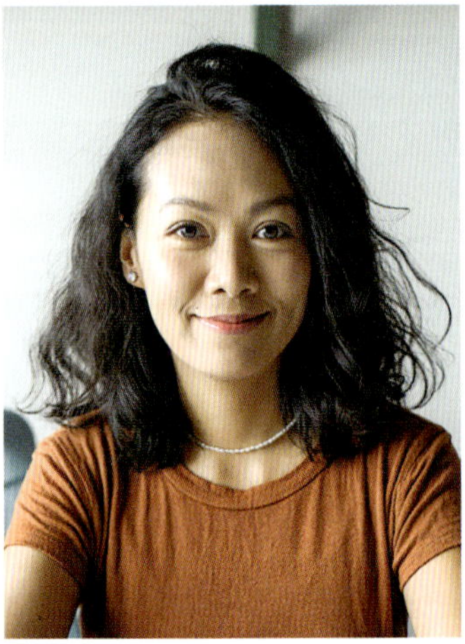

Thanh Huynh is an artist who was born and raised in Vietnam, where she was inspired by the rich culture of food. She graduated with a bachelor's degree in interior design from the University of Architecture in Ho Chi Minh City. Utilizing her knowledge of 3-D space and lighting, Thanh adapts these principles to her food paintings, giving them a highly realistic appearance. Her works are renowned for their "tasty" visual appeal, captivating viewers with their lifelike quality. You can explore more of her artwork on Instagram @foodillustration.studio, where she shares her creations with over 100,000 fellow artists and friends. Stay in touch with Thanh by sharing your practices from the book and using the hashtag #foodillustrationstudio.

Index

Page numbers in **boldface** indicate illustrations.

T

U

V

W

Y